International Design Protection

A Global Handbook

Consulting Editor **Clive Thorne**

Consulting editor
Clive Thorne

Publisher
Sian O'Neill

Commissioning editor
Katherine Cowdrey

Editor
Carolyn Boyle

Marketing manager
Alan Mowat

Production
Natalie Clarke

Publishing directors
Guy Davis, Tony Harriss, Mark Lamb

International Design Protection: A Global Handbook
is published by
Globe Law and Business
Globe Business Publishing Ltd
New Hibernia House
Winchester Walk
London SE1 9AG
United Kingdom
Tel +44 20 7234 0606
Fax +44 20 7234 0808
Web www.globelawandbusiness.com

Printed and bound by CPI Group (UK) Ltd, Croydon, CR0 4YY

ISBN 978-1-905783-75-5

Table of contents

Preface

Clive Thorne
Reynolds Porter Chamberlain LLP

Design protection deals with an uneasy territory concerned with the protection of mass-produced articles which lack the necessary inventiveness to attract patent protection, but whose appearance plays a part in the choice of the article. This may be because the article as a whole has an aesthetically pleasing shape or because the shape carries some form of embellishment.

Similar issues relating to the scope of design protection exist worldwide. The extent of available protection in different jurisdictions reflects the inherent problems associated with design protection. These include the following:

- It has an uneasy interaction with copyright protection. For example, what should the interaction of the term of protection for designs be with the term of protection for copyright? In most jurisdictions, for example, copyright protection has a term of 70 years plus life, whereas design protection rarely exceeds 25 years. The reason for this is that design law is intended to protect consumer products which have a relatively short technical life, whereas copyright is generally concerned with the protection of artistic works which have a meritorious degree of creativity.
- In most jurisdictions there is a difficult balance between the extent of protection available for purely functional designs as opposed to aesthetic designs (which have a degree of aestheticism or 'eye appeal' attached to them). In the United Kingdom, for example, prior to the Copyright, Designs and Patents Act 1988 the extent of protection given to functional designs proved highly controversial, particularly when the term of protection for aesthetic designs was generally considerably less.
- Similar issues arise with regard to originality. In many jurisdictions, originality based on the extent of skill and labour put into the copyright work provides the basis for copyright protection. It is arguable that similar skill and labour generally arise in the creation of aesthetic designs, but are absent in the creation of purely functional designs where the appearance of the article is of no real concern.
- There is a conflict between registered designs and the protection of unregistered designs. This is shown acutely in the United Kingdom in terms of the contrast between registered design protection and UK unregistered design rights. It is by no means unusual for there to be a finding of unregistered design right infringement at the same time as a finding of non-infringement in respect of a registered design.

- Spare-parts protection has also caused great difficulty. The essentially economic argument runs that there should be no design protection for spare parts on the basis that such protection would be anti-competitive and restrict the ability of the owner of an article to repair the product other than by using spare parts provided by the design owner.

These issues were to the fore when the current UK scheme of design protection was introduced by the Copyright, Designs and Patents Act 1988. In an April 1986 White Paper entitled *Intellectual Property and Innovation*, the UK government stated: "British Industry relies to a great extent on its innovative abilities. It is clear that there are many innovative industrial products which are costly to design but which are not truly inventive and which therefore do not qualify for patent protection. Accordingly, the Government has concluded that some protection should be available to give the manufacturer, who has spent money on design, the opportunity to benefit from its investment, thus providing the incentive to further investment. It is also concluded that the protection should extend to spare parts but it readily accepts that the full protection of copyright law will be excessive." This encapsulates the inherent problems associated with design protection. Similar issues have arisen worldwide.

This is the first attempt to produce an international compendium of design law.

The editor is grateful to all of the contributors for their help, the publishers and, in particular, Katherine Cowdrey and also Maame Djaan, Elena Shemilt and his colleagues at Reynolds Porter Chamberlain.

Clive Thorne is a partner in Reynolds Porter Chamberlain's IP, technology and outsourcing group. He practises all areas of IP law, including patents, designs, copyright, trademarks and trade secrets. He has a particular interest in the arbitration of IP disputes. He has been appointed an International Chamber of Commerce arbitrator on an IT dispute and is on the World Intellectual Property Organisation (WIPO) panel of arbitrators. He is also on the WIPO panel of experts for domain name disputes and has been on the Nominet panel of experts. He has been involved in many of the leading IP disputes in the United Kingdom and overseas. He is particularly experienced in multi-jurisdictional litigation. Mr Thorne is admitted in Hong Kong and Australia. He practised in Hong Kong between 1984 and 1987 and continues to retain practice links in Asia. He has extensive experience in all areas of intellectual property and has authored a number of books, including Users Guide to Design Law, Users Guide to Copyright *and* Intellectual Property – The New Law.

Australia

Timothy Webb
Clayton Utz

1. Summary of design protection

In Australia, the law of designs is governed by the Designs Act 2003 (Cth) and the Designs Regulations 2004 (Cth), which provide a regime for the grant and protection of exclusive monopoly rights in registered designs within Australia for up to 10 years. The Designs Act came into force on June 17 2004 and replaced the former Designs Act 1906 (Cth) (the 1906 Act). This was the first major reform in designs law in almost 100 years.[1]

The Designs Act establishes a registration system under which a national Register of Designs is kept by a Registrar of Designs.[2] In practice, the register is maintained by IP Australia, the Australian government agency (part of the Department of Innovation, Industry, Science and Research) responsible for granting patent, trademark, industrial design and plant breeder's rights.[3] Exclusive rights in designs are only acquired by registration under the Designs Act. They do not automatically exist on creation of the design, as with copyright.

Designs law relates to the overall appearance of products resulting from their visual features, and is separate from the protection of original artistic works under copyright legislation and the protection of the way items function, which can be obtained through patent law.

The designs law regime seeks to encourage innovation in Australian industry and to derive economic benefit from having well-designed products. It aims to balance the incentive to create new designs by providing monopolies for registered designs with the economic effects of granting the monopolies. This balance is achieved under the Designs Act by granting only a limited-term monopoly for 10 years.

2. Registered design rights

2.1 Nature of rights

A rights holder has the exclusive right, during the term of registration of the design:

(a) to make or offer to make a product, in relation to which the design is registered, which embodies the design;

(b) to import such a product into Australia for sale, or for use for the purposes of any trade or business;

1 The old law under the 1906 Act continues to apply to designs registered under that act. This chapter focuses on the Designs Act, but does note some key differences under the 1906 Act.

2 Designs Act, Sections 111 and 122.

3 See www.ipaustralia.gov.au/.

(c) to sell, hire or otherwise dispose of, or offer to sell, hire or otherwise dispose of, such a product;
(d) to use such a product in any way for the purposes of any trade or business;
(e) to keep such a product for the purpose of doing any of the things mentioned in paragraph (c) or (d); and
(f) to authorise another person to do any of the things mentioned above.[4]

These exclusive rights are personal property and may be assigned.[5] However, an assignment of all or part of the rights holder's interest in the design must be in writing and signed by, or on behalf of, the assignor and the assignee.[6]

2.2 Qualification

Design registration is intended to protect designs that have an industrial application. To qualify for registration, a design must be a 'registrable design' under the Designs Act, which requires that it be 'new' and 'distinctive' when compared with the 'prior art base' for the design as it existed before the 'priority date' of the design.[7] This is discussed further in section 4 below.

The registered owner of a registered design is the person who is entered in the Register of Designs as the registered owner of the design (which can be one or two or more persons).[8] Only the following persons are entitled to be entered on the Register of Designs as the registered owner of a design:[9]

- the person(s) who created the design;
- an employer of the creator(s), if the design is made in the course of employment;
- a person who contracted the creator(s) to make the design;
- a person to whom the design has been assigned in writing; or
- a person who derives title to the design by devolution by will or the legal personal representative of a deceased person mentioned above.

If two or more persons fulfil any of these descriptions, they are co-owners of the design. Where there are two or more owners of a registered design, each of those owners is entitled to an equal, undivided share in the exclusive rights in the design.[10] A co-owner is entitled to exercise the exclusive rights in the design for their own benefit without accounting to the other owner or owners. However, a co-owner may not assign or license a design without consent from the other owner(s).

2.3 Registration procedure

The Designs Act provides for a streamlined registration system whereby design applications will only undergo a formalities check before being registered, to ensure

4 Designs Act, Section 10(1).
5 *Ibid*, Section 10(2).
6 *Ibid*, Section 11.
7 *Ibid*, Section 15(1).
8 *Ibid*, Section 14(1)
9 *Ibid*, Section 13(1).
10 *Ibid*, Section 14(2).

that the application contains all relevant information.[11] If an application passes this preliminary check, the design is registered and published in the Australian *Official Journal of Designs* and the registered owner receives a certificate of registration.[12]

The Designs Act provides for the process of substantive examination to occur only after registration. Such an examination may occur on the request of any person (which may be the rights holder or a third party), by the registrar on his own initiative or by order of the court.[13] The registrar is required to consider whether the registration should be revoked and removed from the register on the ground that the design is not a 'registrable design' or any other ground prescribed by the regulations.[14]

After examination, if the registrar finds that the design meets all the requirements of the legislation, a certificate of examination will be issued and the design will remain on the register.[15] However, if the registrar finds that the design is not valid, it will be removed from the register.[16]

2.4 Term of protection

In Australia, a registered design gives the rights holder a legally enforceable right exclusively to exploit their design for a maximum of 10 years under the Designs Act, unlike copyright which, in Australia, runs for the life of the author plus an additional 70 years.

The Designs Act provides for an initial registration period of five years from the filing date of the design application, with the potential to apply for renewal of the registration for a further five-year period.[17] If the rights holder does not renew the registration, which is subject to renewal fees, it will expire automatically after the five-year period.

The Australian government has reduced the maximum period (it was formerly 16 years under the 1906 Act – an initial period of one year followed by three five-year renewals) to bring Australian law in line with Australia's international obligations under Article 26 of the Agreement on Trade Related Aspects of Intellectual Property (TRIPs Agreement).

2.5 Infringement

It is the responsibility of the person who has registered a design to protect that design. If someone uses it without permission, they may be infringing the registration.

Infringement proceedings can only be started after the design has been examined and a certificate of examination granted. Proceedings must be commenced within six

11 *Ibid*, Sections 39 to 44.
12 *Ibid*, Section 45.
13 *Ibid*, Section 63.
14 *Ibid*, Section 65. Regulation 5.02 of the Designs Regulations states that a prescribed ground is that, under Section 43 of the act, the design should not have been registered. Section 43 provides that the registrar must refuse to register certain designs, including those prescribed by the regulations (Regulation 4.06 prescribes, eg, designs that are scandalous, or might reasonably be taken to be scandalous).
15 Designs Act, Section 67.
16 *Ibid*, Section 68.
17 *Ibid*, Sections 46 and 47.

years of the day on which the alleged infringement occurred.[18] An action may be brought by the rights holder against any person who infringes the monopoly in the registered design. Proceedings cannot be brought by a licensee.

Infringement is discussed in more detail in section 5 below.

2.6 Damages and other relief

In infringement proceedings, a court may grant an injunction and, at the option of the plaintiff, either damages or an account of profits.[19] The court may award such additional damages as it considers appropriate, having regard to the flagrancy of the infringement and all other relevant matters.[20]

If a successful plaintiff elects for an account of profits rather than an award of damages, the profits that must be accounted for are the infringer's net profits obtained by virtue of the infringing conduct.

A court may refuse to award damages, reduce the damages that would otherwise be awarded or refuse to make an order for an account of profits if the defendant has innocently infringed the registered design. This may occur in the case of 'primary infringement' (ie, the defendant has made or offered to make the product in relation to which the design is registered) if the defendant satisfies the court that, at the time of the infringement, it was not aware that the design was registered and, before that time, took all reasonable steps to ascertain whether the design was registered.[21] In the case of 'secondary infringement' (ie, all other exclusive rights, such as importing, selling or using for the purposes of trade), the defendant must satisfy the court that, at the time of the infringement, it was not aware, and could not reasonably have been expected to be aware, that the design was registered.[22]

2.7 Licensing

The exclusive rights of the rights holder can be licensed just like other forms of intellectual property (IP). The scope of a licence will be governed by the terms of the specific agreement between the licensor and the licensee.

A person does not infringe a registered design if the relevant exclusive act(s) done during the term of registration of the design are done with "the licence or authority of the registered owner of the design".[23] In that context, 'licence' has been held to mean simply 'consent, permission'. It may be express or implied and need not be in writing.[24] However, if there are two or more rights holders of a registered design, none of them can grant a licence to exercise the exclusive rights in the design (or assign an interest in the design) without the consent of the others.[25] Accordingly, if there are two or more rights holders of a registered design, the licence or authority

---

18 *Ibid*, Section 71(4).
19 *Ibid*, Section 75(1).
20 *Ibid*, Section 75(3).
21 *Ibid*, Section 75(2)(a).
22 *Ibid*, Section 75(2)(b).
23 *Ibid*, Section 71(1).
24 See *Interstate Parcel Express Co Pty Ltd v Time-Life International (Netherlands) BV* (1977) 138 CLR 534; *Avel Pty Ltd v Multicoin Amusements Pty Ltd* (1990) 171 CLR 88.
25 Designs Act, Section 14(2)(c).

must be sought from each of the co-owners.

Licensing and exploitation are discussed further in section 7 below.

2.8 Compulsory licences

Under the Designs Act, a person may apply to a prescribed court for an order requiring the rights holder of a registered design to grant the person a licence to do anything falling within the rights holder's exclusive rights.[26] The application must be made within three years of the date of registration of the design,[27] and may not be made unless a certificate of examination has been issued.[28]

The court may order a compulsory licence if it is satisfied that:[29]

- products embodying the design have not been made in Australia, to the extent that is reasonable in the circumstances of the case;
- the rights holder has given no satisfactory reason for the failing to exercise the exclusive rights in the registered design; and
- the applicant has tried for a reasonable period, but without success, to obtain from the rights holder an authorisation to do, on reasonable terms and conditions, anything falling within the rights holder's exclusive rights.

A compulsory licence does not give the licensee any exclusive rights in the design, and is assignable only in connection with an enterprise or goodwill in connection with which the licence is used.[30] The applicant must pay the rights holder an amount agreed between them or, failing agreement, such amount as is determined by the court to be just and reasonable having regard to the economic value of the licence.[31]

A compulsory licence may be revoked by agreement between the rights holder and licensee, or if a court finds that the circumstances that justified the grant of the licence no longer exist and are unlikely to recur and the legitimate interests of the licensee are not likely to be adversely affected by the revocation.[32]

2.9 Validity

As indicated above, a design registration may be revoked by the registrar during the process of examination. In addition, the Designs Act provides two mechanisms for a third party to challenge the validity of a registered design and seek its revocation.

First, a person may apply to the registrar for revocation of the registration of a design on the grounds that a person or persons were entitled persons at the time of the first registration of the design and that one or more of the original rights holders were not so entitled at that time, or that some other person, along with the original rights holders, was also an entitled person at that time.[33]

---

26 *Ibid*, Section 90(1).
27 Designs Regulations 2004 (Cth), Regulation 7.01.
28 Designs Act, Section 90(2).
29 *Ibid*, Section 90(3).
30 *Ibid*, Section 91(2).
31 *Ibid*, Section 92(4).
32 *Ibid*, Section 91(5).
33 *Ibid*, Sections 51 to 56.

Second, a person may apply to a prescribed court for an order revoking the registration of a design.[34] Such an application may be made only after the design has been examined and a certificate of examination has been issued.[35] The grounds on which a court may revoke the registration of the design are that:[36]

- the design is not a registrable design;
- one or more of the original rights holders was not entitled to be a rights holder;
- there were other persons entitled to be rights holders at the time the design was registered;
- the registration of the design was obtained by fraud, false suggestion or misrepresentation; or
- the design is a corresponding design to an artistic work, and copyright in the artistic work has ceased.

If a design was registered under the 1906 Act, the previous law will continue to apply for the purposes of determining the validity of the registration of the design.[37]

3. Unregistered design rights

Copyright protection under the Copyright Act 1968 (Cth) arises automatically on the creation of a work, provided it is original, and there is no registration system for copyright in Australia. The visual features of a product may constitute an artistic work in which copyright subsists under the Copyright Act. 'Artistic work' is defined in the Copyright Act to mean:

(a) a painting, sculpture, drawing, engraving or photograph, whether the work is of artistic quality or not;

(b) a building or a model of a building, whether the building or model is of artistic quality or not; or

(c) a work of artistic craftsmanship whether or not mentioned in paragraph (a) or (b).[38]

Thus, it is possible that a design might be embodied in a 'product' within the meaning of the Designs Act and be an 'artistic work' within the meaning of the Copyright Act. A painting that is applied as part of wallpaper and a sculpture that is mass-manufactured as a decorative item for the home are clear examples.

This potential overlap between the protection offered under the Designs Act and that offered under the Copyright Act has a long and complex history in Australia. It is presently dealt with in Sections 74 to 77 of the Copyright Act. At the same time as the Designs Act came into force on June 17 2004, a separate piece of legislation relating to designs law came into force altering these 'copyright/design overlap' provisions of the Copyright Act.

In simple terms, this technical area of the Copyright Act is designed to remove

---

34 *Ibid*, Section 93(1).
35 *Ibid*, Section 93(2).
36 *Ibid*, Section 93(3).
37 *Ibid*, Section 151(3).
38 Copyright Act, Section 10(1).

copyright protection for certain copyright works which are exploited industrially. However, the previous provisions gave rise to differing interpretations and were subject to criticism. The amendments are designed to provide clarity to this area of the law and to close a number of loopholes and anomalies which had developed.

The intention is that these amendments should better reflect the underlying policy that:

- artistic works which are industrially exploited as three-dimensional designs should be denied copyright protection and instead be subject to design protection; and
- artistic works which are exploited as two-dimensional designs should continue to receive copyright protection and be entitled to dual protection by design registration, where available.

Under the regime applying since June 17 2004, where copyright subsists in an artistic work and a corresponding design is or has been registered under the 1906 Act or the Designs Act it is not an infringement of that copyright to reproduce the work by embodying that, or any other, corresponding design in a product.[39] A 'corresponding design', in relation to an artistic work, is defined to mean "visual features of shape or configuration which, when embodied in a product, result in a reproduction of that work, whether or not the visual features constitute a design that is capable of being registered under the Designs Act 2003".[40] Notably, registration of a corresponding design as a design under the Designs Act does not extinguish the copyright in the artistic work, but provides a defence to infringement allegations as a result of reproduction of the artistic work.

Further, even where a corresponding design has not been registered under the 1906 Act or the Designs Act, there is a defence to actions for infringement of copyright in an artistic work if the corresponding design of a three-dimensional article is 'applied industrially', whether in Australia or elsewhere, by or with the licence of the owner of the copyright in the place of industrial application.[41] The regulations made under the Copyright Act specify that a design is taken to be applied industrially if it is applied to more than 50 articles or to one or more articles (other than hand-made articles) manufactured in lengths or pieces.[42] However, this regulation is a deeming provision only, and industrial application will be found if on the facts one or more products embodying the corresponding design have been made under a manufacturing process for the systematic production of articles.[43]

There are exceptions for artistic works that are buildings, models of buildings or works of artistic craftsmanship.[44] Even if these artistic works are industrially applied, the copyright owner may bring proceedings for infringement of copyright unheeded

---

39 *Ibid*, Section 75.

40 *Ibid*, Section 74(1).

41 *Ibid*, Sections 77 and 77A.

42 Copyright Regulations 1969, Regulation 17.

43 See *Safe Sport Pty Ltd v Puma Australia Pty Ltd* (1985) 4 IPR 120 at 126; *Kevlacat Pty Ltd v Trailcraft Marine Pty Ltd* (1987) 11 IPR 77 at 88 to 89; and *Press-Form Pty Ltd v Henderson's Ltd* (1993) 26 IPR 113 at 121, cited in Lahore, James and Warwick Rothnie, *Copyright and Designs* (3rd revised edn, looseleaf) at [64,500].

44 Copyright Act, Section 77(1)(a).

by the defence in Sections 77 and 77A, unless a corresponding design is or has been registered as a design, in which case the Section 75 defence to copyright infringement will apply.

4. Qualification for protection

4.1 What is a 'design'?

In the Designs Act 'design', in relation to a product, means "the overall appearance of the product resulting from one or more visual features of the product".[45] 'Product' is defined as a thing that is manufactured or hand-made.[46] The Designs Act provides that "visual feature, in relation to a product, includes the shape, configuration, pattern and ornamentation of the product".[47]

Shape and configuration primarily refer to three-dimensional features of the product, such as the form of a vase or the shape of a light bulb. Pattern and ornamentation generally refer to two-dimensional features, as might appear on wallpaper or a carpet. However, there can be overlap between these visual features, as in the case of diagonal ribbing applied to a rubber hot-water bottle[48] or decorative plates applied to a coffin.[49]

The feel of the product, its materials and the repeat features of its pattern or shape are not considered visual features under the Designs Act,[50] nor are features that convey the method or principle of construction.[51]

Importantly, the definition of visual features is non-exhaustive, and colour is an example of an additional, potentially relevant visual feature. As stated by Graham J in *Smith Kline & French Laboratories Ltd's Design Application*:[52] "[c]olour may or may not make a material difference, depending upon the circumstances and nature of the design in question".[53] It is true that normally differences in colour are unlikely to be important. Generally, the alteration of a colour in a design would be regarded as being in the nature of a trade variant. However, in other cases colour may be an essential feature of the design.[54]

While a visual feature may serve a functional purpose,[55] the registration of a design does not protect the function itself. Protection of this nature falls within the domain of patent law.

4.2 What is a 'registrable design'?

To qualify for registration a design must be a 'registrable design' under the Designs

---

45 Designs Act, Section 5.
46 *Ibid*, Section 6(1).
47 *Ibid*, Section 7(1).
48 See *Cow (PB) & Co Ltd v Cannon Rubber Manufacturers Ltd* [1959] RPC 347.
49 See *Re Rollason's Registered Design* (1898) 15 RPC 441.
50 Designs Act, Section 7(3).
51 See *Firmagroup Australia Pty Ltd v Byrne & Davidson Doors (Vic) Pty Ltd* (1987) 9 IPR 353.
52 [1974] RPC 253 at 261.
53 More recently, see *Review 2 Pty Ltd v Redberry Enterprise Pty Ltd* (2008) 79 IPR 214.
54 For a detailed analysis of the role of colour in registered designs, see Webb, Timothy, 'She Comes in Colours Ev'rywhere: law and practice at the intersection of fashion and registered designs' (2009) 79 *Intellectual Property Forum (Journal of the Intellectual Property Society of Australia and New Zealand)* 11.
55 Designs Act, Section 7(2).

Act. A design is a registrable design if the design is new and distinctive when compared with the prior art base for the design as it existed before the priority date of the design.[56]

A design is 'new' unless it is identical to a design that forms part of the prior art base to the design,[57] and is 'distinctive' unless it is substantially similar in overall impression to a design that forms part of the prior art base for the design.[58]

The 'prior art base' for a design consists of designs publicly used in Australia, designs published in a document within or outside Australia and designs disclosed in earlier design applications.[59] The 'priority date' is the filing date of the design application, unless the applicant claims an earlier priority date deriving from an overseas application filed in a convention country (discussed further in section 4.3 below).[60] In Australia, design applications are filed with IP Australia.

In deciding whether a design is substantially similar in overall impression to another design, more weight is given to similarities between the designs than to differences between them.[61] In addition, the person determining whether the design is substantially similar must:[62]

- have regard to the state of development of the prior art base for the design;
- if the design application identified particular visual features of the design as new and distinctive, have particular regard to those features;
- if only a part of the design is substantially similar to another design, have regard to the amount, quality and importance of that part in the context of the design as a whole; and
- have regard to the freedom of the creator of the design to innovate.

The person making the determination must apply the standard of a person who is familiar with the product to which the design relates, or products similar to the product to which the design relates (known as the 'standard of the informed user').[63]

4.3 International obligations

Since 1925, Australia has been a member of the union constituted by the Paris Convention for the Protection of Industrial Property, done at Paris on March 20 1883.[64] In accordance with the convention, once protection has been sought in Australia a rights holder is allowed a six-month period in which to lodge design applications in other member countries to the convention. This avoids the burden of making simultaneous applications in countries in which the rights holder desires design protection.

The filing date of the design application in Australia will be the relevant date from which the design is protected in other member countries, provided the design

---

56 *Ibid*, Section 15(1).
57 *Ibid*, Section 16(1).
58 *Ibid*, Section 16(2).
59 *Ibid*, Section 15(2).
60 *Ibid*, Section 27(1).
61 *Ibid*, Section 19(1).
62 *Ibid*, Section 19.
63 *Ibid*, Section 19(4).
64 See www.wipo.int/treaties/en/ip/paris/trtdocs_wo020.html.

is successfully registered in those other countries. Similarly, the priority date in Australia for an application from a convention country (the 'basic application') will be the date of the basic application if the corresponding Australian application is made within six months of the basic application.

In addition to applications made in Paris Convention countries, Australia currently recognises applications made under the Hague Agreement Concerning the International Deposit of Industrial Designs, done at The Hague on November 6 1925, the Benelux Designs Convention, done at Brussels on October 25 1966, and the Treaty Establishing the European Community, done at Rome on March 25 1957.[65]

Similar advantages to those under the Paris Convention are given to members of the World Trade Organization (WTO) under the TRIPs Agreement. Australia has been a member of the WTO since it started on January 1 1995. Under the TRIPs Agreement, members are to provide for the protection of "independently created industrial designs that are new or original".[66] The rights of owners under the agreement are in similar terms to those under the Designs Act, and members are also required to ensure the protection of textile designs.[67]

Australia classifies design applications using the International Design Classification that was created by the Agreement establishing an International Classification for Industrial Design, signed at Locarno on October 8 1968.[68]

5. Infringement

5.1 Test for infringement

Under the Designs Act, there are five elements that must be proved in order to establish infringement:

- the alleged infringer has done one (or more) of the actions specified under the Designs Act as being the exclusive rights of the rights holder;
- the alleged infringer has done the action(s) without the licence or authority of the rights holder;
- the action(s) were done within the term of the design's registration;
- the action(s) were done in relation to a product for which the design is registered; and
- the products embody the design or a design that is identical to or substantially similar in overall impression to the registered design.[69]

In determining whether a design is substantially similar in overall impression to the registered design, the court must consider the same mandatory factors that apply when determining whether a design is 'distinctive' to be a registrable design.[70]

---

65 Design Regulations, Regulation 3.06(6).
66 TRIPs Agreement, Article 25(1).
67 TRIPs Agreement, Articles 25(2), 26(1).
68 See www.wipo.int/treaties/en/classification/locarno/trtdocs_wo014.html.
69 Designs Act, Section 71(1). The test for infringement under the 1906 Act – which continues to apply for designs registered under it – was significantly different. A person infringed the monopoly in a registered design if they applied the design or any "fraudulent or obvious imitation of it" without licence or authority of the owner.

5.2 Defences to infringement

An alleged infringer may escape liability if it can make out one of the several available defences under the Designs Act.

First, there is a defence for parallel imports. A person does not infringe a registered design if he imports a product which embodies a registered design (or one substantially similar to it) if the product embodies the design with the licence or authority of the rights holder.[71] The intention is that the import of pirate products will constitute infringement but the import of genuine products will not. However, it has been noted that this raises certain complexities.[72] The licence or authority must be the licence or authority of the rights holder of the Australian registered design. If the design is owned outside Australia by someone other than the person entered in the Australian register as the rights holder, the defence for parallel imports will not arise. Also, there is uncertainty about what can be done with the products once imported. The Designs Act specifies only that importation of such products is not an infringement, and it does not specify that selling, offering for sale, or even using or keeping such products for the purposes of trade or business is not an infringement also. Thus, it is possible that those acts are not covered by the defence. Although there has been no judicial consideration of this issue, eminent authors submit that the better view is that products lawfully imported pursuant to the defence may be dealt with by sale, hire, etc in Australia, or else the right to import genuine products would be rendered largely useless.[73]

Second, there is also a defence to infringement for the making of repairs to a 'complex product' – that is, a product comprising at least two replaceable component parts permitting disassembly and reassembly of the product. The Designs Act provides that a person does not infringe a registered design if he uses a product in relation to which the design is registered, the product is a component part of a complex product and the use is for the purpose of the repair of the complex product so as to restore its overall appearance in whole or part.[74] This is sometimes called the 'spare parts' defence.

Third, a defendant in infringement proceedings in respect of a registered design may apply for the revocation of the registration of the design, by way of counterclaim in the proceedings.[75] If the counterclaim is successful and the court makes an order revoking the registration of the design, the primary claim for infringement of that design must necessarily fail.

Fourth, the Designs Act contains Crown use provisions that enable the Commonwealth of Australia or a state, or a person authorised in writing by the Commonwealth or a state, to use a design for the services of the Commonwealth or state.[76] Accordingly, infringement proceedings do not lie in relation to such use of a design.[77] For these purposes, 'state' is defined to include the Australian Capital

70 Designs Act, Section 71(3).
71 *Ibid*, Section 71(2).
72 See Lahore and Rothnie, note 43 above, at [71,055].
73 See *ibid*.
74 Designs Act, Section 72.
75 *Ibid*, Section 74.
76 *Ibid*, Section 96(1).
77 *Ibid*, Section 100.

Territory, the Northern Territory, Norfolk Island and an authority of those territories.[78]

Finally, in contrast to Australian trademarks law, it is no defence to an action for infringement of a registered design that the infringer's product is itself subject to a design registration. While the design registration may form part of the prior art base which could affect the validity of the design alleged to be infringed, if the priority date is not earlier the fact of design registration is irrelevant.

6. Design infringement litigation

6.1 Where actions may be brought

The rights holder of a registered design may bring proceedings against another person, alleging that the person has infringed the registered design.[79] Infringement proceedings may be brought in a prescribed court or in another court that has jurisdiction in relation to the proceedings.[80] The Designs Act defines the Federal Court of Australia or a Supreme Court of a state or of the Australian Capital Territory, the Northern Territory or Norfolk Island to be prescribed courts.[81] However, the jurisdiction of a Supreme Court of a territory is limited to the extent the Constitution permits, or otherwise is conferred only in relation to proceedings instituted by a natural person who is resident in the territory, or a corporation that has its principal place of business in the territory, at the time the proceedings were brought.[82]

The Intellectual Property Laws Amendment (Raising the Bar) Bill 2011 (Cth), which will amend a range of intellectual property laws, has been passed by the Commonwealth Parliament and is awaiting Royal Assent by the Governor General. When it commences, the Federal Magistrates Court – established to provide a cheaper and quicker forum for less complex disputes – will also be a prescribed court given jurisdiction with respect to matters arising under the Designs Act, including claims for infringement of a registered design.

Infringement proceedings must be started within six years of the day on which the alleged infringement occurred.[83] A court may grant the registrar leave to intervene in infringement proceedings.[84]

6.2 Court procedure

The specific procedure of design infringement litigation will depend on the prescribed court in which the proceedings are commenced. In addition to the general rules of court, specific rules apply to IP proceedings, such as Division 34.3 of the Federal Court Rules 2011 (Cth) for the Federal Court, Part 48 of the Uniform Civil Procedure Rules 2005 (NSW) for the Supreme Court of New South Wales and Chapter VIII of the Supreme Court (Intellectual Property) Rules 2006 (Vic) for the Supreme

---

78 *Ibid*, Section 95(2).
79 *Ibid*, Section 73(1).
80 *Ibid*, Section 73(2).
81 *Ibid*, Section 5.
82 *Ibid*, Section 84(2).
83 *Ibid*, Section 71(4).
84 *Ibid*, Section 76.

Court of Victoria. These specify, for example, that in a proceeding for the infringement of a registered design, particulars of the infringement must specify the manner in which the design is alleged to be infringed and give at least one instance of each type of infringement alleged.[85]

Proceedings are usually started by filing a document stating the relief claimed by the plaintiff together with a pleading containing a summary of the material facts on which the party relies. Those documents are served on the defendant, who files a defence to the claim which either admits or traverses each allegation.

Once the issues are defined by the pleadings, there may be a process for the production of relevant documents by each party, commonly known as discovery. However, there has a been a general trend in most courts to limit discovery to the extent necessary to resolve the real issues in dispute, due to the cost and time involved.

The parties then prepare evidence to be relied on at the hearing, which usually is in the form of affidavits. These are written statements made by witnesses who swear or affirm that the statement is true. The affidavits are read at the hearing by the party relying on that evidence, and the deponents of them may be cross-examined by the opposing party.

It is common in IP infringement proceedings, including design infringement, for there to be a separate determination of liability and damages. This is because there is often a clear line of demarcation between liability and damages issues, with the latter being unnecessary if the claim for infringement is not established.

6.3 Relief from unjustified threats

If a person is threatened by another person with infringement proceedings, or other similar proceedings, in respect of a design, an aggrieved person may apply to a court for a declaration that the threats are unjustified, an injunction against the continuation of the threats and the recovery of damages sustained as a result of the threats.[86] The aggrieved person may be someone other than the person who is being threatened, such as a person whose profit-making activities will be affected by the threat of proceedings.

The Designs Act specifies that mere notification of the existence of a registered design does not constitute a threat of infringement proceedings.[87] However, if a certificate of examination has not been issued in respect of a design, a threat to bring infringement proceedings in respect of the design is deemed to be an unjustified threat.[88] While the legislation gives no further guidance on what constitutes a threat, the courts have held that the test is whether or not the language would convey to any reasonable person that the author of the communication intended to bring proceedings against the person threatened.[89] Further, threats may be made by means of circulars or advertisements or by any other means.[90]

---

85 Rule 34.36 of the Federal Court Rules; Rule 48.21 of the Uniform Civil Procedure Rules; and Rule 6.02 of the Supreme Court (Intellectual Property) Rules 2006.

86 Designs Act, Section 77(1).

87 *Ibid*, Section 80.

88 *Ibid*, Section 77(3).

89 See Lahore and Rothnie, note 43 above, at [71,260].

90 Designs Act, Section 77(2).

The defence to an action for unjustified threats is for the person who made the threat to satisfy the court that the threat was justified. This requires the rights holder to establish, first, that the design concerned is registered, has been examined and certificate of examination has been issued and, second, that the acts about which the threats were made infringe, or would infringe, the registered design. As a result, an available tactic in response to an application for relief from unjustified threats is for the respondent to apply, by way of counterclaim, for relief in respect of infringement proceedings.[91] In such an event, the applicant seeking relief from unjustified threats may, without making a separate application, apply for revocation of the registration of the design.[92]

The damages that can be awarded as a result of unjustified threats can be significant. In the decision of *World of Technologies (Aust) Pty Ltd v Tempo (Aust) Pty Ltd*,[93] the court awarded the cross-claimant the sum of A$213,059.96 by way of damages for the cross-respondent's unjustified threats of infringement proceedings. This was made up of A$126,231.38, being the gross profit that would have been made from the sale of an outstanding order that was cancelled on receipt of the threat, and A$86,828.58, being compensation for future orders that might have been placed if the threat had not been made.

6.4 Appeals

A first-instance decision in infringement or unjustified threats proceedings may be appealed to the Federal Court constituted as a Full Court, which usually comprises three judges.[94]

An appeal from a decision of the Full Federal Court lies to the High Court of Australia, but only with special leave of the High Court.[95]

7. Licensing and exploitation

An IP licence grants another entity the right to access and use the intellectual property for an agreed time where such access or use would otherwise infringe the rights of the IP owner. A licence is one of the most common forms of IP commercialisation as it is a flexible option allowing the needs of both licensor (the party allowing the use) and licensee (the party taking the licence) to be accommodated.

A licence does not transfer ownership of intellectual property and it is the owner's responsibility to maintain the registered design, for example by ensuring the renewal fee is paid after the initial five years of registration.

The terms of the licence will depend on the agreement reached between the parties. It may be exclusive or non-exclusive, for a specific period of time or perpetual, restricted to a particular territory or worldwide, and allow or preclude the licensee from sublicensing. A licence may also be granted for a specific set of

---

91 *Ibid*, Section 79(1).
92 *Ibid*, Section 79(2).
93 (2007) 71 IPR 307.
94 *Ibid*, Section 87(1); Federal Court of Australia Act 1976 (Cth), Sections 25 and 14.
95 *Ibid*, Section 87(3).

activities, such as researching, developing, modifying, manufacturing or selling products or services incorporating the intellectual property.

Registered designs can be licensed just like other forms of intellectual property, such as copyright, patents and trademarks. The licence can take several forms, such as direct licensing of the design to an end user (which may be implied as a term of the contract for sale), granting rights to a distributor or retailer (that assists in distributing the products to end users) or licensing the design to a commercialising party that will further develop and commercialise the intellectual property.[96]

However, the designs legislation is notable for what it does not enable licensees to do. An exclusive licensee may suffer greater loss than the rights holder as a result of the infringing acts of other parties, and may be in a better position to enforce those rights. This is reflected in the Copyright Act 1968 (Cth), Patents Act 1990 (Cth) and Trade Marks Act 1995 (Cth), each of which enables exclusive licensees to commence infringement proceedings. In contrast, the Designs Act does not include like provisions, so licensees do not have standing to bring actions for infringement.

96 For more detail on IP management and commercialisation generally, see Spruson and Ferguson, *Intellectual Property Management: A Practical Guide for Electrical and Electronics Related Industries* (2007) at www.sprusons.com.au/pdf/IP_Management_Guide_(lowres).pdf (October 30 2011).

Austria

Roland Deissenberger
Deissenberger Rechtsanwälte

---

1. Summary of design protection

In Austria, designs may enjoy legal protection through patents, industrial designs (or utility models), design protection, trademarks or copyrights. Additional protection may be obtained under competition law, if a legal relationship can be established, using contractual clauses providing confidentiality and/or limitations on use, but this is not discussed in the following.

2. Registered design rights

Protection as patents, industrial designs (which are treated separately from designs), designs and trademarks is obtained through registration at the Patent Office. The requirements and the applicability to designs or design features vary and are discussed below.

2.1 Patent rights

A patent is an intellectual property right which protects technical inventions subject to the legal provisions of the Patents Act. The rights holder enjoys an exclusive right to use the invention protected by the patent and to stop any other party from using it. This includes the manufacture, distribution and sale of products incorporating the invention.

The legal requirements of a patent are that the design is:

- an invention;
- which is new (novelty of the invention); and
- not obvious (inventive step); and
- open for industrial application.

These requirements are identical to the requirements of the European patent filed under the European Patent Convention.

An invention is considered to be new if it is not state of technology. It is or becomes state of technology if was made known to the public before the patent application is filed. Austrian patent law does not provide any period of grace regarding novelty.

There are several limitations to patent protection: patents cannot be granted for surgical and therapeutic treatment methods or diagnostic methods on humans or animals, plant varieties, animal breeds or biological methods of breeding. Discoveries, mathematical methods, scientific theories, aesthetic creations, plans, rules and proceedings for theoretical activities, for games or business activities and software programs are not considered to be inventions and cannot be protected. Beyond that, a patent cannot be granted if the use of the invention infringes public order and morals (eg, cloning or the use of human embryos).

The invention must not be obvious to a person who is skilled in the technology and must contain an inventive step. If an invention cannot be industrially utilised, it will not be granted patent protection.

Only the inventor of a design or his legal successor may apply for a patent. Special rules apply for inventions by employees. If the activity which led to an invention is part of the employee's duties, or the suggestion for the invention arose from his employment, or the invention was assisted by the employer's experience and facilities, and if the employer and employee have an agreement in writing that any invention of the employee should belong to the employer or that the employer should have a usage right regarding an invention, the employee is entitled to receive compensation for his invention and the employer enjoys the rights set out in the agreement. Public institutions (eg, a university) do not need a separate agreement to claim the invention of their employees and enjoy the usage right.

The first step to obtain a patent is to file a patent application at the Patent Office. The application must include:

- the application;
- the title of the invention;
- a description of the invention;
- the claims of the patent, for which protection is applied;
- eventually, drawings to support the description; and
- a summary.

An application may be submitted in German, English or French. If it is not made in German, a German translation must be provided within two months of being requested by the Patent Office. The naming of the inventors is not compulsory, but inventors may be named in the application. A priority can be claimed for an application under the Paris Convention for the Protection of Industrial Property and the Agreement on Trade-Related Aspects of Intellectual Property Rights (TRIPs).

The Patent Office examines the application formally and substantially to ensure it complies with the legal requirements for a patent. The office issues a search report listing earlier publications which the examiner considers to be important for assessment of the patentability. The first opinion of the examiner is usually issued at the same time. The applicant may comment on the opinion of the examiner and the description, the claims, the drawings and the summary of the design may be amended. The application is kept secret for 18 months from the filing date, or for 18 months from the priority date if a priority is claimed, after which the application documents, claims and search report are published. Upon successful completion of the examination a patent is granted, which is confirmed by a certificate, and announced in the Patent Gazette and the patent document is published.

Any party may object to a patent by filing an opposition within four months of its publication. Opposition proceedings are held before the technical department of the Patent Office. The rights holder may submit a response to the opposition. If witnesses are to be heard or a sample is to be inspected, oral proceedings will take place. This may be requested by either party or ordered by the Patent Office. The patent may be revoked completely or partly by opposition proceedings and the decision will be published in the Patent Gazette. The parties to the proceedings must bear their own costs.

Decisions of examination proceedings and opposition proceedings may be appealed to Patent Office's appeals department. Appeals must be filed within two months of the decision. Before the file and the appeal are forwarded to the appeals department, the original decision-maker may conduct preliminary appeal proceedings and issue a preliminary appeal decision. The preliminary appeal decision replaces the contested decision. Either party may request submission of the appeal to the appeals department, within 14 days. Such a request suspends the preliminary appeal decision and the appeal proceedings will be undertaken by the appeals department.

The decision of the appeals department may be appealed to the Supreme Senate for Patents and Trademarks.

The parties have to bear their own costs in all appeal proceedings.

Apart from the deadlines to claim a priority, to file an opposition and to file an appeal, the terms in the proceedings can be extended upon request of the party.

A patent application may be converted to an industrial design application provided no decision on the patent application was made. Reconversion of such an application to a patent application is not permitted. Conversion to an industrial design application is only possible for national patent applications. Such conversion is recommended if the Patent Office examination confirmed the novelty of the invention but the inventive step is disputed.

An industrial design application may be branched off from a patent application. Branching off is possible before the expiry of:

- two months from the date on which the patent application is considered to be withdrawn;
- two months after the decision to reject the patent application became enforceable;
- six months after the patent is considered to be granted if no opposition was filed;
- 11 months after the decision to grant a European patent became enforceable if no opposition was filed; or
- two months after the decision on an opposition became enforceable.

Branching off into industrial design applications is available for national patent applications as well as European and international applications if Austria is mentioned as contracting state.

A patent provides protection for up to 20 years.

Various remedies for infringement of a patent are available under the Patent Act:

- a claim for 'cease and desist';
- a claim for destruction, which includes the objects infringing the patent and the tools and appliances used in the production of the infringing objects;

- a claim for publication of the judgment;
- a claim for adequate compensation, for lost profit or for the profit of the infringer, and for damages;
- a claim for disclosure of accounts data; and
- a claim for disclosure of the origins of the infringing object or service and of distribution channels.

Claims for cease and desist, destruction, compensation, profit and damages may be accompanied by an application for a preliminary injunction. Injunctions may be also obtained to secure evidence. The court may issue injunctions for claims for cease and desist and destruction even if the usual legal requirements for injunctions are not fulfilled.

The Patent Act extends the claim for cease and desist in the case of infringements by employees. Claims for compensation, profit, damages, disclosure of accounts data and disclosure of origins and distribution channels are extended to the owner of a business, unless he was not aware of and did not obtain an advantage from the infringement. The owner of a business becomes liable for the claims for compensation, profit and damages if he knew about the infringement or should have known about it.

Claims arising from infringements of patents and applications for preliminary injunctions are filed exclusively at the Trade Court in Vienna.

The infringement of a patent constitutes a criminal offence which may be prosecuted at the request of the infringed party. The Criminal State Court in Vienna has exclusive competence for such offences.

A rights holder may grant licences for using the invention. The Patent Act provides the possibility of granting compulsory licences in the following cases:

- if an invention cannot be used without infringing an older patent, and the invention brings an important technical progress of relevant commercial importance;
- if an invention is not used in Austria in an adequate scope; or
- in relation to obtaining or using a plant variety right and the need to use a patented invention, which is outside of the scope of the topic of this chapter.

A restriction for semiconductor technology applies.

If a rights holder does not grant a licence within a set time, an application to the Patent Office can be filed. The time limits for application are four years after the patent application is filed or three years after the patent is granted, the later expiry date being relevant. The Patent Office decides on the term and extent of the compulsory licence, the compensation for the rights holder and a security for the compensation. If an invention is in the public interest and is needed due to a state of emergency or extreme urgency, a preliminary licence may be granted without first seeking the rights holder's approval.

Licences, including compulsory licences, may be assigned without the approval of the rights holder if the part of a business which is licensed is transferred.

A patent may be contested by an action for revocation of the patent. First, the

Patent Office will prepare the proceeding by hearing non-local witnesses and/or obtaining expert opinions. An appeal against the decision to the Supreme Senate for Patents and Trademarks is possible.

A declaratory judgment can be requested from the Patent Office to clarify whether an object or a method falls under a patent or not. Such judgment is binding on other courts.

2.2 Industrial designs

The industrial design (or utility model) is sometimes called 'petty patent' because it requires an inventive step, and the protection period is reduced to a maximum of 10 years. It is an additional means of protecting inventions. The legal regulations for industrial designs are provided by the Industrial Design Act.

The legal requirements for an industrial design are similar to a patent – that is, that it requires:

- novelty (although the inventor enjoys a six-month grace period);
- an inventive step (but less demanding than a patent); and
- industrial applicability.

Whereas a patent is granted only after an extensive examination, an industrial design only requires a formal examination of conformity with the legal requirements and a search report to achieve registration.

Upon registration, an industrial design is an intellectual property right, granting the rights holder the same claims against infringers as for a patent.

In Austria, industrial designs are not limited to certain fields. The same restrictions apply as for patents. Unlike patents, an industrial design may be used to protect programming logic used in software and methods of diagnosis and treatment of animals. Microorganisms cannot be protected by an industrial design.

The application requirements for an industrial design are the same as for a patent (see section 2.1 above). The application is only examined formally for compliance with the legal requirements. The novelty of the invention and the inventive step are not examined in substance. Claims made in an application may be amended after reviewing the search report. Once the search report has been issued, the industrial design is registered and published. An accelerated registration is possible before completion of the search report. If the result of the examination results in non-conformity with the legal requirements, then such notice is to be answered within two months. If an application does not meet the legal requirements, it must be amended within two months of notification.

It is possible to claim priority of a patent or an industrial design under the Paris Convention and TRIPs.

As mentioned in section 2.1 above, it is possible to convert a patent application into an industrial design application. Similarly, an industrial design application may be converted into a patent application within two months of the issue of the search report, with the exception of accelerated publication and registration of the utility model. Conversion to a patent will provide a longer period of protection. Branching off an industrial design application from a patent application provides a faster method of obtaining protection than for a patent, which has a relatively long registration procedure.

Claims for infringement of an industrial design are the same as for a patent – that is, for cease and desist, destruction, compensation, profit and damages, and disclosure of the accounts data and of origins and distribution channels. Preliminary injunctions are available in the same way as for patents. Claims for infringements and applications for preliminary injunctions are filed exclusively at the Trade Court in Vienna.

The infringement of an industrial design constitutes a criminal offence which may be prosecuted at the request of the infringed party. The Criminal State Court in Vienna has exclusive competence for such offences.

Actions for nullity, revocation, transfer and declaration of dependency of an industrial design are available. Proceedings are conducted by the Patent Office. An appeal to the Supreme Senate for Patents and Trademarks is possible.

A declaratory judgment may be requested from the Patent Office to clarify whether an object or a method falls under an industrial design. Such a judgment is binding on other courts.

2.3 Designs

Under the definition provided by the Design Protection Act, a design is the appearance of an industrial product or of a part of a product. Registration of a design provides protection of the specific appearance of an object according to the registered sample of the design. In essence, any design of an industrial or handicraft object or part of such object, including packaging or covers, decorations, logos, images and so on, may be design protected.

To qualify for design protection, the design must be:

- new; and
- of individual character.

Software is excluded from design protection. The designer enjoys a grace period of 12 months for the novelty requirement. A design has an individual character if its overall impression differs from the overall impression of products which are already available to the public. Designs are considered to be identical if they differ only in unimportant details. A design cannot be protected if its appearance is solely a consequence of its technical function.

A design application is filed with the Patent Office. The application must contain:

- representations of the design; and
- the specification of the products under the classes of the Locarno Agreement Establishing an International Classification for Industrial Designs.

The representation of the design should show all features of the design clearly and so filing of different views is permitted. A single design may refer to any number of classes or sub-classes. If designs belong only to one class of the international classification, it is possible to combine up to 50 designs in one multiple design application. The design application may be submitted as a secret filing, whereby it will not be published for up to 18 months after the priority date of the design. Priority may be claimed within two months of filing under the Paris Convention and other treaties or in the case of reciprocity.

The application is examined to check that it complies with formal requirements, namely the representation of the design and the classification. Novelty and individual character are not examined. If the design passes the examination, it is registered and published.

Protection of a design is granted for five years, which may be extended in five-year terms to a maximum of 25 years.

Registration grants the rights holder the exclusive right to use the design. Usage covers the manufacture, offering, selling, importing, exporting and using the design for products included in the classification for which it was registered.

In a case of design infringement, similarly to a patent and an industrial design the rights holder may claim for cease and desist, destruction, compensation, profit and damages, disclosure of the accounts data and of origins and distribution channels, and preliminary injunctions. Claims for infringements and applications for preliminary injunctions are filed exclusively at the Trade Court in Vienna. The infringement of a design constitutes a criminal offence, which may be prosecuted at the request of the infringed party. Exclusive competence for such offences lies with the Criminal State Court in Vienna. Similarly to patents and industrial designs, a declaratory judgment can be requested from the Patent Office to clarify whether a product may be classified as a design.

An action is available to nullify or to revoke and transfer a design and to contest that the design fulfils the legal requirements. The proceeding can be started *ex officio* and on application. The proceeding is conducted by the Patent Office. An appeal to the Supreme Senate for Patents and Trademarks is permitted.

2.4 Trademarks

The Trademark Act defines trademarks as special signs serving to distinguish the products and services of a business from those of other businesses. A trademark may consist of words, words and images, or only images. Registration of three-dimensional images and audio trademarks is possible.

The trademark application requires details of:

- the mark (word, word and images, or image only); and
- the products and services for which the trademark is to be used.

The specification of products and services must follow the International Classification of Goods and Services. Marks cannot be registered if they are not distinctive, are merely descriptive or are deceptive. The Patent Act provides additional limitations for trademarks, such as use of coats of arms, official quality marks or signs of international organisations.

The Patent Office examines compliance with the legal requirements – that is, mainly the correct classification of the goods and services and whether the mark is excluded from registration because of lack of distinctiveness or because of its descriptive or deceptive nature. The office will conduct a search for similar trademarks and provide a report to the applicant. Similarity or sameness with a registered mark is not an obstacle to registration but may lead to later disputes and infringements.

Third parties may oppose a trademark registration. The opposition must be filed within three months of publication of the mark.

The rights holder is granted the exclusive right to use the trademark for the goods and services for which the mark was registered, and to forbid third parties from using an identical or a similar mark, which could be misleading for the average consumer, for the same or similar goods and products. However, the rights holder is not entitled to forbid the use of the mark for products or services which were placed and made available in the European Economic Area by the rights holder or with its approval. The trademark must be used within five years of grant to avoid the risk of an action for cancellation due to non-usage.

An action for cancellation of a trademark is available, and may be requested based on any of the following reasons:

- if the mark is similar or identical to an earlier registered mark, by the owner of the earlier registered mark, within five years after becoming aware of the use of the newly registered mark;
- if the owner of a mark had an obligation to protect the business interests of the applicant, and the trademark was registered without consent of the applicant;
- if a non-registered mark is similar or identical to the registered mark, and the non-registered mark had secondary meaning at the time of registration of the new mark, by the user of the non-registered mark within five years after registration of the mark;
- if the registered mark uses a name, a name of a business or a special designation of a business or a designation similar without approval and if use of the registered mark may be misleading, within five years after obtaining knowledge of the use of the mark;
- if the mark is not distinctive or is descriptive or deceptive;
- if a mark has not been used for at least five years; or
- if a registered mark becomes a common designation for a product and service.

The proceeding is conducted by the Patent Office. An appeal against its decision to the Supreme Senate for Patents and Trademarks is possible.

The protection is granted for 10 years and is renewable.

If a trademark is infringed, the rights holder may claim for cease and desist, destruction, compensation, profit and damages, disclosure of the accounts data and of origins and distribution channels, and preliminary injunctions. The infringement of a mark constitutes a criminal offence which may be prosecuted at the request of the infringed party.

If a trademark is infringed by a business, any claim for cease and desist and for destruction may be directed against the owner of the business. Claims for compensation, profit, damages, disclosure of accounts data and disclosure of origins and distribution channels are extended against the owner of the business, unless the owner did not know about and did not obtain an advantage from the infringement. The owner of a business is liable for claims for compensation, profit and damages if it knew or should have known about the infringement.

Licenses for trademarks can be granted exclusively or non-exclusively, for the whole territory of Austria or parts of it, and for all or only some goods and services. A trademark can be assigned in total or partially for some goods and services without the business of the rights holder.

3. Unregistered design rights

Industrial designs may be protected through unregistered rights under the Copyright Act and some regulations of competition law.

3.1 Copyright

The Copyright Act defines 'works' as intellectual creations in the fields of literature, music, the visual arts and cinema. A work is protected as a whole and in its parts under the provisions of the act. Computer programs are explicitly defined as works of literature.

Certain industrial designs meet the requirement of a work under copyright law. The courts interpret the definition of a work according to the Copyright Act – that a work does not require a certain level of creative input, but that generally intellectual creations of various fields enjoy copyright protection. This includes industrial and handicraft products, unless their form and design is only a result of their technical function. The explicit definition of software as a work of literature, including the machine code, also covers software designs.

The creator of a work enjoys the copyright. The copyright includes the exclusive right to utilise the work – to copy, distribute, let and lease, exhibit, broadcast, and perform it. Works of Austrian creators, works published in Austria and works of visual art, which are part of real estate in Austria, are protected. Other works of foreign creators are protected under the Copyright Act in cases of reciprocity or under treaties such as the Berne Convention for the Protection of Literary and Artistic Works, the Universal Copyright Convention and TRIPs).

Under Austrian copyright law, copyright ends 70 years after the creation of the work, if the creator is not named, or 70 years after the death of the creator, if he is named. Registration of a work or its creator is not required. However, it is possible to register a creator in the Creator's Registry, so that the copyright for his work expires 70 years after his death.

If a copyright is infringed, the main claims available to the rights holder are for cease and desist, destruction, publication of a judgment, adequate compensation, profit and damages, disclosure of the accounts data, manufacturer, origins and quantities of infringing goods or services, and preliminary injunctions. If the infringer is a business, the claim for adequate compensation is extended to the owner of the business. If the owner of the business knew or should have known of the infringement, damages and profit claims may be lodged against him.

Copyright infringements constitute a criminal offence. It is an offence for the owner or manager of a business not to prevent an infringement by an employee. The rights holder must request prosecution and in criminal proceedings it is possible to apply for seizure of the infringing goods and supporting devices and their destruction.

The creator of a work can grant rights of utilisation and licences for his work.

3.2 Industrial design protection regulations under the Competition Act

Paragraph 9 of the Competition Act provides for claims for cease and desist, damages, adequate compensation and profit, disclosure of accounts data where:

- a name, a special designation of a business or a registered trademark is used in a way which may lead to confusion with the name or the special designation used by another party; or
- signs and other features of a business, especially features of goods, packaging or covers, or business papers, which are considered as marks of a business by consumers, are used in a similar misleading way.

Accordingly, if designs or certain features of designs used in products or the packaging obtain a secondary meaning, then a claim against the infringer can be established and substantiated based on paragraph 9 of the Competition Act. A claim for cease and desist and for damages may also be brought against the owner of a business, if the infringement was made by a person in this business. The owner of the business must have or should have known about the infringement. The act provides preliminary injunctions for the claims based on its regulations.

4. Qualification for protection

To enjoy protection as an industrial design, either an intellectual property must be established by registration (as a patent, industrial design, design or trademark) or the design must constitute a work under the Copyright Act or have achieved secondary meaning for a business, as discussed above. The requirements for the various means are quite different, and cover a wide range of protection.

If there are no applicable treaties, foreign parties enjoy protection in Austria if Austrian citizens and businesses enjoy protection in the other country (reciprocity). Austria is member and contracting party to most international treaties governing intellectual property rights and copyright, such as (for example, but not limited to) the Paris Convention, TRIPs, the Berne Convention and the Universal Copyright Convention. As a member of the European Union, Austria has implemented all relevant EU directives relating to intellectual property rights, copyright and competition law into national law.

5. Infringement

Whether there is an infringement depends on the scope of property rights or copyright. The better a design is protected, the easier it is to prosecute infringements. The range of claims, including claims for damages, compensation and profit, is discussed above under the individual rights.

6. Design infringement litigation

If registered intellectual property rights or copyrights are infringed, the rights holder can request prosecution of the infringer by the criminal courts. As well as punishment, criminal proceedings may be used to seize the infringing objects and obtain evidence, using police and police investigations, which otherwise are not or not easily available.

In relation to all the property rights discussed above and rights without registrations, it is relatively easy to obtain preliminary injunctions under the legal regime. Injunctions may be obtained even if all the usual requirements for injunctions are not met (eg, for irrecoverable damage or prevention of imminent danger). In most infringement cases, civil proceedings are started by applying for a preliminary injunction against the infringer, and often the matter can be settled in the preliminary proceeding without entering into a main proceeding. An application for an injunction must substantiate the existing rights and the infringing activities. Preliminary injunctions are usually granted within a few hours or a few days if well prepared.

The main proceeding is the same as for any other civil litigation. The plaintiff must substantiate the claim in the writ, the defendant is requested to reply and after the exchange of writs the oral hearings start. Generally, judges request that the parties submit all available evidence at the beginning of the hearing. Procedural law allows the parties also to submit writs in the course of the hearings, but in practice it is more advantageous to be as complete and precise as possible in the first writs. Hearings usually start within two or three months of filing the claim. Proceedings at first instance usually take one to two years, depending on the extent of evidence to be taken. All facts must be presented at the first instance, as appeals do not allow submission of new facts. Depending on the importance of the legal issue to be resolved, a further appeal to the Supreme Court may be granted by the Court of Appeals or may be accepted by the Supreme Court.

The court sets the costs of the proceeding in its judgment, based on the decision. Civil procedure law provides that the successful party's costs are reimbursed by the other party. Costs include the cost of representation, which is assessed under the Austrian lawyers' tariff. The tariff takes into account the value of the claim and all necessary steps in the proceedings (eg, writs, duration of hearings) and provides the fees for all these steps. In an average litigation, the fees set by the tariff cover all or most of the cost of representation. The court fee must be paid by the plaintiff when the claim is filed and is dependent on the value of the claim, which must be stated in the claim.

The enforcement of injunctions and judgments is reasonably efficient and fast.

7. Licensing and exploitation

If property rights or copyrights are not used by the rights holder, licences may be granted to use the rights commercially. All property rights allow rights holders to negotiate and define the term and scope of the licence. Licences may be granted exclusively or non-exclusively, restricted in time or territory, and to the full extent of the right or only parts of it. It is possible to register licences for most property rights, but this is not a requirement for the licence to be valid. See section 2.1 above for compulsory licences.

Belgium

Karel Nijs
Philippe Péters
NautaDutilh Brussels

---

1. Summary of design protection

In Belgium, protection of the outward appearance of a product or a part thereof can be obtained by various means, such as follows:

- *Design*
  The Benelux Treaty on Intellectual Property allows the outward appearance of a product to be protected as a design, provided it is novel and has individual character. These requirements apply to both two-dimensional drawings and three-dimensional forms or shapes. Designs registered under the treaty are valid throughout Benelux – that is, Belgium, the Netherlands and Luxembourg.
- *Copyright*
  A design can be protected by copyright if it fulfils the specific conditions applicable to literary and artistic works under the Copyright Act, whether it is registered or not.
- *Tort/unfair competition*
  In principle, the provisions of unfair competition law could also be relied on, but case law indicates that the courts are reluctant to uphold this type of claim.

Under Benelux law, design rights can only be protected through registration. Copyright protection is not subject to any formalities and vests automatically in the creator of the work. However, specific rules apply for works designed by employees or third (ie, external) parties.

2. Registered design rights

2.1 Nature of the rights

The Benelux Treaty defines a 'design' as the outward appearance of any type of industrial or handicraft product or part thereof, packaging, get-up, graphic symbol or typeface, by incorporation or application. The design should result from features such as the lines, contours, colours, shapes, textures and/or materials of the product, and/or its ornamentation.

Under the treaty, design rights can only be obtained through registration. The holders of registered Benelux designs have an exclusive right to use the design and to prevent any third party from using it. They are protected against both deliberate copying and the independent development of a similar design. Their rights are valid throughout the Benelux.

2.2 Requirements for protection

To qualify for protection, a design must be new and have individual character.

A design is considered to be new if no identical design has been made available to the public prior to the filing date of the application for registration or, if priority is claimed, the priority date. For the purposes of this requirement, a design that differs only in minor respects from the design covered by the application is considered to be identical.

A design is considered to have individual character if the impression it creates differs from that made on an informed user by any other design which has been made available to the public before the filing date or the priority date.

In order to determine whether these requirements are met, the design is compared with those available to the public. A design is deemed to have been made available to the public if it has been published following registration or exhibited, used in trade or otherwise disclosed, before the filing or priority date, unless the design could not reasonably have become known in the normal course of business to the circles specialised in the industrial or commercial sector concerned within the European Union or the European Economic Area. Any disclosure that occurs under the veil of confidentiality is not taken into account. The Benelux Treaty provides for a 12-month grace period to register a design. The period starts to run when the design is first made available to the public and is intended as a remedy that keeps a designer from having to disclose its creations when the product to which it is applied or in which it is incorporated is not yet ready for launch. It enables designers to test the success of their creations first and decide later whether to seek protection as a registered design, since any public display of the design during this period is not deemed to be detrimental to the assessment of its novelty.

In principle, a design may not be registered if it is based solely on a technical function or must necessarily be reproduced in its exact form and dimensions in order to allow the product in which it is incorporated, or to which it is applied, to be mechanically connected to, or placed in, around or against, another product so that either product may perform its function. The same is true for designs that are contrary to public policy or to accepted principles of morality, or use an existing trademark- or copyright-protected component without the consent of the trademark or copyright owner, or make improper use of the items referred to in Article 6 of the Paris Convention (ie, arms, flags and other emblems, abbreviations and names of states or international organisations).

Where the product incorporating the design or to which the design is applied constitutes a component part of a product composed of multiple replaceable components (so-called complex products), the design is only considered to be new and to have individual character if:

- the component part, once incorporated into the complex product, remains visible during normal use of the product by the end user (excluding maintenance, servicing and repair works); and

- to the extent the visible features of the component part themselves meet the requirements of novelty and individual character.

Effective from January 1 2003, a so-called 'repair' clause was introduced into the Benelux Treaty, according to which designs that form part of a complex product and which are used for repair purposes in order to restore the original appearance of the product are no longer protected. The purpose of this clause is to open up the spare-parts market, in particular in the automotive sector. However, in two important decisions of March 7 2011, the Mons Court of Appeal found that, notwithstanding this considerable limitation on the exclusive rights of the rights owner, automotive spare parts are original works protected by copyright. Thus, even when other intellectual property rights are not available, copyright remains an effective means of protection (see below).

2.3 Registration procedure

The institution responsible for the registration of designs in the Benelux countries is the Benelux Office for Intellectual Property (BOIP).

The registration process starts with the submission of a standard application form, available on the BOIP's website, www.boip.int, in the two official languages of the BOIP, namely Dutch and French.

On receiving an application, the BOIP assesses its admissibility by checking that it contains a clear representation of the design, a description of the product in which the design is incorporated or to which it is applied, and the applicant's name. An application fee must be paid. If these minimum requirements are not met, no filing date will be granted and the application will not be processed. A filing date is important as it is used to determine the priority (date) of the design that forms the object of the application.

The BOIP does not conduct a substantive examination, except to verify that the design is not contrary to public policy or accepted standards of morality. The novelty and individual character of the design are not checked.

If the procedural requirements are in order, the design will be registered and published in the Benelux Industrial Designs Gazette. To keep the design from being disclosed to competitors sooner than is necessary, the applicant may ask the BOIP to defer publication by up to 12 months. This delay enables the designer to test the products that incorporate the design in the marketplace, in order to determine whether registration of the design is worthwhile.

2.4 Term of protection

A Benelux design is protected for five years from the filing date of the application. The registration can be renewed for additional five-year terms, up to a maximum of 25 years.

As a rule, renewal must be requested, and the corresponding fee paid, within 12 months before expiry of the registration. However, it is possible to request renewal up to six months after expiry of the renewal deadline, provided an additional fee is paid. The BOIP sends a reminder to the rights holder six months before the renewal deadline.

Unlike a trademark, a design need not be put to use in order for the rights to be maintained.

2.5 Rights

A registered Benelux design confers on its rights holder the exclusive right to use the design and to prevent any third party from using it without his consent. Such use covers the making, offering, putting on the market, selling, supplying, letting, importing, exporting, exhibiting and employing a product in which the design is incorporated or to which it is applied, as well as storing such a product for any of these purposes.

Whilst the scope of protection of a Benelux design is based on the representations in the register and not on the product's actual appearance, such protection nevertheless extends to any design which does not produce a different overall impression on an informed user.

2.6 Infringement

The question of infringement should be analysed from the viewpoint of an informed user. Whilst an informed user need not be an expert or specialist, he usually has in-depth knowledge of the relevant market and the designs in existence on that particular market. It is generally accepted that an informed user is aware of design issues and better informed than the average consumer in matters of trademark law. This means that an informed user can more easily identify the distinctive characteristics that create the design's overall impression.

2.7 Damages and other relief

In the event of infringement, several remedies are available, including damages. The amount of damages is determined by the specific facts of the case, in particular the adverse economic effects of the infringement, such as the injured party's lost profit and the infringer's unlawful gain. Non-monetary factors, such as the moral damage sustained by the rights holder, can also be taken into account. Lump-sum damages, at least equivalent to the royalties the rights holder would have received had the infringer requested permission to use the design, may be awarded.

Other remedies include an injunction, the surrender, destruction or recall of infringing goods (including all materials and equipment used to make them), the provision of information about the origin and/or distribution of infringing goods, and publication of the decision.

2.8 Licensing

Benelux designs may be licensed. Although there is no statutory registration obligation, a licence must be registered with the BOIP in order to be enforceable against third parties.

The licensee may intervene in an action brought by the rights holder against alleged infringers for damage caused as a result of the infringement or take action independently, provided the rights holder has agreed.

2.9 Compulsory licences

Except for the cases mentioned below with regard to copyright, Benelux design legislation does not provide for the compulsory granting of licences.

2.10 Validity issues

(a) *Cancellation*

The Benelux Treaty provides that any interested party, including the public prosecutor, may seek the cancellation of a registered design which does not meet the requirements detailed above.

The validity of a design can be challenged by the holder of a prior international, European Community or Benelux design which is identical to the challenged design or which does not give a different overall impression to the challenged design, or even by the holder of a trademark- or copyright-protected work which has been incorporated into the challenged design without consent.

Finally, the designer or rightful owner of the rights to a design may request cancellation of a registration that has been made at the request of a third party without his consent or, alternatively, claim to become recognised as the legitimate holder of the design. A claim relating to the entitlement of a design is time-barred five years after the publication date of the registration.

Cancellation proceedings can only be started before the competent court of the place where the defendant is domiciled. A claim relating to the entitlement of a Benelux design must be brought before the BOIP.

(b) *Abandonment of rights*

A rights holder can voluntarily cancel his registration at any time. A design will also lapse if the registration expires and the renewal formalities are not completed in time.

3. Unregistered design rights: copyright

3.1 Nature of the rights

As a rule, a design can only be protected in the Benelux countries through registration. However, works of applied art and industry, including designs, can be protected by copyright, regardless of whether they are registered. Belgian copyright law is regulated by the Copyright and Neighbouring Rights Act 1994.

3.2 Requirements for protection

In order to enjoy copyright protection, a design must meet the same two cumulative conditions applicable to literary and artistic works: the design must be fixed in a material form (an idea cannot be protected) and original, meaning it must reflect the personality of its creator. This threshold exceeds a mere display of skill, labour and judgment. In practice, originality stems from the creator's personal, discretionary choices, as opposed to technical or economic constraints.

Following the case law and literature, the concept of originality should be construed broadly, and copyright claims for works of applied art have been widely upheld. Only purely utilitarian items, lacking any research with respect to their appeal or appearance, should be excluded. The artistic merit, genre and/or intended audience are not taken into account. The fact that a work consists of a combination of common elements does not exclude it from being eligible for copyright protection. Novelty is not a separate requirement, but prior art is taken into consideration in assessing whether a work is original.

3.3 Term of protection

Under the Copyright Act, copyright protection extends for 70 years after the author's death.

3.4 Rights

Copyright includes both economic rights and moral or personality rights.

The Belgian Copyright Act does not define moral rights, but such rights are generally deemed to include the right to:

- communicate a work to the public;
- claim or deny authorship of a work; and
- preserve the integrity of a work and prevent the alteration, distortion, mutilation or any other impairment of the work that could be prejudicial to the author's reputation or dignity.

Economic rights include:

- the right to reproduce the work, pursuant to which the author has the exclusive right to authorise or prohibit direct or indirect, temporary or permanent, material or intellectual, reproduction or copying of the work by any means, in any form, in whole or in part, in an identical manner or with differences;
- the right to communicate the work to the public, which enables the author to authorise or prohibit any communication to the public of the work, by wire or wireless means, including the making available to the public of works in such a way that members of the public may access them at an individually selected time and place; and
- the right to distribute the work, in any form, by sale or otherwise.

3.5 Infringement

The relevant test for infringement is whether the allegedly infringing work incorporates all or some of the original features of the original work and creates a similar overall impression, regardless of any likelihood of confusion. The overall or global impression is that which remains in the minds of the normal non-technical and non-artistically educated public. This assessment should be made at first sight, meaning it should be verified whether the average purchaser of the products concerned would spontaneously believe that the allegedly infringing product on the whole resembles the original product.

It is generally accepted that similarities are more important than differences. Of course, if the differences outnumber the similarities and confer a different overall impression, no infringement can be found.

The partial reproduction of an original work in a later work which contains new elements that are not found in the original work can be considered copyright infringement if the copied elements are original and protected. One of the main difficulties with this is distinguishing between the reproduction of original features and the mere application of an idea or concept, which cannot be protected. There is very little published case law on partial copying. The cases that do exist generally concern musical works in which only part of a prior musical work is copied. The originality of the copied excerpt is normally not an issue. The later work will be considered infringing if it can be established that the infringer knew or could have known of the earlier work (in order to protect the independent creation of a similar work).

3.6 Damages and other relief

Under the Copyright Act, the author of a work is entitled to compensation for any damage he has sustained due to infringement of his copyright.

The damages that can be recovered are limited to the injured party's lost profit and actual harm as a result of the infringement.

With respect to lost profit, it should be verified whether the infringement affected the goods and/or services the injured party would otherwise have been able to provide, either himself or through his licensee(s). If lost profit can be established, the damages that can be recovered are limited to:

- the profit he would have earned by selling or providing his own goods or services, or
- the royalties he would have received from his licensees.

Damages for actual harm cover the loss suffered by the rights holder due to the harm to his image or reputation.

If the damage cannot be estimated precisely, a fair and equitable assessment is authorised. It is generally accepted that any difficulty in quantifying damage does not call into question its existence. Nor does any such difficulty release a court from its duty to award compensation for the harm suffered

If the infringing party acted in bad faith, the copyrights holder may claim damages equal to the price the defendant received for the goods – that is, actual turnover.

Other remedies include issuing an injunction, the surrender, recall or destruction of the infringing goods together with all materials/equipment used to make them, the provision of information about the origin and/or distribution of the infringing goods, and publication of the decision.

3.7 Licensing

An assignment of the economic rights of copyright must be agreed in writing with the author of the work. However, this condition should be viewed as an evidentiary requirement rather than a requirement for the validity of the assignment. Specific rules should be followed with respect to the terms of the licence. For instance, an assignment or grant of rights that is worded in general terms will not be valid. Under the Copyright Act, the parties should expressly list all forms of exploitation they want the assignment to cover. For each form of exploitation, the duration and remuneration should be expressly stated. Some scholars add an additional requirement, namely that the geographic scope of the assignment should be mentioned. Contracts can also be concluded with respect to future works, provided the genre of the work is specified and the transfer or assignment is limited in time. A transfer of rights for forms of exploitation that are unknown at the time the contract is concluded will be deemed invalid.

Moral rights (ie, the right to disclose the work to the public, the right to be recognised as the author of the work, the right to the integrity of the work, etc) cannot be assigned. According to certain scholars, the author can waive the exercise of these rights in writing.

3.8 Compulsory licences

Under Belgian law, compulsory licenses, in the narrow sense of the term, only exist for the neighbouring rights of performing artists and producers. In all other cases, the exclusive rights of the author are limited mainly by the following exceptions. The author of a work may not object to (any part of) the work being reproduced in the context of short quotations, news reports, parodies, caricatures and pastiche (provided the rules on fair trade practices are observed). The most important restrictions are the so-called 'private use' exception and the exception for exhibitions held in a public space. 'Private use' encompasses both the use of a copyright-protected work in the family circle and its use for illustration purposes in teaching or scientific research. Recent case law indicates that the exception for public exhibitions extends to any accidental use of a copyright-protected work. A typical example is taking a picture of a person in a public place near a protected building, sculpture or statue – the protected building or sculpture is not the subject of the image. However, the final assessment will be left to the court.

3.9 Unfair trade practices

Article 95 of the Commercial Practices Act prohibits an undertaking engaging in commercial practices that harm or are likely to harm the interests of other undertakings. In the past, this article could be successfully raised as a legal basis for claims of parasitic behaviour against competitors (ie, free-riding on a competitor's product and thus taking unfair advantage of its success). However, recent case law indicates that it is becoming increasingly difficult to succeed on these grounds.

The requirements for a finding of parasitism are very strict since they derogate from the fundamental principle of free competition and freedom to copy. According to these principles, competitors are entitled to carry out the same economic activities, target the same market and even copy each other, including their respective products and services and the manner in which they are offered. This position was recently confirmed by the Supreme Court, which held that a merchant who, without making any creative effort, takes direct advantage of significant investments and efforts made by a competitor in developing a creation with economic value is not necessarily guilty of an unfair trade practice.[1] However, the court can find such behaviour to be illegitimate on the ground that an advantage is gained by means other than mere copying.

In addition, following the Court of Justice of the European Union's ruling in *Plus Warengesellschaft*[2] on the scope of Directive 2005/29/EC concerning unfair business-to-consumer commercial practices, it would be necessary to establish likelihood of confusion. In this case, the court gave a broad definition of business-to-consumer commercial practices, namely any practice that is directly connected with the promotion, sale or supply of a product to consumers. Only those commercial practices that harm exclusively the economic interests of competitors or which relate to a transaction between traders (merchants) are excluded from the directive's scope of application. Therefore, a competitor's parasitic behaviour with respect to the outward appearance of a product sold to consumers is likely to be deemed an unfair commercial practice falling under the scope of the directive. However, it is not contained in the list of practices which are in all circumstances considered unfair by the directive. Thus, as the directive introduced a fully harmonised system and member states are not entitled to implement any measures that go beyond the scope of the directive, the only remaining option would be to establish that the (offer for) sale of imitation products is misleading or is likely to mislead consumers as to the origin of the goods. Causing such confusion is still listed as an unfair commercial practice and thus prohibited. However, this may be difficult to prove, and it remains to be seen whether a claim of parasitic behaviour based on Article 95 of the Commercial Practices Act will still be upheld.

4. Qualification for protection

Rights to a registered Benelux design vest in the designer or his successor in title. If two or more persons have jointly developed a design, the rights vest in them jointly. The person in whose name the design is registered or, prior to registration, the person in whose name the application is filed, is deemed to be the designer.

Any natural person or legal entity may apply for and register a Benelux design.

When a design is developed by an employee in the performance of his duties or in following his employer's instructions, the rights to the design vest in the employer, unless agreed otherwise (Article 3.8.1 of the Benelux Treaty). The same applies when a drawing or model has been designed by a third party for the purpose of being reproduced or used by the commissioning party in the course of trade. Under Article 3.8.2 of the Benelux Treaty, the person or entity that placed the order is considered to be the designer.

Copyright protection is not subject to any formalities and normally vests automatically in the creator from the time the work is fixed on a tangible medium. For registered designs, Article 3.28.2 of the Benelux Treaty provides that the person in whose name the application is filed will be deemed the holder of the copyright. Specific rules apply to works created by employees or external contractors. Under general copyright rules, copyright normally remains with the employer or the external contractor that created the work, unless agreed otherwise in writing. However, his rule is overridden by Article 3.29 of the Benelux Treaty, under which

1 *Noël Marquet & Co v Orac* Cass., May 29 2009.
2 Case C-304/08.

copyright is held by the employer or the person or entity that placed the order.

In a recent decision, the Supreme Court referred a request for a preliminary ruling to the Benelux Court of Justice, to determine which party should be considered the designer of a design created by an external contractor (or employee) which has not (yet) been registered as such under the Benelux Treaty. The relevant question is whether the assumption in favour of the employer or commissioning party extends to unregistered designs. In its decision of June 22 2007, the Benelux Court of Justice held that it does. This decision was welcomed by both legal practitioners and the industry, as it allows employers and commissioning parties to use the product in which the design is incorporated on a commercial scale and have it registered as a design in their own name.

Another development in the case law concerns the ownership of copyright in creations which are not eligible for protection as a registered design. This is, for instance, the case for spare parts, further to the repair clause in the Benelux Treaty (see section 2.2 above). Under the Copyright Act, the person or entity whose name or mark is mentioned on the work is presumed to be the author, unless proven otherwise. In two decisions of March 7 2011, the Mons Court of Appeal held that this presumption can also be raised with respect to spare parts that are integrated into a complex product bearing the maker's mark, such as a car, even if the parts themselves are not marked.

5. Infringement

See sections 2.6, 3.5 and 3.9 above on design and copyright infringement and unfair trade practices.

6. Design infringement litigation

6.1 Procedure

Design and copyright infringement litigation can take various forms, as follows.

(a) Summary proceedings

Summary proceedings are started in order to obtain provisional relief, and there must be a showing of urgency – that is, immediate measures are required in order to avoid irreparable harm to the claimant. In assessing urgency, the court will balance the parties' interests in light of the particular facts of the case. If, for example, the products, methods or process suspected to infringe an intellectual property (IP) right have been available on the market for some time, it may prove difficult to establish urgency. A second condition is that the IP rights relied on must be valid *prima facie*. Finally, the claimant must establish indications of infringement or imminent infringement.

The presiding judge will order provisional relief, pending a decision on the merits. Thus, the relief sought must be interlocutory in nature, typically a temporary injunction subject to a penalty for noncompliance or violation.

It usually takes between three and six months to obtain a decision in summary proceedings. Costs range from €15,000 to €30,000.

(b) ***Cease-and-desist proceedings***

Cease-and-desist proceedings are accelerated proceedings on the merits which are initiated and conducted as summary proceedings, with the difference that a showing of urgency is not required. As the case is examined on the merits, full evidence of the validity of the rights asserted, which may be challenged by way of a counterclaim, and of the infringement is required. The measures that can be obtained are:

- a permanent and immediately enforceable injunction, usually subject to a penalty for non-compliance;
- publication of the decision; and
- any of the measures provided for by design and copyright law (see above), with the exception of damages, which can only be awarded in regular proceedings on the merits (a separate action for damages can be filed at a later date).

A decision is usually rendered within six to 12 months and is immediately enforceable, regardless of the possibility of appeal or payment into court. The costs usually vary between €20,000 and €35,000.

(c) ***Descriptive seizure***

The Judicial Code provides for a specific remedy available to the holders of intellectual property rights, known as a descriptive seizure. A descriptive seizure is ordered on the basis of an *ex parte* application and thus allows the petitioner to take the (alleged) infringer by surprise. Unlike in other EU member states, descriptive seizure proceedings have been available for some time in Belgium and are frequently used.

In the scope of a descriptive seizure, the following measures can be requested:

- the appointment of an independent expert to describe the allegedly infringing goods and methods, any instruments relevant to the infringement and all plans, documents, calculations, writing and so on which serve as evidence of the alleged infringement and the extent of the infringement (so-called descriptive relief); and
- the seizure of any allegedly infringing products which, in practice, can take the form of an injunction prohibiting the marketing or selling of the allegedly infringing products, generally subject to a penalty for non-compliance (so-called seizure or attachment measures).

A number of other measures may also be granted, if requested, including:

- access to all premises where the infringing products may be found on Belgian territory;
- copies of all papers and electronic documents and files necessary for the expert to complete his investigation;
- samples of the infringing products;
- disclosure of access codes, passwords, and so on (which may be useful if certain documents or computer files are secured); and
- the right to have a representative of the petitioner and/or its counsel present during the descriptive raid.

In order to obtain descriptive relief, the petitioner should establish the *prima facie* validity of the IP rights asserted and the existence of indications of infringement or imminent infringement. The requirements for seizure measures are slightly more stringent. Apart from the first condition mentioned above, there must be no *prima facie* grounds to dispute the infringement and the seizure must be reasonably justified in light of the interests of all parties involved, including the public interest.

If seizure or attachment measures are sought, the court may decide first to hear the alleged infringer. The petitioner will be informed of the decision beforehand and it may at that time decide to forgo seizure of the allegedly infringing goods and limit its application to descriptive relief in order to preserve the element of surprise.

When the alleged infringer is served with an order for a descriptive seizure, it has the right to object by filing a motion to set aside the order, which must be done within one month of service of order. The parties subsequently file written pleadings, as in summary proceedings, to prove the existence or, as the case may be, the lack of valid *prima facie* rights and/or a *prima facie* infringement. Either party may appeal the decision rendered in opposition proceedings.

The applicant must initiate proceedings on the merits within the time specified by the court or, if no such time limit is set, within the shorter of either 20 working days or 31 calendar days following submission of the expert's report. If an action on the merits is not started within this time, the order granting the descriptive seizure will cease to have effect and the applicant may no longer rely on it or on the expert's report or make them public, unless the parties agree otherwise.

A descriptive seizure order is generally issued within one week of the filing of the *ex parte* application. It can be executed rapidly, depending on the expert's availability. Opposition proceedings can take between one and six months. The expert's investigation is usually completed within one or two months of appointment, depending on the complexity of the case.

The costs of a descriptive seizure, including possible opposition proceedings, are estimated at €10,000 to €25,000.

(d) *Proceedings on the merit*

Proceedings on the merit allow a rights holder to claim damages in addition to the relief sought in the above proceedings.

Proceedings on the merits cases may not be heard for between six months and one year, or more. Appellate proceedings can take even longer. The delay is attributable in part to the judicial backlog in Belgium.

The costs of proceedings on the merits are more difficult to estimate and will depend on the strategy of the opposing party and the complexity of the case. In general, such proceedings tend to cost between €30,000 and €60,000.

6.2 Jurisdiction

For claims based solely on copyright, jurisdiction will depend on the value of the claim and the capacity of the parties:

- claims with a value of less than €1,860 can only be brought before the justice of the peace of the place where the infringement occurred;

- for claims with a higher value, the competent court will be either the court of first instance or the commercial court of one of five appellate districts in Belgium (Brussels, Antwerp, Ghent, Mons or Liège). If both parties are merchants, the commercial court will have exclusive jurisdiction to hear the case. However, if the defendant is not a merchant, the claim must be brought before the court of first instance, regardless of the claimant's capacity. If only the defendant is a merchant, the claim can be brought before either the competent commercial court or the court of first instance.

If a claim is (also) based on design rights, the commercial court of one of Belgium's five appellate districts will have exclusive jurisdiction, regardless of the value of the claim and of whether the parties are merchants.

6.3 Interim remedies

See the discussion of summary proceedings and cease-and-desist proceedings at sections 6.1(a) and (b) above.

6.4 Final remedies

See the discussion at sections 2.7 and 3.9 above on damages and other forms of relief that can be obtained for each legal ground on which a claim may be based.

6.5 Costs

In addition to what is mentioned in respect of the various types of proceedings, the party that is sanctioned by the court will bear the costs of the proceedings and contribute to the other party's legal costs. Effective from January 1 2008, these costs are fixed at a lump-sum amount, depending on the value of the claim and the complexity of the case, with a maximum of €33,000 for claims with a value in excess of €1,000,000. For claims that cannot be expressed in monetary terms, the minimum contribution is €1,320 and the maximum is €11,000. The court may double the award if it finds that the proceedings were initiated vexatiously and/or frivolously.

6.6 Validity

Cancellation actions can only be brought before a court; the BOIP does not hear validity disputes. A counterclaim for the invalidity of a design can also be made by the alleged infringer.

7. Licensing and exploitation

The licensing of design rights and copyright is discussed at sections 2.8 and 3.7 above. Design rights can be transferred or pledged. In order for the transaction to be enforceable against third parties, it should be recorded in the designs register, in the same way as a licence.

Brazil

Simone Lahorgue Nunes
Levy & Salomão Advogados

---

1. Summary of design protection

The value of intellectual property has increased worldwide as territorial barriers are dismantled in the globalised marketplace. Thus, the legal protection of designs has become even more important.

Industrial property has been protected through legislation in Brazil since 1934. In 1996 the enactment of the new Industrial Property Law introduced a more effective design protection regime.

Article 5(29) of the Federal Constitution 1988 provided temporary privileges for creators of useful industrial goods, stressing the need to consider the social interest and Brazil's technological and economic development. This constitutional protection of industrial property rights, in which designs are included, raised the status of protection to the category of fundamental rights.

The first legal instrument governing design protection was Decree 24,507/1934. This was followed by the former Industrial Property Code, Law 5,772/1971. Both contained similar provisions for the protection of designs. Protection was granted within the patent system, in a separate category from industrial models. The Industrial Property Law 9,279/1996 introduced an important change to the regime. It unified the two categories under the concept of 'industrial designs', and moved industrial design protection into a special regime.

Under this current regime, the creator of an industrial design is protected by a registration system, which is simpler than the patent application process. The Industrial Property Law regulates design protection under a specific title. The applicable articles are Articles 94 to 121 (general rules), Articles 187 and 188 (crimes against such property) and Article 195 (unfair competition).

The patent and utility model regimes also contain provisions that apply to designs – for example, measures against third parties that violate industrial property rights and measures relating to the ownership of designs created under labour relationships.

The Industrial Property Law provides protection for these intellectual works. It grants the authors/owners a temporary privilege and the exclusive right to use, benefit and dispose of their work, and to exploit their work commercially and industrially.

Under Brazilian law, an 'industrial design' is considered to be the ornamental plastic form of an object or any ornamental arrangement, whether three-dimensional or two-dimensional, of lines and colours, which may be applied to an industrial product to produce a new and original visual form that is suitable for industrial manufacture.

To qualify for protection, the article must comply with the validity requirements of novelty, originality and industrial application, as established by Articles 95 to 97 of the Industrial Property Law. Works of a purely artistic nature are not classified as industrial designs.

The National Institute of Industrial Property, based in Rio de Janeiro, is responsible for the registration of industrial designs. It carries out only a formal examination of design protection applications, but does not consider the validity requirements. The applicant may request that these be examined in order to avoid future actions challenging the validity of the registration (Articles 102, 106 and 111 of the Industrial Property Law).

2. Registered design rights

2.1 Nature of rights

The rights provided to a registered industrial design relate to its use. The nature of these rights is controversial. The Federal Constitution uses the term 'temporary privilege' (Article 5) to define such rights, while the Industrial Property Law uses the term 'property' (Article 109) to designate such rights. Some academics define the rights as a legal monopoly, in this case authorised by the Federal Constitution.

Whatever their nature (ie, as a privilege, a monopoly or even as a property), the rights related to industrial property are not absolute. They are limited by other constitutional principles and are exercised in accordance with public interest and the promotion of Brazil's technological and economic development.

Design protection is granted through the Industrial Property Law where the design consists of a work applied to an article with a view to industrial manufacture.

Designs can also be treated as works of art if they are considered as an expression of the author's creativity (in addition to their industrial utility). It has therefore been argued that they should also qualify for copyright protection and, occasionally, trademark protection (where the design identifies a product and distinguishes it from others on the market). Because of their hybrid nature, some say that industrial designs should receive *sui generis* protection.

2.2 Qualification

As previously mentioned, the recognition of a design depends on three basic requirements:

- It must be new;
- It must be original, presenting a visual configuration that differs from any prior art; and
- It must be reproducible on an industrial scale.

The novelty requirement is satisfied whenever a design introduces a characteristic that has not been seen before on the market – that is, something more than the state of the art. The term 'state of art' may be understood as everything made accessible to the public before the date on which the application for registration was submitted to the National Institute of Industrial Property.

In terms of novelty, according to the Industrial Property Law, if a design is disclosed in the 180 days preceding the date of filing the registration form or priority claim (the so-called 'grace period'), it will not be considered to be part of the state of the art, provided that the disclosure was made by the author/creator, the institute or a third party.

By 'originality', Brazilian law means that the design must present a characteristic that distinguishes it from the ordinary concept – that is, it must result in a distinctive visual configuration in relation to other objects. The originality must be identifiable by consumers; from their perspective, there should be something original. A design is also considered original when it embodies an original configuration of known elements.

The Industrial Property Law defines the circumstances in which an industrial design will not be registered, as follows:

- The design is contrary to morals and good customs, offends the honour or image of people, or is contrary to the liberty of conscience, beliefs or ideas, and feelings worthy of respect and veneration; or
- The design is the necessary common or ordinary shape of an object, or is determined essentially by technical or functional considerations.

This analysis involves imprecise evaluations and may lead to different conclusions depending on the case.

As previously stated, works containing artistic features only should not be registered as designs; they are better protected under the Copyright Law.

Under Articles 88 and 121 of the Industrial Property Law, and unless otherwise agreed between the parties of an employment or professional service relationship, an industrial design will belong exclusively to the employer whenever:

- the services are rendered in Brazil; and
- the object of the contract is research or inventive activity, or the design results from the nature of the services for which the person was hired.

Remuneration for the development/creation of the design is limited to the salary or the value agreed in the contract executed by the parties.

The employer may grant the employee a share in the profits resulting from exploitation of the design. This shall not be considered part of the employee's salary.

When an employment or professional services relationship ends, the employee or service provider may not, within one year of the termination, apply for registration of a design. In such case the design will be deemed as having been developed while the contract was in force, unless proven otherwise.

However, the employee or service provider will be the exclusive owner of a design developed or created during a contract if that design is unrelated to the contract and no resources, techniques, materials, facilities or equipment belonging to the employer or contracting party were used during its development.

The ownership of a design will be shared, in equal proportion, whenever it results from the personal contribution of the employee or service provider and the resources, data, means, materials, facilities or equipment of the employer or contracting party. An exception is made for contractual provisions to the contrary;

in such case the employer or contracting party will be entitled to an exclusive licence for exploitation and the employee or service provider will be guaranteed fair remuneration.

In the absence of an agreement between the parties, the employer or contracting party must start using the design within one year of registration. If it does not, ownership is transferred exclusively to the employee or service provider. An exception can be made if the lack of exploitation is for legitimate reasons.

In accordance with Articles 92 and 121 of the Industrial Property Law, all of these provisions apply to the relationship between an independent worker or trainee and the contracting company, and between contracting and contracted companies.

2.3 Registration procedures

The Brazilian design registration system is governed by the Industrial Property Law and Normative Act 161/2002, which stipulates the requirements for obtaining design registration in a more specific manner.

According to the Industrial Property Law and Act 161/2002, an application to the Industrial Design Registry may be made by:

- the author/creator;
- the author/creator's successors;
- an assignee of the rights; or
- anyone whom the law or an employment contract determines to be the owner of the rights over the design.

The Industrial Property Law establishes that an industrial design will belong to the employer whenever:

- it is created or produced in connection with an employment contract in which the services are being rendered in Brazil;
- the object of the contract is research or creation; or
- the design results from the services that the employee was contracted to render.

When created jointly by two or more persons, all or any one of those persons may apply for registration, but all authors/creators should be named.

An application for registration of an industrial design must contain the following:

- registration form;
- specification report, if applicable;
- claims, if applicable;
- illustrations and/or photos of the design;
- application field of the design; and
- proof of payment of the submission fee.

The application form must also include:

- the personal information of the rights holder and of its attorney in fact;
- the title of the request for registration;

- a request for priority and/or privacy, if applicable; and
- other relevant information.

The illustrations and/or photos of design are among the most important documents submitted, since they show the decorative plastic form of the object or the group of decorative lines and colours that may be applied on the product for which registration is being requested.

If the illustrations and/or photos do not clearly define and delimit the design, a descriptive report should also be included. This report can provide further information on the design and its application field. It is mandatory to provide detailed information about the application field in order to inform the National Institute of Industrial Property as to how the design will be applied in the marketplace.

Since registration is a public procedure carried out by a Brazilian federal agency, all data must be presented in Portuguese, Brazil's official language.

Any missing documents must be supplied within five days of the application or the application will be rejected.

Applications must be for a single design, but variations on the design can be included. One registration form may include a maximum of 20 variations of the same design. These variations must have the same purpose as the original design and share the same distinguishing characteristics.

As stated above, the institute does not examine the requirements of novelty and originality when it processes an application. If the form meets all of the requirements outlined above, the registration will be granted and published and a registration certificate will be issued to the applicant. This is a very quick procedure in comparison with the invention registration procedure (patents).

Although the design is not examined before the granting of registration, under the Industrial Property Law regime it can be examined at any time thereafter if a request is made by the rights holder or a third party.

2.4 Term of protection

Industrial designs are protected for 10 years from the date of filing. The protection can be renewed for three successive terms of five years, giving a maximum protection of 25 years. Application for renewal must be submitted within the last year of the registration term.

The certificate of registration grants the rights holder the right to prevent third parties from manufacturing, using, offering for sale, selling or importing the object without the rights holder's consent.

The temporary exclusivity granted by the law is valid in all national territory and is not restricted to a set class of products or services, as occurs with trademarks. However, the owner of an industrial design must indicate the field of its use at the time of application.

A maintenance fee must be paid for the second and subsequent five-year periods, counted as from the filing date, and must be paid at the time of the renewal application.[1]

(a) ***Cancellation of registration and extinction of the registration rights***

A registration may be cancelled through administrative or judicial proceedings.

The National Institute of Industrial Property may cancel a registration via an administrative proceeding, at its own instigation or at the request of any party with a legitimate interest, within five years of granting of registration. Registration will be cancelled if the applicant is not the owner of the design, the object is not considered to be an industrial design, or the validity requirements (novelty, originality and industrial application) or other legal requirements have not been complied with.

Under Article 113 of Industrial Property Law, this proceeding will suspend the effects of the registration if submitted or published within 60 days of the granting of registration. The alleged rights holder will be notified to present a defence within 60 days of publication. After this the institute will give an opinion. Both parties (ie, the alleged rights holder and the third party) must respond within 60 days of the opinion. The institute will then rule on the request, regardless of the presentation of responses.

A rights holder may request adjudication (*adjudicação*) of a registration that was wrongly granted to another person by the institute. A lawsuit must be filed requesting the transfer of the relevant registration entry to the courts.

The institute or any third party with a legitimate interest may request the cancellation of a registration at any time during its term, through a judicial proceeding to the competent federal court. The judge may, as a preventive or interim ruling, suspend the registration, provided that relevant procedural requirements have been met. The defendant has 60 days to present his defence. When the decision on a cancellation becomes final, it is published by the institute.

Registration rights may also be extinguished (i) upon the expiration of the 10-year term, which can be extended up to the maximum of 25 years; (ii) upon the waiver of the rights holder, without prejudice to third parties' rights; (iii) if the registration, renewal or maintenance fee has not been paid; or (iv) if the applicant is domiciled abroad and does not maintain an attorney-in-fact in Brazil with powers to represent him in administrative and judicial spheres, including the power to receive summonses on his behalf.

2.5 Infringement

The Industrial Property Law devotes an entire chapter to crimes against industrial property. It covers crimes against:

- patents, which include the unauthorised manufacture, export, import, sale and display for sale of a product manufactured in violation of a patent (Articles 183 to 186);

---

1 The Industrial Property Law introduces a maintenance fee for industrial design registrations:
Article 120: The registration owner is subject to the payment of a quinquennial fee as of the second quinquennium counted as from the filing date.
§1 Payment of the second quinquennium will be made during the 5th (fifth) year of the term of the registration.
§2 Payment of the subsequent quinquennium fees will be made upon application for renewal referred to in Article 108.
§3 Payment of quinquennium fees may still be made within 6 (six) months after the period established in the preceding paragraph, upon payment of an additional fee.

- designs, which include the same prohibitions applicable to patents, along with punishment against substantial imitation (discussed below) (Articles 187 and 188); and
- trademarks, which include their unauthorised use or amendment, in whole or in part, and the import, export, display for sale and sale of an unauthorised product brand (Articles 189 and 190).

The Industrial Property Law introduces two offences specific to designs. Article 187 prohibits the manufacture of a product that incorporates a registered design, or a substantial imitation that may lead to error or confusion, without the authorisation of the rights holder. The penalty is imprisonment for between three months and one year or a fine, to be determined by the judge on a case-by-case basis.

Under Article 188, it is an offence to:

- export, sell, exhibit or offer for sale, maintain in stock, hide or receive, in order to use for economic purposes, an object that illicitly incorporates a registered industrial design or a substantial imitation that may lead to error or confusion; or
- import a product that incorporates an industrial design registered in Brazil, or a substantial imitation that may lead to error or confusion, for use for economic purposes, and which has not been placed on the external market directly by the rights holder or with its consent.

The penalty is imprisonment for between three months and one year or a fine, to be determined by the judge on a case-by-case basis.

These dispositions apply only to designs that have already been registered with the National Institute of Industrial Property.

Industrial property rights can also be infringed by acts of unfair competition. Article 195 of the Industrial Property Law states that this type of offence is committed by any entity that:

- publishes, by any means, a false statement that might affect a competitor, with the intent of gaining an advantage;
- provides or makes public false information with regard to a competitor, with the intent of gaining an advantage;
- uses fraudulent means to divert, for its own or a third party's benefit, a competitor's clients;
- uses or imitates a third party's slogans or jingles, causing confusion between products or commercial establishments;
- uses, without authorisation, a third party's legal or commercially known name or insignia, or sells, displays or offers for sale or keeps in stock a product with such references;
- substitutes its own name or its company name on someone else's product without consent;
- claims, as a means of advertising, to have been awarded a prize or distinction that was not awarded;
- sells, displays or offers for sale, in a third party's packaging, an adulterated or

falsified product, or uses the third party's packaging to sell a product of the same type, even if has not been adulterated or falsified (which constitutes a more serious offence);
- gives or promises money or some other utility to a competitor's employee so that the employee provides it with some advantage;
- discloses, exploits or uses, without authorisation, confidential techniques, information or data that may be used in industry, commerce or services rendered to which it had access though a contractual or employment relationship, even after termination of the contract (an exception is made for information of public knowledge or which may be obvious to a person with expertise);
- discloses, exploits or uses, without authorisation, confidential information which has been obtained directly or indirectly by unlawful means, or to which it had access by fraudulent means;
- sells, displays or offers for sale a product which it falsely declares to be the subject of a filed or granted patent or design, or falsely refers to such a right, in a commercial announcement or paper, as having been filed or registered; or
- advertises, exploits or uses, without authorisation, the results of tests or other undisclosed data which has involved considerable effort and has been presented to government agencies as a condition for approving the commercialisation of products (an exception being made for disclosures by a government agency which is qualified to authorise the commercialisation of a product that are deemed necessary to protect consumers).

The penalty is imprisonment for between three months and one year or a fine, to be determined by the judge on a case-by-case basis.

One of the features of the laws governing industrial property issues is the repression of unfair competition. Under Article 196, the penalties may be increased by up to 50% whenever:
- the offender has a relationship with the rights holder that allows it privileged access to the registered design, such as a work relationship, a representative relationship, a legal relationship or an agency agreement; or
- the modified, reproduced or imitated trademark is famous, widely known, or a certified or collective trademark.

2.6 Damages and other reliefs

Design infringement is an offence and a civil tort. The owner may apply for injunctive relief in both the criminal and civil courts.

Under criminal law, the owner or its licensee may file a criminal complaint based on industrial design infringement. A licensee can file a complaint only if it has registered its design with the National Institute of Industrial Property.

A criminal complaint must be preceded by a search-and-seizure action, whereby evidence of the offence is seized and presented before two court experts. The experts examine the evidence and provide an official report on their findings. The purpose is to gather irrefutable evidence of the infringement.

As discussed above, the penalty for criminal infringement is up to one year's imprisonment or a fine, which may increase by one-third to one-half if the infringing party is a representative, proxy, agent, partner or employee of the rights holder or its licensee. Such cases are decided by one judge at first instance and by a three-judge panel on appeal.

The police may obtain a warrant to seize the infringing goods. The seizure of counterfeit goods to prove a crime requires only enough samples for forensic analysis (formation of the body of the offence). This contrasts with civil law, where a judge can decide that all of the counterfeit goods and works should be seized, even if this shuts down the infringer's business.

Under civil law, the competent court to review such actions is the state court of the defendant's domicile. In some cases the plaintiff may choose the state court of the place where the infringement has taken place.

An injured party may instigate civil proceedings seeking reimbursement for material and moral damages suffered as a result of the violation. Proceedings must be started within five years of the violation.

A plaintiff may request a temporary or permanent injunction against the infringer, and the judge may grant preliminary relief. Permanent relief is obtained only upon a final decision, subject to appeal.

A civil claim may include a request for compensatory relief, which is standard practice. No punitive damages are awarded. As set down in Article 210 of the Industrial Property Law, the assessment of damages commonly takes into consideration the criteria most favourable to the damaged party from the following:

- the benefits that would have been obtained by the party had the violation not occurred;
- the benefits obtained by the infringer; and
- the remuneration that the infringer would have paid to the rights holder had it been licensed to use the rights lawfully.

Although no opposition procedure is available for designs, once the registration is granted any interested party may, by means of administrative or judicial proceedings, seek the cancellation of a registration if it has been issued in violation of legal applicable provisions (Articles 113 to 117 and 118 of the Industrial Property Law).

A rights holder seeking damages must commence judicial proceedings within five years of the violation.

2.7 Licensing

Under Articles 121, 58 and 59 of the Industrial Property Law, the rights conferred by a design registration can be transferred to third parties through total or a partial assignment. The assignment must be registered with the National Institute of Industrial Property in order to be effective. The institute will register the name of the party to which the rights have been assigned and any encumbrance or limitations to the rights.

In respect of compulsory licences, the Industrial Property Law contains one title on the subject, but this is within the section that expressly refers to patents. Although, as previously mentioned, several provisions not contained in the design section of the Industrial Property Law also apply to designs, including some relating to patents, Article 121 states that only the articles relating to a voluntary licence are applicable to designs. Thus, it is clear that compulsory licences do not apply to designs.

The Copyright Law does not establish any compulsory licences in relation to works protected under that regime.

2.8 International obligations

In an increasingly globalised marketplace, it soon became clear that harmonisation and guidance within the international trade community was needed. For example, the definition of a 'design' differs from jurisdiction to jurisdiction, and the concept of a design is not clearly established within the international community. The industrialised countries have reached consensus on the importance of the legal protection of industrial property rights, including designs, and on their standardisation.

The Paris Convention for the Protection of Industrial Property of 1883, administered by the World Intellectual Property Organization (WIPO), established the International System of Industrial Property. This was the first attempt at the international harmonisation of different national legal systems relating to industrial property. The Paris Convention has undergone periodic revisions – namely Brussels (1900), Washington (1911), The Hague (1925), London (1934), Lisbon (1958) and Stockholm (1967). Brazil was one of the original signatories and by the early 1990s had met the final terms established by the Stockholm review.

The Agreement on Trade-Related Aspects of Intellectual Property Rights (TRIPs) entered into force in Brazil in 1995 (Decree 1,355/1994). Alongside the Paris Convention, the agreement established the standards underlying the legal system for the registration and use of industrial property in Brazil. The TRIPs provisions on industrial designs have been incorporated in the Industrial Property Law.

The Hague Agreement on the International Registration of Industrial Designs[2] establishes an international system for the registration of industrial designs. This system grants the owner of an industrial design the possibility to obtain protection in several countries by filing a single application with WIPO and paying a single fee in one currency. Many countries are members of this system, but Brazil is not. Brazil has adopted the model set out in the Paris Convention.

3. Unregistered design rights

The usual and legal form of protecting industrial designs in Brazil is through registration. However, in some cases it may be possible to apply other forms of protection to industrial designs through copyright – at least theoretically.

Copyright registration is not mandatory; thus, copyright protection is granted

2 The system is based on a combination of three acts: London (1934), The Hague (1960) and Geneva (1999), as amended. These are all connected, but the parties can adhere to each of them separately.

regardless of registration. Registration under copyright principles merely confirms anteriority concerning the design and will mainly emphasise its artistic characteristics. This principle is established in the Berne Convention, which grants copyright protection regardless of registration, and in Brazil's Copyright Law.

Under the Copyright Law, protection for artistic work is granted for the life of the author plus 70 years, starting on January 1 of the year following his death.

It may be argued that when an industrial design is also a work of art, the author may invoke the double protection of the laws because each regime protects different interests and complements the other, and a design may exhibit mixed characteristics of a work of art together with industrial application.

The Industrial Property Law and the Copyright Law take different paths for protection. For an industrial design with artistic features, the rights holder may be entitled to the advantages of copyright protection, thus protecting an unregistered design. If double protection is sought, the industrial design must have the characteristics of both a work of art and an industrial application.

It is also possible to protect a design under the trademark regime. The Industrial Property Law introduced major changes in trademark protection. It states that a visually perceptive, distinctive sign when not prohibited by law is capable of registration as a trademark. However, the necessary, usual shape of a product or its packaging, or shapes that cannot be dissociated from a technical effect, cannot be registered as a trademark. Thus, it is possible to secure registration of trademarks found in the form of the product or in the packaging, provided they are distinctive and have no technical effect. The major advantage is that trademark registration can be renewed indefinitely. However, it is subject to a strict preliminary examination.

There are no regulations protecting trade dress in Brazil. Some judicial decisions have recognised its existence and the need to protect this new approach. In more than one ruling the courts have prohibited third parties from imitating the look and feel of a product. These decisions were mainly based on the unfair competition rules.

4. Infringement litigation

4.1 Overview

The Industrial Property Law provides for the creation of specialised courts to hear cases involving industrial property. Some specialised courts have thus been set up to deal exclusively with all aspects of industrial property.

As mentioned above, in addition to the rights holder, certain other parties may sue an infringer. This right is granted to any party that has the right to explore the design commercially and has suffered damages as a result of the infringement. Some decisions fof the Superior Court of Justice have confirmed this understanding.[3]

The Brazilian courts are sensitive to unfair competition arguments, as illustrated by the following extract:

It does not seem correct that a company spend millions of reais with consumer opinion research, designs, engineering works, marketing to attract customers; and a third party

3 Such as Special Appeals 833098-PR (2010); 466.360-SP (2003); and 590.645-SC (2009).

just copy the final result, commercializing it in the market and competing with the own company that has developed the copied product. It is obvious that Ford has exclusivity on the parts that it has created, developed and produced and there is no disrespect to consumers or Federal Constitution on that.[4]

An interesting case involving designs concerned the violation of the design of the famous Birkin bag, produced and commercialised worldwide by Hermès. Hermès accused Brazilian bag producer Village 284 of copying and selling its industrial property. The lower courts recognised Hermès' rights and awarded moral and economic damages. The judge recognised Hermès' copyright in the bag, under the argument that the bag should be considered a work of art, even though it was mass produced. The court ordered:

- a prohibition on Village 284 producing and commercialising any product that violated Hermès' rights, imposing a fine of R$10,000 for each day of infringement, capped at R$1 million;
- an obligation for Village 284 to disclose the number of bags it produced for calculation of material damages;
- an indemnification for moral damages in the amount of 50% of the material damages;
- an obligation for Village 284 to publish details of the infringement in a widely circulated newspaper; and
- after the decision became final, the destruction of all illicit products.[5]

Similarly, Grendene SA, a company that manufactures and sells footwear, filed judicial proceedings against Ynor Calçados Ltd, Comercial Baldez Araújo Ltd and Injetsul Calçados Ltd, based on infringement of its registration rights and unfair competition. The defendants were selling shoes that were copies of Grendene's models Ipanema Gisele Bundchen and Grendha Adriane Galisteu, which were registered with the National Institute of Industrial Property. The Minas Gerais Court of Appeals decided as follows:[6]

INFRINGEMENT OF INDUSTRIAL DESIGN – VERIFIED – INTERPRETATION OF ARTICLES 42 AND 109 OF LAW NO. 9,279/1996 – ASSUMED LOSSES AND DAMAGES – APPEAL GRANTED

– The Federal Constitution and legislation (Law No. 9,279/1996) ensure property protection of industrial design, being prohibited to third parties to use, produce, offer for sale, sale or import a product that has the same or similar design to another product registered, without the consent of the owner, especially because such practice may lead consumers to mistakenly assume that both products come from the same origin, even if the products involved differ from each other.

– Once proved that the products offered for sale by the defendants are counterfeit products, it is pertinent to judicially prevent the unlawful practice by the offenders that shall refrain from storing, offering for sale and selling such products.

---

4 São Paulo Court of Appeals – TJ/SP; Interlocutory Appeal 541.916.4, December 18 2007.

5 São Paulo Court of Appeals – TJ/SP; Proceeding 583.00.2010.1877075; decided on June 3 2006.

6 Judicial District of Juiz de Fora; Minas Gerais Court of Appeals; Civil Appeal 1.0145.04.158153-2/001, September 13 2009.

– In the case of counterfeiting, the existence of losses and damages is assumed and shall be determined by judicial award.

However, the infringement of a design can be argued in court only by the rights holder – that is, the author/creator, the employer or contracting party or the assignee – as Special Appeal 833098-PR, STJ, described below, confirms.

In 2002 Sier Móveis Ltd, a company that manufactures and sells furniture, filed suit against Silva e Rosastti Ltd. It sought to prohibit Silva e Rosastti from copying, manufacturing and marketing products that had been registered as industrial designs by its partner, Ismael Reis. The grounds were that the drawings had been made using resources, techniques, materials, facilities and equipment pertaining to Sier Móveis, which also had rights related to them based on Article 91 of the Industrial Property Law.

The case was rejected in the lower court. The company appealed to the Superior Court of Justice. The court confirmed that the legitimate party to seek judicial protection of industrial property rights is that which has effectively registered the industrial design with the National Institute of Industrial Property or its representative, and not third parties, as Sier Móveis was. This is because Ismael Reis had registered the design of the products and made no mention that Sier Móveis would be representing it. The court also understood that Articles 91 and 92 of the Industrial Property Law relate specifically to the employment relationship maintained between employee and employer, and cannot be broadly interpreted in order to include commercial partners. The case was again rejected by the Superior Court of Justice.

The Brazilian courts have also decided cases relating to international obligations. In one of those cases[7] Chinese company Kaulin Manufactoring Co Ltd filed suit against Brazilian company Pancostura SA Indústria e Comércio, which had imported sewing machines from China. It argued that the sewing machines were protected by a design which had been registered with the National Institute of Industrial Property and thus could not be imported to Brazil. In support of its argument, it invoked the Paris Convention, a treaty executed between Brazil and China, and Article 188 of the Industrial Property Law.[8]

The ruling of the lower court was based on the interpretation that the subject of the proceedings was not the design itself, but whether the import was legal. Since it was legal, and there is no law in China that grants the exclusive use of a registered design, the judge understood that the registration of a design in Brazil does not prohibit the import of an identical product, but merely its manufacture in the country. Thus, other companies based in China were permitted to manufacture

---

7 São Paulo Court of Appeals – TJ/SP; Proceeding 583.00.2003.032221-1/000001-000; decided on May 18 2006.

8 Article 188 of the Industrial Property Law provides that an offence is committed against an industrial design registration by anyone who:

- exports, sells, exhibits or offers for sale, maintains in stock, hides or receives, in order to use for economic purposes, an object that illicitly incorporates a registered industrial design or a substantial imitation thereof that may lead to error or confusion; or
- imports a product that incorporates an industrial design registered in Brazil or a substantial imitation thereof that may lead to error or confusion, in order to use for economic purposes, and which has not been placed on the external market directly by the owner or with its consent.

sewing machines identical to that created by the rights holder. Under the Paris Convention, a registration effected in Brazil is binding only if the exclusivity right is also granted in the country in which the company is headquartered and registered. The convention aims to protect the exclusivity of foreign products from copies that could be made in other member states, as long as the relevant design has been registered before the competent national authority. It does not aim to ensure the exclusivity of sales in connection with other companies in their own country if that country does not guarantee the right of exclusivity. Thus, if the rights holder did not enjoy the exclusive right to manufacture its sewing machines, which could be produced by other companies in its country of origin, the design registration with the National Institute of Industrial Property guaranteed only that no Brazilian company would manufacture the product. It did not prevent Brazilian traders from importing the product from another Chinese manufacturer.

4.2 Antitrust administrative courts

Law 8,884/1994 regulates infringements against economic order and empowers the Secretariat for Economic Monitoring, the Secretariat of Economic Law and the Administrative Council for Economic Defence to regulate the market and prevent abusive conduct. This encourages the fair development of a market with free competition.

Since industrial propriety rights have the power to grant the rights holder a monopoly that would exclude all others in the market from using the design, this situation, in principle, raises antitrust concerns.

In Brazil, as in many countries, operations involving industrial property are subject to the antitrust authorities' approval if they fall within any of the various hypotheses described in Law 8,884/1994, as for any other merchandise.

In an administrative decision involving industrial designs relating to automotive parts, the Secretariat of Economic Law issued a legal opinion recognising the importance of the protection granted by Law 8,884/1994:[9]

> *Research and development to create new products (in the broadest sense) most of the time requires huge investments. Protecting such products through industrial propriety prevents competitors from copying and commercializing the same for a cheaper price, since they did not incur the costs related to research and development of the product. Therefore, protection is a valuable and indispensable tool to guarantee the return of the invention and industrial creation. During the period of protection of the industrial property right, the owner has the right to exclude non-authorized third parties from manufacturing, commercializing, importing or using the protected object.*

---

9 Preliminary Investigation of SDE No. 08012.002673/2007-51; Complainant: Associação Nacional dos Fabricantes de Autopeças – ANFAPE; Investigated: Volkswagen do Brasil Indústria de Veículos Automotivos Ltd, Fiat Automóveis S/A, Ford Motor Company Brasil Ltd.

Canada

Graeme Deuchars
Stuart C McCormack
Stikeman Elliott LLP

---

1. Summary of design protection

In Canada, industrial designs are protected only if they are registered.[1] Registration grants an owner a monopoly over a design, providing an exclusive right to its use for 10 years. The rights holder is protected from infringing use of the design or a substantially similar design, provided that maintenance fees are paid and the design is used in compliance with proper marking procedures. Rights holders may also assign or license their interest in a design to outside parties.

Qualification for protection is obtained through application for registration of a design with the proper authorities. Proprietors must submit an application in the correct form to the Patent Office, a branch of the Intellectual Property Office located in Ottawa, including a drawing or photograph of the design, a brief description of the design and a declaration that the design is original. The application will be reviewed to ensure it meets the requirements for registration, and the applicant must respond to any defects found during examination. Where an application qualifies as valid, it will be registered and the proprietor will be issued with a certificate of registration.

2. Registered design rights

2.1 Nature of rights

In Canada, industrial design rights fall within the federal jurisdiction, under the authority of the Parliament of Canada. The governing statute for industrial design rights is the Industrial Design Act,[2] which is administered by the Patent Office. The office is responsible for the administration of all Canadian intellectual property rights.

The roots of Canadian design law can be found in the United Kingdom, in a series of early statutes spun off from the common law of copyright.[3] The first mention of design registration in Canada was an 1861 Act of the Province of Canada, which stated:

And whereas it is advisable to make provision for the copy-righting, protecting and

---

1 With the exception of limited protection available under copyright law.
2 Industrial Design Act, RSC 1985, c. I-9.
3 An act for the encouragement of the arts of designing and printing linens, cottons, calicoes, and muslins, by vesting the properties thereof in the designers, printers, and proprietors, for a limited time, 1787, 27 Geo. III, c. 38; Copyright of Designs Act, 1839 2 Vic. c. 17.

registering of new and original designs, ... and every such registration shall be termed a "Copyright"...[4]

This section confirmed that copyright is the historical basis of Canadian design law. Design law was derived from copyright law to create a legal regime for articles reproduced by an industrial process, separate from that for articles of a primarily artistic nature.

In 1868, the Dominion Parliament of Canada passed the Trade Mark and Design Act.[5] The act was amended and consolidated several times[6] until 1970, at which point it adopted the title of Industrial Design Act. The act was further amended in 1994 and in 2001.[7] Its provisions have remained largely unchanged since their enactment in 1868.

Canada is also a signatory to the Paris Convention[8] dealing with industrial property generally, including industrial designs. Canada is a signatory to the 1934 London revision and the administrative provisions of the 1967 Stockholm revision.

2.2 Qualification

In order for an applicant to register an industrial design under Canadian law, the design must meet the requirements set out by the Industrial Design Act. Where the design meets these requirements and does not fall into one of the limitations set out in the act, the design will be registered and a certificate will be issued to the applicant.[9]

Section 2 of the Industrial Design Act provides the following definition of a 'design':

design or "industrial design" means features of shape, configuration, pattern or ornament and any combination of those features that, in a finished article, appeal to and are judged solely by the eye.[10]

Section 5.1 adds a negative limitation:

No protection afforded by this Act shall extend to

(a) features applied to a useful article that are dictated solely by a utilitarian function of the article; or

(b) any method or principle of manufacture or construction.

The act also imposes a requirement of originality. Section 4(1)(b) requires an applicant for registration of an industrial design to declare that: "the design was not, to the proprietor's knowledge, in use by any person other than the first proprietor at the time the design was adopted by the first proprietor". Where it is found that a

---

4 An Act to amend the Act respecting Trade Marks, and to provide for the Registration of Designs, 1861, 24 Vic., c. 21.

5 *Ibid.*

6 Trade Mark and Design Act, 1879, 42 Vic., c. 22; Trade Mark and Design Act, 1891, 54–55 Vic., c. 35; RSC 1906, c. 71; RSC 1927, c. 201; Industrial Design and Union Label Act, RSC 1952, c. 150.

7 Industrial Design Act, RSC 1985, c. I-9, as amended SC 2001, c. 34.

8 International Convention for the Protection of Industrial Property, March 20 1883 (Paris).

9 Sections 2 and 5.1 of the Industrial Design Act. *Kaufman Rubber Co Ltd v Miner Rubber Co Ltd* [1926] Ex CR 26 at 29; *Re Industrial Design Application No 1997-2899* (2003), 29 CPR (4th) 85.

10 These provisions were introduced into the act by the amendments effective from June 8 1988, SC 1988, c. 15.

design is identical to or closely resembles another design already registered, the application may be rejected.

Registration of an industrial design under Canadian law is subject to a time limit. For a design to be protected under the current statute, registration must be applied for within one year from the date of its first publication in Canada or elsewhere.[11]

2.3 Registration procedure

In order to receive protection under the Industrial Design Act, designs must be registered with the Patent Office. The registration must be accompanied by a filing fee payable to the Receiver General of Canada.[12]

The proprietor of a design may apply to register it by completing the application form set out in Schedule 1 to the Industrial Design Regulations. Since 1993, the amended act has provided that a proprietor, "whether the first proprietor or a subsequent proprietor", may apply to register an industrial design.[13] Assignees are not barred from registration.[14]

The application must include the following:

- a drawing or photograph, identifying title and a brief description of the design. Drawings must show the design in well-defined solid lines, with margins of at least 2.5 centimetres, of sufficient quality to allow the features of the design to be clearly and accurately identified. Elements of the drawing used to demonstrate its articles or features, including environment, may be incorporated using stippled lines.[15] The description must describe the features that make up the design or, at a minimum, identify the design as that which is shown in the drawings;[16]
- a declaration that, to the applicant's knowledge, the design was not in use by any person other than himself at the time of his adoption of the design; and
- any prescribed information.[17]

Any document, other than a photograph, submitted as part of an application must be legibly printed on good-quality white paper on one side only, if filed in paper form, or in an electronic format specified by the commissioner in the Patent Office Record, if filed in electronic form.[18]

---

11 Industrial Design Act, Section 6(3).

12 Section 21 of the Industrial Design Regulations, SOR/99-460. The tariff of fees is set out in Schedule 2 to the regulations and the current filing fee is C$400 plus C$10 for each page of drawings in excess of 10 pages.

13 See Section 13 of the Intellectual Property Improvement Act, SC 1993, c. 15 and Section 4 of the Industrial Design Act.

14 *Melnor Manufacturing Ltd v Lido Industrial Products Ltd* [1971] SCR 72 at 78.

15 Section 9.1(5) of the Industrial Design Regulations defines 'stippled lines' as broken lines formed by evenly spaced dots, short dashes or alternating dots and short dashes.

16 For example: "the design is as shown in the attached drawings". See Industrial Design Office Practice Notice, 'Description identifying features that constitute the design', October 5 2008.

17 See Section 4 of the Industrial Design Act and Section 9 of the Industrial Design Regulations.

18 Section 12 of the Industrial Design Regulations. Amendments made to the regulations by SOR/2008-268, s. 4 now permit some documents to be submitted in electronic form. Documents filed in paper form must be on paper that measures between 20 and 22 centimetres in width and between 25 and 36 centimetres in length; thus applications on A4 paper are also accepted.

As a signatory to the Paris Convention,[19] applications made in foreign jurisdictions will be treated as if they were filed in Canada on the date of the earliest foreign application, provided that the Canadian application is filed within six months of the earliest foreign application.[20]

Under Canadian design law, the principle of unity of subject matter of a design prescribes that the statutory protection is for the entire design; it does not protect the design's constituent elements separately.[21] In practice, this means that a separate application must be filed for each individual design, along with the required fee.[22] Where the examiner decides that the application covers two or more designs, the applicant will be required to elect which single design to pursue to registration.[23] Minor variants of a design may appear in one application and will be accepted by the Industrial Design Office.[24]

On receiving the application and the prescribed fee, the office will examine the application to check that it meets the requirements of the Industrial Design Act. For example:

- the design must not be the same as or similar to an already registered design applied to a similar manufactured article;
- the application must not have been filed more than one year after the publication of the design; and
- the design must be original.[25]

If any requirements are not met, the applicant will be sent a report detailing the defects. The applicant must amend the application or contest the examiner's view within four months of the date of the report or the application will be deemed inactive. Inactive applications may be reactivated at a later date by submission of a response and a statement that the design has not been published in Canada for more than one year.

The examiner may reject a design on the grounds that it is contrary to public morality or order,[26] or that the applicant has failed to correct or adequately to contest the deficiencies notified in the examiner's report. The applicant may appeal the examiner's decision to the Patent Appeal Board, which will arrange a hearing and then make recommendations to the Commissioner of Patents. Decisions of the commissioner may be appealed under Section 22 of the act. These appeals are heard by the Federal Court of Canada, Trial Division, which has exclusive jurisdiction to

---

19 International Convention for the Protection of Industrial Property.

20 The foreign country must provide similar privilege to Canadians: Section 29 of the Industrial Design Act.

21 *Holdsworth v McCrea* (18667) LR 2 HL 380 at 388; *Lewis Falk Ltd v Jacobwitz* [1994] 61 RPC 116 at 119; *Kestos Ltd v Kempat Ltd* [1935] 53 RPC 139 at 150.

22 Section 10 of the Industrial Design Regulations.

23 *Ibid.*

24 See *Re Industrial Design Application No 1998-0950* (2001) 14 CPR (4th) 213, where the Patent Appeal Board held that several embodiments in a single application should be considered variants of one design when there are significant similarities between those embodiments.

25 Sections 5 and 6 of the Industrial Design Act. See also *Re Industrial Design Application 1998-2446* (2003) 25 CPR (4th) 256 at 262, where the Patent Appeal Board held that: "what is to be examined is the drawing in conjunction with the description of the design provided by the applicant".

26 Section 6 of the Industrial Design Act.

review any refusal by the commissioner to register the design.[27] Additional evidence may be put before the court, although this does not constitute a new trial.

Where a design meets all statutory requirements, it will be registered and a certificate of registration will be issued to the applicant, indicating that the design has been duly registered in accordance with the act,[28] and recording the date of registration, the name and address of the proprietor, and the registration number.[29]

If a rights holder wishes to make amendments to a registered design, it must apply to the Federal Court of Canada for leave to add to or alter the design in any non-essential detail.[30] The court may refuse or grant leave on terms it deems fit. Notice must be given to the minister, who is entitled to be heard on the application.[31] The court has exclusive jurisdiction to make, expunge or vary any entry in the Register of Industrial Designs made or omitted without sufficient cause, or to refuse an application.[32] An action may be brought by any aggrieved person, including anyone who may possibly be injured by the continuance of the design in its current form and to the extent it is so registered,[33] or the attorney general.

2.4 Term of protection: rights granted

The registration of a design gives the right of absolute monopoly[34] over the design in Canada. Under Section 9 of the Industrial Design Act, the rights holder is granted an exclusive right to the use of the design. Unauthorised use of the design in the ornamentation of articles for sale or publication is prohibited, as is the use of a design not differing substantially from the registered design.[35]

Rights granted last for 10 years starting on the date of registration, with a further five years on payment[36] of a maintenance fee before the expiry of the initial five-year period.[37] If the maintenance fee is paid within the five-year period, registration is maintained for ten years.[38] If the registration is not renewed within the five-year period, a request may be made to the commissioner within six months of expiry, with payment of the renewal fee and a supplementary fee, that the exclusive right be maintained.[39]

---

27 Section 18 of the Federal Courts Act, RSC 1985, c. F-7; *Goodyear Tire & Rubber Co v Commissioner of Patents* [1979] 2 FC 401 (FCTD), appeal allowed on other grounds [1979] 2 FC 588 (FCA).

28 Section 7(a) of the Industrial Design Act.

29 *Ibid*, Section 7.

30 *Ibid*, Section 23(1); Rule 63(1) of the Federal Courts Rules 1998, SOR/98-106, provides that such an application is made by an originating notice of application. The notice must be supported by an affidavit and documentary exhibits within 30 days of its issue (Rule 306).

31 Section 23(2) of the Industrial Design Act.

32 *Ibid*, Section 15(2)(b).

33 *In Re Vulcan Trade Mark* (1915) 51 SCR 411 at 413. The term 'person aggrieved' has been held synonymous with 'person interested'. See *Autosales Gum and Chocolate Co v Canadian Billings and Spencer Co Ltd* (1921) 20 Ex CR 302; *The Billing and Spencer Co v Canadian Billings and Spencer Co Ltd* (1921) 20 Ex CR 405; *Jones v Horton* (1922) 21 Ex CR 330; *Lamont, Corliss & Co v The Star Confectionary Co* (1924) Ex CR 147; *Bartons Inc v Mary Lee Candy Shoppes Ltd* (1950) Ex CR 386; for 'person interested' see *Feingod v Demoiselle Juniors Ltd* (1948) Ex CR 150 at 156.

34 Jeremy Phillips, *Introduction to Intellectual Property Law* (London: Butterworths, 1986) at 264.

35 Section 11 of the Industrial Design Act.

36 *Ibid*, Section 10(1).

37 *Ibid*, Section 10(1), *supra* note 2; see also Section 18 of the Industrial Design Regulations.

38 *Ibid*, Section 10(2).

39 Section 18(2) of the Industrial Design Regulations. The tariff of fees is set out in Schedule 2 to the regulations and is currently C$350 for requests made within the five-year period, plus an additional C$50 for requests made after the period.

For designs registered in Canada before June 9 1993, articles to which the designs are to be applied must be marked with the letters "Rd", along with the year of registration and the rights holder's name. The act has now been amended to state that the rights holder may, but is not required to, mark the articles to which the design is applied with the capital letter "D" in a circle and its name or usual abbreviation.[40] If the rights holder is an assignee, only the assignee's name should be marked.[41]

It had been understood that failure to mark leads to a loss of protection,[42] but the 1993 amendments provide that the failure to mark only has an impact on protection insofar as it supports an argument by an infringer that he was not aware and had no reasonable grounds to believe that a design was registered.[43] This defence does not apply if most of the articles were marked.[44]

2.5 Infringement

Section 15 of the Industrial Design Act provides that an action for infringement of the exclusive right may be brought in any court of competent jurisdiction by the rights holder or by an exclusive licensee of any right therein, subject to any agreement between the rights holder and the licensee.

Infringement of a registered industrial design under the act is by way of negative limitation. Section 11 of the act provides that:

11.(1) During the existence of an exclusive right, no person shall, without the license of the proprietor of the design,

(a) make, import for the purpose of trade or business, or sell, rent, or offer or expose for sale or rent, any article in respect of which the design is registered and to which the design or a design not differing substantially therefrom has been applied, or

(b) do, in relation to a kit, anything specified in paragraph (a) that would constitute an infringement if done in relation to an article assembled from the kit.

Thus, the act provides for four basic infringements:

- making;
- importing for the purposes of trade or business;
- selling or renting; or
- offering or exposing for sale or rent,

a registered design in Canada.

Infringement applies only to an article to which the design (or a design not differing substantially from the design) has been applied, and production or sale of the infringing article must take place within Canada.[45]

The test for infringement applied by the courts focuses on the features appealing

40 *Cimon Ltd v Bench Made Furniture Corp* (1965) 1 Ex CR 811 at 846 to 847. See also *Melnor Manufacturing Ltd v Lido Industrial Products Ltd* (1969) 1 Ex CR 76 at 87, aff'd (1971) SCR 72.

41 *Cimon Ltd v Bench Made Furniture Corp* (1965) 1 Ex CR 811 at 846 to 847.

42 *Mainetti SPA v ERA Display Co Ltd* (1984) 80 CPR (2d) 206 (FCTD).

43 Section 17 of the Industrial Design Act.

44 *Ibid*, Section 17(2).

45 *Edmund Potter Co v Braco de Prata Printing Co Ltd* (1891) 8 RPC 218; cf. *Haddon & Co v RP Bannerman & son* (1912).

to, and judged solely by, the eye.[46] Infringement is a question of fact,[47] which the court will judge by the 'instructed' eye.[48] The courts have applied different tests to determine infringement: the 'threefold test', the 'side-by-side test' and the 'distance test'.[49]

2.6 Damages and other relief

The Industrial Design Act grants the court considerable latitude in administering relief for findings of infringement under Section 15. Courts are empowered to make any "such orders as the circumstances require", including but not limited to orders for relief by way of injunction and the recovery of damages or profits. Discretion is also granted to award punitive damages and costs. The court may issue an order for the disposal for any infringing article or kit.[50]

2.7 Assignment and licensing

The Industrial Design Act provides for both the assignment and licence of designs. A design may be assigned, in whole or in undivided interest,[51] by a written agreement recorded at the office of the Commissioner of Patents and with the payment of a prescribed fee.[52] A design may also be licensed to another party for an unexpired term of the rights holder's exclusive right or any portion of it.[53] While an exclusive licence must be recorded with the commissioner's office, non-exclusive licences do not need to be recorded if they are executed in writing.[54] There appears to be no penalty for failing to record.

2.8 Compulsory licences

Canadian law does not provide for compulsory licensing of designs for specific purposes.

2.9 Validity issues

See section 6.6 below.

3. Unregistered design rights

Canadian law does not provide protection to unregistered industrial designs beyond remedies that may be available under copyright law, trademark law or passing off.

---

46 *Algonquin Mercantile Corp v Dart Industries Canada Ltd* (1984) 1 CPR (3d) 75 (FCA); *Carr-Harris Ltd v Reliance Products Ltd* (1969) 58 CPR 62 (Ex Ct); cf. *Societé Anonyme Les Cuirs Meillon v Brumer* (1974) 18 CPR (2d) 102 at 106, aff'd by Q/C/A/ in 25 CPR (2d) 153. See also *Dunlop Rubber Co Ltd v Golf Ball Development Ltd* (1931) 48 RPC 268 at 279; *Marsden Mfg Co Ltd v The Vono Co* (1934), 51 RPC 282 at 287; see generally HG Fox, *Canadian Law of Copyright and Industrial Design*, 2nd edn (Toronto: Carswell, 1967) at 683 to 684 and *Holdsworth v McCrea* (1867) LR 2 HL 380.

47 *Ingram & Kemp Ltd v Edward Brothers* (1904) 21 RPC 463; *Chudzikowski v Sowak* (1957) 74 RPC 111.

48 *Algonquin Mercantile Corp v Dart Industries Canada Ltd* (1984) 1 CPR (3d) 75 (FCA); *Dunlop Rubber Co Ltd v Golf Ball Developments Ltd* (1931) 48 RPC 268.

49 See generally, Robert E Mitchell, "Infringement of Registered Industrial Design" (1988) CIPR Vol. 4, No. 2, at 278 to 294.

50 Section 15(1) of the Industrial Design Act.

51 *Ibid*, Section 13(1) of the Industrial Design Act.

52 Section 19 of the Industrial Design Regulations.

53 Section 13(2) of the Industrial Design Act.

54 *Ibid*, Section 13(3); see also R Hughes, *On Copyright and Industrial Design* (Toronto: Butterworths, 1984) Section 16 at 1672.

Under the Copyright Act,[55] where copyright would subsist in a design applied to a useful article or in an artistic work from which the design is derived, if more than 50 of the articles are reproduced, the act offers no protection from infringement of the copyright or moral rights.[56] The reasoning is that industrial design protection should cover articles produced in numbers of 50 or more. There are exceptions to this rule in relation to certain categories of works and, accordingly, copyright may protect certain works, including graphic or topographic representations applied to the face of an article, trademarks and representations of real or fictitious beings, events or places.[57] However, outside this limited selection, any unregistered design applied to a useful article in a quantity of 50 or more will not receive protection under Canadian copyright law.

Passing off may be available to the extent that a particular design has acquired a reputation in the minds of the Canadian public, such that an article of similar design would lead to confusion.

4. Qualification for protection

In order to qualify as for protection under the Industrial Design Act, a design must meet the requirements of the definition of 'design' in the act. Under Section 2, a design is (a) a shape, configuration, pattern or ornament (b) in a finished article (applied to an article) which (c) appeals to the eye and is (d) not a method or principle of manufacture or construction and is (e) not dictated solely by utilitarian function. The act also imposes a requirement of originality, and the design must be registered within the set time limits.[58]

4.1 Shape, configuration, pattern or ornament

The terms 'shape' and 'configuration' have been held by the courts to be synonymous for practical purposes.[59] While both terms signify the three-dimensional aspect of an article,[60] the courts have noted that the word 'shape' refers primarily to the external form of the article, while 'configuration' imports the arrangement by which the shape of a composite article is arrived at.[61] 'Pattern' and 'ornament' may similarly be considered as practically synonymous,[62] and are used to describe the two-dimensional aspects of a design rather than its three-dimensional aspects. They typically consist of something that is placed on an article for its decoration.[63]

4.2 In a finished article

The Industrial Design Act defines an 'article' as anything that is made by hand, tool or machine.[64] A design may be protected under the act only in reference to a physical

---

55 Copyright Act, RSC 1985, c. C-42.
56 Section 64(2) of the Copyright Act.
57 *Ibid*, Section 64(3).
58 Section 6(3) of the Industrial Design Act.
59 Fox, note 46 above, at 653, and the cases reported therein.
60 *Ibid.*
61 *Gramophone Co Ltd v Magazine Holder Co* (1910) 27 RPC 152 at 159.
62 *Kestos Ltd v Kempat Ltd* (1936), 53 RPC 139 at 152.
63 HG Fox, *Fox on Canadian Law of Copyright and Industrial Designs*, 4th ed. 2011 – Release 2 by John S McKeown (Toronto: Thomson Reuters, 2009) at 31 to 37.

article, even though the two are considered to be separate. The idea or concept of the design itself is not registrable, and the design must be committed to a concrete form, similar to principles under copyright law. The design need not be fixed to a functional article to be considered a design; rather, any artistic work may be considered an article under the definition in the act. The act only requires that the design be embodied in a physical form, separating it from a "mere scheme or preliminary conception".[65] Generally, an industrial design is registered along with its actual application to a specific article or class of articles.

While older decisions interpreted the requirement that a design be 'applied' to an article to mean that a design could only relate to something applied to the surface of the article, modern courts have recognised that the external shape or configuration of the article itself is protectable under the act. The design must be ornamental so as to give the article an individual appearance[66] capable of being distinguished from the general form dictated by its function.[67]

4.3 Appeal to the eye

In order to receive protection under the Industrial Design Act, a design must appeal to and be judged by the naked eye. This requirement imports two aspects: visibility and the aesthetic quality of the design. For visibility, the design's aesthetic features must be visible in the finished article.[68] Rights may not be claimed in designs that are transient in nature,[69] and there is "some doubt" as to whether a design "so small that the naked eye cannot fairly discern" can be registered.[70]

Canadian courts have held that the 'eye' from which a design is to be considered is that of the informed consumer.[71] The design must be judged separately from the article's utilitarian features,[72] and must be such as to cause a person to choose a particular article over another of the same kind.[73] The design need not have artistic merit, but it must be appreciated by a prospective buyer for its elements other than "underlying features of function or construction" common to other articles of the same type or class.[74] It must be noticeable and have some perceptible appearance of an individual character.[75]

---

64 Section 2 of the Industrial Design Act.

65 *Milliken & Co v Interface Flooring Systems (Canada) Inc* (1998) 3 FC 103 (Fed. TD), additional reasons at (1998) 149 FTR 125 (Fed. TD), aff'd (2000) 5 CPR (4th) 209 (Fed. CA).

66 *Global Upholstery Co Ltd v Galaxy Office Furniture Ltd* (1976) 29 CPR (2d) 145 at 162 (FCTD); *R v Premier Cutlery Ltd* (1980) 55 CPR (2d) 134 at 137 (Ont. Prov. Ct); *Algonquin Mercantile Corp v Dart Industries Canada Ltd* (1983) 71 CPR (2d) 11 (FCTD), aff'd (1984) 1 CPR (3d) 75 FCA.

67 Fox, note 46 above, at 657 to 658.

68 Russell-Clarke, *On Copyright in Industrial Designs*, 5th edn by Michael Fysh (London: Sweet & Maxwell, 1974) at 18.

69 *Re Industrial Design Application No 1997-2899* (2003) CPR (4th) 85.

70 Fox, note 46 above, at 653.

71 Fox, note 63 above, at 31 to 388, and the cases reported therein.

72 Fox, note 46 above, at 653.

73 Sections 2 and 5(1) of the Industrial Design Act.

74 Russell-Clarke, note 68 above, at 20.

75 *Harvey & Co Ltd v Secure Fittings Ltd* (1996) RPC 515 at 518.

4.4 **Not a method or principle of manufacture or construction**

Section 5.1 of the Industrial Design Act provides that features applied to a useful article that are a method or principle of manufacture or construction will not be protected. Loosely defined, these terms refer to a process or operation by which a shape is produced.[76] To allow registration of such general characteristics would extend to the designer a monopoly on features imposed by the necessity of the article itself.[77] However, if under the court's interpretation a method of construction or principle of manufacture is an incidental or secondary element of the design, it may be validly registered.[78]

4.5 **Not dictated solely by utilitarian function**

Section 5.1 of the Industrial Design Act provides features applied to a useful article that are dictated solely by a utilitarian function of the article are not protected. The act defines 'utilitarian function' as a function other than merely serving as a substrate or carrier for artistic or literary matter.[79] This does not mean that design protection is not available for functional objects, but rather that the design must relate to the ornamentation of the article and not to its utilitarian function.[80] Designs in which some of the shape or configuration is dictated by the function of the article, provided it is not solely dictated by these aspects, may be registered.[81]

4.6 **Originality**

Under Section 4(1)(b) of the Industrial Design Act, an applicant for registration of an industrial design must provide a declaration that "the design was not, to the proprietor's knowledge, in use by any person other than the first proprietor at the time the design was adopted by the first proprietor". Section 7(3) of the act specifically refers to the "originality of the design" as one of the essential elements constituting a certifiable industrial design. The industrial design law regime requires not only that the design be an original creation of the author,[82] but that the design be new in comparison with previous designs for the purpose of ornamenting the article in issue.[83]

The courts have applied various tests to determine whether a design is original in comparison with a pre-existing design. Novelty may be established by the application of a design to an article of manufacture, even where the design has been taken from a common source.[84] In these circumstances, the existence of an earlier

---

76 Russell-Clarke, note 68 above, at 3.

77 Fox, note 46 above, at 654, citing *Vandervell & Co v Lundberg & Sons* (1916) 33 RPC 60.

78 Fox, note 46 above, at 655 to 656; Immanuel Goldsmith, *Trade Marks and Industrial* Designs (Toronto: Carswell, 1982) at 248, Section 415 and the cases cited therein.

79 Section 2 of the Industrial Design Act.

80 WL Hayhurst, "Recent Developments in Canadian Law: Intellectual Property" (1988) 19 *Ottawa Law Review* 137 at 182.

81 Section 5.1 of the Industrial Design Act; *Wells v Attache Case Mfg. Co Ltd* (1932) 49 RPC 113 at 119; *Gandy v Pat. Commr* (1980) 47 CPR (2d) 118 (FCA); *Re Industrial Design Application 1998-2446* (2003) 25 CPR (4th) 256 (PAB).

82 Hayhurst, note 80 above, at 184; *Les Habitations du Boise d'en Haut Inc v Yves Bilodeau Dessinateur Inc* (1989) RJQ 405.

83 *Clatworthy & Son Ltd v Dale Display Fixtures Ltd* (1928) Ex CR 159 at para 6, aff'd (1929) SCR 429.

84 *Saunders v Weil* (1893) 10 RPC 29 at 33.

design does not stop the registration of a subsequent design incorporating the same subject matter: the design will only fail to meet the originality requirement if its purpose is analogous to its previous application.[85] The new application of the design must be substantially different from previous applications,[86] and trivial changes will not count as new, original applications. It is not necessary for the entire design to be original. It has been held that it is sufficient for a part of a design to be original,[87] and new combinations of old features have been upheld as original designs.

Ultimately, the test of a design's originality is the novelty of its appeal to the eye. The eye judging the design is the eye of the tribunal[88] acting as the consumer, and the court will allow expert evidence to assist it in explaining the drawings.[89]

4.7 Time constraint

Section 6(3) of the Industrial Design Act provides that:

(3) The Minister shall refuse to register the design if the application for registration is filed in Canada

(a) more than one year after the publication of the design in Canada or elsewhere, in the case of an application filed in Canada on or after the day on which this subsection comes into force; or

(b) more than one year after the publication of the design in Canada, in the case of an application filed in Canada before the day in which this subsection comes into force.

Therefore, for a design to be protected under the act, the application must be submitted within one year of the date of its first publication, either in Canada or abroad. Publication is deemed to have occurred when the article embodying the design is disclosed to the public by giving it knowledge of the design.[90] The only conditions for publication are that the public has easy access to the publication[91] and that the publication provides the information necessary to make the design.[92] This incorporates any commercial offering or distribution of products incorporating the design or distribution of printed publications showing the design.[93]

The design may be disclosed without activating the one-year publication period if the disclosure is made in confidence. The disclosure must be made for a limited

---

85 *Clatworthy & Son Ltd v Dale Display Fixtures Ltd* (1928) Ex CR 159; *Carr-Harris Product Ltd v Reliance Products* (1969) 58 CPR 62 at 76 to 79 (Ex Ct), aff'd (1969) 65 CPR 158 (SCC); *Simmons v Mathieson & Co Ltd* (1911) 28 RPC 491; *Allen West & Co Ltd v British Westinghouse Electric & Mfg. Co Ltd* (1916) 33 RPC 157; *Re Clarke's Registered Design* (1896) 2 Ch 38; *Anonymous Application* 106 CPOR, June 27 1978; *Re Industrial Design Application 2001-1238* 30 CPR (4th) 571.

86 *Simmons v Mathieson & Co Ltd* (1911) 28 RPC 491; Fox, note 46 above, at 665; Goldsmith, note 78 above, at para 423; R Hughes, *On Copyright and Industrial Design* (Toronto; Butterworths, 1984) Section 6; Russell-Clarke, note 68 above, at 40 to 41.

87 *Wells v Attache Case Mfg. Co Ltd* (1932) 49 RPC 113; *Rollason's Design* (1898) 15 RPC 447.

88 *Overman Atiebolag's Application* 104 CPOR September 7 1976.

89 *Werner Motors Ltd v AW Gamage Ltd* (1904) 2 Ch 580; *Re Monotype Corp Ltd Application* (1939) 56 RPC 243; *R V Premier Cutlery Ltd* (1980) 55 CPR (2d) 134 (Ont. Prov. Ct).

90 Fox, note 46 above, at 669.

91 *Otto v Steel* (1886) 3 RPC 109; *Plimpton v Malcolmson* (1876) 3 Ch D 531.

92 *Plimpton v Malcolmson* (1876) 3 Ch D 531.

93 Russell-Clarke, note 68 above, at 45 to 47; Fox, note 46 above, at 669; *Harris v Rothwell* (1887) 4 RPC 225; *Otto v Steel* (1886) 3 RPC 109; *Plimpton v Malcolmson* (1876) 3 Ch D 531; *In the Matter of Sherwood's Design* (1892) 9 RPC 268; *Ribbons (Montreal) Ltd v Belding Corticelli Ltd* (1961) Ex CR 388, 36 CPR 65; *Durable Electric Appliance Co Ltd v Renfrew Electric Products Ltd* (1926) 59 OLR 527 at 537 (CA), aff'd (1928) SCR 8; *Kangol v Centrokomise (London) Ltd* (1937) 54 RPC 211.

purpose, to an individual who is not free to use his knowledge of the design as he pleases in order for pass the confidence requirement.[94] Similarly, a secret[95] or experimental[96] use is not a publication if the party shown the design is not free to use its knowledge for its own or a third party's benefit. However, disclosure made in anticipation of commercial distribution (eg, disclosure of a design made to potential customers to determine whether they would be interested[97]) does not imply a confidential relationship and is not excepted. The broad definition of the 'public' adopted in the industrial design law regime to include "those who are apt to be interested in taking up the offer of the design or to take advantage of its availability"[98] suggests that all disclosures in anticipation of commercial distribution constitute publication.

5. Infringement

The design law regime provides for four infringements:

- making;
- importing for the purposes of trade or business;
- selling or renting; or
- offering or exposing for sale or rent,

a registered design that enjoys an exclusive right.[99] The production or sale of infringing articles must take place within Canada.[100] It is not an offence to apply a design that is similar or identical to the design for which protection has been registered to a substantially different article or in a new or novel manner.[101]

Infringement is a question of fact,[102] to be determined by the court. The test for infringement focuses primarily on the features appealing to, and judged solely by, the eye.[103] The courts have applied three different tests in determining whether an act of infringement has taken place.

The first test, the threefold test, incorporates three elements: whether one design would be confused with another; whether the defendant's design would exist in the absence of the plaintiff's design; and whether the defendant's design was any nearer to that of the plaintiff's than any prior user.[104] The threefold test was rejected by the Federal Court of Appeal in 1984, and so its viability is still debatable in Canadian law.[105]

---

94 Fox, note 46 above, at 669; *Allaire v Hobbs Glass Ltd* (1948) Ex CR 171 at 144.

95 *Young and Neilsen v Rosenthal & Co* (1884) 1 RPC 29; *Bristol-Meyer Co (Johnson's) Application* (1973) RPC 157 (CA), aff'd by House of Lords (1974) FSR 43.

96 *Cornish v Keene* (1835) 1 WPC 501; *Betts v Neilsen* (1868) LR 3 Ch App 429; *Boyce v Morris Motors* (1927) 34 CPR 105; *Newall v Elliott & Glass* (1858) 4 CB (NS) 269.

97 *Blank v Footman, Pretty and Co* (1888) 5 RPC 653 at 656.

98 *Algonquin Mercantile Corp v Dart Industries Canada Ltd* (1983) 71 CPR (2d) 11 (FCTD), aff'd (1984) 1 CPR (3d) 75 (FCA).

99 Section 11(1) of the Industrial Design Act.

100 *Edmund Potter Co v Braco de Prata Printing Co Ltd* (1891) 8 RPC 218; cf. *Haddon & Co v RP Bannerman & Son* (1912).

101 *Clatworthy & Son Ltd v Dale Display Fixtures Ltd* (1928) Ex CR 159 at 431.

102 *Ingram & Kemp Ltd v Edward Brothers* (1904) 21 RPC 463; *Chudzikowski v Sowak* (1957) 74 RPC 111.

103 *Algonquin Mercantile Corp v Dart Industries Canada Ltd* (1984) 1 CPR (3d) 75 (FCA); *Carr-Harris Ltd v Reliance Products Ltd* (1969) 58 CPR 62 (Ex Ct); cf. *Societé Anonyme Les Cuirs Meillon v Brumer* (1974) 18 CPR 62 (Ex Ct).

The second test is the side-by-side test. This involves placing the two designs side by side to allow the eye to judge whether one is an imitation of the other.

Finally, while no Canadian court has expressly applied the third, distance test[106] in an infringement context, it could be adopted by Canadian courts in the future. The test requires that the designs are viewed separately or at a distance to allow for a viewer's imperfect observation, not side by side. In doing so, it rejects important differences that would not be relevant to the consumer.

The intention of the defendant is irrelevant in proving infringement.[107] If material infringement of the exclusive right is proved, an intention in good faith will not clear the defendant's liability.[108] However, Section 17 of the Industrial Design Act provides that the absence of knowledge and the absence of reasonable grounds for suspecting that the design was registered may provide a valid defence to an award of damages by the court, although not to injunctive relief.

The registration of an infringing design is not a defence to an infringement claim.[109] Canadian law does not provide procedures for opposing or challenging registrations; in their absence, a claim of registration does not contribute to a contention of non-infringement.[110] While sufficient to provide evidence of originality of a design in the absence of proof to the contrary, registration is not sufficient to bar proceedings to remove the design from the register.[111]

The defences available to a defendant in an infringement claim include the following:

- delay in filing suit: under Section 18 of the act, no remedy will be awarded for an infringement committed over three years before the action for infringement was filed. The three-year period is deemed to begin when the infringement was, or ought to have been, detected;[112]
- invalidity of the design registration;[113]
- failure to mark: the plaintiff's entitlement to any remedy other than an injunction may be challenged on the basis of the plaintiff's failure to mark all or substantially all of the article; and
- personal or experimental use: importation for personal uses is a valid defence, as the act only protects against importation for purposes of trade or business.

---

104 Fox, note 46 above, at 682.
105 *Algonquin Mercantile Corp v Dart Industries Canada Ltd* (1984) 1 CPR (3d) 75 (FCA).
106 See generally, Mitchell, note 49 above, at 278 to 294; this test is also sometimes referred to as the 'imperfect recollection' test.
107 *Corbron Foundries Ltd v FX Drolet Inc* (1982) 65 CPR (2d) 151 at 151 to 152 (FCTD).
108 *Mitchell v Henry* (1880) 15 Ch D 181; *Walker, Hunter & Co v Hecla Foundry Co* (1888) 5 RPC 365 at 367, aff'd 14 App. Cas. 550.
109 *Mainetti SPA v ERA Display Co Ltd* (1984) 80 CPR (2d) 206 at 221 to 222 (FCTD).
110 *Ibid.*
111 *Ibid*, at 222.
112 *Warner Bros-Seven Arts Inc v CESM-TV Ltd* (1969) 58 CPR 97 at 107 to 110 (Ex Ct).
113 See section 6.6 below on validity.

6. Design infringement litigation

6.1 Procedure

An action for infringement of an exclusive right may be brought in any court of competent jurisdiction by the rights holder or by an exclusive licensee of any right therein, subject to any agreement between the rights holder and the licensee.[114] The rights holder must be a party to any action for infringement of the exclusive right.[115]

In any action for infringement, the burden of proof of authorship and infringement of a design falls upon the plaintiff.[116] Expert evidence is admissible if it relates to similarities and dissimilarities between the designs, what is common to the trade and what has been disclosed in previously published designs.[117]

The certificate issued on registration presents *prima facie* evidence of its contents – that is, evidence of the name of the rights holder, of the term of the registration and of the originality of the design.

6.2 Courts

The Industrial Design Act grants the Federal Court of Canada concurrent jurisdiction with other provincial courts to hear and determine any action for the infringement of a right, and any claims regarding the ownership of the design or any right to a design.[118] The decisions of the Federal Court and the relevant provincial courts may be appealed to their respective appellate bodies.

6.3 Interim remedies

An infringement may be stopped during the period leading up to trial by the grant of an interlocutory injunction.[119] The principles for the award of an interlocutory injunction are based on the case of *RJR-MacDonald Inc v Canada* (Attorney General):[120] the need to assess whether there is a serious question to be tried; whether the applicant would suffer irreparable harm if the application were refused; and which of the parties would suffer greater harm from the granting or refusal of the injunction pending a decision on the merits.

A defendant may be ordered to keep an account of all profits of the allegedly infringing act.[121]

6.4 Final remedies

Section 15.1 of the Industrial Design Act grants the court considerable latitude to make any orders it sees fit, including orders for relief by way of injunction and the recovery of damages. The usual measure for damages is the lost profit which would have accrued

---

114 Section 15(1) of the Industrial Design Act.
115 *Ibid*, Section 15(2).
116 Fox, note 63 above, at 31 to 41 and cases noted therein.
117 *Ibid*.
118 Section 15(2) of the Industrial Design Act.
119 *Slim Line Design Ltd v Pacific Northwest Manufacturing Inc* (1999), 86 CPR (3d) 498 (BCSC); *Knowles & Co v Bennett & Sons* (1895) 25 RPC 615.
120 (1994) 1 SCR 311 (SCC).
121 *Whitelock v Automatic Phonograph Co* (1908) 25 RPC 615.

to the plaintiff had the plaintiff sold the articles instead of the infringer.[122] However, the damages may also be measured as a reasonable royalty on infringing sales.[123] The onus is on the plaintiff to demonstrate that it has suffered a loss. In the absence of satisfactory evidence of loss, the court is entitled to award only nominal damages.[124]

In general, punitive damages are awarded only to punish or deter, and where the existing damages do not achieve this.[125] The court may make any orders appropriate for the circumstances, including the disposal of any infringing article or kit.[126]

6.5 Costs

The awarding of costs is at the court's discretion.[127] Litigants should make reference to the practice and procedure of the court involved concerning the awarding of costs and the effect of offers to settle.[128]

6.6 Validity

A defendant may challenge the validity of the registration on the grounds that:

- the design was not proper subject matter for registration within the meaning of 'design' under Section 2 and the limitations in Section 5.1 of the Industrial Design Act;
- the design was published more than one year before application for registration, in violation of the time-limit under Section 6(3);
- the declaration made by the proprietor accompanying registration was false; or
- the design is not original.[129]

The registration will lapse if the maintenance fees set by Section 10 are not paid. This provides another ground to challenge the validity of a registration.

A claim of invalidity may be raised in the course of an infringement action – it need not be raised in a separate procedure.[130]

7. Licensing and exploitation

Section 13(1) of the Industrial Design Act provides that every industrial design is assignable by written agreement.[131] The design may be registered or in the process of registration, and may be assigned in whole or in an undivided interest. The original assignment or its notarised copy[132] is recorded in the Commissioner of Patents' office

---

122 *Consolidated Wafer Co v International Cone Co* (1926) 59 OlR 205 (Ont. SC); *Lightning Fastener Co v Colonial Fastener Co* (1935), (1936) Ex CR 1 (Can. Ex. Ct), varied (1936), (1937) S/C/R/ 36 (SCC).

123 *PB Cow Ltd v Cannon Rubber Mfrers Ltd* (1961) RPC 236.

124 Fox, note 63 above, at 31 to 44.

125 *Vorvis Insurance Corp. of British Columbia* (1989) 1 SCR 1085 at 1107 to 1108 (SCC); *Hill v Church of Scientology of Toronto* (1995) 2 SCR 1130 (SCC); *Lubrizol Corp. v Imperial Oil Ltd* (1996) 67 CPR (3d) 1 (Fed. CA); *Profekta International Inc v Lee* (1997) 75 CPR (3d) 369 (Fed. CA).

126 Section 15.1 of the Industrial Design Act.

127 *Ibid*, Section 15.1.

128 Fox, note 63 above, at 31 to 46 and cases noted therein.

129 Fox, note 63 above, at 31 to 45.

130 *Clatworthy & Son Ltd v Dale Display Fixtures Ltd* (1928) Ex CR 159.

131 Section 13(1) of the Industrial Design Act.

132 Section 19 of the Industrial Design Regulations.

on payment of a prescribed fee.[133] Once a registered design has been assigned, all articles to which the design is applied by the assignee should display the name of the assignee, not the former rights holder, for the purposes of Section 17(2).

The rights holder also has a statutory right to license the design to others. Section 13(2) of the act provides that every rights holder may grant and convey an exclusive right to make, use, sell and grant to others the right to make, use and sell the design. Such a grant, or licence,[134] may be for an unexpired term of the proprietor's exclusive right or any portion of it. A licence granted under this section applies throughout Canada, but does not grant rights to apply the design in foreign jurisdictions.

An exclusive licence must be registered with the office of the Commissioner of Patents,[135] following the same procedure as that for assignment. The section refers only to exclusive licences, but this is based on the nature of the rights holder's rights under the act and should not be interpreted to its rights to the grant of exclusive licences only. Non-exclusive licences may be granted.[136] They do not need to be registered if the grant is a written agreement.[137] It is not clear whether a licence may be made by parole.[138]

133 Section 13(1) of the Industrial Design Act. The fees are currently C$100 for each design in the assignment (Schedule 2 to the Industrial Design Regulations).

134 Section 13(1) of the Industrial Design Act: "A grant or conveyance under subsection (2) shall be called a license, and shall be recorded in like manner and time as assignments."

135 *Ibid*, Section 13(1).

136 Fox, note 63 above, at 31.

137 Section 13(3) of the Industrial Design Act; see also R Highes, *On Copyright and Industrial Design* (Toronto: Butterworths, 1984) Section 16 at 1672.

138 Fox, note 63 above, at 31.

China

John Ng
Vivien Chan & Co

1. Summary of design protection

It has become increasingly popular to use design patents to protect industrial designs in China. In 2010, the State Intellectual Property Office (SIPO) received 421,273 design patent applications, more than double the number of applications in 2006.

In China, industrial design protection is governed by both the Patent Law and the Copyright Law.[1] In order to obtain protection under the Patent Law regime, design owners must register their designs with SIPO.[2] The Copyright Law offers automatic protection to industrial designs without the requirement of registration.

2. Registered design rights

Designs may be protected through registration under the Patent Law.

2.1 Qualification

(a) Qualifying designs

Article 2 of the Patent Law defines 'design' as:

> *any new design of the shape, pattern or a combination thereof or the combination of colour and shape or pattern, of a product, which creates an aesthetic impression and is fit for industrial application.*

Thus design patents are limited to the artistic elements of a product. In order to apply for a design patent, the following requirements must be met:

- The carrier of a design must be a product.[3] Products which cannot be reproduced are not patentable – for example, livestock products, handicraft, agricultural products and naturally existing products.[4]
- The design to be registered must be in the *shape, pattern, a combination of shape and pattern, or a combination of colour and shape or pattern of a product.*[5] The colour of a product alone cannot constitute a design unless the product consists of a few colours combined to create a pattern.[6] According to the

---

1 Patent Law of the People's Republic of China (Third Amendment) 2008 (the Patent Law), Article 2; Copyright Law of the People's Republic of China (Second Amendment) 2010 (the Copyright Law), Article 3.
2 Patent Law, Article 27.
3 Patent Examination Guide 2010, Part I, Chapter 3, Section 7.1.
4 *Ibid.*
5 Patent Examination Guide, Part I, Chapter 3, Section 7.2.
6 *Ibid.*

> Patent Examination Guide, the combinations that may constitute a design include "the shape of a product; the pattern of a product; the shape and a pattern of a product; the shape and colour of a product; the pattern and colour of a product; the shape, pattern and colour of a product".[7]

According to the Patent Examination Guide, 'shape' refers to "the external structure of the product, as shown by the movement, changes, and combination of the external elements, e.g. dots, lines, and surfaces".[8] 'Pattern' refers to "the figure created on the surface of the product by means of the arrangement or combination of lines, characters, symbols or colour".[9] The pattern of a product should be permanent and visible. 'Colour' refers to the colour or combination of colours applied on the product.

Designs may be either two-dimensional or three-dimensional. For two-dimensional designs, the applicant should submit an orthographic projection of the relevant side only. For three-dimensional designs, the applicant should submit an orthographic projection of the views from all six sides. In addition:

- The design must create an *aesthetic impression*.[10] When considering whether a design creates an aesthetic impression, SIPO will use the standard of a normal consumer's view of the "visual sensation of the appearance of the product", and not the functional or technical effect of the product.[11] This is a subjective test. The only objective test is that the design must be visible to the eye.
- The design must be *fit for industrial application*.[12] A design must be used in industry and be capable of reproduction. It must be considered independently of value. Based on case law, artistic works which are unique and cannot be reproduced do not fulfil this requirement.

(b) *Non-qualifying designs*

The following are expressly listed as products that are not registrable as a design patent:

(a) Any fixed building, bridge or similar structure that is constructed for its specific geography and cannot be rebuilt elsewhere, such as a villa built by a particular lake or hill;

(b) Any product that has no fixed shape, pattern or colour because it contains a substance that has no fixed shape, such as a gas, liquid or powder;

(c) Any component part of a product that cannot be sold or used separately, such as the heel of socks, the peak of a hat, the handle of a cup or a chess piece;

(d) In the case of any product consisting of several component parts that have different shapes or patterns, a component part that is not a product with independent use value is not protectable subject matter. For example, a jigsaw puzzle consisting of interlocking pieces of varied shapes is protectable

---

7 *Ibid.*
8 *Ibid.*
9 *Ibid.*
10 Patent Examination Guide, Part I, Chapter 3, Section 7.3.
11 *Ibid.*
12 *Ibid.*

subject matter only when one application is filed for the design patent relating to the entire puzzle, including all the pieces;

(e) Any product that cannot be visually perceived or viewed by the naked eye, or whose shape, pattern or colour can only be distinguishable by means of specific instruments, for example, a product whose pattern is only visible under an ultraviolet lamp;

(f) Any design that is not the normal state of a product, for example the shape of an animal made by folding a handkerchief in a certain way;

(g) Any design that is the original shape, pattern or colour of a naturally existing object;

(h) Any work that belongs wholly to the field of fine arts;

(i) Any design that consists only of geometric shapes or patterns common in the field of the relevant product;

(j) Pronunciations or meanings of words and numerals; and

(k) Any pattern which is shown only when the product is electrified, such as the pattern on an electronic watch dial, the pattern on the screen of a mobile phone, software interface, etc.[13]

(c) Other circumstances where a design patent will not be granted

Article 5 of the Patent Law stipulates three situations where patent applications will be denied. These provisions are rarely invoked by SIPO as a basis for rejecting applications. The three situations are as follows:

- if a design violates the laws of China.[14] This refers to the laws announced by the National People's Congress and the Nationalities Committee of the National People's Congress only. For example, if a design contains the pattern of the Chinese national currency or graphics of gambling venues, SIPO will not grant a design patent;[15]
- if a design is contrary to social morality,[16] that is, considerations relating to social stability and standards of behaviour generally believed to be appropriate and accepted by the public in the China.[17] This clause would prohibit, for example, designs which contain drawings or photographs of pornography, violence, murder and so on.[18] Apart from the more apparent examples above, there have been cases where more conservative examiners have relied on this clause to reject patent applications that are suggestive – for example, the shape of a bottle which is in the shape of a woman's body;
- if a design is detrimental to public interest,[19] that is, "the exploitation or use of the design may harm the interests of the public or society or may affect the normal order of the State and the society".[20] The Patent Examination Guide

13 Patent Examination Guide, Part I, Chapter 3, Section 7.4.
14 Patent Law, Article 5.
15 Patent Examination Guide, Part I, Chapter 3, Section 6.1.1.
16 *Ibid.*
17 Patent Examination Guide, Part I, Chapter 3, Section 6.1.2.
18 *Ibid.*
19 Patent Law, Article 5.
20 Patent Examination Guide, Part I, Chapter 3, Section 6.1.3.

explicitly prohibits the use of famous buildings, portraits of a national leader, the Chinese national flag and the Chinese national emblem in design patents.[21]

2.3 Examination of applications: preliminary examination

Design patent applications are only subject to a preliminary examination by SIPO. A design patent will be granted provided the design is not identical or similar to any earlier published designs and does not conflict with any other earlier legal rights which are known to the examiner.

(a) Documents accompanying an application

Foreign persons or enterprises with no habitual residence or place of business in mainland China must engage a patent agent to file a design patent application.[22] The application form must be submitted to the Application Receiving Department of SIPO and must be accompanied by:

- a power of attorney (for foreign applicants);[23] and
- drawings or photographs showing the details of the design.[24]

(b) Quality of drawings

The shape of the design must be shown using solid lines of even thickness.[25] Dotted lines, shadow lines, indicative lines, central lines and size lines may not be used.[26] The only exception is that two parallel, double-dotted lines may be used to show the omitted part of a long, thin product.[27]

(c) Brief description

The scope of protection provided by a design patent is subject to the drawings or photographs submitted. Under an amendment to the Patent Law in 2008, design patent applicants must also submit a brief description indicating:

- the title of the product;
- the use of the product;
- the essential features of the design; and
- which drawing or photograph best shows the essential features of the design.[28]

This brief description requirement is intended to help examiners understand the design features incorporated in the product. In the past, some design patent applications were rejected simply because the examiners were not able to discern the design features solely from the drawings or photographs provided. The 2008 amendment was introduced to address this problem.

---

21 *Ibid.*
22 Patent Law, Article 19.
23 Implementing Rules, Article 15.
24 Patent Law, Articles 16, 27 and 28.
25 Patent Examination Guide, Part I, Chapter 3, Section 4.2.2.
26 *Ibid.*
27 *Ibid.*
28 Implementing Rules, Article 28.

The court and administrative authorities may refer to the brief description to interpret the scope of the design patent,[29] so it should be as broad as possible to cover all claims. Failure to include a particular element in the brief description may lead to its exclusion from the scope of protection. For example, if colour is an essential part of a design, a colour claim must be stated in the brief description of the design application. This will also strengthen the patentee's argument in any infringement proceedings.

(d) ***Classification of design***

SIPO uses the International Classification for Industrial Designs (the Locarno Classification) to classify patent applications for designs. At present, these classifications are designated by the examiners; the applicant does not participate in the designation of the class.

(e) ***Multiple designs***

In general, a design patent application is limited to one design.[30] However, under the Third Amendment to the Patent Law 2008 two or more similar designs may be submitted in one application if they have the same design concept.[31] This amendment was introduced to rectify the situation whereby a later application for two or more similar and affiliate designs was not allowed due to an earlier design application. For similar designs to qualify under one design application:

- it must be shown that the designs relate to the same product or belong to a set;
- the application must designate one design as the fundamental design, of which the affiliate designs are derivatives; and
- no more than 10 designs may be included in the application.[32]

The affiliate designs and the fundamental design must have the "same concept of design", which refers to the unity of style of design of each product.[33] This means that the design of the shape or pattern and their combination or the combination of colour with shape or pattern of each product must be unified. If the affiliate designs and the fundamental design have the same or similar features with only slight differences in fine detail or a change of the colour element, they will be considered similar designs.[34] For example, a design consisting of a coffee pot decorated mainly with orchids and a coffee cup decorated mainly with pandas will not be considered similar since the selected subject matter is not the same. Similarly, if the designs involve three teapots and one teacup, a multiple design application may not be allowed as the designs will not be sold or used concurrently.[35]

---

29 Interpretations of the Supreme People's Court concerning Certain Issues on the Application of Law for the Trial of Cases on Disputes over Infringement on Patent Rights, Article 3.

30 Patent Law, Article 31.

31 *Ibid.*

32 Patent Examination Guide, Part I, Chapter 3, Section 9.1.

33 Patent Examination Guide, Part I, Chapter 3, Section 9.2.4.

34 *Ibid.*

35 *Ibid.*

(f) ***Degree of similarity with existing designs***

Under Article 23 of the Patent Law, SIPO will grant a design patent if:

- the design is not attributable to any designs existing before the date the application is filed. 'Existing design' is defined as any design known to the public. Public knowledge may be through publication, use, broadcast or any other means, in China or abroad, before the filing (priority) date;[36]
- no entity or individual has filed a patent application for same design with SIPO before the filing (priority) date of the application;
- the design is distinctively different from existing designs or a combination of existing designs; and
- the design does not conflict with any existing legal rights, including and not limited to trademark rights, copyright and so on.

The Third Amendment to the Patent Law 2008 introduced an absolute novelty requirement for design patents, raising the threshold for obtaining design patents. This means that the relevant design should not have been made available to the public anywhere in the world before the application filing date. Under the revised law, it is now easier to invalidate junk patents since new designs must contain noticeable differences from pre-existing designs. This addresses circumstances in the past whereby design patents were easily granted due to the low threshold required in the preliminary examination.

In determining whether a design is the same as an existing design, SIPO compares the design with existing designs. If there is no existing design that is identical or substantially similar to the design, SIPO will grant the design patent.[37]

In determining whether a design is identical or substantially similar to existing designs, SIPO adopts the standard of a normal consumer viewing the design. If a normal consumer paying normal attention is unlikely to notice the differences between two designs, the two designs will be regarded as identical or substantially similar and a design patent will not be granted.[38]

(g) ***No substantive examination requirement for a design patent***

There is no substantial examination procedure for design patents. If a design patent application complies with the above-mentioned criteria, SIPO will grant the design patent, issue a patent certificate and announce the grant. The design patent takes effect on the date of announcement.[39]

2.4 Re-examination of applications

If a design patent applicant does not satisfy the examiner during the preliminary examination, SIPO will issue a notification for rectification and the applicant will be given an opportunity to respond to the notification within a prescribed period from the date of receipt of the notification. If the response still fails to satisfy the

36 *Ibid*; Patent Examination Guide, Part IV, Chapter 5, Section 2.
37 Patent Examination Guide, Part IV, Chapter 5, Section 5.
38 Patent Examination Guide, Part IV, Chapter 5, Section 5.1.2.
39 Patent Law Article 40.

examiner, SIPO will reject the application. The applicant will then have a right to request a re-examination by the Patent Re-examination Board.[40] The request must be submitted in writing within three months of the date of receipt of the rejection decision[41] and must state the arguments to be made and be in the prescribed form.[42]

On reviewing the application, the Patent Re-examination Board may decide either that:

- the request for re-examination is not allowed and the decision of rejection is upheld; or
- the request for re-examination is allowed and the decision is revoked.[43]

The board's decision is not final and is subject to appeal to the Beijing Intermediate People's Court.[44]

2.5 Rights of the patentee

Rights holders enjoy the exclusive right to exploit a patent.[45] This includes the exclusive right to make, offer to sell, sell or import the patented product for production or business purposes.[46]

Rights holders may also assign[47] or license the design patent to other parties.[48] The parties to the assignment must conclude a written contract and record the assignment with SIPO.[49] The assignment of the patent or the patent application will take effect on the date of recordation.[50]

(a) Term of protection

A design patent is protected for 10 years starting on the date of application.[51] Timely payment of the annual renewal fees is required to maintain the validity of a design patent.

(b) Right to use the patented product

Unlike invention patents and utility model patents, design patentees do not have the exclusive right to use the patented product. Therefore, the use of a patented product will not be considered infringement.

3. Unregistered design rights

In addition to the Patent Law, the Copyright Law offers some protection to industrial designs, and it affords protection to designs without any requirement for registration.

---

40 *Ibid*, Article 41.
41 *Ibid*; Implementing Rules, Article 60.
42 Implementing Rules, Article 60.
43 Patent Examination Guide, Part IV, Chapter 1, Section 7.
44 Patent Law, Article 41.
45 *Ibid*, Article 11.
46 *Ibid*, Article 11.
47 *Ibid*, Article 10.
48 *Ibid*, Article 12.
49 *Ibid*, Article 12.
50 *Ibid*, Article 12.
51 *Ibid*, Article 42.

The focus of the two laws is different: while the Patent Law aims to protect the invention of technology, the Copyright Law protects the expressions of ideas, verbal and artistic, fixed on any tangible medium. China became a member of the Berne Convention for the Protection of Literary and Artistic Works on October 15 1992 and recognises copyrights created in all member states.

3.1 Subject matter

Any copyrightable work will automatically be protected by the Copyright Law on the completion of its creation.[52] There are no further requirements for protection to be granted (subject to the copyright recordation system for the enforcement of copyright, discussed below).

However, not all works are copyrightable. In the context of industrial designs, there are usually two types of copyrightable works:

- the drawings for engineering designs and product designs; and
- the industrial designs themselves.

The former is expressly protected under the Copyright Law[53] and the latter is internationally recognised as belonging to 'works of applied art'. Although there are no provisions in relation to the protection of this type of work in the Copyright Law, works of applied art are expressly protected under the Berne Convention.[54] As a party to the Berne Convention, China is obliged to protect the copyright of works of applied art originating from other member states. The Provisions on the Implementation of International Copyright Treaties contain an article stipulating the terms of protection of these works.[55]

3.2 Requirements of a copyrightable work

In order to be copyrightable, a work must be original. This is a lower threshold than the novelty requirement under the Patent Law. The originality requirement only requires the work to be independently created by the author. Even if the work is substantially similar to an existing copyrighted work, it is not an infringement if the author can prove that the work was independently created.

There is an additional requirement for works of applied art – that the work must have more artistic quality than practicability. Although, as mentioned above, the Copyright Law does not define 'works of applied art', the court would regard works of applied art as original intellectual creations with both artistic quality and practicability.[56] While the practicability aspect is not protected, the artistic elements are.[57]

When considering whether a product is a work of applied art in relation to its artistic outlook, the court has stated that consideration must be given to whether the

52 Regulation on the Implementation of the Copyright Law of the People's Republic of China, Article 6.
53 Copyright Law, Article 3(7).
54 Berne Convention, Article 2.
55 Provisions on the Implementation of the International Copyright Treaties, Article 6.
56 *Inter IKEA Systems BV v Taizhou Zhongtian Plastic Co, Ltd* (2009) and *Inter Lego AG v Coko (Tianjian) Toy Co, Ltd* (1999).
57 Regulation on the Implementation of the Copyright Law of the People's Republic of China, Article 4(8).

work could be regarded as art from an aesthetic point of view, taking into consideration the artistic ideas of other general products and the means of expression of such art.[58] The test for whether a product is practical is whether it can be used in real life with an actual function, rather than solely viewing or enjoyment, such as with a work of fine art.

3.3 Copyright ownership

In general, copyright is vested in the author of the copyrighted work, and the individual who created the work will be deemed to be its author.[59] Copyright of a work created jointly by two or more authors will be owned by the co-authors jointly.[60]

The ownership of a copyright in a commissioned work vests in the commissioned party unless expressly agreed otherwise and provided in a contract between the two parties.[61]

Ownership of the copyright of works created by employees in the course of their employment depends on the nature of the work, the agreement between the employer and the employee and the legal framework of the Copyright Law. Normally, copyright in the work created by employees during the course of their employment would vest in the employees themselves, subject to the prior right of the employer to use the work within the scope of its business.[62] However, the employee may not, within two years of the creation of the work, allow any third party to use the work in the same way as the employer, without the employer's consent.[63] If the employer consents to the use of the copyrighted work by a third party within the two-year period, the employer and the employee must agree the proportionate shares of the remuneration arising from such licensing.[64]

However, in the context of industrial designs the situation is slightly different. Under the Copyright Law, for drawings of engineering designs, drawings of product designs, maps, computer software or any other similar works that are created mainly by using resources of the employer and for which the responsibility lies with the employer, the employee owns the right of attribution of the authorship only and the employer owns all other copyrights.[65] The resources in this context include funds, equipment and materials specifically provided by the employer for the completion of the work.[66]

3.4 Rights of copyright holders

Under the Copyright Law, copyright holders enjoy the rights of publication, attribution, revision, integrity, reproduction, distribution, rental, exhibition,

58 Shanghai 2nd Intermediate People's Court in *Inter IKEA Systems BV v Taizhou Zhongtian Plastic Co, Ltd* (2009).
59 Copyright Law, Article 11.
60 *Ibid*, Article 13.
61 *Ibid*, Article 17.
62 *Ibid*, Article 16(1).
63 *Ibid*, Article 16(1).
64 Regulation on the Implementation of the Copyright Law of the PRC, Article 12(2).
65 Copyright Law, Article 16(2).
66 Regulation on the Implementation of the Copyright Law of the PRC, Article 11(2).

performance, projection, broadcast, communication via an information network, cinematisation, adaption, compilation of the copyrighted work, and the right to license and assign the copyrighted work to others.[67]

The rights of reproduction and distribution are the most relevant to industrial designs. For the right of reproduction, a rights holder enjoys the exclusive right to make copies of the design by printing, photocopying, making a rubbing, making a recording and other means.[68] For the right of distribution, a rights holder has the exclusive right to provide the original or reproductions of their work to the public by means of sale or gift.[69]

The above apply to rights holders who are citizens or legal entities in China. For foreign copyright holders to enjoy the same rights in China, they must fulfil one of the following requirements:[70]

- the work must be first published in China;
- the owner, in accordance with an international treaty acceded to by both its home country or country of habitual residence and China, enjoys copyright in a work that it has published outside China; or
- the work is first published in a member country of an international treaty of which China is also a member.

3.5 Term of protection

The author's rights of attribution, revision and integrity continue indefinitely.[71] Apart from these rights, if the author is an individual, the term of protection is the author's lifetime plus 50 years, ending on December 31 of the 50th anniversary of the author's death.[72] If the author is a corporation, the term of protection is 50 years after the date of first publication.[73]

Works of applied art are protected for 25 years from the creation of the work.[74]

3.6 Infringement

The Copyright Law provides a list of infringing activities.[75] The most relevant infringing activities are publishing a work without permission from the rights holder, plagiarising another's work and using another's work without paying due remuneration.[76] These more relevant provisions may be used to enforce design patent rights, for example, against products incorporating patented design features which can also be covered by copyright.

3.7 Voluntary recordation of copyright works

Copyright is an automatic right arising upon the completion of a work, without any

---

67 Copyright Law, Article 10.
68 *Ibid*, Article 10.
69 *Ibid*, Article 10.
70 *Ibid*, Article 2.
71 *Ibid*, Article 20.
72 *Ibid*, Article 21.
73 *Ibid*, Article 21.
74 See note 4 above.
75 Copyright Law, Article 47.
76 *Ibid*, Article 47.

formal requirements of registration. Therefore, one of the greatest difficulties facing copyright holders is proof of ownership when they wish to enforce their rights.

China offers a system of voluntary recordation of copyright works. The system is voluntary – that is, non-recordation of works will not affect the copyright protection. Recordation of the copyright works is *prima facie* evidence of ownership in a work. This evidence is useful in establishing a claim when infringement occurs, and therefore facilitates enforcement actions (whether through the administrative or the judicial route).

Recordation of copyright is a process handled by the Copyright Protection Centre of China (CPCC) under the National Copyright Administration of China (NCAC). The recordation procedure requires the following documents to accompany an application:

- the identity certificate of the applicant (copyright holder);
- a brief description of the work;
- a pledge letter of right;
- a sample of the work; and
- a power of attorney and the identity document of the local agent.

On receipt of the application and a fee, the CPCC will examine the application and issue a registration certificate.

The courts are not bound by the recordation of the CPCC and have a discretion to decide on the legality and validity of a registration certificate and ownership of the copyright work when adjudicating copyright dispute cases. Should the copyright be challenged, the alleged rights holder faces strict conditions to prove ownership of the rights and their validity, even if the copyright has been recorded. However, as discussed above, evidence of recordation with the CPCC may expedite the acceptance of the statement of claim at the courts as it provides *prima facie* evidence of ownership. Recordation of copyright may also assist in applications for interim injunctions.

3.8 Enforcement

When faced with infringement of copyrighted work, rights holders may enforce their rights through the following routes.

(a) Criminal proceedings

Copyright infringement may be subject to criminal sanction. Under the Criminal Law, the copying or distributing of a copyrighted work without permission of the rights holder will be a crime if the number of the copies or the illicit gain generated exceeds the threshold stipulated in the Judicial Interpretation of the Supreme People's Court.[77] In cases where the volume of infringing copies is between 500 and 2,500 or the amount of proceeds arising from the illegal turnover is between Rmb50,000 and Rmb250,000, the infringer will be subject to a maximum sentence of three years' imprisonment if the illicit gain is between Rmb30,000 and

77 Interpretation of the Supreme People's Court and the Supreme People's Procuratorate Concerning Some Issues on the Specific Application of Law for Handling Criminal Cases of Infringement upon Intellectual Property Rights (2004 and 2007).

Rmb150,000.[78] In cases where the volume of infringing copies involved is more than 2,500 or the proceeds arising from the illegal turnover are more than Rmb250,000, the infringer will be subject to a sentence of three to seven years' imprisonment if the illicit gain is more than Rmb150,000.[79]

It is a crime for any party knowingly to sell infringing works for the purpose of profit and to make a profits of Rmb100,000 or more. The penalty is a maximum of three years' imprisonment and/or a fine equivalent to one to five times the amount of the illegal income, or half of the full amount of the illegal turnover.[80]

(b) Administrative proceedings

As discussed in section 2 above, enforcement against infringement through administrative measures is usually more expedient and more cost-effective. It is not necessary to pursue an administrative complaint through the NCAC. Local copyright administrations are authorised to investigate and adjudicate on straightforward cases of infringement. NCAC involvement is only necessary for infringements that have national impact.[81] The delegation of work between state and local administrative bodies makes investigations more time-effective.

The Copyright Law empowers local administrative bodies to issue warnings, stop infringement activities, confiscate unlawful proceeds, destroy or confiscate pirated reproductions, confiscate the equipment for installation or storage of infringing products, and confiscate the materials, tools and equipment used in the manufacture of the infringing reproductions.[82] Local administrative bodies may also impose a fine of up to three times the illegal proceeds on the infringer. If the amount of proceeds is not ascertainable, a fine of up to Rmb100,000 may be imposed.[83] Local administrative bodies may also investigate whether the act constitutes a crime and any criminal liabilities.[84] However, the administrative measures mentioned above are exhaustive, and the rights holder cannot claim for damages against the infringer.

A copyright infringement complaint must be filed with the local administration body where the infringing act occurred. The complainant must submit a complaint form and provide evidence to substantiate the complaint, such as a copyright holders' certificate (if any), the recordation certificate from CPCC (if any) or a copy

---

78 Criminal Law, Article 217: Interpretation of the Supreme People's Court and the Supreme People's Procuratorate Concerning Some Issues on the Specific Application of Law for Handling Criminal Cases of Infringement upon Intellectual Property Rights (2004), Article 5; and Interpretation II of the Supreme People's Court and the Supreme People's Procuratorate Concerning Some Issues on the Specific Application of Law for Handling Criminal Cases of Infringement upon Intellectual Property Rights (2007), Article 1.

79 *Ibid.*

80 Criminal Law, Article 218; Interpretation of the Supreme People's Court and the Supreme People's Procuratorate Concerning Some Issues on the Specific Application of Law for Handling Criminal Cases of Infringement upon Intellectual Property Rights (2004), Article 6; and Interpretation II of the Supreme People's Court and the Supreme People's Procuratorate Concerning Some Issues on the Specific Application of Law for Handling Criminal Cases of Infringement upon Intellectual Property Rights (2007), Article 4.

81 Regulation on the Implementation of the Copyright Law of the PRC, Article 37.

82 Art 4, Measures for the Implementation of Copyright Administrative Punishment (2009), Article 4 and Copyright Law, Article 48.

83 Regulation on the Implementation of the Copyright Law of the PRC, Article 36.

84 Copyright Law, Article 18.

of the infringing work. The complainant may also provide other information that can assist the investigation. The administrative body will investigate the complaint and decide whether the products in question are infringing. The limitation period for the copyright administrative department to impose punishment for infringing acts is two years from the date of the infringing act.[85]

(c) *Customs recordation*

A copyright holder enjoys the same rights as a design patentee to record his rights with the customs authorities. The customs recordation will be effective for the life of the copyright.

(d) *Judicial proceedings*

If the copyright holder pursues the judicial route and initiates proceedings against infringers in the court, he may first obtain an interim injunction against the infringing act[86] and request the court to preserve the evidence of infringement and the property of the defendant.[87] The copyright holder may also obtain damages. Upon a successful adjudication of the claim, the quantity of damages will based on the actual loss of the rights holder, taking into account the reasonable expenses incurred by the rights holder in stopping the infringement.[88] If the actual loss is not ascertainable, the court may impose damages up to a maximum of Rmb500,000.

To initiate a legal proceeding at court, the copyright holder must submit a written complaint, documents identifying the rights holder and the infringer, evidence of copyright ownership and the infringement, and a power of attorney if a local agent is instructed.

4. Qualification for protection

An inventor or a designer has the right to apply for a design patent.[89] Article 13 of the Implementing Rules for Patent Law 2010 (the Implementing Rules) defines an 'inventor' or 'designer' as the "person who makes a creative contribution to the essential features of a design". Article 13 excludes persons who are engaged solely in an organising or supporting role during the inventing or creative stage.

For designs created by employees, the employer has a right to apply and obtain a patent right for the design.[90] A design created by an employee is defined by Article 6 of the Patent Law to be a design made by a person in the performance of the tasks instructed by his employer, or a design made by him using mainly the materials and technical resources of his employer. 'Materials or technical means of the employer'[91] here refer to where the employee uses the employer's funds, equipment, raw materials or confidential technical information to create the design.[92]

---

85 Measures for the Implementation of Copyright Administrative Punishment (2009), Article 19.
86 Copyright Law, Article 50.
87 *Ibid*, Article 51.
88 *Ibid*, Article 49.
89 Patent Law, Article 6.
90 *Ibid*, Article 6.
91 Patent Law, Article 6(3).
92 Implementing Rules, Article 12.

To qualify as a design created by an employee, one of the following conditions must be met:

- the design has been created in the course of employment;
- the design has been made in the performance of an assigned task other than in the course of employment; or
- the design is made within one year of the employee's retirement, transfer or termination of labour relations in connection with duties or tasks assigned to him.[93]

5. Infringement

A rights holder's rights are infringed if any party:

- manufactures, sells, offers to sell or imports any product incorporating the patented design for business purposes without authorisation;[94]
- licenses the patented design to other parties without authorisation;[95]
- affixes the patented mark and registration number on its product to pass it off as a patented product;[96] or
- produces counterfeit or fake patent certificates, patent documents or patent application documents.[97]

Any party that manufactures and/or imports a patented product without the permission of the rights holder infringes the design patent even if it has no knowledge of the existence of the design patent.

However, specific protection applies to any party who produces or sells end products containing patent-infringing product parts. In particular, a *bona fide* producer of an end product that incorporates infringing product parts is regarded as 'using' the product and not 'making' the product, thereby qualifying for protection under Article 70 of the Patent Law, and may be exempted from paying compensation.

Warning letters will be effective evidence to prove a collaborative relationship between the maker of the infringing part and the seller of the product which incorporates it, in which case both the producer and the seller of the end product will be liable for damages.

In instances of infringement, rights holders may seek to enforce against the infringer through various routes:

- criminal proceedings;[98]
- administrative proceedings;[99]
- customs recordation; or
- judicial proceedings.[100]

---

93 *Ibid*, Article 12.
94 Patent Law, Article 11.
95 *Ibid*, Article 12.
96 Patent Implementing Rules, Article 84.
97 *Ibid*, Article 84.
98 Criminal Law (1997), Article 21.
99 Patent Law, Article 63.
100 *Ibid*, Article 63.

5.1 Administrative proceedings

Administrative proceedings refer to the ability of rights holders to complain of certain breaches of the law to the local administrative authority. Administrative proceedings are generally more expedient with enforcement. Any breaches of the Patent Law, including infringement complaints, may be submitted to the local administrative authority. The jurisdiction of administrative authorities depends on where the infringement took place.[101]

The new Rules on Administrative Enforcement of Patent Rights (the Administrative Enforcement Rules) were introduced by SIPO on December 29 2010 and became effective on February 1 2011. The rules codify the practice and act to strengthen the local administrative authorities' powers, thereby increasing the effectiveness of administrative actions in the enforcement of patents.

Under Article 28 of the Administrative Enforcement Rules, the local administrative authorities are given the power to seize suspected counterfeiting products after obtaining the approval of the senior administrative authorities. The rules also increase a complainant's ability to collect evidence. Article 35 prescribes that the infringed party may ask the local administrative authorities to collect evidence for patent infringement disputes if it is not able to collect it independently. The local administrative authorities decide whether to investigate and collect relevant evidence. During the investigation and collection of relevant evidence, and upon demonstrating the possession of administrative enforcement certificates, all parties must cooperate to provide correct information, and may not refuse to do so or obstruct the investigation or the collection of evidence. The local administrative authorities may also seek assistance from customs authorities for the investigation of the import and export of seized products.[102]

If the local administrative authority considers that there is an infringement, it may order the infringer to stop the infringing act immediately,[103] confiscate the illegal income and impose fines of up to four times the gains of the infringement.[104] The infringer may bring a civil action to set aside the orders.[105] If the infringer does not appeal and does not comply with the orders, the authority may approach the court to request a compulsory execution of its orders.[106]

Parties may also ask the local administrative authority to mediate over disputes relating to:

- patent infringements;[107]
- the quantum of damages under an infringement order granted by SIPO;[108]
- the ownership and rights relating to a patent;[109]

---

101 Rules on Administrative Enforcement of Patent Rights (2010), Article 2.
102 Administrative Enforcement Rules, Article 40.
103 Patent Implementing Rules, Article 85.
104 Patent Law, Article 63.
105 *Ibid*, Article 60.
106 *Ibid*, Article 60.
107 *Ibid*, Article 60.
108 *Ibid*, Article 60.
109 Patent Implementing Rules, Article 85.

- the qualifications of inventors and designers;[110] and
- other patent disputes.[111]

5.2 Customs recordation

Apart from filing a complaint to the administrative bodies, a rights holder may have its rights recorded with the customs authorities, and will then be informed whenever any potentially infringing goods are discovered at a customs port. The rights holder will have the option to have the goods seized upon payment of a bond. The customs authorities will conduct further investigation to verify the infringement. The procedure of customs recordation is relatively straightforward and the recordation will be effective for the same term as the design patent. A customs recordation covers exports from and imports to all ports in China.

5.3 Invalidation orders

Invalidation may be used by rights holders as a strategic defence in infringement proceedings. Any party or individual may file an invalidation request with the Patent Re-examination Board.[112] The petitioner must state the specific reasons for invalidation and attach supporting evidence.

The grounds for invalidation are as follows:

- the subject matter does not create an aesthetic impression or is not a design feature of a product;[113]
- the design lacks novelty;[114]
- the design conflicts with prior legal rights (eg, existing registered trademarks);[115]
- the brief statement of the design patent does not clearly define the scope of patent protection; and
- the drawings or photographs of the design do not clearly display the design features of the product.

The petitioner may adduce physical evidence and documentary evidence.[116] For physical evidence, the petitioner may submit samples of pre-existing products with similar designs as proof of prior arts. For documentary evidence, the petitioner may submit registration certificates of registered trademarks or other registered rights that are similar to prove that the design conflicts with existing legal rights.

If the board declares a patent to be invalid, the patent will be deemed to never have been applied for.[117]

Invalidation orders are subject to appeal to the courts in China.[118]

---

110 *Ibid*, Article 85.
111 *Ibid*, Article 85.
112 Patent Law, Article 44.
113 *Ibid*, Article 65.
114 *Ibid*, Article 23.
115 *Ibid*, Article 23.
116 Patent Examination Guide, Part IV, Chapter 3, Section 3.3.
117 Patent Law, Article 47.
118 *Ibid*, Article 46.

Invalidation orders do not have any retroactive effect on any judgment delivered or mediation agreement reached with respect to patent infringements before the invalidation order.[119] However, if damages, royalties or patent transfer fees were ordered, and not refunding these would constitute a blatant violation of the principle of fairness, a partial or full refund will be ordered.

5.4 Declaration of non-infringement

In response to the increasingly common practice of alleged infringers confronting rightful owners with actions in response to a cease-and-desist letter issued by the rights holder, the Interpretations of the Supreme People's Court concerning Certain Issues on the Application of Law for the Trial of Cases on Disputes over Infringement on Patent Rights of 2010 has stipulated certain criteria for claiming non-infringement declaratory judgments to prevent frivolous claims by alleged infringers.[120]

Before a court can accept an application for a declaratory judgment, the rights holder must have failed to respond to the alleged infringer's response within one month of receiving it or within two months of it being issued. This ensures that the rights holder has sufficient time to withdraw its cease-and-desist letter or to institute court proceedings.

6. Design infringement litigation

6.1 Criminal proceedings

Under the Criminal Law, a party found guilty of infringement may be sentenced to a fixed term of imprisonment of no more than three years and may have fines imposed[121] if any one of the thresholds below are met:[122]

- the amount of illegal business operations is more than Rmb200,000;
- the amount of illegal proceeds is more than Rmb100,000; or
- the economic loss of the rights holder is more than Rmb500,000.

Rights holders may submit a complaint to the local public security bureau asking it to investigate the complaint. The bureau has wide powers of investigation and prosecution in its areas of jurisdiction, including:[123]

- detaining suspects;
- collecting evidence of infringement; and
- prosecuting the infringers in the courts.

---

119 *Ibid*, Article 47.

120 Interpretations of the Supreme People's Court concerning Certain Issues on the Application of Law for the Trial of Cases on Disputes over Infringement on Patent Rights, Article 18.

121 Criminal Law (1997), Article 216.

122 Interpretation of the Supreme People's Court and the Supreme People's Procuratorate Concerning Some Issues on the Specific Application of Law for Handling Criminal Cases of Infringement upon Intellectual Property Rights (2004 and 2007), Article 4.

123 Supreme Court's Interpretation on Criminal Liability 2011, Articles 1 and 2.

6.2 Judicial proceedings

Any interested party may initiate civil proceedings in the courts to resolve patent disputes or to challenge invalidation orders or injunctions made by SIPO.[124] Before commencing a civil proceeding, rights holders must obtain a design patent search report from SIPO to show that the design patent has novelty.[125] SIPO will provide a search report within two months of receipt of a request.[126] Although this is not a mandatory requirement, in practice courts will only accept claims supported by search reports. As design patent registrations do not pass through substantive examination, courts will not have any means of verifying the validity of the design patent. The search report will confirm the validity of the design for the courts.

(a) Determination of similarity between designs

The determination of similarity between two designs is key to an infringement action. The court applies a two-part test. The first test is whether the alleged infringing product is the same or a similar type of product as the product of the registered design.[127] In determining the similarity of the products, the court may refer to the brief description of the design, the International Classification for Industrial Designs, the function and sales channel of products and the application of the design.[128] If the court considers that the alleged infringing product is not the same or a similar class of product as the registered design, no infringement will be found.

The second test is whether the design itself is considered the same or similar. The standard is based on the "knowledge level and cognitive ability of the average consumers of the requisite product".[129] The court will conduct a comprehensive review based on the design features of the patented design and the infringing design along with their overall visual effects.[130] The court may refer to the claims, brief description, drawings and photographs of the design in determining the case. However, it will not consider the mere technical functions or the internal structures that do not affect the overall visual effect of the design.[131]

(b) Prior arts defence

A prior arts defence may be pleaded if it can be shown that the patented design belongs to an existing design.[132] If the evidence submitted is sufficient to show this, the court will hold that there is no infringement. The evidence submitted should demonstrate that the prior arts have been published before the filing date of the requisite design patent.

---

124 Article 60, Patent Law.
125 Patent Law, Article 61.
126 Patent Implementing Rules, Article 57.
127 Supreme Court's Judicial Interpretations of Certain Issues on the Application of Law on Disputes over Infringement on Patent Rights 2009, Article 8.
128 Supreme Court Interpretation, Article 9.
129 *Ibid*, Articles 10 and 11.
130 *Ibid*, Article 11.
131 *Ibid*, Article 11.
132 Patent Law, Article 62.

(c) ***Interim injunction***

Before filing an action, a rights holder may apply to the court for an interim injunction against the infringing act.[133] To apply for an interim injunction, the rights holder must show that:

- the design patent right has been infringed; and
- the infringing act will cause irreparable damage if prompt action is not ordered.[134]

The rights holder must provide security in the form of a bond to the court and must commence the legal action against the infringer within 15 days of the date of issuance of the interim injunction order.[135]

(d) ***Remedies***

A rights holder may claim damages in design patent infringement proceedings.[136] The quantum of damages is determined based on the actual loss suffered by the rights holder.[137] If the actual loss is difficult to quantify, damages are determined on the basis of the profits made by the infringer.[138] Where the infringing products are packaging materials, the court will calculate damages based on the value of the packaging materials and their function in the realisation of profits of the sale of the packaged products.[139]

Where it is not possible to establish the quantum of damages, the court has a statutory right to grant damages of between Rmb10,000 and Rmb1,000,000.[140]

(e) ***Limitation of patent infringement claims***

If a rights holder does not bring legal proceedings with respect to infringing acts within two years from the date of becoming aware of or having constructive knowledge of the infringement, the claim will be time barred.[141]

7. Licensing and exploitation

Rights holders enjoy the right to licence their patents.[142] They may grant ordinary licences, exclusive licences, sole exploitation licences and cross licences to any party and the terms may be freely agreed between the parties.

SIPO issued a Circular on the Measures for the Filling of Patent Exploitation License Contracts (the Patent License Measures) in August 2011. The measures stipulate certain legal requirements which must be met before the patent licence is effective.

---

133 *Ibid*, Article 66.
134 *Ibid*, Article 66.
135 *Ibid*, Article 66.
136 Patent Law, Article 65.
137 *Ibid*, Article 65.
138 *Ibid*, Article 65.
139 Supreme Court Interpretation, Article 16.
140 Patent Law, Article 65.
141 *Ibid*, Article 68.
142 *Ibid*, Article 12.

First, a patent licence contract must be in writing and must comply with the Contract Law.[143] In particular, the contract should include the names and addresses of the parties, the title of the invention or design, the patent registration number, the date of grant and the date of announcement of authorisation of the patent rights, and the period of the licence.[144]

Secondly, the patent licence contract must be recorded with SIPO within three months of the execution of the contract.[145] The parties should submit an application form signed by the licensor, a copy of the licence contract, proof-of-identity documents and a power of attorney.[146]

Although the Patent Law includes provisions for granting of compulsory licences, these only expressly prescribe the scope to include inventions or utility models and are silent on design patents.[147]

143 Patent Licence Measures, Article 4.
144 *Ibid*, Article 9.
145 *Ibid*, Article 5.
146 *Ibid*, Article 8.
147 Patent Law, Article 48.

Denmark

Claus Barrett Christiansen
Bech-Bruun

---

1. Design protection

In Denmark, design protection is regulated by the Designs Act (1259/2000), as amended up to January 28 2009.[1] The act implemented the EU Designs Directive (98/71/EC). The EU Community Designs Regulation (6/2002) has a direct effect in Denmark.

A design right is created by the first party to file or use the design within the jurisdiction. If a design is new and has individual character, it may be registered either as a national design under the Designs Act or as a registered Community design under the Community Design Regulation.

If the design is new, has individual character and has been made public within the relevant jurisdiction, it may also be protected as an unregistered Community design under the Community Design Regulation effective for Denmark.

2. Registered design rights

2.1 Nature of rights

Under Section 1 of the Designs Act, the creator of a design may acquire an exclusive right to the design by registration in accordance with the act. 'Design' means the appearance of a product or part of a product resulting from the features of the product itself or its ornamentation, in particular with respect to lines, contours, colours, shape, texture or materials.[2]

2.2 Qualification

A design right will be granted only if the design is new and has individual character. A design is considered to be new if no identical design has been made available to the public before the application for registration is filed or the date of priority, if priority is claimed. A design is considered to have individual character if the overall impression it produces on an informed user differs from any design made available to the public before the filing of the application for registration or the date of priority, if priority is claimed.[3]

---

1 See the Consolidated Designs Act (89/2009).
2 Section 2 of the Designs Act.
3 *Ibid*, Section 3.

2.3 Registration procedure

Provisions on the application and registration procedure of Danish designs are contained in Chapter II of the Designs Act and in the Order on Application and Registration of Designs (1099/2008).[4]

Applications for the registration of a design must be filed with the Danish Patent and Trademark Office.[5] No formal requirements exist for the application, which may be filed as a paper version or submitted online. Standard application forms are available from the office. An application must contain the following details, set down in Section 2 of the order:

- the name or firm and postal address of the applicant;
- reproductions illustrating the design and a specimen of the design, where applicable;
- an indication of the product in relation to which the design is intended to be used (product specification);
- an indication of the appropriate class or classes of the product according to the Locarno Agreement Establishing an International Classification for Industrial Designs;
- a request for priority if the applicant wishes to claim priority;
- the name or firm and postal address of the agent if the applicant is represented by an agent, and a power of attorney – if the applicant is represented by a trademark/design agent or lawyer, no power of attorney is required;
- the name and postal address of the designer, including designer group or firm, if a request is made for the recording of one or more designers in the Register of Designs;
- information as to who will be authorised to receive communications from the Patent and Trademark Office on behalf of all the applicants if the design registration is applied for by several applicants jointly and they are not represented by an agent;
- a statement of the period for which publication of the registration is to be deferred if the applicant requests deferment; and
- a statement that the design is to be registered in colour if the protection is to comprise the design in colour.

The Patent and Trademark Office has stated that the registration of a design in black and white will usually confer protection on all colour combinations of the design.

The application will only be granted legal effect from the date that either a reproduction or a specimen of the design is included in the application.[6] A design may only be granted protection from an earlier date if so claimed in the application.

An application may contain more than one design provided that the designs

---

4 The application and registration procedure for a Community design is identical to the Danish procedure. However, the application is filed with the Office for Harmonisation in the Internal Market. See Titles IV to V of the Community Design Regulation.

5 Section 13 of the Designs Act.

6 *Ibid*, Section 14, paragraph 1.

applied for can be referred to the same class in the Locarno Classification.[7] It is possible to separate out a multiple design registration.

Deferment of the publication may be requested only in the application; later requests will be disregarded. Request for deferment may concern only some of the design in a multiple application. Deferment of publication is possible for up to six months and the applicant is asked to include a fixed date for publication in the request for deferment.

The Patent and Trademark Office will examine an application when it is filed. The application is checked mainly for formalities. No substantive examination[8] is carried out – that is, no search is made for novelty or individual character except to verify that the application relates to a design and that the design is not contrary to public policy or morality. If requested by the applicant, and upon payment of a fee, the Patent and Trademark Office will perform an extended examination,[9] which includes a search with respect to existing design registrations as well as pending design applications. However, an extended examination is not a substantive examination since the Patent and Trademark Office does not submit any conclusions as to whether earlier registrations or applications are considered harmful to the novelty or individual character of the design applied for.

If the application complies with the formal requirements, the design will be registered. If the application does not meet the formal requirements, an objection will be raised by the Patent and Trademark Office. The applicant will be notified of this and will be allowed to file its observations or take steps to correct the application within a time limit stipulated by the Office.[10] This will lead either to an amendment of the application and thereby registration or to its refusal in the case of non-compliance with the formal requirements.

2.4 Term of protection

A design registration is valid for five years from the filing of the application. The term of protection is always from the day of the application, even if priority is claimed. The registration may be renewed for four consecutive periods of five years on request, providing a total term of protection of 25 years.[11] In relation to spare parts, the term of protection is limited to a total of 15 years. A request for the renewal of a design registration is made by payment of the renewal fee to the Patent and Trademark Office. The payment may be made within three months before and six months after expiry of the registration period.[12]

2.5 Rights granted

Protection under the Designs Act means that no other person may exploit the registered design without explicit consent from the rights holder. No other

7 Section 15 of the order.
8 Section 17 of the Designs Act.
9 *Ibid*, Section 17, paragraph 2.
10 *Ibid*, Section 19, paragraph 1.
11 *Ibid*, Section 23, paragraph 1.
12 *Ibid*, Section 24, paragraph 1.

individual or company can make, offer, market, import, export or use a product for which the design is applied or stock such a product for one of these purposes.[13]

The exclusive rights of the rights holder are limited in respect of:

- acts done for private purposes;
- acts done for experimental purposes;
- acts of reproduction for the purpose of making citations or for the purpose of teaching, provided that such acts are compatible with fair trade practice and do not unduly prejudice normal exploitation of the design, and provided that the source is acknowledged;
- the equipment on ships and aircraft registered in another country when these temporarily enter Danish territory; and
- the importation to Denmark of spare parts and accessories for the purpose of repairing and the execution of repairs on such ships and aircraft.[14]

A principle of European Economic Area regional exhaustion applies to designs under the Designs Act.[15]

2.6 Infringement

Any design that does not produce on an informed user a different overall impression constitutes an infringement of the design already registered. The scope of protection of the design is determined by the description of the design in the registration and the classes for which the design is registered. The degree of freedom of the designer in developing his design will be taken into consideration.[16]

2.7 Damages and other relief

Under Section 37 of the Designs Act, any person or legal entity intentionally or negligently committing design infringement is liable to pay reasonable compensation for the exploitation of the design and damages for any further injury the infringement has caused, taking loss of profit suffered by the injured party and the illicit profit obtained by the infringer into consideration. However, it can be seen from the case law that compensation and damages are usually inadequate, not even equalling the profits obtained by the infringer. Liability under the Designs Act corresponds to the general principles of liability in tort, requiring negligence, causality and adequacy.

Design infringement may involve criminal liability. If a person or legal entity intentionally or with gross negligence infringes a design right, they may be fined. If the infringement has been committed under aggravating circumstances, the penalty for a person may be increased to a term of imprisonment for up to 18 months.[17]

A preliminary injunction is available under the Administration of Justice Act for cases concerning infringement of intellectual property rights, to prevent future infringement.

---

13 *Ibid*, Section 9, paragraph 1.
14 *Ibid*, Sections 10 and 11.
15 *Ibid*, Section 12.
16 *Ibid*, Section 9, paragraph 2.
17 *Ibid*, Section 36.

2.8 Licensing

The design right may be licensed, but the Designs Act does not contain any provisions on licences and, consequently, under Danish law there are no formal requirements for licences. Licences are governed by the general principles applying to intellectual property licences.[18] On request, the grant of a licence will be entered in the Register of Designs.[19]

2.9 Compulsory licences

There is no general limitation on the scope of protection in the Designs Act in respect of licences. The act does not contain any provisions on compulsory licences.

2.10 Validity issues

If the design is not renewed within the time limit stipulated, or renewal is not possible because the maximum term of protection has been exceeded, the design registration is no longer valid and it is cancelled.

A design registration may be cancelled by the Patent and Trademark Office or by way of a court decision.[20]

3. Unregistered Community designs

3.1 Nature of rights

In Denmark, the design law regime does not contain any provisions on unregistered designs. A design must be registered in order to be protected under the Designs Act.

However, since the Community Design Regulation has direct effect in Denmark, an unregistered Community design does enjoy protection in Denmark.[21]

The meaning of a 'design', 'product' and 'complex product' is the same for unregistered Community designs, and also the protection requirement/qualification. The two main differences between registered and unregistered designs are that unregistered designs will only be infringed by direct or indirect copying and that the term of protection is only three years from the date the design was first made available to the public.[22]

3.2 Qualification

In order for an unregistered Community design to be granted protection, the same requirements apply as for registered designs: the design must be new and have individual character on the date when the design for which protection is sought is made available to the public.[23]

However, an additional requirement set down in Article 11 of the Community Design Regulation must be fulfilled for unregistered Community designs. The

---

18 See section 7 below.
19 Section 51, paragraph 1 of the Designs Act.
20 An unregistered Community design cannot be subject to administrative proceedings in Denmark. An objection must be filed with the Danish courts.
21 Article 27 of the Community Design Regulation.
22 *Ibid*, Article 11.
23 *Ibid*, Article 6, paragraph 1.

Community Design Regulation stipulates that unregistered Community design protection is not established until the design has been made available to the public within the European Union – that is, it has been published, exhibited or otherwise made public in a way that the design, in the normal course of business, could reasonably have become known to the circles specialising in the sector concerned.[24] If the design is first made available outside the European Union, it is not protected as an unregistered Community design.

3.3 Term of protection

An unregistered Community design is protected for three years from the date when the design was first made available to the public. Registration of an unregistered Community design may be applied for within one year of it first being made available in the European Union.[25]

3.4 Rights granted

An unregistered Community design enjoys the same rights as those granted to registered designs and is subject to the same limitations (see section 2.5 above). The rights holder has the exclusive right to use the design and can prevent any third party from using the design in a commercial setting without its consent.[26]

However, a holder of an unregistered Community design right may only prevent third parties from using the design if the contested use results from direct or indirect copying of the design. It is not sufficient that the contested design produces the same overall impression on an informed user as the unregistered Community design. It is not considered copying if the design is an independent work of creation by a designer who may reasonably be thought not to be familiar with the design made available to the public by the rights holder.[27] Thus, the protection granted to an unregistered Community design is not a priority right, but only a protection granted against copying.

3.5 Infringement

An unregistered Community design may be infringed by the same types of acts that constitute infringement of registered designs. However, in theory it has to be proved that the alleged infringer has copied an unregistered Community design since independently created designs do not constitute infringement of an unregistered Community design (see section 3.4 above). Case law indicates that Danish courts apply similar infringement criteria irrespective of whether the allegedly infringed design is registered or unregistered.

3.6 Damages and other relief

The Community Design Regulation does not include any provisions on sanctions for

---

24 *Ibid*, Article 11, paragraphs 1 and 2.

25 However, protection under the Designs Act does not preclude protection from copyright. Therefore, protection could possibly be granted under the Copyright Act when the term of protection of a design has expired.

26 Article 19, paragraph 1 of the Community Design Regulation.

27 *Ibid*, Article 19, paragraph 2.

infringement, so the laws of the country in which the infringement was committed will apply to an unregistered Community design.

This means that the same sections regarding damages and other reliefs for a national registered design and a registered Community design apply to the unregistered Community design (see section 2.7 above).

3.7 Licensing

An unregistered Community design right may be licensed under Article 32 of the Community Design Regulation. Article 32 does not contain any formal requirements in relation to licences, so the licensing of an unregistered Community design is governed by the general principles applied to intellectual property licences[28] in the various jurisdictions covered by the licence. Since the right is not registered, the grant of a licence cannot be entered in the Register of Designs.

3.8 Compulsory licences

There are no rules regarding compulsory licences in the Community Design Regulation. Thus, an unregistered Community design is not subject to compulsory licensing, as for other intellectual property rights.

4. Qualification for protection

The conditions for protection are novelty and individual character for the registered design rights (see section 2 above), as well as having been made available to the public for the unregistered Community design.

4.1 Novelty

A design has been made available to the public if it has been published or if it has been exhibited, used in trade or otherwise disclosed. However, a design is not deemed to have been made available to the public if the design – even though it has been published – could not reasonably have become known in the normal course of business to the circles specialising in the sector concerned and operating within the European Union.[29] Thus, even if a design is published, it has not necessarily been made available to the relevant public and is not necessarily a hindrance for registration. The design is not made available to the relevant public if it has been disclosed to a third party under explicit or implicit conditions of confidentiality.[30]

Section 6 of the Designs Act stipulates a grace period. A design will retain its novelty if disclosure of the design occurs no later than 12 months before the date of filing an application for registration or the date of priority. This gives the rights holder time to consider whether the design should be registered or whether an unregistered Community design offers adequate protection.

A design of a component part of a complex product may only be considered to be new and to have individual character provided that the component part, once it

---

28 See section 7 below.
29 Section 5, paragraph 2 of the Designs Act.
30 *Ibid*, Section 5.

has been incorporated into the complex product, remains visible during normal use of the product, and the visible features of the component part comply with the requirements of novelty and individual character.[31]

4.2 Individual character

A design can only have individual character if it differs from the overall impression of designs already published. The design does not have individual character if it consists of ordinary, fully accessible design elements used in designs already published. Whether a design has a different overall impression, and thereby complying with the individual character requirement, thus depends on two factors: whether the informed user considers the designs to be similar, and the degree of freedom for the designer in developing a new design.

An informed user is neither a professional nor an expert in the area, but will have some knowledge of the product, its purpose or its functions.

In developing a design, the designer may be limited by the specific functional requirements of the product. A design right may not be obtained for those features of the appearance of a product which are exclusively dictated by the technical function of the product.[32]

4.3 Limitations in qualification for protection: spare parts

Spare parts are protectable under Section 4 of the Designs Act. Under Section 8 of the act, a design right may not be based on features of the appearance of a product which must be reproduced in their exact form and dimension to enable the product to which the design relates to be mechanically connected to, or placed in, on, around or against, another product, or to enable either product to perform its function[33] – the 'must-fit' exclusion. Design protection will not be granted to must-fit components, since protection would create a monopoly in respect of spare parts. However, a design right may be obtained for a component if the design allows the multiple assembly or connection of products within a modular system consisting of mutually interchangeable parts.[34]

In addition to must-fit components, a design will not be granted protection as either a registered or an unregistered Community design if it is a 'must-match' component. Thus, protection cannot be granted to a design of a component which is used for the repair of a complex product so as to give the product its original appearance. However, the 'must-match' rule only applies to Community designs. It is possible to obtain a registered design for must-match components in Denmark, although the protection is limited by the components subject to the must-fit rule. Must-match components can be protected for a maximum of 15 years.[35]

---

31 *Ibid*, Section 4, paragraph 1.
32 *Ibid*, Section 8, paragraph 1 (i).
33 *Ibid*, Section 8, paragraph 1 (ii).
34 *Ibid*, Section 8, paragraph 2.
35 *Ibid*, Section 23, paragraph 2.

4.4 International obligations

Denmark is a member of the Agreement on Trade-Related Aspects of Intellectual Property Rights under the World Trade Organization, the Paris Convention, the Geneva Act of the Hague Agreement Concerning the International Registration of Industrial Designs 1999 and the Locarno Agreement Establishing an International Classification for Industrial Designs.

5. Infringement

As mentioned in sections 2.6 and 3.5 above, any design that does give the informed user a different overall impression from a design already registered constitutes an infringement. For an unregistered Community design, it has to be proved that the alleged infringer has copied the design since independently created designs do not constitute infringement of an unregistered Community design – see section 3.4 above and Recital 21 of the Community Design Regulation.

Under the Community Design Regulation, proof of knowledge is not required for infringement of registered designs. In relation to unregistered design rights, Article 19 of the Community Design Regulation states that an independent work of creation by a designer who may reasonably be thought not to be familiar with an earlier unregistered design is not copying, implying that knowledge regarding the design is a relevant aspect in determining whether a use infringes an unregistered Community design right.

5.1 Dealing with infringement

(a) Knowledge and negligence

Case law of the Supreme Court suggests that use of a design without the consent of the rights holder constitutes infringement, even if an alleged infringer of an unregistered Community design did not have knowledge of it and did not show negligence. Lack of knowledge and negligence may result in the rights holder not being awarded any compensation, damages or recovery of profits.[36]

(b) Scope of protection

It has been discussed in Danish legal theory whether the copying requirement for unregistered Community designs narrows the protection down to protection against identical imitations or whether the scope of protection also encompasses close imitations. Case law from the Maritime and Commercial Court supports the view that a close, although not identical, imitation of an unregistered Community design may constitute infringement, especially if the characteristic design elements of the unregistered Community design are copied and the differences are immaterial.[37] Furthermore, as a substitute for knowledge, the court has stated that, provided that it is difficult to "imagine" that a later design has been designed and produced without knowledge of the earlier unregistered Community design, this strongly

---

36 See Case 2007/1112 of January 30 2007.
37 See Case V-62/04 of July 1 2005.

supports a conclusion that the earlier design has been infringed even though knowledge on the part of the infringer has not been proved. Even so, the scope of protection of unregistered Community designs is still narrow and requires a high degree of similarity, although not identity. A mere conceptual identity does not constitute infringement.[38]

(c) *Novelty and individual character*

The Maritime and Commercial Court has stated that a "normal" combination of already known, ordinary and fully accessible design elements does not constitute individual character.[39] However, case law in general shows that the threshold for novelty and individual character is not very high – even minor changes in everyday items and known design elements may suffice.

6. Design infringement litigation

6.1 Procedure

Infringement claims, requests for injunctions and search proceedings may only be dealt with by the court.

Application for cancellation of registered designs may be dealt with either by the court or by the Patent and Trademark Office. Design decisions from the office must be appealed to the Patent Board of Appeal before further appeal to the court system.

A request for cancellation may not be filed with the Patent and Trademark Office if any proceedings before a court have not been settled. Where proceedings concerning a design are brought before the court before a final decision of the Patent and Trademark Office has been given, the Patent and Trademark Office or the Patent Board of Appeal will put on hold consideration of the request ending the final settlement of the proceedings, unless the request has been filed by the rights owner.

6.2 Courts

(a) *Ordinary court proceedings*

The Community design court of first instance is the Maritime and Commercial Court, and the Supreme Court is the court of second instance.[40]

The district courts are generally the courts of first instance for ordinary court proceedings. The Maritime and Commercial Court is also competent to deal with proceedings involving national design registrations, provided that design law is essential to the case. It will hear such cases if a claimant submits a case before it or if one of the parties requests that a case be referred from the district courts to the Maritime and Commercial Court and no conflicting prior agreement has been entered into between the parties.[41]

Decisions made by the Maritime and Commercial Court may be appealed to the

---

38 See Case V-142/03 of March 28 2006.
39 See Case V-123/08 of December 14 2009.
40 Designs Act, Section 42.
41 Section 225, paragraph 2(iii) of the Administration of Justice Act.

Supreme Court. Decisions made by the district courts may be appealed to the courts of appeal, the Danish High Courts. Further appeal from the High Courts to the Supreme Court requires permission from the Appeals Permission Board. Provided an appeal is submitted within two weeks of the decision of the lower court, it will generally suspend the lower decision.

In cases of infringement, if a counterclaim for declaration of invalidity is made, the Community design court (ie, the Maritime and Commercial Court) may, upon application by the rights holder and after hearing the other parties, stay the proceedings and ask the defendant to submit an application for a declaration of invalidity to the Office for Harmonisation in the Internal Market (OHIM).[42] In a recent case,[43] a rights holder claimed that the matter was to be decided by the office under Article 86, paragraph 3 of the Community Design Regulation. The defendant did not agree that the matter needed to be brought before OHIM. The court stated that, according to Article 24 of the regulation, a Community design can be declared invalid either after application to OHIM or by making a counterclaim in infringement proceedings. The alleged infringer has the choice of whether to take the invalidity question to OHIM or keep it in the national court. An application by the rights holder to take the matter to OHIM can be complied with only where the same question is pending before several national courts or where special circumstances are present; otherwise, the national court would disclaim the jurisdiction stipulated by the Community Design Regulation.

(b) Injunction proceedings

The courts of first instance for injunction proceedings involving registered national designs are the district courts. The Maritime and Commercial Court is the court of first instance for injunction proceedings involving registered and unregistered Community designs.

Decisions on injunctions made by the Maritime and Commercial Court and the district courts may be appealed to the courts of appeal, the High Courts. Further appeal to the Supreme Court requires permission from the Appeals Permission Board. Appeals do not suspend the decision of the lower court.

If an injunction is granted, the plaintiff must file a confirmatory action within two weeks, since an injunction is a provisional remedy. The purpose of this procedure is to establish that the granting of the injunction was justified. The plaintiff may include a claim for damages in the confirmatory action. It will take between one and two years from filing for the court of first instance to deliver its judgment, which is appealable.

If the confirmatory action is not filed in due time, the injunction will not be upheld and the defendant will be awarded costs. However, if the defendant waives its right to have a confirmatory action filed, the injunction will remain in force and no action need be filed.

---

42 Article 86, paragraph 3 of the Community Design Regulation.
43 Case V-91/08 of September 22 2009.

6.3 Interim remedies: injunction

Injunctions are one of the most important remedies for infringement available to a rights holder. The Designs Act does not contain any provisions on injunctions – they are regulated by the Administration of Justice Act. Under the act,[44] injunctions may be granted if it is proved or shown probable that:

- the acts against which the injunction is sought infringe the rights holder;
- the alleged infringer has performed the acts against which the injunction is sought; and
- the benefit will be lost if the design holder has to enforce its right through normal legal proceedings.[45]

The burden of proof lies with the rights holder. Adequate security, fixed by the court on the basis of an assessment of the potential damages inflicted on the defendant, is usually required for an injunction to be granted.

When so requested due to the risk of further infringements, the court may decide that goods infringing a design right must be:

- withdrawn from the market;
- removed definitively from the market;
- destroyed;
- surrendered to the injured party; or
- altered in a specified manner for the purpose of preventing further infringements of the design.[46]

Injunction proceedings may take place without giving prior notice to the defendant if there is a risk that it will destroy or remove infringing copies. However, the defendant is usually notified before the proceedings take place in court and the defendant will always be notified of the date of the proceedings.

In general, the granting of an injunction (and the subsequent seizure of any infringing copies) will be conditional upon provision of security by the rights holder. The purpose is to secure coverage of a potential claim for damages by the defendant if it is found, during any subsequent confirmatory action, that the conditions for granting the injunction were not satisfied.

A confirmatory lawsuit has to be filed within two weeks of the grant of the injunction. If the confirmatory lawsuit is not filed in due time, the injunction will not be upheld and the defendant will be awarded costs. However, if the defendant waives its right to have a confirmatory action filed, the injunction will remain in force and no action need be filed.

6.4 Final remedies: damages, delivery up, find injunction

Under the Administration of Justice Act, evidence may be secured using *ex parte* search proceedings in cases involving the infringement of intellectual property

---

44 See Consolidated Act 1063/2011.
45 Section 642 of the Administration of Justice Act.
46 Section 38, paragraph 1 of the Designs Act.

rights, including but not limited to design infringements. The rights holder must either prove or render probable that an infringement has taken place and that evidence of the infringement is in the defendant's possession. As a general rule, any evidence may be presented, but the enforcement court may reject evidence based on the *ex parte* search being a provisional remedy.

If a search order is granted, the enforcement court will carry out a search. The search usually takes place without prior notice to the defendant to avoid removal or destruction of evidence. It takes between four and six weeks from filing of the application to the search taking place when the infringement in question is clear. If urgency is proved, the search can take place within a few days. However, it may take longer in other circumstances.

Under the rules on *ex parte* searches, it is possible to secure evidence relating to the extent of the infringements that have already taken place. Infringing material such as invoices, other records, proof of orders and so on may be seized to provide evidence of the extent of infringement.

The enforcement court will appoint an impartial expert to carry out a search. The expert appointed will be appropriately qualified for the specific search – for example, if bookkeeping material is to be reviewed, an accountant will be appointed. Both the plaintiff and the defendant will be sent a copy of the expert's report.

Securing of evidence is usually conditional upon provision of security by the rights holder. The purpose is to secure coverage of a potential claim for damages by the defendant if it is found, during any subsequent confirmatory action, that the conditions for granting the injunction were not satisfied.

A confirmatory action has to be filed within four weeks of the court finalising and confirming the search proceedings. Appeals in search proceedings may suspend the proceedings.

Under Section 37 of the Designs Act, any person or legal entity intentionally or negligently committing design infringement is liable to pay reasonable compensation for the exploitation of the design and damages for any further injury caused by the infringement. The loss of profit suffered by the injured party and the illicit profit obtained by the infringer is taken into consideration. Case law indicates that compensation and damages are usually inadequate, often not even matching the profits obtained by the infringer. Liability under the Designs Act is the same as the general principles of liability in tort, requiring negligence, causality and adequacy.

Design infringement may involve criminal liability if a person or legal entity intentionally or through gross negligence infringes a design right. The penalty for criminal infringement is a fine or, if the infringement was committed under aggravating circumstances, imprisonment for up to 18 months.[47]

6.5 Costs

The successful party in court proceedings will usually be awarded costs. However, the amount is generally small and does not cover costs incurred.

No costs are awarded in proceedings before the Patent and Trademark Office.

---

47 *Ibid*, Section 36.

6.6 Validity

If a design is not renewed within a specified time limit, or if renewal is not possible because the maximum term of protection has been exceeded, the design is no longer valid and will be cancelled.

The Patent and Trademark Office or a court may make an administrative decision to cancel the registration,[48] provided the request is based on one of the following:[49]

- the product is not a design;[50]
- the design is not new;[51]
- the design does not have individual character;[52]
- the design conflicts with public policy or accepted principles of morality;[53]
- the design conflicts with a prior design that was made available to the public after the filing date of the application or, if priority is claimed, the date of priority, provided that the application date of the prior design precedes the application date of the design in question;
- where the design, in an unauthorised way:
    - constitutes use of any of the items listed in Article 6c of the Paris Convention for the Protection of Industrial Property, or other badges, emblems and escutcheons not covered by Article 6c, which are of particular public interest;
    - includes a trademark, trade name or distinctive sign of real property of another person;
    - constitutes use of a work protected by copyright laws; or
    - contains a prior design;
- the design has been altered so as to relate to a design other than the design stated in the application;
- the registration comprises more than one design not relating to the same Locarno class; and
- the design is solely dictated by its technical function or must be reproduced in its exact form and dimensions in order to permit the product for which the design is applied to be mechanically connected to or placed in, on, around or against another product, to enable either product to perform its function unless the design allows for multiple assembly or connection of products within a modular system, consisting of mutually interchangeable parts.

7. Licensing and exploitation

7.1 Practice

There is no licensing practice in Denmark.

---

48 An unregistered Community design cannot be subject to administrative proceedings in Denmark. An objection must be filed with the Danish courts.
49 Section 25 of the Designs Act.
50 *Ibid*, Section 2.
51 *Ibid*, Sections 3 to 6.
52 *Ibid*, Sections 3 to 6.
53 *Ibid*, Section 7.

7.2 Registration of licence requirements

The design right may be licensed, but the Designs Act does not contain any provisions on licences and, consequently, under Danish law there are no formal requirements for licences. Licences are governed by the general principles applying to intellectual property licences. On request, the grant of a licence must be entered in the Register of Designs.[54]

An unregistered Community design right may be licensed under Article 32 of the Community Design Regulation. Article 32 does not contain any formal requirements in relation to licences, so the licensing of an unregistered Community design is governed by the general principles applied to intellectual property licences in the jurisdictions covered by the licence. Since the right is not registered, the grant of a licence cannot be entered in the Register of Designs.

---

54 Section 51, paragraph 1 of the Designs Act.

Finland

Kukka Tommila
Juridia Ltd

---

1. Summary of design protection

In Finland, designs that have been registered are fully protected. Registration can be obtained through national registration, registration of a Community design, or designation of Finland or the European Union in an international design registration.

Registered designs are protected against both copying and the independent development of a similar design. As well as the design itself, the protection covers all designs that do not give a different overall impression to the informed user.

Following Council Regulation 6/2002/EC on Community Designs, designs may be protected without registration after they have been made available to the public within the European Union. This form of protection is limited: unregistered Community designs are protected only against copying and only for three years after publication of the design.

A design must be new and have an individual character in order to qualify for protection.

Design protection is granted to the creator of the design or his successor. Rights holders may be natural persons or any legal entity. Joint applications by more than one natural person or legal entity are possible.

2. Registered design rights

Finland has three systems for registering design rights:

- national registration;
- Community design registration; and
- international design registration in which Finland or the European Union is designated.

2.1 National design registration

National design registrations are processed by the National Board of Patents and Registration (often abbreviated to the Patent Office) and are regulated by the Registered Designs Act (221/1971, as amended). The act is based on the Design Directive (98/71/EC), which harmonises design protection across EU member states.

(a) Qualification for protection

A design is protectable under the national legal regime if the outward appearance of its product results from the lines, contours, colours, shape, texture, materials and/or its ornamentation. Non-separable parts of products can obtain independent design protection.

The product can be for any industrial or handicraft use, including packaging, get-up, graphic symbols and typographic typefaces. Parts of complex products qualify for protection. However, computer programs cannot be protected as designs.

A design must be new and have individual character in order to qualify for protection.

'New' means that no identical design has been made available to the public before the filing date or priority date.

'Individual character' means that the overall impression of the design to an informed user is different from the overall impression of earlier designs. The degree of freedom of the designer in developing the design is taken into consideration.

The design must be a result of creative work. Thus, simple and commonplace designs, such as basic geometrical forms or ordinary stripes, cannot be registered. However, the design does not need to be artistic.

National design registration is not available for coats of arms, flags or other emblems, official marks and inspection marks, trade names and trademarks, surnames, titles of copyrighted works and utility models.

(b) *Registration procedure*

The registration procedure starts with a written application in Finnish or Swedish. It is not possible to file an application electronically. An application is not considered filed and is not given a filing date until the application fee has been paid.

Applicants domiciled in Finland can either file an application themselves or through a representative. Applicants who are not domiciled in Finland must have a representative in the European Economic Area. The representative must submit a power of attorney with the application.

The name and address of the creator of the design must be given in the application. The creator is always a natural person. If the applicant is a company or a successor of the creator, the applicant must confirm in the application form that the design rights have been assigned to it.

The common name of the product for which registration of the design is sought must be given in the application. The applicant may suggest an appropriate Locarno class, but the Patent Office will decide the correct classification.

The application may contain several designs, provided that the products belong to the same Locarno class.

The extent of protection is determined by the representations filed in the application. Anything not shown in the representations will not be protected. The applicant may attach a specimen of the design to the application, if its size and material allow. The specimen and the representations must present the same design in every detail.

At the request of the applicant, the application can be kept secret for up to six months from the filing date or, if priority is claimed, from the priority date. The request must be made when the application is filed. If the application is dismissed, rejected or withdrawn during the secrecy period, the documents will not be made public.

The Finnish Patent Office checks the application to ensure that it meets the formal requirements and that the conditions for registration – such as novelty and individual character – are fulfilled. The examination covers all applied and registered designs in Finland.

If no obstacles to registration are found, the design is registered and published.

A two-month opposition period is open from the date of publication. Anyone may file an opposition if they consider that the design should not have been registered because it is not new or does not have individual character, or is contrary to law and good policy, or protection has been sought for characteristics which cannot obtain protection. If the ground for opposition is that registration has been sought by someone other than the person entitled to it or that the design is in conflict with an earlier right, only people whose right is violated by the registration may file an opposition.

(c) Term of protection

Design registration is valid for five years from the application date, and it may be renewed for five-year terms up to a maximum of 25 years from the filing date.

However, if the design is a component part of a complex product and is used to restore the original appearance of the complex product, the maximum term of protection is 15 years.

(d) Rights granted

A registered design gives the rights holder an exclusive right to use the design and any design which does not produce a different overall impression on an informed user.

The rights holder is entitled to prevent any third party from making, offering, putting on the market, using, importing, exporting or stocking for these purposes a product which matches the design or in which the design is incorporated.

2.2 Community design registration

Community design registrations are dealt with by the Office for Harmonisation in the Internal Market (OHIM). Community designs have equal effect across the European Union.

Registration is based on the Regulation on Community Designs. The regulations governing the definitions of a design and a product and the requirements for novelty and individual character are the same as in both the Design Directive and the Registered Designs Act (see section 2.1 above).

However, the OHIM does not stipulate the creativity in a design that is required by the Patent Office. Simple and commonplace designs may be registered as Community designs.

(a) Registration procedure

The registration procedure starts with filing an application, either directly with the OHIM or through the national patent office of any EU member state. Electronic filing is possible through the website of the OHIM. The application must include payment of the appropriate fees.

There is no nationality requirement for applicants – any natural person or legal entity from anywhere in the world may file an application.

An applicant domiciled in, or having its principal place of business or a real and effective industrial or commercial establishment in, the European Union can file an application on its own behalf or use a representative. Other applicants must be represented by a professional representative approved by the OHIM or by a legal practitioner who is entitled to represent before a national patent office. A power of attorney does not need to be filed.

It is not mandatory to give the name of the designer in the application.

An application may contain several designs if the products belong to the same Locarno class.

A representation of the design suitable for reproduction must be included in the application. If the application is for a two-dimensional design and deferment of publication has been requested, a specimen may be provided in place of the representation.

The application must contain a description of the product. A proposal for Locarno classification may be submitted, but the OHIM will decide the correct class. The type of product and its classification do not affect the scope of protection of a Community design.

The OHIM conducts only a formal examination of the application. If no deficiencies are found, the design is registered and published immediately. The registration date will be the same as the filing date. At the applicant's request, publication may be delayed for up to 30 months from the filing date or, if priority is claimed, from the priority date. The request for deferment must have been made on the application form.

There is no formal opposition period, but invalidity proceedings can be brought against registered Community designs at any time after their registration. An application for a declaration of invalidity can be filed either with the OHIM or in a community design court as a counterclaim to infringement proceedings. The most common grounds for invalidity are that the design does not fulfil the requirements for novelty and individual character. An application for a declaration of invalidity must include an indication and reproduction of the earlier design that is an obstacle to the novelty or individual character of the registered Community design.

(b) Term of protection

Design registration is valid for five years from the application date, and it may be renewed in five-year terms, up to a total term of 25 years from the date of filing.

(c) Rights granted

The rights granted by a registered Community design are the same as those enjoyed by a national registered design.

2.3 International design registration

Finland and the European Union are contracting parties to the Geneva Act (1999) of the Hague Agreement Concerning the International Registration of Industrial

Designs, so Finland or the European Union can be designated in an international design registration.

International design registrations are handled first by the World Intellectual Property Organisation (WIPO) for the formal part. The process is completed either by the Finnish Patent Office, if Finland is designated, or by the OHIM, if the European Union is designated.

International designs are treated identically to national Finnish designs or registered Community designs. An International design registration in force in Finland has the same effect as a national design registration. An International design registration in force in the European Union has the same effect as a registered Community design.

(a) *Registration procedure*

An application can be filed either in paper format or by electronic filing on the WIPO website. Finnish applicants may file paper applications through the Finnish Patent Office, but the OHIM does not accept international applications.

An application must list the contracting states in which protection is sought. There are some special requirements, depending on which contracting states are designated.

An applicant must be a national of or have domicile, habitual residence or a real and effective industrial or commercial establishment in a contracting state. Multiple applicants are allowed provided all of them are entitled to file the application.

An applicant may appoint a representative. There are no restrictions as to who may act as a representative before the WIPO.

An application may contain several designs if the products belong to the same Locarno class.

The scope of protection is defined by a reproduction of the design, and only elements visible in the reproduction will be protected.

The creator of the design must be identified in any application for international design registration in which Finland is designated.

If the European Union is designated in an international application, publication may be deferred on request for up to 30 months from the filing date or from the priority date if priority is claimed, provided that the application is not designated to a contracting state which either has a shorter deferment period or does not offer deferment.

If Finland is designated, a maximum of six months from the filing date or, if priority is claimed, from the priority date is allowed.

The WIPO checks only that an application complies with the formal requirements. If it does, the design is registered and published in the *International Designs Bulletin*.

After publication, the patent offices of the designated contracting states undertake a substantive examination – the same as that for national design applications.

The Finnish Patent Office's examination of the application is identical to that for national design registration – that is, whether the design is new and has individual character and whether there are other obstacles to registration.

The OHIM does not examine the novelty or individual character of a design filed for international design registration. If a third party believes that the design is not new or does not have individual character, or that there are other reasons why the design should not have been registered, it must bring invalidity proceedings. The rules are the same as for registered Community designs.

(b) *Term of protection*

An international design registration may be kept in force for a maximum of 25 years. However, if the design is a component part of a complex product and is used to restore the original appearance of the product, the maximum term of protection is 15 years when Finland is designated.

(c) *Rights granted*

A registered international design enjoys identical protection to national design registrations.

3. Unregistered design rights

Unregistered designs enjoy protection based on the Community Design Regulation. The requirements for qualification are the same as for registered Community designs.

Protection as an unregistered Community design is granted to all designs that qualify for design protection and are made available to the public within the European Union. The protection is more limited than the protection of registered national or Community designs. An unregistered Community design enjoys the right to prevent commercial use of the design only if the use is a result of copying. If a later design results from an independent work of creation by a designer who was not aware of the existence of the unregistered Community design, use of the later design cannot be prevented.

Unregistered Community designs are protected for only three years from the date on which the design was first made available to the public.

Designs can enjoy protection under the Copyright Act without registration if the design is considered to be an artistic work. If the design qualifies for copyright protection, its creator has the exclusive right to make copies of the design.

Copyright protection runs for 70 years after the death of the creator.

4. Qualification for protection

4.1 Definition of design

In order to qualify for protection, a design must meet the criteria of a design set out in the legislation. The application must be for the appearance of the whole or a part of a product resulting from the features of, in particular, the lines, contours, colours, shape, texture and/or materials of the product itself, and/or its ornamentation.

The product can be for any industrial or handicraft application, such as packaging, get-up, graphic symbols and typographic typefaces. Parts of a complex, multi-component product which can be replaced, allowing disassembly and reassembly, qualify for protection. However, computer programs cannot be protected as designs.

A component part may only be protected as a design if it remains visible during normal use of the product and if its visible features fulfil the requirements for protection. 'Normal use' in this context does not include maintenance, servicing or repair work.

Design protection is not granted to features that are solely dictated by technical function. This is interpreted to mean features which for technical reasons cannot be implemented in any other way.

Design protection is not granted to features that must be reproduced in their exact form and dimensions in order to permit a product to be mechanically connected with another product so that either product may perform its function. However, this does not prevent protection of designs whose purpose is to allow multiple assembly or connection of mutually interchangeable products in a modular system.

If a design includes features that are excluded from protection, those features are not be taken into consideration when assessing whether other features of the design fulfil the requirements for protection.

A design will not be granted protection if it is contrary to public policy or to accepted principles of morality.

4.2 Novelty and individual character

To qualify for protection, a design must be new and possess individual character.

'New' means that no identical design has been made available to the public before the filing or priority date. 'Identical design' in this context does not require absolute identity, but designs that differ only in immaterial details are considered identical and thus prevent protection.

A design is deemed to have been made available to the public if it has been published, in the registration procedure or otherwise, or if it has been exhibited or used in trade, or it has otherwise become known. The design is not considered to have been made available to the public only if it could not reasonably have become known in the normal course of business within the European Union.

The owner of a design may delay applying for registration for up to 12 months after publication and the design will still considered to be new.

A design is considered to have individual character when its overall impression to an informed user is different from the overall impression of earlier designs. When the individual character is considered, the type of the product and the freedom of design are taken into consideration.

4.3 Impediments to registration

Under the Registered Designs Act, a design will not be registered as a national design if it without permission includes:

- the coat of arms, flag or other emblem, or the designation or abbreviation of the designation of a state, municipality or an international intergovernmental organisation, or a figure, designation or abbreviation of a designation that may be confused with such an emblem, sign, designation or abbreviation of a designation;

- an official mark or stamp of inspection or guarantee for the same or similar articles as those for which the design is intended;
- anything that may be understood to be another person's trade name or a trade symbol or trademark established for another in Finland or the surname, pseudonym or similar name or the portrait of another, unless the name or portrait manifestly refers to a person long since deceased;
- anything that may be interpreted as the title of another person's protected literary or artistic work, provided that the title is distinctive, or anything which infringes another's copyright to such a work or his right to a photographic illustration; and
- anything that does not substantially differ from a design or utility model registered in Finland in the name of another person.

Since International designs designating Finland are treated identically to national designs, these criteria will also invalidate an international design in Finland.

5. Infringement

A design right will be infringed if a third party uses the design in a commercial setting without the consent of the rights owner. Unauthorised use of a design that does not produce a different overall impression on an informed user is also an infringement.

For a registered design, the level of protection is determined by the representations filed with the application or by the specimen if one was filed. The protection covers only what can be seen in the representations or the specimen.

Unregistered designs enjoy protection of the outward appearance of the design as it can be seen from the product which is the design or in which the design is incorporated.

If a later design is not identical to the protected design, the two designs will be compared to establish whether they produce the same overall impression for an informed user, taking into consideration the designer's degree of freedom in developing the design.

The concept of 'informed user' is important when the infringement of a design right is considered since an informed user is different for different product categories. In each case it must be considered who would be an appropriate informed user.

The General Court of the European Union has ruled that that the informed user is neither a manufacturer nor a seller of the products (Decision T-097). The informed user must be someone who is particularly observant and has some awareness of the state of the prior art.

For example, if the designs are for bread, the informed user is someone who is a user of bread. He is not a designer, a manufacturer or a specialist in the food industry, but someone who regularly consumes bread and is has knowledge of the ingredients in bread, how bread is made and served, and the overall appearance of bread.

The overall impression of a design produced on the informed user is a question of law, which the judge decides. No person is heard as an informed user.

The degree of freedom of the designer must also be taken into consideration and can be different for different product categories. For example, the technical function of a product or statutory requirements applicable to the product may restrict the designer's degree of freedom in developing a design. Restrictions may result in standardisation of certain features, which will be common to all designs in the relevant product category. The more the designer's freedom in developing the contested design is restricted, the more likely it is that minor differences between designs will be sufficient to produce a different overall impression on the informed user.

Infringing use is, in particular, making, offering, putting on the market, importing, exporting or using a product in which the design is incorporated or to which it is applied, or stocking such a product for those purposes.

The private use of a design for non-commercial purposes and acts of reproduction for demonstration or teaching are not infringements, provided that such acts are meet fair trade practice, do not unduly prejudice the normal exploitation of the design and the source is acknowledged.

The exclusive right does not cover equipment on ships and aircraft registered in another country when they temporarily enter Finland, the importation into Finland of spare parts and accessories for the purpose of repairing such craft, or the execution of repairs on such craft.

It is not possible to take action in respect of threatened infringement of design rights.

6. Design infringement litigation

6.1 Courts

Design litigations are heard at the Helsinki District Court in the first instance. Decisions of the district court may be appealed at the Helsinki Court of Appeal. The decisions of the Court of Appeal can be appealed to the Supreme Court only if the Supreme Court grants leave to appeal. Leave to appeal may be granted if a decision of the Supreme Court is necessary to clarify the application of law, to ensure the consistency of case law or to correct a serious error in the Court of Appeal's decision.

These courts also hear all litigation concerning registered and unregistered Community designs. Under the Community Design Regulation, Finnish courts will apply national law on all matters which are not covered by the regulation. Therefore, the procedure is the same whether the design right is based on a national design registration, a Community design or an international design registration.

6.2 Procedure

Design infringement litigation proceedings are started by an applicant filing a written application for summons. The application will state the demands and the grounds, and significant written evidence is usually attached.

The court serves the claim on the defendant, who is summoned to file a written response. After the response is filed, the judge decides whether more written observations are required from the parties.

Once the written part of the proceedings is complete a preparatory hearing is arranged, in which the parties outline their main arguments and what evidence will be presented and submit their witness lists. The preparatory hearing will also clarify which questions are disputed and which are not. The judge will ask whether there is any possibility of settling the matter at this stage.

In the main hearing the demands and the grounds of both parties are presented along with the written evidence, and witnesses are heard. It ends with a closing statement from both parties.

The decision is given at a later date, usually one or two weeks after the main hearing.

6.3 Interim remedies

A rights owner may ask the court to issue a preliminary injunction before the main proceedings have been decided. In principle, the defendant must be heard before a preliminary injunction is granted. The court will grant an interim injunction without hearing the defendant only in very serious cases where the purpose of the preliminary injunction could be compromised. This will remain in force until the defendant has been heard and the decision on the preliminary injunction can be given.

Preliminary injunctions are granted only if the infringement is very obvious. If there are doubts, the application for a preliminary injunction will be rejected.

An application for a preliminary injunction is decided in a completely written procedure and no hearing is arranged.

The preliminary injunction remains in force until the main case has been decided or until the court cancels it. The main claim decision will include a decision on how long the preliminary injunction is to remain in force. If the main claim is dismissed, the court may order that the preliminary injunction will remain in force until the decision becomes final.

If the preliminary injunction proves to be unjustified, the defendant is entitled to compensation for any damage it has caused.

6.4 Final remedies

If the court considers that a design right has been infringed, the defendant will be prohibited from continuing or repeating the infringing action.

If an infringement is intentional or the result of negligence, the infringer will have to pay a reasonable compensation for the use of the design and compensation for the damage caused by the infringement.

If the negligence is found to be minimal, the amount of compensation may be reduced.

If there is no intent or negligence found, the infringer will have to pay only reasonable compensation for use of the design.

Compensation must be claimed within five years of the damage or the right to compensation will be forfeited.

The amount of the damages is set taking into consideration all relevant issues, such as a decrease in sales and profits of the rights owner. It is often difficult to prove exactly what damages have been caused and the courts will estimate an appropriate compensation, generally based on what royalty the infringer would have had to pay if it had purchased a licence.

The court may order that infringing products must be altered or deposited in safe custody for the remainder of the period of protection, or destroyed. If the infringing articles have been illegally manufactured or imported, the court may order them to be surrendered, against remuneration, to the rights owner.

Design infringement litigation is usually heard as a civil dispute, but if the infringement has been intentional it may be deemed a criminal offence, punishable by a fine or a prison sentence of up to two years.

6.5 Costs

In principle, the courts order the losing party in design litigation proceedings to reimburse the successful party's costs. Costs include reasonable lawyer's fees, court fees and other costs and expenses related to the proceedings. If both parties are successful on some counts but not on others, they will usually be ordered to bear their own costs.

6.6 Validity

Decisions concerning national design registrations and international design registrations designating Finland are valid only in Finland.

However, if the decision concerns the infringement of a Community design and the case is heard in Finland because the domicile of the defendant is in Finland, the prohibition to continue the infringement should be considered to extend throughout the European Union. This interpretation would be consistent with the ruling of the European Court of Justice in *DHL v Chronopost* (Case C-235/09). Although the decision concerned infringement of a Community trademark, there is no reason why decisions concerning Community designs should have a narrower effect.

7. Licensing and exploitation

A rights owner is entitled to license the design right. The licence may be exclusive or non-exclusive. If the licence is for a Community design, it may be effective throughout the European Union or in part of it.

Licences of registered national designs and registered Community designs may be recorded in the appropriate design register; they cannot be recorded in the international design register.

Registration of a licence agreement is not mandatory: a licence agreement will be valid even without registration. The legal effect of the registration of a licence is that it becomes binding towards third parties. If the licensor assigns design rights to a third party, the assignee will only be bound by a previously existing licence agreement that has been registered or that the assignee has been aware of. Otherwise, the assignee is not bound by the licence.

A licence agreement is valid even without a written agreement. Oral and implied agreements are binding on the parties.

However, in order to register a licence, a written agreement, or at least a written confirmation of the relevant parts of the licence, must be drafted, signed and attached to the request for registration.

France

Stefan Naumann
Hughes Hubbard & Reed LLP

1. Summary of design protection

The concept of unity of art is a fundamental feature of the protection of designs in France. It allows designs to enjoy protection both under French and EU design laws and under French copyright law, provided the designs meet the criteria for protection. A practical result is that where a registered design is invalidated, copyright may still be used to protect the design.

France and the European Union are members of the Geneva Act of the Hague Agreement concerning the international registration of industrial designs. Thus, the same design may be protected in France by up to four separate rights:

- as a registered French design under the Intellectual Property Code, Part 2, Book 5 and, if applicable, under Article 14 of the Hague Agreement;
- as a registered Community design under EU Regulation 6/2002;
- as an unregistered Community design under EU Regulation 6/2002; and
- as a work protected by copyright under the Intellectual Property Code, Part 1, Book 1 and Book 3, Title III.

Each statute, regulation or treaty has specific requirements for a design to qualify for protection and to determine infringement, and different terms of protection. Jurisdiction for Community designs litigation differs from that of the other types of protection. In spite of these differences, French courts and legal commentators consider that copyright and design law protection in the same design can be cumulated where a design meets the respective criteria for protection.

2. Registered and unregistered design rights

2.1 French registered designs

To qualify for protection as a French registered design, a design must be registered by its author or his successor in interest. French design law creates a rebuttable presumption that the party that registers the design qualifies for protection. The registered design is protected for five years from the date of filing, renewable four times to give a total of 25 years' protection. French registered designs filed before October 1 2001 are protected for a single 25-year period from the date of filing or from their date of renewal if an extension was requested before October 1 2001.

The registration of a design protects the appearance of the product, any part of the product and for its ornamentation, characterised by its lines, contours, colours, shape, texture or material, provided that the design is new and has an individual character. There is an exception for computer programs and for designs where the appearance is exclusively the result of the technical function of the product or is required to attach the product to another (must fit).

Although the author of an industrial design in principle enjoys the benefit of moral rights through its protection by copyright, the courts take into account the intended commercial purpose of industrial designs to allow rights holders considerable leeway in modifying a design to fit its commercial purpose.

2.2 Community registered and unregistered designs

The requirements for protection of Community designs are the same as those discussed above, except that an unregistered Community design may qualify for protection as of first public disclosure in the territory of the European Union. An unregistered Community design is protected for three years from the date it is disclosed to the public for the first time in the European Union. A registered Community design is protected for five years from the date of filing, renewable four times, giving 25 years' protection.

2.3 International registered designs

An international registered design will qualify for protection in France if it meets the criteria for protection of a French registered design and the registrant is a national of, a habitual resident of or has a real and effective establishment in a contracting state of the Hague Agreement. International registered designs are usually protected for five years from the date of registration, renewable twice to give a total of 15 years' protection. However, under Article 17(3)(b) of the Geneva Act, in France such designs would be protectable for the same total duration as French registered designs, provided they are renewed when necessary.

2.4 French copyright protection

Unlike a registered or unregistered design, under French copyright law a design qualifies for copyright protection by virtue of its creation, even if it is incomplete, so long as it is original. French case law interprets the requirement of originality to mean that a design must reflect the personality of its author. Except for collective works, the author of a design must be a physical person. French copyright law does not provide an equivalent to the US 'work made for hire' doctrine. There is a limited exception for collective works in which the contribution of the individual authors cannot be identified, none of the individual authors has separate rights in the overall design and the design was published and disclosed at the initiative of the legal entity that owns it. In France, legal entities also benefit from a rebuttable presumption that they own the copyright in any design that they publicly exploit.

Copyright protection covers the life of the author plus 70 years from January 1 of the year following the author's death. Copyright law provides for extensions of protection for the two World Wars and for authors who died for France during these conflicts, if this is indicated on their death certificate. Where such rights are vested, they allow a work that would otherwise have already fallen into the public domain to benefit from the 70-year post-death protection.

2.5 Scope of protection

A rights holder may prohibit the manufacture, offer, putting into commerce, importing, exporting, or using or holding for these purposes, of a product that incorporates a French registered design or a design that does not create an overall different visual impression for an attentive observer. There are exceptions for private, non-commercial and experimental uses, and for the reproduction of a design for teaching purposes or as illustration, provided the reproduction or illustration identifies the registered design and the rights holder, conforms to loyal commercial practices, and does not prejudice the normal exploitation of the design.

Registered Community designs are expressly given the same scope of protection as French registered designs. Unregistered Community designs are only protected against the acts of infringement set out above if the contested use results from copying.

A rights holder may prohibit the partial or total reproduction, representation or adaptation of a copyright-protected design. The author of a copyright-protected design enjoys moral rights in his work that are non-transferrable except to his heirs. Thus, it is important to define carefully the scope of the right of adaption in any agreement between the rights holder and its successor in interest, so as to ensure that the legal entity exploiting a copyright-protected design may use and modify the design without violating the author's moral rights. Registered Community designs limit the moral right of the author to the right to be cited as such before the Office for Harmonisation in the Internal Market and in the register.

French copyright law provides a detailed list of exceptions to the scope of copyright protection that may become relevant when a design is only protected by copyright, either because it was not registered as a design or because the registration has been cancelled or has expired. The application of copyright exceptions to an unregistered Community design has not yet been litigated in France.

3. Qualification for protection

Although there is an overlap between copyright and registered design protection under French law, the substantive qualifications for protection differ significantly. Case law decided under the earlier French registered design law of July 14 1909 and under the modifications to that law following the incorporation on July 25 2001 of Directive 98/71/EC discusses the requirements for each type of protection. The transposition of the directive into French law profoundly modified French registered design law. Registration is now a substantive requirement to qualify for protection. Under the previous registered design law, registration was viewed as having a merely declaratory effect.

Copyright law and registered design law do not protect ideas, and neither law permits the courts to take into account the merit of the work for which protection is sought in order to decide whether or not it qualifies for protection. Registered design protection requires the existence of a product. In other words, a design that does not correspond to a product or its ornamentation cannot benefit from registered design protection. Practical examples are that an interior design or works of art that exist in a single copy cannot be protected as registered designs.

The courts have consistently held that a registered design cannot protect a genre. As a result, the courts have invalidated designs that simply reflect current fashion in an otherwise common piece of clothing. However, the courts have consistently upheld the validity of registered designs that combine elements of the public domain or variations on a known theme, provided the rights holder has given a personal and/or original interpretation. The same holds for designs inspired by elements of nature, so long as they show a personal interpretation by their author. Registering multiple designs with similar characteristics does not constitute an attempt to protect a genre. Where a design combines elements of the public domain, only the specific combination of these elements qualifies for protection. A single colour or a change in destination or materials does not qualify for protection as a registered design.

A design must be new to qualify for protection as a registered design. Case law interprets this to mean that no earlier identical designs may exist. The novelty requirement is both objective and nearly absolute. Any earlier identical or nearly identical design would disqualify a registered design from protection and invalidate the registration. Thus, any earlier art could in principle destroy the novelty of a design without limitation in time or location. For example, an emblem commonly used by freemasons or a design that was disclosed in previous utility patents would fail the novelty test. The registered design law regime limits this very general rule by providing that a design has been disclosed only if it could reasonably be known by following current commercial practices in the relevant sector by professionals within the European Union, but not if it had only been disclosed subject to confidentiality. Although this limitation may appear to exclude many older designs, the burden of proof rests on the rights holder to show that an old design and/or a design from a distant location had been forgotten.

In litigation, it would in practice be difficult for the rights holder to show that its registered design possesses an individual character when compared by an attentive observer with an earlier, rediscovered design. Yet to be valid, a design must have an individual character. 'Individual character' means that the design must create a globally different visual impression on an attentive observer compared with earlier designs.

The design of a part meets these two requirements only if it remains visible once it is included in a complex product during the normal use of that product by the end user. French design law excludes from protection those parts that would only be visible during maintenance or repair.

The novelty and individual character requirements must be fulfilled by the visible elements of the part included in a complex product. However, designs of modular products can qualify for protection.

Thus, novelty alone is not sufficient to qualify a design for registered design protection. A design must also have an individual character. Under French law, this individual character is an objective criterion, unlike the requirement of originality under copyright law, which is based on a subjective link between an author and his work. The objective criterion results from the visual impression on an attentive observer, thereby allowing the courts to carry out a detailed comparison of a design with earlier art.

The registered design statute codifies French case law, which has consistently found that if the appearance of a product is the result of purely technical choices, the design does not qualify for protection. In deciding whether the appearance is determined by technical choices, the courts examine whether other shapes will achieve the same technical result. The burden of proof rests on the defendant to show that the appearance and technical result cannot be dissociated. A functional design may qualify for registered design protection even if it is patented to the extent that the functional elements or their results can be dissociated from the shape.

3.1 International obligations

France is a member of the Paris Convention of 1883 and a contracting state to the Hague Agreement. As a result, French registered design law allows persons established or domiciled in the European Economic Area to own French registered designs, and persons outside the European Economic Area to own these designs provided their country's law provides a reciprocal protection for French registered designs.

The application of the criteria of reciprocity remains largely theoretical. Article 2, paragraph 7 of the Berne Convention on copyright allows member states that apply copyright to designs to refuse to recognise registered designs where another member state only protects such designs by a specific law and not by copyright. In this situation, a member state would apply copyright law to the design. This system does not apply within the European Union even though the rule on cumulating copyright and registered design protection varies among EU member states.

4. Infringement

A French registered design is infringed by any identical or similar design that is incorporated in a product and that does not produce on an informed user a different overall impression. Thus, the reproduction of the design of a perfume bottle in an online advertisement has been held not to constitute a design infringement since it is not incorporated in a product. In contrast, Regulation 6/2002/EC on Community designs prohibits the unauthorised use of a design, and only lists the making, offering and so on of a product in which the design is incorporated as a particular type of design infringement. For unregistered Community designs, an alleged infringer could attempt to show that the similarity is not the result of copying but of an independent development, in order to avoid a finding of infringement. Infringement is determined on the basis of resemblances, excluding those that result from elements that are in the public domain, such as elements that are common to designs of the same style, fashion or subject matter. In this context, infringement is determined by a side-by-side comparison of the designs, irrespective of the industrial sector of the products (so, by way of example, the shape of a bottle may be infringing even where it is used in different sectors such as beverages and personal care products).

The rights conferred by a registered design do not cover private, non-commercial use, experimental use or the reproduction of the design for illustration or teaching purposes, provided the latter identify the registered design and the name of its owner, conform to loyal commercial practices and do not prejudice the design's normal exploitation. The registered design law regime does not provide for an exception for the prior good-faith use of a design, unlike Community designs.

French copyright law prohibits the total or partial reproduction of a design, as well as its adaptation, and includes a number of exceptions to the scope of copyright protection.

Community design law limits the scope of protection of unregistered Community designs to acts of copying.

The case law has shown that a risk of confusion is not one of the elements required for a finding of infringement, but confusion is often found to result from the resemblances. The resemblances must be a result of the reproduction of the characteristics of the design, and not a result of the use of elements that are in the public domain or that are common to the genre to which the registered design belongs. Good-faith use of an infringing design is not a defence in civil trials, whereas criminal prosecution requires an element of intent to find infringement.

5. Overview of design infringement litigation in France

5.1 Courts

Cases involving French registered designs and copyrights are brought before the civil courts that have territorial jurisdiction.

Cases are heard by a panel of three judges, who are career civil servants. The Paris courts have chambers that specialise in intellectual property (IP) matters and have exclusive jurisdiction for all Community IP rights and for patents. Proceedings may take up to 15 months. Court rules have been implemented to speed up the process.

As is customary in infringement litigation in France, the same court will determine the validity of a design or copyright and the issue of its infringement, except in criminal proceedings. Criminal courts do not have the power to cancel a registered design, but may find that the material element of the criminal violation is not met where they consider a registered design to be invalid.

Under the rules of civil procedure, an appeal is a second trial on the merits and an appeal court makes its own findings of fact and law in deciding a case. Either party may appeal an appeal court judgment to the Supreme Court, which will review the appellate decision for errors of law. If the Supreme Court overturns a judgment, it will return the case to another appeal court. In contrast to common-law jurisdictions, the Supreme Court and appeal courts' judgments are not binding precedents, with the exception of judgments of the Supreme Court following a second appeal.

5.2 Remedies

Relief in the event of infringement includes interim remedies, such as injunctions and product recalls, and final remedies, such as compensatory damages, destruction of infringing stock, recall of products, publication of the judgment at the defendant's costs and reimbursement of some or all of the successful party's legal fees.

In civil proceedings, damages do not include punitive damages but may take into account an infringer's profits in determining the amount of damages. The courts may appoint an expert to determine the amount of damages. A court-appointed expert will hold hearings and prepare a report, which is not binding on the court.

If a design has not been exploited, either directly or through licences, by the rights holder, he may nevertheless be entitled to damages based on loss of royalties.

Courts may order any interim remedies needed to prevent a violation of the registered design rights or to stop an infringing act. In theory, interim measures may be requested unilaterally, but courts have required that plaintiffs show that an adversarial proceeding would prevent the interim measure from being effective, for example where a delay in obtaining the interim measure would cause irreparable harm to the plaintiff.

As with other intellectual property rights, an infringement constitutes a criminal violation, punishable by a fine of up to €300,000 and a prison term of up to three years. Fines can be increased to €500,000 and the prison term increased to five years where the infringing merchandise is dangerous for the health or safety of humans or animals, or where the infringement has been committed by organised crime.

A criminal court may order the total or partial, final or temporary closing of an establishment used to commit the acts of infringement. Since the closing of an establishment may lead to the loss or suspension of employment contracts or financially damage salaried employees, this remedy is rarely granted.

Criminal prosecution for infringement is fairly uncommon as it requires proof of intent and also because infringement cases are not given a high priority. However, criminal prosecution resulting from customs withholdings or seizures of infringing products are routinely heard by the criminal courts.

These remedies also apply to infringements of Community designs and copyright-protected designs.

5.3 Procedure

Design and copyright infringement are both civil torts and criminal offences. The statute of limitations for civil registered-design infringement actions is three years from the date of the alleged infringing act and that for copyright infringement is 10 years. Criminal prosecution is time-barred after three years.

Design infringement seizures allow evidence of an alleged infringement to be collected. A rights holder may request a court to authorise a bailiff, assisted by law enforcement officers and experts, to enter the premises of an alleged infringer to gather evidence of the origin, scope and destination of the infringement, including the seizure of samples. The bailiff's infringement seizure report is considered reliable evidence of the facts since bailiffs, even though instructed and paid by a party, are officers of the court. The courts routinely grant infringement seizure authorisations and use the infringement seizure reports and samples in litigation.

Although infringement seizure reports are a commonly used form of evidence, they are not a prerequisite for bringing an infringement action. Plaintiffs may submit other types of evidence to prove infringement. In civil litigation, courts rarely admit oral testimony, relying instead on written documents to prove facts. Affidavits are not considered a reliable source of evidence unless they are substantiated by extrinsic evidence.

With the transposition into French law of the EU Enforcement Directive, a plaintiff may request the court to order the defendant or third parties to submit as evidence documents or information showing the origin and distribution networks of the infringing products, specifically the names and addresses of producers, manufacturers, distributors, suppliers, wholesalers and retailers, the quantities produced, commercialised, delivered, received or ordered, and their price.

This right to information has resulted in significant litigation. Case law holds that courts may order the production of documents and information before a finding of infringement, which is in conformity with the EU directive. Generally, a plaintiff must show an infringement seizure has been carried out but did not yield this information.

6. Licensing and exploitation

French copyright law only provides for the assignment of copyright, which thus cannot be licensed. In practice, this and other formal requirements mean that careful drafting is needed for the effective assignment of copyrights in a work including a design.

Registered designs can be assigned or licensed, and can be used as collateral. Any act affecting the rights in a registered design must be recorded with the Industrial Property Office in order to be enforceable against third parties. For international registered designs, only a change of ownership may be recorded at the World Intellectual Property Office. Acts that affect rights in a registered Community design must be registered, except where the registered design is transferred together with its rights owner.

There is no provision for compulsory licences under either registered design law or copyright law. However, under copyright law a court may order the disclosure of a copyright-protected work where the rights holder interferes with an author's right to disclose his work. This specific rule is of limited relevance to designs, and most of the case law relates to undisclosed or unfinished audiovisual works.

Germany

Moritz Hüsch
Katharina Scheja
Heymann & Partner Rechtsanwälte

1. Summary of design protection

1.1 Introduction

In Germany, designs are protected through design patents under the Act on the Protection of Designs and Models (the Design Act). A design may also be protected under the EU Community Design Regulation (6/2002), which includes protection in the territory of Germany. Further legal means available to protect designs include trademark and copyright protection (see below).

In general, design patents cover designs relating to two- or three-dimensional products, which are specified by the features of lines, contours and colours, the shape, the surface structure, or the materials of the product or its decoration. For example, the designs of mobile phones, web pages, computers, other technical devices, chairs, cars, glasses and baby equipment may be protected as design patents under the Design Act.

In 2010, roughly 47,000 design patents were registered in Germany, an increase of 5.5% compared with 2009. About 38,000 of these registrations were of domestic origin. The proportion of design patents filed by applicants based in foreign countries was 20% in 2010. The majority of design patent applications by foreign applicants were from Austria (9.6%), Italy (5.7%) and Switzerland (1.4%). The largest numbers of design patents (18.0%) were filed in Class 02, 'articles of clothing and haberdashery'.[1]

These numbers illustrate that industrial designs are of growing importance in a world which looks not only for the best available technological devices but also demands outstanding designs. Apple's iPad is one example, and while industrial designs rarely generate high-profile cases, on September 9 2011 the Landgericht Düsseldorf decided a landmark case of *Apple v Samsung*, confirming an earlier preliminary order against Samsung to cease and desist from further selling the Galaxy tablet. The decision was first based on Apple's Community design with effect all over Europe but was subsequently restricted to apply only for Germany.[2] the final decision should be handed down in September 2012 – something to watch out for. A potential European-wide effect under the Community Design Regulation is one of the many attractive aspects of design protection.

1 www.presse.dpma.de/presseservice/datenzahlenfakten/statistiken/geschmacksmuster (accessed September 9 2011).

2 *Landgericht* Düsseldorf, September 9 2011, case 14c O 194/11; *Oberlandesgericht* Düsseldorf, January 31 2012, case I 20 U 175/11.

1.2 Design protection

In Germany, industrial designs can in principle be protected by a design patent, and also under trademark, copyright and unfair competition law.

(a) *Design patent*

Most prominently, protection for designs may be granted under the Design Act, which came into force on March 12 2004. The act governs the requirements for protection of designs, in particular the registration process, as well as the scope of protection, infringement claims and remedies with respect to the designs. Further regulation is provided by the Regulation on the Protection of Designs and Models (the Design Bylaw), which contains detailed provisions regarding the application and registration procedure to complement more general provisions of the Design Act. Unlike in other jurisdictions, registration is mandatory for protection of a design under the Design Act; merely publishing a design is not sufficient to obtain any protection under the act. However, where a design has been published, but not (yet) registered, it may enjoy protection as an unregistered Community design under the Community Design Regulation. Once registered, a design is protected under the Design Act for up to 25 years.

(b) *Trademark*

A design may be protectable as a trademark. Trademark protection is obtained either by registering a German trademark with the Patent and Trademark Office (this is also possible through World International Property Office proceedings) or a European trademark with the Office of Harmonisation for the Internal Market. Trademarks may cover three-dimensional designs such as the shape of goods or their packaging and other get-ups. One key requirement for trademark protection is that the design is capable of distinguishing the goods or services of one company from the goods or services of other parties. Protection as a trademark may also be achieved through actual usage – that is, without any formal requirements (see also below). Once trademark protection is granted, the rights holder has the exclusive right to use and exploit the trademark (eg, through the grant of licences). However, this right is limited to the classes of goods and services for which protection has been granted. Protection of a registered trademark begins on the application filing date and lasts for 10 years. It may be renewed for further periods of 10 years by payment of renewal fees.

(c) *Copyright*

A design may also enjoy protection under copyright law if it is the result of a personal and intellectual creation. There are no formal or other requirements for copyright protection. In particular, the Copyright Act does not require registration of the copyright protected work. A copyright is protected for 70 years after the creator's death.

(d) *Unfair competition*

Where a design is not specifically protected under intellectual property law as a design, trademark or copyright, its creator cannot prohibit third parties from copying and using the design for their own purposes.[3] However, where the use of a copied design would constitute an act of unfair competition, the creator of the design (or its successor or licensee) could, subject to further requirements, object to such use and claim damages and other remedies under the Unfair Competition Act. A greater infringement than the mere copying of an otherwise unprotected design is needed to prove unfair competition – for example, if a competitor offers goods or services that imitate goods or services of another party where:

- such use avoidably misleads consumers as to the corporate origin of the goods or services;
- such use constitutes an unfair use of or otherwise damages the reputation of the goods or services imitated; or
- the competitor has gained the knowledge or documents necessary to imitate the goods/services in bad faith or through illicit acts.[4]

The requirements for enjoying unfair competition law protection are strict. While Section 4 of the Unfair Competition Act in principle is not enumerative and further circumstances could be introduced that violate other provisions of the act, it is used as a last resort to defend against illicit copying.

(e) Order of precedence

A design may enjoy protection as a design patent, a trademark and a copyrighted piece of work at the same time. The claims resulting from the different protections may be raised in one legal action, but competence of the appropriate courts differs. This should be borne in mind when deciding on legal strategies for an infringement action. The protection that may be available in addition under the Unfair Competition Act is of secondary importance and will apply to the use of copied designs only in cases where the design is not specifically protected under intellectual property law (see above).

2. Registered design rights

2.1 Nature of rights

A design may be protected for a limited time under design law. In Germany, this protection may be obtained under the Design Act and under the Community Design Regulation. The Design Act came into force in 2004 to implement the EU Directive of 1998 into German law. The 2004 act replaced the old Design Act, which was first enacted in 1876 – one of the oldest pieces of statutory law in Germany. Under the Design Act, the protection of a design is limited to the territory of Germany. The Community Design Regulation came into force in 2002, under which it possible to obtain protection for designs in all 27 member states of the European Union. Since the costs for the registration of a Community design are relatively low, the

3 Piper/Ohly/Sosnitza, *German Unfair Competition Act*, 5th edition, 2010, line item 80.
4 Unfair Competition Act, Section 4, No 9.

Community design has become popular, while design protection under the Design Act has lost some of its importance.[5]

2.2 Qualification

In order to register a design under the Design Act, the design must qualify as a 'design' as defined in the act: it must be a: "two-dimensional or three-dimensional appearance of the whole or part of a product resulting from the features of, in particular, the lines, contours, colours, shape, texture or materials of the product itself or its ornamentation".[6] Additionally, the design must be new and must have an individual character.[7]

(a) Novelty

The novelty requirement is met when no identical design has been made available to the public before the date of filing the application. Designs are considered to be identical if they either do not differ at all or if they differ only in immaterial details.[8] The disclosure of a design to the public before application is not relevant for the question whether a design is new if the disclosure was made within 12 months before the date of application (or the date of priority), either by the creator of the design, his successor, or, in limited cases, even by a third party.[9] In this way, the creator is able to test a design in the relevant market before he decides whether to apply for design patent registration. For assessment of whether a design is new, each of its elements will be compared with earlier art separately, without assessing the overall impression.

(b) Individual character

A design must have an individual character to be protectable under the Design Act;[10] To fulfil this requirement the overall impression the design produces must differ from the overall impression produced by other designs available to the public in the same sector before the filing date (or the date of priority). Where there are no or a limited number of known designs in the same sector, the design may have to meet stronger requirements than in situations where the number of known designs in the same sector is high. In other words, the more known designs there are, the easier it will be for slight deviations to be sufficient to provide an individual character.[11] This is because informed users may attach more value to slight deviations where there is already a variety in existing designs. The nature of the product to which the design relates and the sector in which the design will be used will be taken into account for the assessment. The question whether a design has an individual character will be answered based on the overall impression of the appearance of the design, but not on the appearance of the particular elements of the design.

---

5 Klett/Sonntag/Wilske, *Intellectual Property Law in Germany*, 1st edition, 2008, Chapter 4.
6 Design Act, Section 1.
7 *Ibid*, Section 2.
8 Klett/Sonntag/Wilske, note 5 above, Part 1, Chapter 4, B, I, 2.
9 Design Act, Section 6.
10 *Ibid*, Section 2.
11 Klett/Sonntag/Wilske, note 5 above, Part 1, Chapter 4, B, I, 2.

2.3 Registration procedure

An application must be filed with the Patent and Trademark Office to obtain protection of a design under the Design Act. The office will conduct a formal examination, which does not go too much into detail. In particular, the office will not examine whether the design is new and individual. The law leaves it to other rights holders to oppose the application or registration when they become aware the new design.

The application must be filed on the application form published by the Patent and Trademark Office,[12] which is available on the office's website.[13] The application can be filed by post, electronically using the online service DPMAdirect, or by delivery in person to the Patent and Trademark Office in Munich, Jena or Berlin or at a number of patent information centres. Applications can also be filed by fax, but the office advises against filing by fax due to the loss of quality caused by fax transmissions. The application form must include the following documentation and information:

- the application form, which contains formal information regarding the applicant, its representative, the date of the application and information on the product(s) for which the design will be used;
- a copy of the design in a publishable quality; and
- a list of attachments if more than one application is being filed.

While not required by law, it is advisable to commission a legal advisor (a patent attorney) to support and control the filing of an application.

The Patent and Trademark Office will only examine the application to establish whether:

- the design is a 'design' under the provisions of the Design Act;
- the application contains the required documentation and information and all other formal requirements (signature, payment of fees, etc); and
- the design does not contain elements that:
  - form part of the design solely for technical reasons (the technical elements);
  - must be copied exactly for technical reasons to allow assembling with other parts or products;
  - are contrary to public policy; or
  - are contrary to accepted principles of morality.[14]

If these formal requirements are met, the office will register and publish the design as a design patent. The cost of registering a German design is relatively low.[15] The basic application fee is €70 for an application to protect one design for five years. Collective applications of up to 100 designs in one application are permitted against payment of an additional fee of €7 for each design (10 designs are already included in the basic application fee). In addition to the application fee, a publication fee of

12 Design Bylaw, Section 4.
13 Available at: www.dpma.de/geschmacksmuster/formulare/index.html (accessed September 7 2011).
14 Design Act, Section 16.
15 Klett/Sonntag/Wilske, note 5 above, Part 1, Chapter 4, C, I.

€12 is charged for each design. The fees for renewal of a design registration are higher: the first renewal of a design (from year 5 to year 10) costs €90 for each design; the second renewal (from year 11 to year 15) costs €120 a design; the third renewal (from year 16 to year 20) costs €150 a design; and the final renewal (from year 21 to year 25) costs €180 a design.

The registration process generally takes between two and three months. This is relatively quick, so filing a design application in Germany can be helpful to set the priority for further applications of the same design in other jurisdictions under the international application procedure.

2.4 Term of protection

The protection of a design under the Design Act starts on registration and lasts for 25 years, subject to payment of the renewal fees.[16] Once registered, the rights holder enjoys exclusive protection under the design patent, including the exclusive rights to manufacture, offer, distribute, import, export and use the products for which the design is being used (in line with the registration).[17] The rights holder is also entitled to grant exclusive and non-exclusive licences within Germany or parts of Germany and has the right to prohibit third parties from using the design in Germany.[18]

The Design Act does not provide for any obligation to grant compulsory licences under a design patent. Where a rights holder hinders competitors that are trying to enter the market and excludes them from competition, the competitors may seek a compulsory licence under the provisions of anti-trust law, subject to further requirements. Such a compulsory licence will be imposed only in exceptional cases – for example, where a rights holder stops the distribution of spare parts, claims unfair prices for them or refuses to supply them on unreasonable grounds.[19] However, the mere refusal to grant a licence under a design patent is not sufficient for the imposition of a compulsory licence under anti-trust law. There have not been any cases where compulsory licences have or could have been claimed to obtain a legal licence in order to use a protected design.

The protection of a design patent covers only those parts of the design that were disclosed in the application process. Any changes made to the design thereafter do not enjoy protection, unless a second application is filed (and granted) for a new, modified design. If an applicant is not the creator or its successor and is not otherwise entitled to apply, the actual rights holder – that is, the creator or its successor – can ask for the register to be corrected.[20] The right to claim correction is limited to three years after publication of a design, except in cases where the registrant acted in bad faith. In this case, there is no time limit for requesting correction of the register.

If an employee creates a design in the course of his employment or on the instruction of his employer, all rights in the design will vest with the employer unless the parties have explicitly agreed otherwise.[21] Thus, it is important for companies that

---

16 Design Act, Section 27.
17 *Ibid*, Section 27.
18 *Ibid*, Section 38.
19 EuGH GRUR Int 90, 140 Rn 18 – CICRA/Régie Renault, GRUR Int 90, 141 Rn 9.
20 Design Act, Section 9.

create industrial designs to ensure transfer of full ownership by describing the scope of employment and the employee's tasks accurately in the employment contract and to document the projects in which the employee is involved. To ensure the transfer of ownership in designs created by freelance workers, the company commissioning the freelance worker should include an appropriate transfer provision in the commissioning agreement, although this is not required by law.

2.5 Validity issues

(a) *Incorrect application*

As set out above, the application for registration must contain certain mandatory information and the applicant must have paid the registration fee. Protection under the Design Act will not be granted if these formal requirements are not met. In such case, the Patent and Trademark Office will ask for the missing information and/or the payment of the fee within a grace period.[22] If the applicant does not provide the missing information and/or does not pay the fee within this grace period, the office will reject the application.

(b) *No payment of renewal fees*

The protection of a registered design patent ends after expiry of the term of protection for which the protection fee has been paid if the rights holder does not pay the renewal fee. Deadlines and notification letters from the Patent and Trademark Office should be observed.

(c) *No 'design' according to the Design Act definition*

The Patent and Trademark Office conducts only a formal review, with no in-depth examination that would guarantee protectablity by itself. Even where a design has been registered, its protection may be invalidated if it does not meet the definition of 'design' provided by the Design Act.[23] The design will be pronounced invalid by a court in a declaratory judgment, whereas the invalidity claim may be filed by any party.[24] Therefore, applicants should evaluate the protectablity of the design and should undertake their own research of older designs before they file an application, so as to avoid unnecessary filing and legal enforcement costs.

(d) *Existing third-party rights*

A third party is entitled to request invalidation of a design patent if it interferes with the party's rights in signs with a distinctive character to the extent that such signs have been incorporated into the design patent, copyright-protected works to the extent that such works have been incorporated into the design patent, or to the extent that the design patent falls within the scope of protection of another design patent with a better priority.

---

21 Trademark Act, Section 7, paragraph 2.
22 Design Act, Section 16, paragraphs 3 and 5.
23 *Ibid*, Section 1.
24 *Ibid*, Section 33.

(e) *Proceedings*

A design may be invalidated only through proceedings before a German court. Unlike the Trademark Act, the Design Act does not provide for an administrative invalidation process.

3. Unregistered design rights

3.1 Unregistered Community designs

Under the European Design Act, it is possible for a design to enjoy protection as a Community design for three years if it is made available to the public – for example, on the internet, in brochures or in the press. In this case, and for this period, no registration is required.

3.2 Unregistered protection under German law

Under German law, a design can enjoy protection without registration as a non-registered trademark, as a copyright or under unfair competition law.

(a) *Trademarks*

A design can be protected as a trademark under the Trademark Act through its use in Germany, provided that the design has acquired a secondary meaning as a trademark within the applicable market, which is a condition that is difficult to meet.[25] Trademarks can be, for example, any signs and designs, even three-dimensional signs and designs, including the shape of goods and their packaging. For a design to enjoy protection as a trademark, it must be possible to distinguish between the goods and services it is applied to and goods and services of other sources. A design cannot enjoy trademark protection where it exclusively consists of a shape that:

- results from the nature of the goods themselves;
- is necessary to obtain a technical result; or
- gives substantial value to the goods.[26]

Moreover, the Trademark Act defines a number of absolute grounds for refusal, under which a design will not be granted trademark protection. These are that the design:

- has no distinctive character with respect to the goods or services;
- consists exclusively of signs or indications that may serve in business to designate the kind, quality and other particulars of the goods or services;
- consists exclusively of signs or indications, which have become customary in day-to-day language; or
- can mislead the public, in particular, as to the nature, quality or geographical origin of the goods or services.[27]

---

25 Trademark Act, Section 4, paragraph 2.
26 *Ibid*, Section 3.
27 *Ibid*, Section 8.

The protection of a design as a non-registered trademark ends when the design has lost its secondary meaning as a trademark.[28]

(b) *Copyright*

A design can enjoy protection as a copyright under the Copyright Act if it is the result of a personal and intellectual creation. If this requirement is met, literary, scientific and artistic creations are protectable under the act. The act provides a list of examples of creations that may in principle enjoy protection, such as written works, computer programs, works of fine art, works of architecture, and scientific or technical illustrations. The list is intentionally non-exhaustive so that other types of creations, such as designs, may also enjoy protection as a copyright.[29] However, it will be difficult in most cases to prove the creativity requirement for industrial designs. If the creator can prove that a design is above the creativity threshold, no further formal requirements (such as a registration or application) need to be met. There is no office or other public authority that registers creations for protective measures, such as proof of the date on which a creation has been made. As a result, many copyrights owners deposit their creation with a notary to provide evidence of the date of creation should it come into dispute. A copyrighted design enjoys protection during its creator's lifetime and for 70 years after his death.

(c) *Unfair competition*

A design may be protected under the Unfair Competition Act if it is not specifically protected under intellectual property law as a design patent, trademark or copyright. As set out above, the circumstances of use of the copied design must make the use an unfair act – for example, if the use would mislead customers or would damage the reputation of the rights holder. If the use of a copied work constitutes an unfair act under the Unfair Competition Act, the rights holder may prohibit such use and claim damages and other remedies under the act.

4. Qualification for protection

A party qualifies for protection through application for registration of the design with the Patent and Trademark Office. If the applicant is not the creator of the design, the applicant must have obtained the rights in the design from the creator or its successor. The office will not check this during the registration process,[30] but it is necessary in order to avoid any disputes with the creator or its successors or licensees. In this regard, it is of particular importance for companies to ensure the proper transfer of a design from their employees and freelance workers.

5. Infringement

The rights holder in a design has an exclusive right to manufacture, offer, distribute, import, export and use the products for which the design is being used (in line with

---

28 Fezer, *Trademark Law*, 4th edition, 2009, Section 4, 214.
29 Klett/Sonntag/Wilske, note 5 above, Part 1, Chapter 3, B, I.
30 Design Act, Section 8.

the registration). The manufacture, offering, distribution, importing, exporting and use by a third party of products for which the design enjoys protection will constitute an infringement.[31]

6. Design infringement litigation

6.1 Proceedings

If a design is infringed, the rights holder can bring civil law actions against the infringing party. The rights holder may require the infringer to cease and desist the infringement and may claim damage compensation if the party was acting at least negligently.[32] The rights holder may also require the party to recall and destroy all of the products it has manufactured and distributed under the infringement.

The courts offer comparatively fast proceedings at a reasonable cost (also providing for reimbursement of the costs of the successful party). The cost is calculated under a statutory system based on the value under dispute, and incorporates the legal costs of enforcement. German judgments also receive high attention in other (not only European) jurisdictions. Over the past decade, German courts have begun to take a leading position in Europe in certain areas and are increasingly regarded as the first choice for bringing a legal action for design infringements in Europe.

In addition to civil law actions, a rights holder may also initiate criminal proceedings and file a complaint with the competent prosecutor's office. The rights holder may request customs seizure at the European and/or German borders if it has filed a border seizure application under EU Directive 2004/48/EC on the Enforcement of Intellectual Property Rights.[33] The directive has been incorporated into German law by the Act on the Improvement of the Enforcement of Intellectual Property Rights.[34] There are subtle differences between the European and the German customs seizure provisions, but these are not discussed here. Customs seizure applications require thorough documentation of rights, sample material and pictures, and constant updating efforts; they are among the most efficient means of fighting product piracy.

Design act cases are heard by the regional court of the competent court district. The forum is usually either the seat of the infringer's business or the place where infringement shows its legal effects.[35]

6.2 Preliminary and main proceedings

In urgent cases, a rights holder may apply for preliminary injunctions and seizures. Where such preliminary proceedings do not resolve the action, in particular through a settlement, main proceedings will follow.

Preliminary injunctions may be filed at the competent chambers. When markets

---

31 *Ibid*, Section 42.
32 *Ibid*, Section 42.
33 Available at: http://eur-lex.europa.eu/LexUriServ/LexUriServ.do?uri=OJ:L:2004:157:0045:0086:EN:PDF (accessed September 12 2011).
34 Available at: www.bmj.de/SharedDocs/Downloads/DE/pdfs/Gesetz_zur_Verbesserung_der_Durchsetzung_von_Rechten_des_geistigen_Eigentums.pdf?__blob=publicationFile (accessed September 12 2011).
35 Eichmann/von Falkenstein, *German Design Patent*, 4th edition, 2010, sec. 52, line item 4.

are held, the courts will provide dedicated competency offering 24/7 application support if counterfeited material is discovered. The applicant may apply for the seizure of allegedly counterfeited goods and for a 'cease and desist' from further sale to be ordered. All other claims (particularly for information of infringing sales and damages) must be settled in main proceedings. Proof is evidenced through affidavits and photographic and other business material. An injunction may be obtained *ex parte* without the attendance, involvement and knowledge of the alleged infringer, and may be issued during a fair within hours, although the issue generally takes between two and five days. The injunction may be appealed by the defender. The law provides for damages claims against the applicant for an injunction should the injunction prove to be incorrect or is revoked.

Damages claims in cases that are ambiguous and not fully clear at the outset may be avoided by using main proceedings. Thus they are often brought instead of preliminary injunctions if the case is not urgent or the plaintiff is looking for a thoroughly reasoned decision.

In design patent cases the patent chambers in each federal state are competent to hear main proceedings if local competence is given.

6.3 Damages and other relief

The full range of available damages may only be dealt with in main proceedings: cease and desist from further sales, destruction of infringing goods, information on the volumes of infringing products sold, and damage claims. Under the legal regime, three methods of damages calculation may be applied at the request of the rights holder, based on:

- a hypothetical licence fee;
- the infringer's profit; and
- the rights holder's lost profit.

The rights holder's lost profit is applied only rarely since it requires the rights holder to submit proof of its cost calculation. A more common approach is to ask for information on the profit of the infringer (requiring the opponent to submit its commercial calculation base) and the number of infringing products sold. The rights holder may then decide which kind of damages compensation is most favourable. The hypothetical licence fee generally prevails. This is based on the average licence fee for the design patent if it were properly licensed, based on available industry data, market research or expert opinion. Punitive damages will not be awarded.

7. Licensing and exploitation

The rights holder has an exclusive right to grant exclusive and non-exclusive licences under the design patent within Germany or parts of Germany.[36] There is no requirement under the Design Act to register licences granted under a design patent, and no requirement to enter into a written agreement. However, it is advisable to execute a written agreement with the licensee to provide proof of the existence and

36 Design Act, Section 31.

scope of a licence. Such an agreement should cover the licence granted and all details necessary to protect both parties' interests. In particular, the agreement should state whether the licence is exclusive, whether it is temporary or indefinite (ie, for the term the design patent is valid), whether it may be assigned, sub-licensed or transferred, whether it is revocable or terminable, whether it is royalty bearing, and whether it is limited to the territory or valid throughout Germany. The agreement should also specify the products and further purposes for which the licensee will be entitled to use the design patent and should, at least, cover the terms and conditions on liability, the term and termination, and boilerplates.

Hong Kong

Anna Mae Koo
Vivien Chan & Co

---

1. Summary of design protection

In Hong Kong, most industrial designs are registered with the Designs Registry of the Intellectual Property Department and enjoy protection as registered designs under the Registered Designs Ordinance (Cap 522). This is a separate field of intellectual property rights from patents, which are governed by the Patent Ordinance (Cap 514). Designs not registered under the Registered Designs Ordinance may be protected under the Copyright Ordinance (Cap 528).

2. Registered design rights

The current Registered Designs Ordinance came into force on June 27 1997, repealing the previous legislation, the UK Designs (Protection) Ordinance, which had extended to Hong Kong the rights of the owners of designs registered in the United Kingdom under the Registered Designs Act 1949.

The Registered Designs Ordinance provides for two types of registered design:

- those registered under the ordinance;[1] and
- those deemed to be registered under the ordinance, which include:
  - designs registered in the United Kingdom under the 1949 act before the ordinance came into force and the rights subsisted on that date;[2] and
  - designs registered in the United Kingdom on or after the commencement date with the application pending immediately before that date.[3]

The previous ordinance and the 1949 act are still applicable to designs that are deemed to be registered designs under the current ordinance in two ways:

- the validity of designs deemed registered is determined under the 1949 act, which only considered novelty on the basis of whether the designs had been published in the United Kingdom before application (but are now subject to an additional ground of invalidity under the Copyright, Designs and Patents Act 1988, whereby the designs must not have been published in Hong Kong before application); and
- acts of infringement taking place before the commencement date are determined under the 1949 act.

---

1 Registered Designs Ordinance, Section 25.
2 *Ibid*, Section 91(1).
3 *Ibid*, Section 91(2).

2.1 Nature of rights

Registered designs are a form of personal property and can be assigned, mortgaged or licensed.[4]

Rights holders of registered designs enjoy the exclusive right to:

- make in, or import into, Hong Kong, for sale or hire or for use for the purpose of trade or business; or
- sell, hire or offer or expose for sale or hire in Hong Kong,

any article in respect of which the design is registered and to which that design or a design not substantially different form it has been applied.[5]

However, these rights do not extend to acts done privately for non-commercial purposes or acts done for the purpose of evaluation, analysis, research or teaching.[6]

The register will provide evidence of anything required or authorised by the Registered Designs Ordinance to be registered.[7] The certificate of entry in the register or a certified extract of the register will be evidence of the application and registration of a design or any mortgage or licence of it.

2.2 Qualification

A design is something capable of being applied to an article, not the article itself.[8] To fulfil the requirements for registration, it must meet the statutory definition of 'design' and be novel.

2.3 Exceptions to registrability

Certain designs are not registrable under the Registered Designs Ordinance, even if they meet all the requirements for registration – for example:

- designs relating to an article the appearance of which is not material (ie, if aesthetic considerations are not normally taken into account to a material extent);[9]
- designs contrary to public order or morality;[10]
- computer programs and protected layout-designs (topographies);[11] and
- designs for articles of a primarily literary or artistic character[12] (see section 3 below on Copyright law).

2.4 Identity of applicant

Under the Registered Designs Ordinance, any person claiming to be the owner of a

---

4 *Ibid*, Section 32.
5 *Ibid*, Section 31(1).
6 *Ibid*, Section 31(3).
7 *Ibid*, Section 65(1).
8 *Re Deyhle's Design Applications* [1982] RPC 526.
9 Registered Designs Ordinance, Section 6.
10 *Ibid*, Section 7.
11 *Ibid*, Section 8.
12 *Ibid*, Section 8.
13 *Ibid*, Section 5(1).
14 *Ibid*, Section 2(1).
15 *Ibid*, Section 3(1).

design may apply for it to be registered.[13] Generally, the person who creates a design[14] is treated as its owner.[15]

If two or more persons create a design, they are treated as co-owners and are entitled to an equal share in the design, subject to any contrary agreement.[16] If a design is generated by computer with no element of human design, the person who makes the arrangements necessary for the creation of the design is the designer.[17] If a design is created under a commission for money or money's worth, the person commissioning the design will be treated as the original owner of the design, subject to any contrary agreement.[18] If a design is created by an employee in the course of his employment, his employer will be treated as the original owner of the design, subject to any contrary agreement.[19]

2.5 Registration procedures

Under Section 12 of the Registered Designs Ordinance, an application to the Designs Registry for the registration of a design must contain the following information:

- a request for registration of the design;
- a representation of the design suitable for reproduction;
- the name and address of the applicant (ie, the design owner);
- a statement explaining the applicant's rights in the design (where he is not the designer); and
- an address in Hong Kong for service of documents.

Each representation of the design filed must bear a statement of novelty, in both English and Chinese, describing the features of the design which the applicant considers to be new.[20] The information should be provided on or attached to Designs Form D1.

Two or more designs can be filed together in one application if the designs relate to the same class of article under the Locarno Classification, or to the same set of articles.[21] A 'set of articles' means two or more articles of the same general character that are ordinarily sold together or intended to be used together.[22]

The filing date of the application is the date on which the request for registration, representation of the design and name and address of the applicant are filed, and the prescribed filing and advertisement fees are paid.[23] Registration and the date for determining the novelty of the design start on the filing date. An applicant may take advantage of the priority of an earlier application. In this case, the applicant files a statement of priority and a copy of the previous application with the registrar, and the filing date of the prior application will be regarded as the filing date of the application in Hong Kong.

The Designs Registry will examine an application to check that it meets the

---

16 *Ibid*, Section 33(1).
17 *Ibid*, Section 3(5).
18 *Ibid*, Section 3(2).
19 *Ibid*, Section 3(3).
20 *Ibid*, Section 8.
21 Registered Designs Rules (Cap 522A), Section 16.
22 Registered Designs Ordinance, Section 2(1).
23 *Ibid*, Section 14.

formal requirements. The applicant will be notified in writing of any deficiencies[24] and must correct these within a specified period or the application will be deemed to have been withdrawn.[25]

As the registry does not conduct a substantive examination, once any deficiencies have been corrected the Registrar must register the design. On registration, the details of the design and the name of the applicant as owner are entered in the register, a certificate of registration is issued, the registration is advertised and a representation of the design is published in the *Official Journal*.[26]

The registrar has discretion to refuse an application if the design is not new or is not registrable.[27] The applicant will be given notice of the refusal,[28] but will continue to enjoy the priority right, if any, before the refusal.[29]

2.6 Term of protection

A design is initially registered for five years, beginning on the application filing date.[30] The registration may be extended by the rights holder for further five-year periods up to a total of 25 years.[31] Renewal is effected by payment of a renewal fee, which may be paid up to three months before the end of the current registration term.[32] Renewal is possible up to six months from the end of the previous term, with an additional late payment fee, and the registration is treated as having been continuous.[33]

2.7 Infringement

The rights owner enjoys certain exclusive rights under Section 31(1) of the Registered Designs Ordinance, namely the right to make in, or import into, Hong Kong for sale or hire or for use for the purpose of trade or business and to sell, hire or offer or expose for sale or hire in Hong Kong any article in respect of which the design is registered and to which that design or a design not substantially different from it has been applied.[34]

Under the ordinance, infringement of registered design rights includes:

- any act in breach of Section 31(1);
- making anything to enable an article referred to in Section 31(1) to be made in Hong Kong;
- doing anything in relation to a kit which would constitute infringement if done in relation to the assembled article; and
- making anything for enabling a kit to be made or assembled, in Hong Kong or elsewhere, if the assembled article would be an article referred to in Section 31(1).[35]

---

24 *Ibid*, Section 24(2).
25 *Ibid*, Section 24(3).
26 *Ibid*, Section 25.
27 *Ibid*, Section 26(1).
28 *Ibid*, Section 26(2).
29 *Ibid*, Section 26(3).
30 *Ibid*, Section 28(1).
31 *Ibid*, Section 28(2).
32 *Ibid*, Section 28(3).
33 *Ibid*, Section 28(4).
34 *Ibid*, Section 31(1).

These rights do not extend to acts done privately for non-commercial purposes or to acts done for the purpose of evaluation, analysis, research or teaching.[36]

The main issue in an alleged infringement is whether the design in question is substantially different from the registered design. The decision will be based on a visual comparison of the two designs by non-expert consumers,[37] with the two articles being compared both side by side and separately.[38] The court will take into account any imperfect recollection of the articles by consumers as they rarely compare the articles side by side but usually look at the articles at different times.[39] However, the hypothetical consumer should have an interest in the design; otherwise the ambit of infringement would be unduly wide.[40]

2.8 Damages and other relief

An infringement of a registered design right is actionable by the rights holder, who may be entitled to all available relief, by way of damages, injunction, account of profits or otherwise as directed by the court.[41] However, the court will not both award damages and order an account of profits in respect of the same infringement.[42] For registered designs owned by two or more rights holders, each will be entitled to bring proceedings in respect of any infringement of the design.[43]

There are other remedies available to the rights owner, such as a court order for delivery up of the infringing articles[44] and an order for disposal, destroying or forfeiture of the articles,[45] as discussed in more detail in section 6 below.

2.9 Licensing and compulsory licences

A registered design is personal property and can be transferred, created or granted.[46] The right may be mortgaged, assigned or licensed as for other personal properties, and this is common practice. See section 7 below.

2.10 Validity issues

Any party may apply to the court for the revocation of a registered design on grounds that the design was not new at the time of application or was not restorable for any other reason.[47] There is no time limit for applications for revocation.

A party having or claiming a proprietary interest in a registered design may refer to the court the questions of:

- who is the true owner of the design;

---

35 *Ibid*, Section 31(2).
36 *Ibid*, Section 31(3).
37 *Tang Fung Kee Manufacturing Co Ltd v Fortuna Plastic Manufacturing* [1980] HKLR 184.
38 *Sonway Manufacturers Ltd v Wai Fat Electronics Co* HCA 5085/1980.
39 *Valor Heating Co Ltd v Main Gas Appliances Ltd* [1973] RPC 871.
40 *Sommer Allibert (UK) Ltd v Flair Plastics Ltd* [1987] RPC 599.
41 Registered Designs Ordinance, Section 48(1).
42 *Ibid*, Section 48(2).
43 *Ibid*, Section 49(1).
44 *Ibid*, Section 53(1).
45 *Ibid*, Section 54(1).
46 *Ibid*, Section 32(2).
47 *Ibid*, Section 45.

- whether the design should have been registered in the name of the person in whose name it was registered; or
- whether any right in it should be transferred or granted to any other party.[48]

A person found by the court to be entitled to be registered as the owner may apply to have the registration revoked on the ground that the person whose name is entered in the registry is not so entitled.[49] However, if reference was commenced after two years from the date of registration of the design, the court may not order revocation of the registration unless the applicant shows that the person whose name is entered in the register knew at the time of its registration that he was not entitled to be registered as the owner.[50]

A person found by the court to be entitled to be registered as the owner may apply to have the registration revoked on the ground that the person whose name is entered in the registry is not so entitled.[51] The application must be filed within two years of the date of registration of the design, and the court may not order revocation of the registration unless the applicant shows that the person whose name is entered in the register knew at the time of its registration that he was not entitled to be registered as the owner.[52]

Any party may at any time after registration of the design apply to the registrar for revocation of the registration on the ground that it is contrary public order or morality.[53] The registrar may refer the question to the court for determination.[54] If the Registrar or the court determines that the design is not registrable on this ground, the registration will be revoked.[55]

If a design registration is revoked, the register will be amended and the registration will be deemed never to have been made.[56]

3. Unregistered design rights

As well as the rights provided by the Registered Designs Ordinance, industrial designs enjoy some protection under the Copyright Ordinance (Cap 528). The Copyright Ordinance affords protection to designs without any requirement for registration.

3.1 Subject matter

To qualify for copyright protection, the subject matter must be a work that falls within one of the nine categories of work specified in Section 2(1) of the Copyright Ordinance. For industrial design protection, the most relevant category of work is artistic work. Section 5 of the Copyright Ordinance defines 'artistic work' as:

(a) a graphic work, photograph, sculpture or collage, irrespective of artistic quality;

---

48 *Ibid*, Section 41.
49 *Ibid*, Section 46(1).
50 *Ibid*, Section 46(3).
51 *Ibid*, Section 46(1).
52 *Ibid*, Section 46(3).
53 *Ibid*, Section 44(1).
54 *Ibid*, Section 44(3).
55 *Ibid*, Section 44(4).
56 *Ibid*, Section 47.

(b) a work of architecture being a building or a model for a building; or
(c) a work of artistic craftsmanship.

Section 5 further defines 'graphic works' as
(a) any painting, drawing, diagram, map, chart, or plan; and
(b) any engraving, etching, lithograph, woodcut or similar work.

Although the name of this category is 'artistic work', the law explicitly states that an artistic quality is not required for a graphic work, photograph, sculpture or collage.[57] For example, a simple line sketch of a hand putting a cross on a ballot paper was held to be protected under the copyright law.[58]

3.2 Requirements for copyright

If a work falls into one of the nine categories under the Copyright Ordinance, the only other requirement is the originality of the work. A copyrightable work must be an original created by its author and must not be copied from another work.[59] However, the law requires only very little originality in order to establish copyright existence.[60] For example, the courts have held that a translation of a foreign work,[61] a photograph of a picture[62] and a report of a speech[63] are protected under copyright law. If the work contains more original features, it will be entitled to broader scope of protection.[64]

Copyright law has no formalities requirements. An original work is automatically protected upon creation of the work. There is no requirement for copyright registration.

3.3 Copyright holder

The author of a work is the person who created the work[65] and is the first owner of any copyright in the work.[66] However, the law provides two exceptions to the first ownership rule. First, if a copyright work is made by an employee in the course of his employment, the copyright belongs to his employer, subject to any prior contrary agreement.[67] Secondly, for commissioned works, if there is an agreement between the author and the commissioner of the work which expressly provides for the entitlement to the copyright, the copyright in the commissioned work belongs to the person who is entitled to the copyright under the agreement.[68]

---

57 Copyright Ordinance, Section 5.
58 *Kenrick v Lawrence* (1890) 25 QBD 99.
59 *Ibid.*
60 *Ibid.*
61 *Byrne v Statist Co* [1914] 1 KB 622.
62 *Graves' Case* (1869) LR 4 QB 715.
63 *Walter v Lane* [1900] AC 539.
64 *Ibid.*
65 Copyright Ordinance, Section 11(1).
66 *Ibid*, Section 13.
67 *Ibid*, Section 14.
68 *Ibid*, Section 15.

3.4 Rights of copyright holder

The rights holder of a copyright work has the exclusive right to do the following acts ('acts restricted by copyright'):[69]

- to copy the work;
- to issue copies of the work to the public;
- to rent copies of the work to the public;
- to make available copies of the work to the public;
- to perform, show, or play the work in public;
- to broadcast the work or include it in a cable programme service; and
- to make an adaptation of the work or do any of the above acts in relation to an adaptation.

The author of a copyright work has the following rights:

- the right to be identified as author;[70]
- the right to object to derogatory treatment of work; and[71]
- the right not to have a work falsely attributed to another person.[72]

3.5 Term of protection

The usual duration of copyright protection is the life of the author plus 50 years.[73] However, where a manufactured article incorporates a design corresponding to an artistic work of copyright ('corresponding design'), the design protection under copyright law will be shorter. If the corresponding design is registered under the Registered Designs Ordinance, it will be protected for 25 years from the end of the year in which the article incorporating the corresponding design is first marketed.[74] If the corresponding design is not registered under the Registered Designs Ordinance, it will be protected for 15 years from the end of the year in which the article incorporating the corresponding design is first marketed.[75]

3.6 Infringement

(a) *Primary infringement*

Any person who does or authorises another to carry out an act restricted by copyright without the licence of the rights holder infringes the copyright in the work,[76] if the act relates to the whole work or any substantial part of the work.[77]

---

69 *Ibid*, Section 22.
70 *Ibid*, Section 89.
71 *Ibid*, Section 92.
72 *Ibid*, Section 96.
73 *Ibid*, Section 17(2).
74 *Ibid*, Section 87(2).
75 *Ibid*, Section 87(3).
76 *Ibid*, Section 22(2).
77 *Ibid*, Section 22(3).
78 *Ibid*, Section 38.
79 *Ibid*, Section 38.
80 *Ibid*, Section 39.
81 *Ibid*, Section 39.
82 *Ibid*, Section 39.

However, the law provides fair-dealing exceptions for research,[78] private study,[79] criticism,[80] review[81] and news reporting.[82]

(b) *Secondary infringement*

The copyright in a work is infringed by a person if he deals with infringing copies without a licence and has reason to believe that he is dealing with infringing copies.[83]

Infringing dealing includes:

- importing or exporting infringing copies into or from Hong Kong;[84]
- possessing infringing copies for trading or business purposes;[85]
- selling or offering for sale infringing copies;[86]
- exhibiting infringing copies in public or distributing infringing copies for trading or business purposes;[87]
- providing the means for making infringing copies;[88]
- permitting the use of premises for infringing purposes;[89] and
- provision of apparatus for infringing actions.[90]

4. Qualification for protection

As mentioned above, a design must fulfil the statutory definition of 'design' and be novel in order to be registered.

4.1 Definition of 'design'

Under the Registered Designs Ordinance, 'design' is defined to mean:

> *features of shape, configuration, pattern or ornament applied to an article by any industrial process, being features which in the finished article appeal to and are judged by the eye, but does not include (1) a method or principle of construction; or (2) features of shape or configuration of an article which (i) are dictated solely by the function which the article has to perform; or (ii) are dependent upon the appearance of another article of which the article is intended by the designer to form an integral part.*[91]

There are some terms in the definition that require explanation. There is no statutory definition of 'shape', 'configuration', 'pattern', or 'ornament', but it has been held that shape and configuration apply to three-dimensional articles and pattern and ornament apply to two-dimensional articles.[92] Thus, icons of an operating system software which appear on a computer screen have been held to be features of pattern or ornament applied to the computer, as the icons were in two dimensions.[93]

'Article' means any article of manufacture and includes any part of an article if

---

83 *Ibid*, Sections 30 to 34.
84 *Ibid*, Section 30.
85 *Ibid*, Section 31(a).
86 *Ibid*, Section 31(b).
87 *Ibid*, Section 31(c).
88 *Ibid*, Section 32.
89 *Ibid*, Section 33.
90 *Ibid*, Section 34.
91 Registered Designs Ordinance, Section 2(1).
92 *Lambretta Clothing Co Ltd v Teddy Smith (UK) Ltd* [2003] RPC 728.
93 *Apple Computer Inc's Design Applications* [2002] FSR 602.

that part is made and sold separately.[94] This definition leaves unclear whether a spare or replacement part which can only be incorporated in another product can be regarded as an article. This question is also relevant in deciding whether an item is dependent upon the appearance of another article to form an integral part. It has been held by the House of Lords that an item designed for incorporation is different from one designed for general use, and that a spare part can be qualified as an article if it has an independent life as an article of commerce and is not merely an adjunct of some larger article of which it forms part.[95] Thus, items such as main body panels, doors, bonnet lids, boot lids and windscreens of vehicles are items designed for incorporation, and hence are not articles. However, items such as wing mirrors, seats and wheels, which have a commercial life of their own, may be regarded as articles. Moreover, an article must not be "dictated solely by the function which the article has to perform", meaning that an article must perform some function other than merely carrying the design.[96]

'Appeal to and are judged solely by the eye' means that the finished article must have eye appeal from a consumer's perspective and the appeal is created by a distinctiveness of shape, pattern or ornamentation calculated to influence the consumer's choice.[97] The requirement to meet this threshold is not high, and it has been held that a design will be regarded as having eye appeal unless the whole of it is dictated solely by functional considerations.[98] However, the design should show some new effect clearly distinguishable by the eye from earlier designs.[99]

4.2 Novelty of the design

As well as meeting the requirements of a design under the Registered Designs Ordinance, a design must also fulfil the requirement of novelty.[100] There is no statutory definition of 'new', but under the Registered Designs Ordinance a design is not regarded as new if it is the same as a prior registered design, no matter whether the design applies to the same article, or if it has been published in Hong Kong or elsewhere before the filing date of the application, no matter whether the publication was in respect of the same article.[101] Moreover, a design is not new if it differs from earlier designs only in immaterial details or in features that are variants commonly used in the trade. 'Immaterial details' are those that have no significant visual impact on the design.[102] However, a design may be new even if its constituent parts are old[103] if the combination process has involved some artistic or intellectual effort.[104]

Publication of a design occurs when non-confidential disclosure of clear and

94 Registered Designs Ordinance, Section 2(1).
95 *Ford Motor Co Ltd's Design Application* [1994] RPC 545 (Divisional Court).
96 *Re Littlewoods Pools Ltd's Application* (1949) 66 RPC 309.
97 *Interlego AG v Tyco Industrices Inc* [1989] AC 217.
98 *Ibid.*
99 *Kestos Ltd v Kempat Ltd and Fitch Kemp* (1935) 53 RPC 139.
100 Registered Designs Ordinance, Section 5(1).
101 *Ibid*, Section 5(2).
102 *Household Article's Ltd's Registered Design* [1998] FSR 676.
103 *Heinrichs v Bastendorff* (1893) 10 RPC 160.
104 *Phillips v Harbro Rubber Co* (1919) 36 RPC 79.

unmistakeable directions on making an article having the features of the design is made to a third party.[105] It is sufficient for a publication to be made verbally, provided that the party can see the design in his mind's eye without the need for any originality on his part.[106] However, confidential disclosures by the rights holder or disclosure by another party in breach of good faith will not render the design unregistrable.[107]

4.3 International obligations

If a party files an application for registration of a design in a Paris Convention country or a World Trade Organization member, that party or its successor in title enjoys a right of priority for six months from the filing date of the application in the original country.[108] The filing date of the previous application is taken to be the filing date of the application in Hong Kong for the purpose of determining whether the design is new. Therefore, publication of the previous application after its filing date in that country will not invalidate a subsequent application in Hong Kong on the issue of novelty.[109]

5. Infringement

5.1 Infringement under the Registered Design Ordinance

As mentioned above, the Registered Designs Ordinance confers certain rights to the rights holder on registration. The exclusive rights do not extend to acts done privately for non-commercial purposes[110] or to acts done for the purpose of evaluation, analysis, research or teaching,[111] so not all acts will be regarded as infringement.

Although the Designs Registry in Hong Kong is responsible for the registration of designs in Hong Kong, it does not deal with infringement actions. There is no administrative proceeding available in Hong Kong for infringement of a registered design. Thus, the rights holder,[112] the co-owner[113] or the exclusive licensee[114] (as the case may be) may only initiate legal proceedings in respect of any infringement of the design.

Under the Registered Designs Ordinance an infringement is a civil liability only. Unlike other types of intellectual property infringement, the infringement of a registered design does not constitute an offence (no criminal liability is created). Therefore, a rights holder cannot seek help from government authorities for enforcement or ask the customs and excise department to take action (eg, seizure of the infringing products) solely on the basis of infringement of a registered design.

---

105 *Rosedale v Airfix* [1957] RPC 239.
106 *Ibid.*
107 Registered Designs Ordinance, Section 9(1)(c).
108 *Ibid*, Section 15(1).
109 *Ibid*, Section 17(3).
110 *Ibid*, Section 31(3)(a).
111 *Ibid*, Section 31(3)(b).
112 *Ibid*, Section 48.
113 *Ibid*, Section 49.
114 *Ibid*, Section 50.

5.2 Infringement under the Copyright Ordinance

As mentioned above, the Copyright Ordinance provides for two types of copyright infringement: primary and secondary infringement, both of which are actionable by the rights holder.[115] An infringement of copyright action may be started in the district court or the Court of First Instance.

In addition to the right to initiate civil proceedings against the infringer for copyright infringement, the Copyright Ordinance makes it an offence for a party, without the licence of the rights holder in a copyright work, to:[116]

- makes an infringing copy of the work for sale or hire;
- import an infringing copy of the work into Hong Kong otherwise than for his private and domestic use;
- export an infringing copy of the work from Hong Kong otherwise than for his private and domestic use;
- sells, let for hire, or offer or expose for sale or hire an infringing copy of the work for the purpose of, or in the course of, any trade or business;
- exhibit in public or distribute an infringing copy of the work for the purpose of, or in the course of, any trade or business which consists of dealing in infringing copies of copyright works;
- possess an infringing copy of the work with a view to acts of the two points above; or
- distribute an infringing copy of the work to such an extent as to affect the copyrights holder prejudicially.

An officer authorised by the Commissioner of Customs and Excise may exercise powers given under Section 122 of the Copyright Ordinance to search for and seize any infringing copy of a copyright work. Thus, in order to protect the copyright of an industrial design under the Copyright Ordinance, the rights holder may, in addition to initiating civil proceedings against the infringer, record its rights and report the infringing case to the customs and excise department for potential seizure and prosecution.

When reporting a copyright-infringing activity, the rights holder should provide adequate information to the customs and excise department, in particular:

- information on the copyright work and the copyright owner;
- a sample of the copyright work and the infringing work;
- an letter appointing a competent and authorised person to conduct subsequent seizure identification and undertake to give evidence and testify in court; and
- an affidavit of evidence supporting the subsistence and ownership of copyright, and the potential criminal prosecution.

The Copyright Ordinance provides the customs and excise department with wide-ranging powers and may be regarded as the best option for protecting the

115 Copyright Ordinance, Section 107(1).
116 *Ibid*, Section 118.

exclusive rights of the rights holder. The power of seizure will stop the infringing acts immediately and the costs of recording with and reporting to the customs and excise department are substantially lower than the costs of litigation.

6. Design infringement litigation

In general, there is no particular procedure that should be followed for initiating a copyright or registered designs infringement action: no specific procedure is prescribed under the law.

Following relatively recent civil justice reform, it is advisable in most litigations to issue a pre-action letter to the infringer to avoid adverse cost consequences should the court consider the act of bringing proceedings without a pre-action letter unreasonable. Furthermore, especially for copyright infringement, it may be necessary to prove that the defendant has knowledge of the infringing copy. A pre-action letter will amount to notice to the potential defendant and provide evidence should the infringing act continue after the pre-action letter.

Should the infringer fail to respond satisfactorily to the pre-action letter, the rights holder may start legal proceedings in the courts. Both the district court and the Court of First Instance have jurisdiction to hear infringement cases. In practice, intellectual property infringement cases will be started directly in the Court of First Instance.

It is preferable for a rights holder to lodge a claim directly with the Court of First Instance if the exact amount of its monetary claim against the infringer is not known before the action starts, since it is possible that the amount will exceed the jurisdiction of the district court, currently HK$1 million. The rights holder may choose between an account of profit and damages, and the final monetary claim may only be established after disclosure of evidence during the proceedings.

Another advantage of starting the action in the Court of First Instance is the potential to obtain interim remedies such as interlocutory injunctions, which are not available through the district court.[117] Interim remedies allow the rights holder to protect its rights during the proceedings, before the decision is given. There is a set of specific Practice Directions governing the procedure for seeking an interlocutory injunction in the Court of First Instance.[118]

The rights holder may seek an interlocutory injunction to restrain the infringing acts immediately, if applicable. It will need to show that there is a serious issue to be tried.[119] The court will not grant an interlocutory injunction if damages are an adequate remedy for the plaintiff and the defendant is in a position to pay. An interlocutory injunction will be granted if damages are an adequate remedy for the defendant and the plaintiff is in a position to pay. If damages are an adequate remedy for both parties, the court will consider all the circumstances of the case and decide whether an interlocutory injunction should be granted.

Reliefs such as damages, injunction and account of profits are available to the rights holder under the Registered Designs Ordinance,[120] and the rights holder may

117 Practice Direction 27.
118 Practice Direction 5.3.
119 *American Cyanamid Co v Ethicon Ltd* [1975] AC 396.
120 Registered Designs Ordinance, Section 48.

apply for delivery-up[121] and disposal.[122] Similarly, relief by way of damages, injunction and account of profits is available to the plaintiff under the Copyright Ordinance,[123] and the plaintiff may apply for delivery-up[124] and disposal.[125]

The plaintiff may apply for either damages or an account of profits, but not both. The court will not award damages and order an account of profits[126] in respect of the same infringement. For copyright infringement, the court may grant an award of additional damages under Section 108(2) of the Copyright Ordinance. It will take into account the flagrancy of the infringement, any benefit accruing to the defendant from the infringement, the completeness, accuracy and reliability of the defendant's business accounts and records, and all other circumstances of the case.

Unlike other remedies, damages and account of profits are not always available in infringement cases. If the defendant was not aware, and had no reasonable ground for knowing, that the design was registered or that copyright subsisted in the work[127] (innocent infringement), no damages and no order for an account of profits will be awarded. In such circumstances, the pre-action letter will inform the defendant about its infringing acts. For public awareness, a registered design must show its registration number accompanied the word 'registered' or a similar abbreviation. The word 'registered' or a similar abbreviation only will not suffice.[128]

As with other legal proceedings, the successful party is usually entitled to an award for the costs of the legal proceedings. However, the court will take into account the conduct of the parties and retain discretion to vary the costs order in appropriate cases. The court may disallow costs or order the successful party to pay costs incurred as a result of improper or unnecessary conduct or misconduct in the proceedings. Following the civil justice reform, in exercising the discretion on costs the court will take into account any unreasonable failure of a party to engage in mediation.[129]

A common defence to an infringement action under the Registered Designs Ordinance is to attack the validity of the registration, generally on the ground of novelty or that the subject matter is not registrable (see section 4 above for the qualification of registered design rights). Similarly, in a copyright infringement action the defendant may dispute the existence of copyright (as there is no registration requirement for copyright). In order to challenge the registration or the existence of right, the defendant will have to allege the same in the particulars.

7. Licensing and exploitation

The right in a registered design can be assigned or mortgaged. A co-owner may not assign or mortgage a share in a registered design without the consent of each of the other co-owners, subject to any contrary agreement.[130]

---

121 *Ibid*, Section 53.
122 *Ibid*, Section 54.
123 Copyright Ordinance, Section 107.
124 *Ibid*, Section 109.
125 *Ibid*, Section 111.
126 Registered Designs Ordinance, Section 48.
127 *Ibid*, Section 51(1); Copyright Ordinance, Section 108(1).
128 *Ibid*, Section 51(2).
129 Practice Direction 31.

The right in a registered design can also be licensed.[131] Similarly, a licence or sub-licence may be assigned or mortgaged.[132] Again, for designs owned having more than one owner, the consent of each co-owner must be granted for the right to be licensed.[133]

Any assignment or mortgage (or any assent in relation to) a registered design or any right in it will be void unless it is in writing and is signed by or on behalf of the assignor, mortgagor or party granting such assent. In case of a corporate body, the document must be signed under the corporate seal.[134] An assignment of a registered design or a share in it, and an exclusive licence granted under any registered design, may confer on the assignee or licensee the right to bring proceedings.[135]

Although there is no statutory requirement that any assignment, mortgage or licence has to be registered, any party that claims to have acquired a right in a registered design by any transaction will be entitled against any other person who claims to have acquired that right by an earlier transaction if no application for the registration of particulars concerning the earlier transaction has been made, or if the party claiming under the later transaction did not know of the earlier transaction.[136] It is advisable that any transaction affecting the right of the registered design be registered as soon as possible so as better to protect the rights of the assignee, mortgagee or licensee.

Copyright is also transmissible by assignment, by testamentary disposition or by operation of law as other personal property. An assignment of copyright must be in writing, signed by or on behalf of the assignor.[137] Licensing of copyright is also possible, and the licence is binding on every successor in title, with the except of a purchase in good faith for valuable consideration and without notice, actual or constructive, of the licence.[138] While there are no formal requirements for granting a licence, an exclusive licence must be in writing and signed by or on behalf of the licensor.[139]

---

130 Registered Designs Ordinance, Section 33(3).
131 *Ibid*, Section 32(4).
132 *Ibid*, Section 32(4).
133 *Ibid*, Section 33(3).
134 *Ibid*, Section 32(6).
135 *Ibid*, Section 32(7).
136 *Ibid*, Section 34(1).
137 Copyright Ordinance, Section 101(3).
138 *Ibid*, Section 101(4).
139 *Ibid*, Section 103(1).

India

AL Mary
Archana Shanker
Anand and Anand

---

1. Summary of design protection

In India, design rights are governed by the Designs Act 2000, which came into effect on May 11 2001, replacing the old law of 1911 to provide more effective protection to registered designs and to encourage design activities.

The purpose of the 2000 act is to protect novel designs that are applied to or govern the shape of an article which is to be manufactured and marketed on a commercial scale. The emphasis is on the visual impact of the finished article. The act grants protection to the rights holder, who may enjoy an exclusive right to the embedded commercial value of its design.

The Designs Act grants the owner or proprietor of a registered design an exclusive right to:

- sell;
- license;
- assign; and
- use,

the design in any product.

An industrial design applied to an article may enjoy protection through registration if it is new or original, provided that it is a non-functional feature of shape, configuration, pattern, ornamentation or a composition of lines or colours, whether in two- or three-dimensional form or both, by any industrial process or means, whether guide, mechanical or chemical, separate or combined.

The Designs Act uses a 'first to file, first to get' system: the inventor or creator of a design must file the application for registration to prevent other persons claiming rights on that particular design. A design is considered to be new if no identical design has been made available to the public before filing date or priority date. The act changed the standard of novelty and uniqueness applied to an article when considering its design for registration. Novelty is now determined on a worldwide basis rather than the territorial novelty criterion provided under the old act.

1.2 Enforceable rights

Once a design is registered, the rights holder has a legal right to bring proceedings against any third party (natural or legal entity) that infringes or counterfeits the design. The action to stop the exploitation and to claim any damages to which the rights holder is legally entitled must be filed with a court at the district court level or higher. If a design is not registered under the Designs Act there will be no legal right to take any action against the infringement.

1.3 Qualification for protection

The creator of a design, or any other person or company assigned by the creator, may apply for and obtain registration of the design.

A design must possess the following attributes in order to qualify for protection:

- it should possess an aesthetically pleasing appearance, which should appeal to the eye;
- it must be applied to articles;
- it should be new or original;
- it should not have been disclosed to the public anywhere in India or in any other country;
- it should be significantly different from other known designs or a combination of known designs; and
- it should not contain any scandalous or obscene material.

(a) Appeal to the eye

The design must be capable of being applied to an article in such a way that it will be seen and perceived by the eye. The particular shape, configuration, pattern or ornamentation must have an embedded visual appeal – the feature to be registered must "appeal to the eye" and be "judged by the eye". This implies that the design must appear on, and should be visible on, the finished article. Thus, any design that is applied to the inside of, for example, a box or money purse may not meet the criteria, as this type of article is generally marketed closed, not open. The key distinction is: "external visibility to the eye/viewer at first instance". It may be argued that the appeal to the eye will apply at the time of sale of the article to which the design is applied and therefore an interior arrangement of a design might be registrable.

(b) Design must be applied to articles

A design is a manifest creative expression that is applied to an article, not the article itself. It may be incorporated in the article in a shape or configuration that is three-dimensional (eg, the shape of a bottle or flower vase) or as the decoration of a two-dimensional article (eg, the design on a bed sheet or wallpaper). The article to which a design is to be applied must be something that is sold as a finished product. Thus, designs of industrial plans, layouts and installations are not registrable under the Designs Act.

The design should be applied or applicable to an article by an industrial process. Normally, designs of an artistic nature such as paintings or sculptures that are not produced in bulk by an industrial process are excluded from the scope of the act.

(c) Novelty or originality

In order to be registrable, a design must be new or original and must not have been published in India before the application is filed. A design of an already-known pattern will be registrable if it is applied to a new article.

In *Reckitt Benckiser (India) Ltd v Wyeth Ltd*,[1] the court disposed of an appeal against a finding that a prior registration of a design in the United Kingdom, the United States and Australia will be considered as prior disclosure under Section 4(b) of the Designs Act. The court stated that if a registered design is intentionally brought into the public domain it is no longer new.

Other decisions on registrability have held as follows:

- The shape of an apple applied to school bag will be registrable. In *Pilot Pen Co v Gujarat Ind P Ltd*, it was held that registration would not be effective unless the design is new and original and not of a pre-existing common type.
- The known shape of 'Qutub Minar' is registrable when applied to a cigarette holder. However, if the process of design for which an application is filed does not involve any significant intellectual effort, registration may not be granted. In *Rotela Auto Components (P) Ltd v Jaspal Singh*, it was held that the test for novelty and originality is dependent on determining the level of intellectual activity involved in developing the design.
- If the design is merely a trade variation of an earlier design, a designer may make some changes under permissible variations. There should be some original intellectual application involved when developing a new design. The novelty or originality of a particular part of the article may be sufficient to import the character of novelty and originality to the whole. A combination of previously known designs can be registered if the visual impact of the combination as a whole is new.

Any mode or principle of construction or operation, or anything which is in substance a mere mechanical device, would not be registrable as a design. For instance, a key that's only novelty is the shape of its corrugation or bend at the portion that engages with levers inside the lock cannot be registered as a design under the act. However, when a design suggests any mode or principle of construction or mechanical or other action of an operation, a suitable disclaimer in respect of this must be inserted on its representation, provided there are other registrable features in the design. The design should not include any trademark, property mark or artistic work as defined under the Copyright Act 1957.

2. Registered design rights

2.1 Nature of rights

Designs are governed by the Designs Act and the Design Rules 2001. A design registration grants the rights holder the exclusive rights of selling, importing and applying the design to any product. India has adopted the 'first to file' system, so applications should be filed at the earliest opportunity to prevent other parties claiming rights in the intended design. Any person can apply to register a design provided that it is new, it has not previously been published anywhere in the world, it is reproducible by an industrial process, it meets the principles of public order, it

1 FAO(OS) 458/2009.

is distinct from all known designs, it does not contain obscene material and it qualifies for the benchmark standard of 'eye catching'.

The registration of a design grants the copyright in the design to the rights holder for the period of registration. Copyright means the exclusive right to apply the design in respect of the article for which it is registered.

Section 15(2) of the Copyright Act precludes the subsistence of copyright in a design that is registered or is capable of being registered as a design under the Designs Act 2000. Thus, there is a clear overlap between the Copyright Act and the Designs Act. Further, even though the protection afforded by a copyright and a design right are mutually exclusive, if a copyright exists in an article, or in a design applied to an article, and the article is reproduced more than 50 times, the owner of the copyright loses its right to prevent unauthorised use of the copyright.

Design rights are granted on a country-by-country basis. An Indian registration provides protection only in India and its territories. If a rights holder wishes to protect its design in other countries, it must seek protection in each country separately under the local laws.

The Paris Convention provides certain privileges to member countries for design protection. A party who files a design application in a member state may, within six months of the filing date, file applications in other member countries claiming the priority of the first application. If the design is accepted for registration, it will be deemed to have been registered from the same date that the application was made in the home country.

2.2 Registration procedure

(a) Who can apply for a design registration?

Any person who claims to be the proprietor of a new or original design that has not been published previously in any country may apply for registration of a design in India.

A proprietor may be:

- the author of the design;
- the person who has acquired the design;
- the person for whom the design has been developed by the author; or
- the person on whom the design has devolved.

In the case of a design claiming priority, the applicant must be the person or entity that has applied for protection of the design in any other convention country or group of countries that are members of intergovernmental organisations, or its legal representatives, alone or jointly with any other person. The Indian design law regime provides for six months' priority from the date of the earliest application.

(b) Application document

An application for registration of a design must be in the format prescribed under the Designs Act and the Designs Rules.

(c) ***Contents of application***

Application form: a design application must be filed in the form prescribed under the Designs Rules along with the registration fee.

E-filing: an e-filing facility for design applications and all subsequent documents is to be made available in India soon.

Class: the class to which the article belongs must be stated correctly in the application form. Under the Designs Rules, articles are classified based on the Locarno Classification.

Section 6(3) of the Designs Act provides that if a design has been registered for any article in one class, the rights holder may apply to register it in respect of one or more other articles in the same class and the registration will not be invalidated:

- on the ground that the design is not new or original, by reason only that it was so previously registered; or
- on the ground that the design has previously been published in India or in any other country, by reason only that it has been applied to article in respect of which it was previously registered,

provided that the later registration does not extend the period of copyright in the design beyond that of the original registration.

If the applicant has already registered one or more designs in any other class, details of the earlier registrations and their registration numbers must be supplied, using Form-1.

An application must be signed either by the applicant or by his authorised agent or legal representative.

Representation of design: an application must include four copies of the representation of the design.

A representation comprises exact drawings, photographs, tracings, including computer graphics, or specimens of the design. In rare cases, the controller may require a specimen of the article to be submitted at the time of examination.

Cross-sectional views, dimensions or engineering symbols, trademarks, words, letters or numerals not forming the essence of the design, extraneous matter or background, dotted, discrete/phantom lines and shadings are not permitted.

If a colour combination is the essence of a design as it is applied to an article, the combination should be depicted clearly in the representation. Colour may be used to highlight the novel portion of black-and-white designs. Descriptive text and reference letters/numerals denoting the components may be included.

The date of registration of the design will be the date of the application for registration or the priority date, as the case may be.

(d) ***Examination***

When an application for registration of a design is filed, it is referred by the Controller of Designs to an examiner of designs, who will examine:

- whether the application and the documents satisfy the formal requirements; and
- whether the design as applied to an article is registrable.

(e) ***Allowance***

The applicant must submit an application within six months of filing it in India in order for it to be granted.

2.3 Grant

On registration, the controller will issue a certificate of registration to the proprietor of the design. The registration process takes approximately 12 months.

2.4 Term of protection

A registered design enjoys protection for 15 years from the filing date or priority date. The registration is valid for an initial term of 10 years and may be renewed for a further five-year term.

A rights holder may apply for the five-year extension as soon as the design is registered. If the extension fee is not paid before the end of the initial 10-year term, the registration will lapse. A lapsed registration may be restored by filing a request along with the prescribed fee within one year of the registration lapsing, stating an acceptable ground for the late payment.

2.5 Licensing

The copyright in a registered design may be extended to or transferred to a third party by assignment, transmission or the operation of law. An interest in a registered design may be transferred through a mortgage, licence or other means.

An application for registration of the title must be filed within six months of its execution. The period is extendable by a maximum of six months. The registered rights holder will have absolute power over assigning and licensing the design. An unregistered instrument will not usually be admissible in any court as proof of title to copyright in a design or to any interest therein.

An industrial design is licensed when the rights holder (licensor) grants permission to another person (the licensee) to use the design for a mutually agreed purpose. A licensing agreement or contract will usually be signed between the two parties, specifying the terms and scope of the agreement.

Licensing contracts often include limitations on the territory in which the licensee may use the design, the time for which the licence is granted and the type of products for which it may be used.

If a design is to be licensed for use abroad, design protection must first be obtained, or at least applied for, in the countries or region concerned.

2.6 Compulsory licences

There is no provision for compulsory licences under the Designs Act.

2.7 Validity issues

The criteria for a registered design to be valid are as follows:

- It should be novel and original.
  If a design is not new, it can still be registered provided it is original. As stated in *Bharat Glass Tube Limited v Gopal Glass Works Limited*,[2] in relation to a design, the term 'original' means originating from the author (or creator) of the design and includes designs which though old in themselves are new in their application.
- It should not have been disclosed to the public anywhere in India or in any other country.
  In *Reckitt Benckiser (India) Ltd v Wyeth Limited*,[3] the Delhi High Court confirmed an earlier decision[4] that prior foreign registration would amount to publication of a design and that its availability in the public domain in India or abroad should be significantly distinguishable from known designs or combination of known designs.
- It should not comprise or contains scandalous or obscene matter.

The validity of a registered design can be challenged at any time after its registration on the ground that the design:

- was previously registered in India and has been published in India or in any other country before the registration date;
- is not new or original;
- is not registrable under the Designs Act; or
- does not meet the definition of 'design' in clause (d) of Section 2 of the Designs Act.

3. Unregistered design rights

There is no concept of or scope for unregistered design rights under the Designs Act.

4. Qualification for protection

4.1 International obligations

The protection of intellectual (IP) property rights was strengthened by the passage in 1999 of legislation to protect IP rights in harmony with international practices and in compliance with India's obligations under the Agreement on Trade-Related Aspects of Intellectual Property Rights (TRIPs) of the World Trade Organization (WTO). In India, protection of IP rights will be granted in accordance with TRIPs, as adopted in the applicable national laws.

The legal regime in India provides for five broad categories of IP rights: trademarks, copyrights, patents, industrial designs and geographical indications.

As a signatory to the following conventions, protection of IP rights in India

---

2 (2008) (37) PTC 1 (SC).

3 Decision of October 8 2010.

4 *Reckitt Benckiser (India) Ltd v Wyeth Ltd* FAO(OS) 458/2009.

meets the stipulated thresholds of the international system:

- the Berne Convention (copyright), since 1928;
- the Hague Agreement/Geneva Act (designs), non-member;
- the Madrid Protocol (trademarks), accession planned since 2009;
- the Paris Convention for the Protection of Industrial Property (priority rights), since 1998;
- the Patent Cooperation Treaty (patents), since 1998; and
- the WTO/TRIPs (IP rights in general), since 1995.

(a) *TRIPs*

TRIPs members are under an obligation to provide for the protection of industrial designs that are new or original.

TRIPs mandates that members grant the owner of a protected design the right to prevent third parties from making, selling or importing articles bearing or embodying a design which is a copy, or substantially a copy, of the protected design without the rights holder's consent, when such acts are undertaken for commercial purposes. The minimum term of protection granted to a rights holder under TRIPs is 10 years.

(b) *Paris Convention*

The Paris Convention 1833 was the first international convention to address the concept of industrial property and its protection. The convention was amended in 1979 to protect industrial designs. It also introduced a provision to place a duty on member states to provide protection to industrial designs without any forfeiture if the design does not work and protection against the import of articles of the same design.

(c) *Hague Agreement/Geneva Act*

The Hague Agreement on the international registration of industrial designs, which governs the WIPO, administers a global protection system for registering designs.

The Geneva Act of the Hague Agreement concerning the international registration of industrial designs was adopted in 1999. The Hague system provides an international registration of designs and a mechanism for registering a design in countries and intergovernmental organisations that are party to the agreement. It is administered by the international bureau of the WIPO. An international registration obtained under this agreement produces the same effects in each of the designated countries, as if it was registered in that country.

India has not ratified the Geneva Act so it has no application in India – wide protection is available under the Designs Act.

(d) *Locarno Agreement*

The Locarno Agreement 1979 establishes an international classification for industrial designs.

Although India is not a contracting party to the Hague Agreement, it follows the international classification for industrial designs based on the Locarno Agreement.

5. Infringement

5.1 Establishing infringement

Infringement of the copyright in a design is known as 'piracy of the design'. The rights holder enjoys the right to prohibit other parties from using the design for commercial gain during the copyright term. The rights holder, or its licensee or assignee, may grant permission to use the design to other parties.

The following acts, if done in relation to a copyright-protected design without the permission of the rights holder, are considered to be piracy, or infringement:

- applying the design or any fraudulent imitation of it to any article for sale;
- importing for sale any article to which the design, or a fraudulent or obvious imitation of it, has been applied; and
- publishing or to exposing for sale any article knowing that the design or any fraudulent or obvious imitation of it has been applied to it.

Section 22 of Designs Act provides that to establish infringement of a registered design it must be proved that:

- the design is registered under Section 11; and
- for the purpose of sale or import for sale and without the consent of the rights holder, the design or a fraudulent imitation of it has been applied to an article in any class of articles in which the design is registered, or an act has been done to enable the design to be so applied; or
- the infringer has published or exposed for sale the article knowing that the design or any fraudulent or obvious imitation of it has been applied.

If the design is not registered under the Designs Act, its proprietor will have no legal remedy or right to take action against the infringer.

The protection granted to the rights holder is based on civil remedy under Section 22 of the Designs Act. The onus is on the rights holder to identify acts of infringement and to file infringement proceedings. The reliefs available under the Designs Act are injunctions (interim or final) and damages; no criminal action against the infringer is available.

5.2 Damages and other relief

Under Section 22(2) of the Designs Act, a party found guilty of infringement may be fined up to Rs25,000. The rights holder may file for recovery of damages, provided the total claim does not exceed Rs50,000, or for an injunction.

Examples of remedies awarded by the courts include the following:

- In *Officine Lovato SPA v Pravinbhai Jagjivandas Mehta*,[5] the plaintiff applied for cancellation of the registration of the defendant's design, under Section 19 of the Designs Act, on the ground that it was not new or original as the same design had been published India and abroad before its registration. The court directed that the registration be cancelled.

5 (2006) 32 PTC 569.

- In *Hindustan Lever Ltd v Nirma Pvt Ltd*,[6] the plaintiff filed for an injunction to stop the defendant using a label on a soap carton, alleging infringement of its registered design and passing-off. The defendant claimed that the label was a design, capable of being registered under Designs Act, and that under Section 15(2) of the Copyright Act 1957 copyright in the label had expired. The court held that a label put on a carton cannot be regarded as a design within the meaning of Section 2(5) of the Designs Act 1911.
- In *Dabur India Ltd v Emami Ltd*,[7] the plaintiff alleged a violation of an interim injunction prohibiting the use of a similar bottle design, which it claimed was damaging the effectiveness of its TV commercials. The defendant stated that it had changed the design of its bottles and the case was dismissed.

(a) Jurisdiction

Proceedings for infringement or passing-off are heard in either the district court or the High Court, depending on the value of the claim.

(b) Validity

A rights holder must demonstrate that the alleged infringing act involves a design that is identical or similar to its registered design and that the infringement interferes with its right of exclusive use or causes economic loss.

(c) Statute of limitation

Under the Limitation Act, a rights holder must start proceedings within three years of an infringement. Design infringement is a continuing offence since the infringer violates the rights holder's exclusive right each time it commits a discrete infringing act, so the limitation period will restart with each new infringing act. Nevertheless, it is advisable to start legal action against the infringer as soon as possible in order to limit the damage and to establish the seriousness of the rights holder's intent before the court.

(d) Ex parte interlocutory injunction

Most Indian courts will grant an *ex parte* interlocutory injunction if the rights holder is able to establish its rights, to show the gravity of the offence and to demonstrate that the infringement merits immediate consideration. It is a temporary injunction, granted for the duration of the trial, restraining the infringer from using the infringing design. The injunction is granted without notice to the infringer.

(e) Appointment of a local commissioner

Depending on the facts of the case, the rights holder may ask the court to appoint a local commissioner to raid the premises of the infringer and seize the infringing goods.

---

6 AIR 1992 Bom 195.
7 (2006) 32 PTC 125.

(f) *Provisions under the customs laws*

In addition to civil remedies, some relief is available through the customs regime, which offers provisions to prohibit the import of infringing goods or counterfeits. Under the Intellectual Property Rights (Imported Goods) Enforcement Rules 2007, rights holders may record their registered designs with the customs authorities and customs officials are authorised to seize infringing goods without obtaining court orders.

A rights holder must give notice in writing to the Commissioner of Customs, or a customs officer authorised by the commissioner at the port of import, requesting that goods infringing its registered design be seized. The commissioner must inform the rights holder whether its notice has been accepted or rejected within a specified time. If the notice is accepted, the request will be registered and customs authorities will prevent the import of infringing goods, classifying them as prohibited goods under the Customs Act 1962. The registration and protection usually lasts for one year.

Customs officers have the authority to suspend the clearance of such prohibited goods either based upon the information received by the rights holder or by filing their own action, provided they have *prima facie* evidence or reasonable grounds to believe that the imported goods infringe the design registration.

The customs authorities will inform the rights holder when infringing goods are seized. The rights holder must execute a bond and join the proceedings against the importer within a specified time or the suspended goods will be released.

The rules permit customs officers to destroy any seized goods or to dispose of them outside the normal channels of commerce if the goods are found to have infringed the registered design and there is no legal proceeding pending in relation to them.

The rules prohibit the re-export of infringing goods in an unaltered state.

5.3 Recent case law

(a) Microfibers Inc v Girdhar & Co[8]

The plaintiff, a US company, owned a US copyright for the artistic work vested in an upholstery fabric design. The plaintiff claimed that the second defendant was manufacturing upholstery fabric that violated its copyright under Section 51 of the Copyright Act 1957 and was marketing it through the first defendant.

The plaintiff claimed to own the artistic rights in the upholstery fabric under the Copyright Act and relying on the Berne Convention. The defendants claimed that the design was a work and should be protected under the Designs Act. The court concluded that the protection available to the plaintiff fell under the Designs Act, not the Copyright Act.

Section 15 of the Copyright Act provides that copyright subsists in any design that has been registered under the Designs Act. At the time the plaintiff registered its design, the Designs Act 1911 was applicable. The plaintiff admitted that it had

8 Decision of May 28 2009.

registered the same design under the UK Designs Act. The court found that the plaintiff would have been entitled to protection under the old or new act, but that it had not registered its design under the new act.

The plaintiff's case was based on infringement of the copyright in the artistic work. The court held that the plaintiff's design should have been registered under the Designs Act and since it was not, no relief could be claimed.

(b) Dart Industries Inc v Techne Plast[9]

This case provides a clear example of the overlap between the Copyright Act and the Designs Act. The court held that once drawings of a final product design are made, copyright in the drawings cannot be claimed under the Copyright Act. The underlying message is that copyright in industrial design is governed by the Designs Act. If a design is registered under the Designs Act, it is not eligible for protection under the Copyright Act and the copyright in it ends.

(c) Marico Ltd v Raj Oil Mills Ltd[10]

This case concerned the registration of a design for a bottle cap. The issue was whether an article that forms part of a product is entitled to enjoy protection as a registered design. The court held that although the cap forms part of a product, it may be manufactured and sold separately and so is entitled to separate protection as a registered design under the Designs Act.

The Designs Act 2000 now covers: "any part of an article capable of being made and sold separately". Thus, once a part of an article falls within the definition of an article and is capable of being made and sold separately, then whether the article or only a part of it has a commercial identity of its own is immaterial. It is the exclusive privilege of the rights holder to choose whether to sell it separately or not.

5.4 Developments in design protection

Following extensive consultation between the Department of Industrial Policy and Promotion and the industrial sector, it is anticipated that a national design policy will be introduced soon. The proposals include:

- strengthening design education at all levels;
- encouraging the use of designs by small-scale and cottage industries and craftsmen;
- encouraging and facilitating the active involvement of industry and designers in the development of the design profession;
- better design management within India and overseas;
- enhanced design service exports; and
- developing an environment that recognises and rewards original designs.

This will create a strong reliance on licensing under the Designs Act and will produce a designs regime that is compliant with the international benchmarks.

---

9 Decision of June 4 2007.

10 (2008) (37) PTC 109 (Bom) (DB).

6. Design infringement litigation

See sections 5.2 and 5.3 above.

7. Licensing and exploitation

See section 2 above.

Ireland

Anne Bateman
Philip Lee Solicitors
David Brophy
FRKelly

---

1. Summary of design protection

In Ireland, designs may be protected as registered national designs, as registered or unregistered Community designs, or under copyright.

National and registered and unregistered Community design rights may arise in respect of any aspect of the design of a product, defined according to the harmonised definitions provided under EU Regulation 6/2002 on Community designs, provided that the design is novel and has individual character. National and Community registered designs enjoy protection for 25 years, while unregistered designs are protected for three years.

Copyright has limited application in design protection, but will arise in respect of items which qualify as artistic works, including works of architecture, sculptures and artistic craftsmanship. Copyright also subsists in original graphic works, and such works may be applied as surface decoration to a product.

The shape and configuration of industrially produced objects that are not artistic works (eg, sculptures, works of artistic craftsmanship) are not entitled to copyright as a three-dimensional work, and the copyright in a drawing of such an item is not infringed when the item itself (as opposed to the drawing) is copied.

1.1 Qualification for protection

A party qualifies for protection under the national and Community (both registered and unregistered) design regimes by virtue of being the designer or the designer's successor in title. If two or more parties have jointly developed a design, the right to the design vests in them jointly. However, if a design is developed by an employee in the execution of his duties or following the instructions given by his employer, the right to the design vests in the employer, unless otherwise agreed.

There are no nationality or residence requirements to qualify for protection under the registered or unregistered design regimes.

For copyright, there are national qualification criteria based on nationality, residence or place of first publication. However, as the qualification requirements embrace all countries that are members of at least one of the World Trade Organization, the Berne Convention, the Universal Copyright Convention or the World Intellectual Property Organization (WIPO) Copyright Treaty, it is rare for a work not to qualify for protection under Irish law.

For artistic works, the first owner of copyright is the author, unless the work is made by an employee in the course of employment, in which case the employer is the first owner of any copyright in the work, subject to any agreement to the contrary.

2. Registered design rights

2.1 Nature of registered rights

Registered design rights (both national and Community) provide the rights holder with the exclusive right to use the design and to authorise others to use it, including the right to make, offer, put on the market, import, export or use a product in which the design is incorporated or to which it is applied, or to stock such a product for those purposes.

The design right in a registered design also extends to any design which does not produce on the informed user a different overall impression, taking into consideration the degree of freedom the author had in developing the design.

Infringement of a registered design does not require any element of copying – that is, the registration is enforceable against any third party that has arrived independently at the infringing design.

2.2 Qualification

To qualify for protection as a registered design, the same criteria apply under both the national and Community regimes. A design must meet the definition of 'design' in EU Regulation 6/2002/EC: it must be novel and have individual character, and it must not be excluded under any of the exclusion criteria.

(a) *Definitions*

A 'design' is defined as the appearance of the whole or a part of a product resulting from the features of, in particular, the lines, contours, colour, shape, texture or materials of the product itself or its ornamentation.

Since the design must relate to the appearance of a product, this definition also must be considered: 'product' means any industrial or handicraft item, including parts intended to be assembled into a complex product, packaging, get-up, graphic symbols and typographical typefaces, but not including computer programs.

A 'complex product' is a product that is composed of multiple components which can be replaced, permitting disassembly and reassembly of the product.

(b) *Novelty and individual character: general considerations*

Both novelty and individual character are assessed in relation to similar earlier art, namely whatever has been made available to the public before the filing date of the application for registration of the design for which protection is claimed or, if priority is claimed, the priority date.

A design is 'made available to the public' if it has been published following registration or otherwise, or exhibited, used in trade or otherwise disclosed, before the application filing date (or priority date if claimed), except where these events could not reasonably have become known in the normal course of business in the circles specialising in the sector concerned, operating within the Community.

Certain disclosures are not taken into consideration:

- if the design was disclosed to a third person under explicit or implicit conditions of confidentiality;
- if the design has been made available to the public by the designer, his successor in title or a third person as a result of information provided or action taken by the designer or his successor in title during the 12 months before the filing date of the application or, if a priority is claimed, the priority date; or
- if the design has been made available to the public as a consequence of an abuse in relation to the designer or his successor in title.

(c) ***Novelty***

A design will be considered to be new if no identical design has been made available to the public before the filing date of the application for registration of the design for which protection is claimed or, if priority is claimed, the priority date.

(d) ***Individual character***

A design will be deemed to have individual character if the overall impression it produces on an informed user differs from the overall impression produced by any design that has been made available to the public before the filing (or priority) date of the application for registration. The degree of freedom of the designer in developing the design will be taken into consideration when individual character is assessed.

The concept of the 'informed user' was considered in the High Court decision in *Karen Millen v Dunnes Stores,*[1] in which Justice Finlay Geoghegan followed the observations of Lord Justice Jacob for the UK Court of Appeal in *Procter & Gamble v Reckitt Benckiser,*[2] that the informed user has more extensive knowledge than the average consumer of trademark law, but is not a designer or manufacturer.

(e) ***Special considerations for component parts of complex products***

A design which subsists in the appearance of a component part of a complex product is only considered to be new and to have individual character if the component part remains visible during normal use of the complex product (ie, during use by the end user, excluding maintenance, servicing or repair work) and to the extent that those visible features of the component part fulfil in themselves the requirements as to novelty and individual character.

(f) ***Exclusions***

The features of the appearance of a product which are solely dictated by its technical function are not registrable. The test to be applied in these circumstances is not clear. There is judicial precedent from the United Kingdom and from Europe for both the *Amp v Utilux*[3] interpretation and the 'multiplicity of forms' interpretation. The *Amp*

1 [2007] IEHC 449.
2 [2007] EWCA Civ 936.
3 1972 RPC 103 (UK HL).

v Utilux interpretation is that a design is excluded if it is dictated only by technical considerations, with no evidence that the designer provided any further aesthetic input to the design and even if other designs would also fulfil the same technical function. The multiplicity-of-forms interpretation is that a design is excluded only if it is the sole design which could achieve the function required for the product. It should be noted that, as at March 2012, this point had not been the subject of a decision by the Irish courts and there is no settled view across Europe as to the correct standard to apply.

A second exclusion comprises the so-called 'must fit' features – that is, features of the appearance of a product that must be reproduced in their exact form and dimensions in order to permit the product in which the design is incorporated or to which it is applied to be mechanically connected to or placed in, around or against another product so that either product may perform its function.

A third exclusion (under Community law but expressed as a ground for refusal under Irish law) is for designs that are contrary to public policy or to accepted principles of morality.

A fourth exclusion (under Irish law but expressed as a ground for invalidity under Community law) is for designs which are in conflict with an earlier design – that is, a registration filed before the invalidated design which is only published after the filing or priority date of the invalidated design application or registration.

There are further exclusions for designs that infringe third-party copyright or trademark rights.

2.3 Registration procedure

Registrations are granted subject to the application being made in the prescribed form and payment of the required fee. The application must identify the applicant and the author of the design and identify the product to which the design is to be applied, and must contain paper representations in the prescribed form. The applicant may pay an additional fee to defer publication of the registration for up to 30 months.

Community design applications require similar information to be supplied, but may be filed in fully electronic form as well as on paper. Like national designs, deferment of publication may be requested for up to 30 months.

In both cases an application may be filed in respect of multiple designs provided that they are all in the same Locarno class. There is a limit of 100 designs in one application under the national system and no limit for Community design registrations.

Applications for both national and Community design registrations are not submitted to substantive examination for the criteria of novelty and individual character, and thus registrations are granted subject only to a formality examination.

2.4 Term of protection

Registered designs are protected for an initial term of five years, which may be renewed four times to provide a maximum of 25 years' protection from the filing date. Although the Industrial Designs Act 2001 provides that the date of registration is deemed to be the priority date (apparently having the effect that renewal and duration should be calculated from the priority rather than filing date), in practice the Patents Office ignores this anomaly and treats the filing date as being the starting point for calculating the duration and renewal dates of a registration, in line with the practice of the Office for the Harmonisation in the Internal Market.

2.5 Rights granted

The rights granted to the owner by the registration are the exclusive right to use the design and to authorise others to use it, including the right to make, offer, put on the market, import, export or use a product in which the design is incorporated or to which it is applied, or to stock such a product for those purposes.

2.6 Infringement

Any person doing any of the exclusive acts reserved for the rights holder without permission while the registration is in force infringes the registration. Accordingly, infringement occurs when the design is used without permission, including making, offering, putting on the market, importing, exporting or using a product in which the design is incorporated or to which it is applied, or stocking such a product for those purposes.

For further details and for a discussion of secondary infringement, see section 5 below.

2.7 Damages and other relief

In an action for infringement of a registered design. all relief by way of damages, injunction, account of profits or otherwise is available to the plaintiff – as it is in respect of the infringement of any other property right.

In addition to or as an alternative to awarding compensation to a plaintiff for financial loss, the court may award aggravated or exemplary damages or both aggravated and exemplary damages.

If at the time of the infringement the defendant did not know and had no reason to believe that the design was registered, the plaintiff is not entitled to damages against the defendant and no order will be made for an account of profits. The plaintiff may still obtain an injunction.

3. Unregistered design rights

3.1 Unregistered Community design right

To a large extent the unregistered Community design shares many of the rights of the registered Community design, as described in section 2 above. The following sections indicate the points of difference and it may be assumed that in all other regards the rights are the same as the registered rights. As copyright is entirely different it will be discussed separately.

(a) Nature of rights

Infringement only occurs when there has been copying, and this must be proved in an action for infringement.

(b) ***Qualification***

The definitions are identical, as are the exceptions to protection. For the substantive requirements of novelty and individual character, the only differences are that the date used for assessing the state of the art is the date when the designer (claiming protection under the unregistered right) first made the design available to the public, rather than the filing or priority date used for the registered rights, and there is no grace period for the designer's own disclosure, as the making available to the public triggers the start of the term of protection.

(c) ***Term of protection***

The term of protection is three years from the date on which the design was first made available to the public within the Community. This includes the design being published, exhibited, used in trade or otherwise disclosed in such a way that, in the normal course of business, these events could reasonably have become known to the circles specialised in the sector concerned, operating within the Community.

(d) ***Rights granted***

The rights granted to an unregistered Community design are the same as those for a registered design other than that the right is limited to the prevention of acts occurring as a result of copying.

(e) ***Infringement***

Infringement occurs when any of the acts which are exclusively reserved for the unregistered rights holder are carried out without permission and as a result of copying.

(f) ***Damages and other relief***

There is no legislative entitlement to aggravated or exemplary damages. All of the normal reliefs available for infringement of intellectual property rights are available, including interlocutory and permanent injunctions, orders for delivery-up and destruction of infringing goods, and a choice between damages and an account of profits.

3.2 Copyright

While copyright is intended to have limited application within the field of industrial design under Irish law, it has some relevance, especially if the design has original surface decoration which has been copied or if the original design started life as an artistic work in itself, such as a sculpture.

Copyright in an original artistic work (whether two-dimensional, such as an original drawing, or three-dimensional, such as a sculpture) provides the copyright owner with the exclusive right to copy the work, to make the work available to the public and to make an adaptation of the work. Infringement only occurs when there has been actual copying, and the copying must be of a substantial part of the original work.

While the general rule is that copying includes reproduction in three-dimensional form of a two-dimensional work and vice versa, this is qualified in the case where the copyright artistic work is a design document, defined as follows under Section 78A of the Copyright and Related Rights Act 2000: 'design document' means any record of a design of any aspect of the shape or contours (whether internal or external) of the whole or part of a product, other than surface decoration, whether in the form of a drawing, a written description, a photograph, storing the work in any medium or otherwise such as a drawing or model for an industrially produced work.

In such cases, and provided that the design document records a design "for anything other than an artistic work", then copyright is not infringed by the making of a product to the design or the copying of a product made to the design.

This provision has two important consequences.

First, if a design document or model records a design for an artistic work (eg, a sculpture in the normal meaning of the word, or a work of artistic craftsmanship such as a stained-glass window), then copying the article in question infringes copyright both in the item itself as an artistic work and in the design document.

Secondly, because the definition of design document excludes surface decoration, the copyright in an original graphic work, applied as surface decoration to a product, is infringed when reproduced on another product. For an illustration, see the UK decision in *Flashing Badge Co v Groves*.[4]

If a copyright work is exploited industrially – by making and selling more than 50 products incorporating the work – after 25 years from the end of the calendar year in which the products were first marketed the work may be copied by making products of any description, or doing anything for the purpose of making products of any description, and anything may be done in relation to products so made, without infringing the copyright in the work.

4. Qualification for protection

There are no nationality or residence qualification requirements for any of the design rights under Irish law.

As Ireland is a member of the Berne Convention, the Universal Copyright Convention, the World Trade Organization and the WIPO Copyright Convention, qualification can occur with reference to any of the member states of any of these agreements (the qualifying countries).

An artistic work can qualify for copyright in Ireland in either of the following ways:

- the author (or one of the joint authors) is a citizen or subject of, or an individual domiciled or ordinarily resident in a qualifying country; or
- the work was first lawfully made available to the public in a qualifying country, or was made available in a qualifying country within 30 days of being first made available elsewhere.

4 [2007] EWHC 1372 (Ch).

5. Infringement

5.1 National registered design rights

Infringement of a national registered design is divided between primary and secondary acts of infringement.

The primary acts of infringement consist of the undertaking, without permission and while the design right is in force, of any act which is within the exclusive right of the rights holder. The 'exclusive right' is defined (in broad terms) in Section 42(4) of the Industrial Designs Act 2001 as the: "exclusive right to use the design and authorise others to use it, including the right to make, offer, put on the market, import, export or use a product in which the design is incorporated or to which it is applied, or to stock such a product for those purposes". In assessing infringement, it is also essential to consider the scope of protection which is afforded to the design, namely that the design right in a registered design will also apply to any design which does not produce on the informed user a different overall impression, taking into account the degree of freedom the author had in developing the design.

There are exceptions to this exclusive right, in particular the 'repair' exception, under which the design right will not apply to the use of a component part of a complex product for the purpose of repair of the product so as to restore its original appearance. Nor is the design right infringed by reproducing a feature of the design which is not taken into account in determining whether the design is registrable, namely those components of complex products which are not visible to the observer or features of the appearance of a product which are solely dictated by the product's technical function. The exhaustion defence also applies.

Other exceptions are specified, namely:

- acts done privately for non-commercial purposes;
- acts done for experimental purposes. Although not specifically stated, and despite there being no clarifying case law on this exception, the scope of this exception is generally considered to cover experimental acts even when carried out with a commercial purpose; and
- acts of reproduction for the purposes of making citations or of teaching, provided that such acts are compatible with fair trade practice and do not unduly prejudice the normal exploitation of the design, and that mention is made of the source.

The legislation also caters for specific exemptions in relation to the use of equipment on ships and aircraft registered outside the state when they temporarily enter the state, and in relation to the importation and use of spare parts and accessories for the purposes of repairing these craft and the actual execution of repairs to them.

Secondary infringing acts are specified, relating to the sale, rental, or exposure for sale or rental of products which infringe the design, importing these into Ireland other than for private and domestic use, or having possession, custody or control of such infringing products in the course of a business, trade or profession. However, the would-be infringer must have intent – that is, he must know or have reason to believe that the relevant product is an infringing product. Secondary infringement also applies to infringing articles – that is, an article which is specifically designed or adapted for applying the protected design to products. The making, selling, rental, offering or exposing for sale or rental, importing or having possession, custody or control of such an article is an infringement of the protected design. Again, intent is relevant to whether there is actionable secondary infringement in relation to infringing articles: the would-be infringer must know or have reason to believe that the relevant article is an infringing article.

The judgment as to whether an act of infringement has occurred, including whether the protected design has been used or replicated in the allegedly infringing design, is a matter for the trial judge alone, taking into account and weighing up all of the evidence (including expert evidence) which is before him as to the identities and similarities between the two designs. Depending on the circumstances, it may be relevant for the court to consider the scope of protection, as outlined above, and in particular expert evidence as to the impression of the so-called informed user, a fictional person into whose shoes the court must step, and the degree of freedom of the designer in the particular field of design. Whilst expert evidence may be offered to the court on these points, it is ultimately the trial judge who must decide whether the protected design is infringed, taking these matters into account.

The Industrial Designs Act 2001 makes provision for 'groundless threats' actions. Such an action can be taken by any person, other than the manufacturer or importer of an allegedly infringing object, who is aggrieved by threats of proceedings for infringement of the design right. The person aggrieved by the threats is entitled to relief unless the person threatening action (whether the rights holder or another) can prove that:

- the acts in respect of which the proceedings were threatened constituted, or if undertaken would have constituted, infringement of the design right; and
- the person threatened fails to show that the registration of the design is invalid.

The relief in this case is a declaration that the threats were unjustifiable, an injunction against continuance of the threats and damages, if any, that may have been sustained by the person in relation to the making of the threats. A notification of the existence of a design registration does not of itself constitute an actionable threat.

Infringement of the design is actionable by the rights holder. No proceedings can be taken in respect of any infringement committed before the date on which the certificate of registration of the design was granted.

The 2001 act also provides for criminal offences of design infringement, very similar in terms to the civil secondary infringement provisions. It is also a criminal offence to make or cause, with intent, a false entry in the design register and/or falsely to claim, again with intent, something to be a copy or reproduction of an entry in the design register or to produce or offer this in evidence. It is also a criminal offence falsely to represent that a design, which is disposed of by a person in Ireland for value, is registered where the person knows or has reason to believe that this representation is false. The Irish police force will usually investigate the alleged offence and make the initial decision as to whether to prosecute summarily (ie, treating the offence as a minor offence, with lower penalties) or to refer the case for prosecution as a serious offence, with heavier penalties.

5.2 Copyright

If a design is protected by copyright, infringement will occur when any of the acts which are within the copyright owner's exclusive control are undertaken by the would-be infringer without permission, namely any of the acts of reproduction, adaptation, making available to the public or communication to the public and/or first distribution of the work. Secondary acts of infringement, including dealings with infringing copies of works, are also specified. Numerous exceptions are also provided for under the Copyright and Related Rights Act 2000, including rights of fair dealing for the purposes of research or private study, criticism or review or reporting current events, incidental and transient uses and educational uses, among others. The key issue to consider in determining whether copyright infringement has occurred is to examine what part or amount of the work has been taken or used by the alleged infringer, and whether this is substantial. In this regard, infringement is assessed on the basis of the quality, rather than the quantity, of what is taken.

6. Design infringement litigation

6.1 Procedure and court forum

The procedure adopted for design or copyright infringement litigation (and, in particular, the court forum) depends on the type of right which is alleged to be infringed.

If the proceedings relate to allegations of infringement of a national registered design right or of copyright, there is a choice of court forum available to the plaintiff, depending on the level of damages or lost profits that the plaintiff assesses are at issue in the proceedings (ie, attributable to the infringement). If the amount of damages or lost profits in such a case does not exceed €6,348.69, the plaintiff must issue its proceedings in the district court, Ireland's lowest court of original jurisdiction. If the amount of damages or lost profits exceeds the district court's monetary jurisdiction but does not exceed €38,092.14, the plaintiff must issue its proceedings in the circuit court. If the plaintiff assesses that its damages or lost profits exceed €38,092.14, it must issue its proceedings in the High Court. If the plaintiff chooses the wrong forum, and at trial is awarded a sum of damages or lost profits which is less than the relevant court's monetary jurisdiction, a costs penalty may be imposed: the plaintiff may only recover legal costs at the level specified before the lower court in which the proceedings should have been issued and it may be required to pay the higher legal costs incurred by the defendant in being forced to defend proceedings (more expensively) before the higher court. Appeals from decisions of the district court lie in the first instance with the circuit court; appeals from decisions of the circuit court lie in the first instance with the High Court; and appeals from decisions of the High Court lie with the Supreme Court.

If the proceedings relate to or involve allegations of infringement of a

Community registered resign or of an unregistered Community design right (a 'Community design' as collectively defined in EU Regulation 6/2002/EC), under Article 80 of the regulation the Irish High Court is designated as the 'Community design court' for Ireland. Proceedings for infringement of a Community design must be issued in the High Court, irrespective of the amount of damages or lost profits claimed by the plaintiff.

Within the High Court, there is an option for either the plaintiff or the defendant to apply to have the case dealt with by the Commercial Division of the High Court. This is a specialist division of the High Court which has remit to hear cases with a particular commercial focus, usually where the value of the case exceeds €1 million. However, the division, in the presiding judge's discretion, may also admit and deal with intellectual property infringement cases which do not meet this €1 million threshold, as long as the proceedings fall under the High Court's monetary jurisdiction generally. The advantages of successfully applying to have the proceedings admitted to the Commercial Division's list are that they will be case-managed by the presiding judge to trial, with the likelihood of obtaining a quicker trial date (in some cases between three and six months after proceedings are issued) than would be achieved in the normal High Court list.

Proceedings for design or copyright infringement are plenary proceedings, and are instituted by means of an originating document called a plenary summons. This means that, following the issuing and service of the plenary summons, there will be a full exchange of formal pleading documents between the parties (including a statement of claim and a defence) and, if required, of discovery/documentary disclosure, and evidence will be provided orally by relevant witnesses rather than by documentary witness statements or affidavits. Proceedings are heard and determined by a judge alone, rather than by a judge and jury. The procedure for exchange of pleadings and all other matters relating to the proceedings are primarily set out in the published rules of the relevant court.

6.2 Remedies: interim and final

The Industrial Designs Act 2001, and Irish law in general, permits a plaintiff to seek interim and interlocutory relief, including in the form of prohibitory and/or mandatory injunctions, in respect of copyright or design right infringements pending full trial. The main criteria for seeking interlocutory relief are that:

- there is a fair question to be tried between the parties to the dispute (which does not mean that the court undertakes a detailed examination of the merits of the claim and defence, but rather that it is satisfied that the claims in the proceedings and the defence to them are stateable);
- damages are not an adequate remedy for the plaintiff should it fail to obtain the interlocutory injunction but ultimately succeed at trial; and
- the balance of convenience favours the granting of the injunction.

The court will also examine the behaviour of the parties, and particularly the party seeking the injunction, as they must come to court 'with clean hands'. The court will also examine the urgency with which the party seeking the injunction addressed the infringement and came to court, taking into account when it first learned of the infringement. Any delay in this regard may affect the party's ability to secure an injunction. In respect of interim relief, and in addition to meeting the criteria specified above, the plaintiff must demonstrate a particular urgency to persuade the court to grant interim relief without first hearing the defendant's side of the case. Interim relief is generally only granted for a few days, until the court can hear from the defendant. Following an interlocutory hearing, the interim relief may be discharged or it may be turned into interlocutory orders pending full trial.

Irish law also provides for other interim and interlocutory remedies in appropriate circumstances, including Mareva orders (permitting the freezing of the defendant's assets), Anton Pillar orders (a type of urgent search-and-seizure order), Norwich Pharmacal orders (requiring the disclosure of names and addresses of the identities of infringers) and the orders specifically provided for under Directive 2004/48/EC. This directive, to the extent the reliefs were not already contained in Irish law, has been fully transposed into Irish law by the EC (Enforcement of Intellectual Property Rights) Regulations 2006. The 2006 regulations allow for orders to be granted, either pending or following full trial, for the disclosure to the plaintiff of information regarding the origin or distribution networks of infringing goods, and of the names, addresses and other relevant details of alleged infringers and others who may be involved with them.

In terms of final remedies, the Copyright and Related Rights Act 2000 and the Industrial Designs Act 2001 make provision for the award of damages, injunctions and account of profits. They also permit the award of aggravated and/or exemplary damages depending on the behaviour of the defendant, although such awards are rarely made. The defendant may also avoid the payment of damages or an account of profits in relation to registered design or copyright infringement if it can successfully claim innocent infringement of the design or copyright – that is, if it can show that at the time of infringement it did not know and had no reason to believe that the design was registered or that copyright subsisted in the work.

The plaintiff may also obtain delivery-up of infringing products or articles. In relation to the 2001 Act, if the court grants an order for delivery-up, it will also make an accompanying order for disposal (eg, destruction) of the infringing products or articles. Both acts also make provision for the plaintiff to apply to the district court for orders to seize infringing goods. These provisions are generally used to seize counterfeit goods that are being traded on the street rather than out of permanent, fixed premises, although the provisions also permit the making of orders in relation to the search of fixed premises.

Additional reliefs may be obtained under the 2006 regulations, specifically orders for recall, removal from trade channels, or destruction of infringing goods or any material or implement principally used in their creation or manufacture. The court may also order the dissemination and publication of the judgment made against the defendant, at the defendant's expense.

6.3 Legal costs

The award of legal costs at the conclusion of any interlocutory injunction applications or following trial is at the discretion of the hearing judge. However, the general rule is that costs follow the event – that is, that the winning party will obtain an award for its legal costs. This will include the costs of engaging experts to assist it and to provide evidence at trial. Costs are awarded on what is called a 'party and party basis' – that is, to reflect the costs of dealing with the other side, rather than interactions for instructions with the winning party's own legal team. This means that the winning party may not be covered in respect of 100% of its actual legal costs in all cases.

6.4 Validity

As a defence to any infringement claim, or as a pre-emptive strike, a defendant or alleged infringer may claim invalidity of any registered design which is in issue. If validity claims are made outside the forum of proceedings, those claims are filed and determined by the relevant registry.

7. Licensing and exploitation

7.1 Licensing: registered design rights

Registered designs may be licensed exclusively or non-exclusively, and the licence may be partial in the sense of applying to some but not all of the acts for which the rights holder is entitled to an exclusive right. A licence is not effective unless it is in writing and signed by or on behalf of the licensor. If the licensor is a body corporate, this requirement may be satisfied by the affixing of its seal.

Until a licence is recorded in the register, it is ineffective against third parties acquiring a conflicting interest in the design.

A licensee (including a non-exclusive licensee) is entitled to ask the rights holder to take infringement proceedings in respect of any matter which affects the licensee's interests, from the date on which an application was made to record the licensee's interests. If the rights holder refuses to take action or fails to do so within two months, the licensee may bring the proceedings in its own name as if it were the registered rights holder. The rights holder must be joined either as a plaintiff or defendant in any such action taken by the licensee, although interlocutory relief may be granted on an application brought by the licensee alone without the rights holder being named in the action.

An exclusive licensee has, from the date of application for recording the licence, the same rights and remedies occurring after grant of the licence as if the licence were an assignment, other than against the rights holder.

7.2 Validity issues

In general, each of the criteria listed in section 4 above may be used as grounds for invalidating a design registration, with a further ground for invalidation being that the rights holder was not entitled to the design. This ground may be invoked only by the rightful owner.

7.3 Licensing: unregistered design rights

An unregistered Community design may be licensed for the whole or part of the

Community. A licence may be exclusive or non-exclusive. Without prejudice to the provisions of the licensing contract, the licensee may bring proceedings for infringement of a Community design only with the rights holder's consent. However, the holder of an exclusive licence may bring proceedings if the rights holder, having been given notice to do so, does not itself bring infringement proceedings within an appropriate period.

7.4 Compulsory licences

(a) Registered design rights

Compulsory licences for registered designs may be granted to any person on the ground that:

- a demand in the state for a product incorporating the design is not being met or is not being met on reasonable terms; or
- a demand in the state for a product incorporating the design is being met by importation other than from a member of the World Trade Organization.

(b) Unregistered design rights

Compulsory licences are not available in respect of unregistered design rights.

Israel

Shlomo Cohen
Dr Shlomo Cohen & Co

1. Summary of design protection

In Israel, the regime for registration and protection of designs has remained relatively unchanged for more than 80 years. It is governed by the Patents and Designs Ordinance 1925, which is based on the UK Patents and Designs Act 1919, and several amendments have been made over the years.[1]

Under the ordinance, designs are protected by registration. Registration is governed by the Registered Design Regulations 1925. Some protection for unregistered designs has been offered in the courts under the laws of unjust enrichment and unfair competition. A distinctive two- or three-dimensional design may also be protected by trademark or by passing off.[2]

The ordinance defines a design as:

The features of shape, configuration, pattern or ornament applied to any article by any industrial process or means; whether manual, mechanical or chemical, separate or combined, which in the finished article appeals to and is judged by the eye, but does not include any mode or principle of construction or anything which is in substance a mere mechanical device.[3]

An 'article' is: "any manufactured article, or any substance, artificial or natural, or partly artificial and partly natural".[4]

A registered design grants the exclusive right to use the design for every article listed or included in the registration for five years. The protection may be extended for up to 15 years.[5]

In spite of efforts to modernise the design protection regime, no results have yet been achieved. The most recent blueprint was published in 1998. Its main aims were to broaden the definition of a design, including functional and ornamental designs; to align Israel with international treaties; and to expand the definition of novelty. The blueprint also proposed granting a limited protection to unregistered designs for a term of five years, on condition that the designs were registrable.

---

1 Patents and Designs Ordinance 1925. First amendment on January 18 1951; second amendment on June 12 1952; third amendment on January 4 1961; fourth amendment on August 17 1967; fifth amendment on December 30 1999; sixth amendment on November 23 2000; seventh amendment on June 13 2002; eighth amendment on November 25 2007; ninth amendment on June 16 2008.

2 Possibly only upon acquired secondary meaning: see CA 733/95 *Arpel Aluminum v Kalil Industries* (1997) IsrSC 51(3) 577, 590, 612.

3 Patents and Designs Ordinance, Section 2.

4 *Ibid*, Section 2.

5 *Ibid*, Section 33.

2. Registered design rights

Under the Patents and Designs Ordinance, a design must be registered in order to be protected. The criteria for protection are that the design must be novel or original and not have been published or used publicly in Israel prior to the application date.[6]

The design may be two-or three-dimensional,[7] and must appeal to the eye of a consumer.[8] Any mode or principle of construction or operation, or anything which is solely a mechanical device, will not qualify as a registered design.[9] Designs that are purely functional (ie, designs that are dictated by the function they are intended to perform) are not registrable, although they may be registered as patents.[10]

This topic is discussed further in section 4 below.

2.1 Registration procedure

(a) The registry

The owner of a design is the "author of a new and original design",[11] who must apply to the Division of Design at the Patent Office to register the design. The application is closed to the public for two years,[12] during which time only the owner of the design, or a person appointed by it in writing, has the right to inspect the design.[13] After the two-year protection period, designs are made available the public.[14]

If an application for registration is denied by the registrar because the design is identical to a previously registered design, the applicant may inspect the pre-existing registered design.[15]

The registrar will refuse to register a design if it finds it to be contrary to law, morality or public order.[16] The decision may be appealed before a district court.[17]

Registration of a design creates a presumption of validity.[18]

(b) Application for registration

The application for registration must include a clear description of the design, including the products for which it is intended and the materials it is made of,[19] and provide photographs or diagrams of the design – from different angles[20] if the design is three-dimensional. A short statement explaining the originality of the design may be attached to each sketch.[21] Failure to describe the original features of the design may pose a risk to the registration process and undermine the validity of the design.[22]

---

6 *Ibid*, Section 30.
7 CA 11487/03 *August Strock KG v Alfa Intuit* (2008) (unpublished).
8 CA 3406/96 *Sela v Akerstein* (1999) (unpublished), 2.
9 Patents and Designs Ordinance, Section 2.
10 CA 430/67 *Sharnoa Ltd v Tnuva* (1968) IsrSC 22(1) 113, 116.
11 *Ibid*, Section 2.
12 Designs Regulations, Section 58.
13 Patents and Designs Ordinance, Section 35.
14 *Ibid*, Section 35(2).
15 *Ibid*, Section 35(1).
16 *Ibid*, Section 30.
17 *Ibid*, Section 44.
18 *Ibid*, Section 3(5).
19 Designs Regulations, Section 16.
20 *Ibid*, Section 16.
21 *Ibid*, Section 17.

(c) ***Registration fee***

An application must be accompanied by a registration fee, as specified in the Designs Regulations 1925.[23]

2.2 Scope of protection

Registration of a design grants exclusive right to the design, for any article made by any industrial process or means, whether manual, mechanical or chemical, separate or combined. The right is limited to the products specified in the registration.[24]

Exclusive right in the design includes the right to:

- use the design for specified goods;
- import goods of the design;
- sell or rent out goods of the design; and
- make kits and components to produce goods of that design.[25]

2.3 Term of protection

A registered design is valid for five years from the date of filing.[26] The registration may be renewed for two consecutive five-year periods, giving a maximum protection of 15 years.[27]

Application for renewal must be submitted before or within six months of the end of the first five-year period.[28]

2.4 Priority date

Israel has been a member of the Paris Convention for the Protection of Industrial Property since March 24 1950. Applications filed in any state that is a member of the Paris Convention or the World Trade Organization may claim priority on applications filed in Israel if the design is essentially similar.[29]

The filing date of the first application will be the Israeli filing date for the purpose of preserving novelty.[30] The Israeli application must be filed within six months of filing the parallel application in the other state.[31]

2.5 Designs executed on behalf of third parties

If "the author of a design, for good consideration, executes the work for some other person, this person is deemed to be the proprietor of the design". Thus, where a design is created by an employee in the course of his employment, the employer will be the rights holder.[32]

---

22 CC (Tel-Aviv) 100619 *A Golan Communication v Cohen Isaac* (2005) (unpublished), 14.
23 Designs Regulations, Section 3.
24 Patents and Designs Ordinance, Section 2.
25 *Ibid*, Section 33 and CA 7125/98 *Mifromel v Kalil* (2001) IsrSC 57(3) 702, 710.
26 Patents and Designs Ordinance, Section 33(1).
27 *Ibid*, Section 33(2) and (3).
28 *Ibid*, Section 33(4).
29 *Ibid*, Section 52.
30 Request for cancellation of a registered design 38326, *Promociones Premier International, SA v Pepsico Inc* (February 7 2005) (unpublished).
31 Patents and Designs Ordinance, Section 52.
32 *Ibid*, Section 30.

2.6 Assignment of design rights

Rights in a registered design can be assigned.[33] Rights can only be assigned fully, not partially.[34] If the assignment of rights in a design is not recorded, a court will not admit any evidence regarding claims of rights over a design. However, a judge may decide to admit such evidence if he deems it fit to do so.[35]

2.7 Licensing

A right to a registered design may be licensed, exclusively or non-exclusively. A licence agreement must be in writing in order to be registered.[36]

When a licence to use a registered design is granted, a note of the licence is included in the design's registration.[37]

The licensee, as well as the rights owner, may seek injunctions if the right to the design is infringed.[38]

Licensing and exploitation are discussed further in section 7 below.

2.8 Compulsory licensing

A specially appointed minister may grant a government department or organisation the right to use a registered design on the grounds of national security or for providing essential goods and services.[39] A special committee will be set up to determine royalties.[40]

The government may, by written contract, grant the right to use the design to any person or entity.[41]

2.9 Cancellation of registration

A registered design may be cancelled on the ground that the design was published or used publicly in Israel before the registration date.[42]

A third party may petition for cancellation of a registered design at any time after registration of the design.[43] The petition for cancellation is subject to an appeal with the district court.[44]

The Supreme Court has ruled that, while not specifically mentioned in the Patents and Designs Ordinance, a district court has the authority to order the cancellation of a registration on the ground that the design does not meet the criteria for registration set out in the ordinance or that the design was registered by a person not entitled to register it.[45]

---

33 *Ibid*, Section 43.
34 *Ibid*, Section 43(2).
35 *Ibid*, Section 43(3).
36 *Ibid*, Section 37(1).
37 *Ibid*, Section 3(3).
38 *Ibid*, Section 37.
39 *Ibid*, Section 39A.
40 Patents Law 1967, Section 106.
41 Patents and Designs Ordinance, Section 39A(b).
42 *Ibid*, Section 36.
43 *Ibid*, Section 36.
44 *Ibid*, Section 44.
45 CA 733/95 *Arpel Aluminum v Kalil Industries* (1997) IsrSC 51(3) 577.

3. Unregistered design rights

Unregistered designs are not protectable under the Patents and Designs Ordinance. However, several court rulings have granted the owner of an unregistered design permission to seek compensation for loss of profit caused by imitation of the design.[46]

Courts have granted the owners of unregistered designs permission to seek compensation under the Unjust Enrichment Law 1979.[47] The proprietor must prove three elements:

- enrichment – whether the beneficiary received any property, service or other benefit;
- whether the enrichment came at the expense of the proprietor; and
- whether the enrichment was unlawful.[48]

The Supreme Court has considered the question of violations of patents that are pending registration. It ruled that under the Unjust Enrichment Law no compensation will be granted for violations of a patent pending registration.[49] It is not yet clear whether the decision is applicable to design law, as the court based its decision on consideration of the balance between multiple and complex interests inherent in patent law.[50]

A design that is registrable under the ordinance will not be eligible for copyright protection, unless no industrial use is to be made of it.[51] When a product is eligible for both copyright and design protection, the court examines whether the ornamental component can be isolated from the article itself.[52]

Imitation of a design may be unfair competition or passing off under the Commercial Torts Law 1979. To succeed in a passing-off action, the owner of the design must prove that it has built a reputation in the design, and that the action of the defendant is likely to cause public confusion regarding the manufacturer of the product. There is no need to prove actual public confusion. The design does not have to include the proprietor's name in order to prove loss of reputation caused by the defendant.[53]

4. Qualification for protection

A design is protected only through registration. It must meet the criteria set out in this section to obtain registration under the Patents and Designs Ordinance.

4.1 Appeal to the eye

A registered design refers to the features of shape, configuration, pattern or ornamentation of an article that appeal to the eye.[54] The design must be visible in the finished article for which it is intended.[55]

---

46 LCA 5768/94 *ASIR v NG Forum* (1998) IsrSC 52(4) 289, 364.
47 *Ibid*, at 497.
48 *Ibid*, at 363.
49 LCA 6025/05 *Merck & Co Inc v Teva Pharmaceutical Industries Ltd* (2011) (unpublished), 22.
50 *Ibid*, at 22.
51 Copyright Law 2007, Section 7.
52 CA 360/83 *Stroski Ltd v Vitman Ice Cream* (1985) IsrSC 40(3) 340, 342 to 343.
53 CC (Tel-Aviv) 100619 *A Golan Communication v Cohen Isaac* (2005) (unpublished), 22.
54 CA 3406/96 *Sela v Akerstein* (1999) (unpublished), 2.
55 CA 7125/98 *Mifromel v Kalil* (2001) IsrSC 57(3) 702, 718.

The shape of the article should appeal to the eye of the relevant consumer so as to influence his choice. A 'relevant' consumer is an average consumer for whom the article is intended; in some cases, the relevant consumer is a professional who uses the article regularly.[56] The reasonable relevant consumer should be able to distinguish between the design's article and other articles of its kind. Likelihood of confusion is an indication of lack of appeal to the eye.[57]

4.2 Not merely functional

The ordinance states that: "any mode or principle of construction or operation, or anything which is in substance a mere mechanical device, does not qualify to be a registered design".[58]

Purely functional designs, or features of a design which are solely the result of functional requirements, are not protectable. If an ornament cannot be separated from its function or utility, the design is not registrable.[59] 'Functionality' has also been interpreted more narrowly. In one case, the Supreme Court ruled that when all of the features of a design are dictated by the function they are intended to perform, thus making the design entirely functional, the design is not registrable.[60]

Letters and words arranged in a certain way on paper, which do not comprise a three-dimensional shape or figure and are not attached to any other decorative element, do not qualify for registered design protection.[61] Words and letters must be removed from the sketches of a design submitted with its application. An inscription that is an integral part of the design may be registered, subject to a waiver of exclusive right of use of the inscription.[62]

4.3 Two- or three-dimensional articles

Two- and three-dimensional designs are registrable. The definition of a design does not exclude the registration of a two-dimensional design provided it contains decorative elements.[63]

4.4 Novelty or originality

A design can be registered if it is novel or original or has not been used publicly or published in Israel.[64] Novelty means that the shape of the article is new. Originality refers to the application of an old and known shape to a new article. Changes in the article cannot be trivial.[65]

A design is compared with earlier art featured in designs already published or used in Israel to determine novelty. Any publication or use of a design in Israel before the filing date will result in the rejection of an application.[66]

---

56 *Ibid*, at 711.
57 *Ibid*, at 712 to 714.
58 Patents and Designs Ordinance, Section 2.
59 CA 430/67 *Sharnoa Ltd v Tnuva* (1968) IsrSC 22(1) 113, 116.
60 *Ibid*, at 117.
61 CC (Tel-Aviv) 2377/98 *Israeli Center of Discs v Ya'il DCS* (2000) (unpublished).
62 Design Regulations, Section 24.
63 CA 11487/03 *August Strock KG v Alfa Intuit* (2008) (unpublished).
64 Patents and Designs Ordinance, Section 30.
65 CC (Tel-Aviv) 1187/94 *Sela v Akerstein* (1996) (unpublished), 3.

5. Infringement

Provided a registered design is valid, it is unlawful to reproduce it, make any use of it, or offer to sell it, or any imitation of it, without authorisation.[67]

The question of whether an article infringes a registered design is judged by visual appearance, as seen by a relevant consumer.[68] The court will then examine the character of the article, noting how the product is put up for sale and the use being made of it.[69] It will consider the overall impression given by the registered and alleged infringing articles in the eye of a relevant consumer.[70] When the articles are similar in their appearance, the court will examine whether there is a likelihood of confusion for the relevant consumer.[71]

A defendant may challenge the validity of a registered design on grounds of novelty or originality.[72]

A new design is one that consists of a shape, configuration, pattern or ornament previously unknown. Originality is when known elements are applied to an article in a new way. In practice, small changes and additions to an article will constitute a new or original design.[73]

6. Design infringement litigation

Claims for infringement of a design are heard in the district courts.[74]

Injunctions are granted at submission of *ex parte* applications, or in the presence of both parties. Injunctions are granted for providing security, or in the matter of costs and losses.

The defendant may challenge the validity of a registered design on grounds of novelty or originality. If the defendant is successful, the court may order the cancellation of the registered design.[75]

7. Licensing and exploitation

A right in a registered design may be licensed, exclusively or non-exclusively. Partial licences are possible for terms of protection, geographic extent, and the purpose or use of a work. A licence agreement must be in writing in order to be registered.[76]

If a design registration has been cancelled, the cancellation will not have a retroactive effect, and royalties already paid will not be restored, unless otherwise agreed between the parties. This does not apply if a design registration was obtained fraudulently.[77]

The licensee, as well as the rights owner, may seek injunctions in cases of

---

66 Patents and Designs Ordinance, Section 36.
67 *Ibid*, Section 37.
68 CA 7125/98 *Mifromel v Kalil* (2001) IsrSC 57(3) 702, 710.
69 *Ibid*, at 711.
70 CA 3406/96 *Sela v Akerstein* (1999) (unpublished), 3.
71 CA 7125/98 *Mifromel v Kalil* (2001) IsrSC 57(3) 702, 713 to 714.
72 CA 733/95 *Arpel Aluminum v Kalil Industries* (1997) IsrSC 51(3) 577, 612.
73 CA 3406/96 *Sela v Akerstein* (1999) (unpublished), 2.
74 Copyright Law, Section 51.
75 CA 733/95 *Arpel Aluminum v Kalil Industries* (1997) IsrSC 51(3) 577, 612.
76 Patents and Designs Ordinance, Section 37(1).
77 CA 427/86 *Blass v Kibuts Hashomer Hatzair 'Dan'* (1989) IsrSC 43(3) 323, 334 to 335.

infringement.[78] The rights owner may seek injunctions on contractual grounds if the licence has been exploited.

78 Patents and Designs Ordinance, Section 37.

Italy

Massimiliano Pappalardo
La Scala

---

1. Summary of design protection

The definition of design includes any appearance of a product that can be seen during its ordinary use. According to Italian law, a 'design' may result from the features of the lines, contours, colours and shape defining a product. It may result also from the texture and materials of the product, as far as such elements are able to change its appearance. A design is constituted by any element capable of affecting the appearance of a product or of a part thereof.

'Product' means any industrial or handicraft item, including component parts intended to be assembled into a complex product, packaging, get-up, graphic symbols and typographic typefaces.

Pursuant to the International Classification for Industrial Designs (the Locarno Classification), designs may be classified in three main categories:

- designs related to the shape of three-dimensional products;
- designs related to building units and construction elements; and
- two-dimensional graphic symbols and logos applied to a product.

Under Italian law, a design may be protected by a set of different intellectual property (IP) rights, characterised by a different acquisition procedure, by a different territorial effectiveness and by a different term.

Access to the different levels of protection will depend on the specific features of the design.

The author is entitled to register the design as a national title or as a title valid and effective within the entire territory of the European Union. Even without registration, under particular circumstances the aesthetic features of a product may be protected as an unregistered design.

These protections may be granted to any design that has an individual character. Following recent legislative changes, it is no longer required that the design is able to confer an outstanding aesthetic value on a specific product in order for it to be protected: an appreciable degree of difference from earlier designs will be sufficient.

An additional and extended protection may be granted solely to those designs that are considered a creative work of the author, provided with an artistic value. In such cases, the industrial design will be treated as an artistic work and, therefore, also covered by copyright law.

Under the legal framework:

- registered national designs are regulated by the Intellectual Property Code

(Law 30/2005) and, in particular, by Articles 31 to 44;
- registered and unregistered Community designs are regulated by Council Regulation 6/2002/EC of December 12 2001 on Community designs; and
- copyright is regulated by the Copyright Act (Law 633/1941).

In the rare cases where the design of a specific product is so unusual that it acquires a distinctive character and is associated with a specific manufacturer by the public, the design can be protected as well as a shape trademark and the slavish copy of it can be prosecuted as an act of unfair competition.

In order to obtain a registered title – a national or Community design – the author must file an application before the competent authorities: for protection in Italy, the Italian Trademark and Patent Office (ITPO); for protection within the European Union, the Office for the Harmonisation in the Internal Market (OHIM).

Protection as an unregistered design may be granted without any formalities, simply by making the design available to the public.

There are no requirements in order to obtain copyright protection. The creation of the intellectual work will be sufficient to acquire the relevant right, although the author will need to be able to prove the paternity and the priority of its creation.

2. Registered design rights

The registration option is primarily used to protect particularly innovative designs or features, and those related to products which might be expected to last on the market for several years. For instance, in the fashion industry, where a design usually lasts only few months, a registered title and the burden related to meeting the requirements for registration are often not the most appropriate means of protecting articles of clothing. Most of the designs registered by fashion houses are not related to apparel, but to accessories such as watches, bags and sunglasses.

A design can be registered as a national or a Community design if it is new and has an individual character. The requirements to obtain protection as a national or a Community registered title are basically the same.

In principle, the protection can also cover accessories and components of a complex product. However, a design for a component part of a complex product used solely for the repair of the complex product so as to restore its original appearance cannot be protected. There has been intense debate within legal circles regarding what is a component part covered by the 'repair' clause and what is an accessory excluded from the scope, particularly in the automotive industry.

A design will be considered new if no identical designs have been made available to the public. The required degree of diversification is quite low. It is sufficient that the design to be registered is not an identical copy of a design already on the market or otherwise disclosed to the public.

In order to assess novelty, a design is compared with any earlier design(s) in the product's specific sector.

A design will be deemed to have been made available to the public if it has been published through registration or exhibited, used in trade or otherwise disclosed, except where these events could not reasonably have become known in the normal course of business to the circles specialised in the sector concerned, operating in the European Union.

A design will not be considered to have been made available to the public if it has been disclosed only to a third party under explicit or implicit conditions of confidentiality.

The design will be considered new if it has been disclosed to the public by its author in the 12 months before the application. This grace period allows the author to test in advance the success of a new design on the market before starting the registration procedure.

A design will not be deemed to have been made available to the public if it has been disclosed by a party other than the author in an abusive manner or if it is likely that – notwithstanding past presentations – the experts in the field are not aware of the design.

In order to be considered to have individual character, the overall impression produced by the design on an informed user should differ from the overall impression produced on the user by any design which has been made available to the public. Thus, the scope of protection granted by a registered design will include any design which does not produce on the informed user a different overall impression.

The comparison between the designs should be carried out taking into consideration the overall appearance of the product, not each single element of identity or diversification.

For the purposes of such a comparison, the reference is represented by the informed user – that is a person that is not an expert in the field (such as a technician), but who is not an average consumer. Under the case law, such a definition makes reference to an user of the product under consideration, but a particular kind of user: a user that has a deep knowledge of the different products available in a specific market and, as a consequence, is much more attentive to the details and able to see differences that an average consumer could not perceive.

In order to obtain legal protection, a design must not rely on features of the appearance of a product which are merely dictated by its technical function. The design may grant exclusive rights to the appearance of a product, but it may not create exclusive rights on the functioning of the product.

Thus, those features are not protectable that have to be reproduced in their exact form and dimensions for the product in which the design is applied to be mechanically connected to another product so that either product may perform its function.

A design cannot be validly registered whenever it is contrary to public policy or to accepted principles of morality.

If the above-mentioned requirements have been met and there are no possible impediments, the shape of a product may be protected within Italian territory under a national registered design or under a Community registered design.

The designer (or the rights holder) must file the relevant application(s) with the competent authority (ITPO and/or OHIM). If a design is developed by an employee in the execution of his duties, the rights to the design vest in the employer, unless otherwise agreed by the parties, and the application must be filed by the employer.

The employee will retain the moral right to be recognised as the author of the design.

The application for a registered design can be filed by a natural person or by a legal entity, either directly or through a patent attorney.

If an application for a national design has been filed with the ITPO, the applicant is entitled to obtain a Community registered design, within six months of the date of the first application, using the national priority. In this case, a cumulative protection, based on the Community and on the national title, can be granted to the rights holder. Any party that has filed an application to obtain a registered design in a member state of an international convention ratified by Italy that grants the right of priority has a right of priority of six months starting from the date of the filing of the first application in accordance with the provisions of the Paris Convention for the Protection of Industrial Property.

The application must specify the class of goods, under the Locarno Classification, where the design's protection is to be granted.

Several designs may be submitted in one application, provided they are related to goods included in the same class of the Locarno Classification. Each of the designs contained in a multiple application or registration may be dealt with separately from the others. In particular each may be enforced and exploited (licensed, assigned etc) separately from the others.

A registered design grants the rights holder the exclusive right to use it and to prevent any third party from using it (making, offering, putting on the market, importing, exporting a product in which the design is incorporated or to which it is applied) without the rights holder's consent.

The protection granted by a registered design lasts for five years from the date of filing the application. The rights holder may renew the protection for one or more periods of five years each, up to a total term of 25 years starting from the date of filing.

The exclusive rights conferred on the rights holder will be exhausted when the goods protected by a registered design have been put on the market by the rights holder, or with its consent, within Italian territory or within the territory of the European Economic Area (EEA).

Thus, once put on the market with the rights holder's authorisation, the goods can circulate throughout the EEA; and the rights holder will be not be entitled to stop the circulation unless a legitimate reason exists.

3. Unregistered design rights

The provisions regulating unregistered Community designs have been set out in order to grant an effective protection to designers that become concerned about protection only after becoming a victim of counterfeiting.

Although fewer formalities are required to obtain an unregistered right, the protection of the design is more limited than that granted to registered titles, as is the duration of the protection.

An unregistered Community design can be obtained, without formality, simply by making the design available to the public. A design is deemed to have been made available to the public within the European Union if it has been published, exhibited, used in trade or otherwise disclosed in such a way that, in the normal course of business, these events could reasonably have become known to the circles specialised in the sector concerned, operating within the European Union.

The protection granted to an unregistered design is basically the same as that granted to a registered design. However, in the absence of the publicity provided by a registration process, enforcement of the unregistered design involves a stricter burden of proof for the rights holder.

An unregistered design confers on the rights holder the right to prevent third parties from exploiting it only if the challenged use results from copying the protected design. The contested use will not be deemed to result from copying the protected design if it results from an independent work of creation by a designer who may be reasonably thought not to be familiar with the design made available to the public by the rights holder.

An unregistered design is protected for only three years, whereas a registered design may be protected for up to 25 years.

3.1 Copyright

Following a change in copyright law implemented on April 19 2001, an industrial design under particular circumstances may also be entitled to copyright protection. Such a protection does not require a registration process or any criteria to be met. The creation of the work is sufficient to give rise to the copyright.

However, copyright is granted only to outstanding industrial designs that can be said to have an artistic value. Therefore, unlike other works (such as books, paintings and sculptures), the creative step is not sufficient to obtain copyright protection.

According to the more recent case law, the assessment of the artistic value should take into consideration whether the product is perceived by the public as a long-lasting icon. This in-depth assessment will be based on objective factors, such as whether the design has been exhibited in art galleries, displayed in museums or mentioned or represented in art books as a piece of contemporary art.

Thus, the scope of copyright protection for industrial designs is much stricter than for other creative works, where copyright is dependent on any assessment of the artistic value of the work.

The exclusive rights to exploit an industrial design protected by copyright last for the life of the author plus 70 years following his death or the death of the last surviving co-author.

There is some debate between the opposing lobbies of the major brands in the furniture market and of the independent art crafts concerning the protection to be granted to industrial designs created before the provision extending copyright to industrial designs was adopted on April 19 2001 that have subsequently been made available to the public after the registration ceases to have effect.

Currently, third parties that manufactured or marketed, within the 12 months before April 2001, products manufactured in conformity with industrial designs at that time available to the public after a registration has expired will not infringe copyright after that date. The provision is limited to products manufactured or purchased before April 19 2001 and (according to a very recent reform of the provision) products manufactured within the following 13 years, and on the condition that such activity remains within the extent of the earlier use, including that of quantity.

4. Qualification for protection

Under certain circumstances, the reproduction of a design may represent an act of unfair competition and be subject to regulation.

However, under Article 2598(1) of the Civil Code the requirements to enforce the unfair competition rules are quite strict. In order to be sanctioned as an act of unfair competition, the copying must have produced confusion in the market concerning the source of a product. Thus, in principle the design must not only have been made available to the public, but an effective awareness of the public about the shape of the product and the distinguishing function of the product must be proved.

Enforcement of the protection should be limited and reserved solely to shapes that have a distinctive character. A shape should be original and arbitrary, such that it may be remembered by the public and associated with a specific manufacturer. Consequently, protection will be granted mainly, although not exclusively, to those manufacturers that have made the shape of their products well known on the market and conferred on them a distinctive character, usually by means of considerable marketing investments.

In practice, the case law indicates that assessment of the distinctive character of a design is not always this strict and protection is often extended to ephemeral shapes provided with a low degree of distinctiveness.

The shape of a product provided with a distinctive character, that does not have a technical function and does not confer to the product a substantial value, may also be protected by a registered or an unregistered shape trademark. Under recent case law, the protection of a shape as a design and as a trademark can be cumulative, not solely alternative.

5. Infringement

The manufacture, importing, marketing and/or promoting of a product the same as a registered design – as well as complementary activities – will constitute infringement of the protected design.

If the exclusive rights of the rights owner are infringed, the infringing party may be penalised under the civil liabilities regime and, in certain circumstances, may be subject to criminal sanctions. Under Article 517*ter* of the Criminal Code, if a party is aware of a registered design, the manufacture or industrial use of infringing products is punishable by up to two years' imprisonment and a fine of up to €20,000.

The same penalties may be applied to an infringer that, in order to gain a profit, imports into or sells in Italian territory infringing goods.

Under Article 473 of the code, the counterfeiting of designs or the use of counterfeited designs may be punished by up to four years' imprisonment and a fine of up to €35,000.

A suspension procedure before the customs authority provides an out-of-court means to prevent the import of suspected infringing products. Under Regulation 1383/2003/EC, a rights holder may apply in writing to the Italian customs department to request its intervention when goods are suspected of infringing the registered design.

The customs office will suspend the goods before they are released for circulation or export or when they are found during checks on goods entering or leaving the Community customs territory. It will allow the applicant to inspect them.

A technical analysis of samples to assess whether the goods do indeed infringe is carried out under the sole responsibility of the rights holder. The rights holder must begin a judicial procedure in order to assess the infringement.

The owner, importer, holder or consignee of the suspended goods will be able to obtain their release if:

- the customs office has been notified that a procedure has been initiated to assess whether an IP right has been infringed under national law;
- the judicial authority has not ordered precautionary measures; and
- all customs formalities have been completed.

6. Design infringement litigation

Under civil remedies, a claim to enforce the IP rights granted to an industrial design must be filed before the competent national judicial authority. In Italy, claims on IP rights are heard by specialised judges in a limited number of tribunals: formerly, the IP Specialised Courts and, according to a very recent reform, the Enterprise Tribunals.

IP rights may be enforced through a civil action on the merits or, subject to grounded reasons of urgency, through an interlocutory proceeding.

The procedure for obtaining an interim remedy is quick and efficient, but the procedure for an action on the merits is more complex and time-consuming. An interlocutory proceeding usually lasts for one or two months, although it may last for up to six months. An action on the merits may last for between two and four years (for the initial proceeding), depending on the complexity of the matter.

6.1 Interim remedies

An interim remedy may be claimed if the plaintiff is able to provide solid evidence of the infringement of its exclusive rights and to demonstrate that the time needed to obtain a final decision on the merits would cause irreparable harm to those rights.

Possible interim remedies include an interlocutory injunction intended to prevent any imminent infringement of the intellectual property rights, the seizure of the goods suspected of infringing the IP rights, and publishing of the decision.

A judge may impose penalty payments in the case of non-compliance with orders or a delay.

If summoning the defendant would jeopardise the effectiveness of the interim remedy, the provisional measures can be taken without the defendant having been heard, on request of the claimant. In this case, the defendant will be informed immediately after the execution of the measures, at the latest.

Interlocutory proceedings, as well as the proceedings on the merits, entitle the claimant to obtain information about the goods involved in the infringement and the extent of the counterfeiting activity.

Upon a grounded and proportionate request by the claimant, it may be ordered that that information on the origin and distribution networks of the goods or services which infringe an IP right be provided by the infringer and any other person who is:

- found in possession of the infringing goods on a commercial scale;
- found to be using the infringing services on a commercial scale;
- found to be providing on a commercial scale services used in infringing activities; or
- indicated by anyone referred to in the above points as being involved in the production, manufacture or distribution of the goods or the provision of the services.

The information will, as appropriate, provide the names and addresses of the manufacturers, distributors, suppliers and other previous holders of the goods or services, as well as the intended wholesalers and retailers, and the quantities produced, manufactured, delivered, received or ordered, and the price obtained for the goods or services in question.

The information must be specifically requested by the claimant and is obtained by judicial examination.

6.2 Final remedies

Should the decision on the merits find an infringement of the exclusive rights of the claimant, the judicial authority may issue against the infringer a final injunction prohibiting the continuation of the illegal activity (manufacturing, marketing or use of the infringing goods) and recalling the infringing goods. The sanctions can be issued also upon any intermediary, summonsed in the civil action and whose services have been exploited in order to infringe the IP rights.

Provision for a penalty payment may be issued with the injunction and the order of recalling, with a view to ensuring compliance.

The court may order the destruction of the infringing goods, with the expenses to be borne by the infringer. Such a measure is limited by a number of exceptions. The destruction cannot be ordered if it would prejudice the national economy. In this case the rights holder may only claim restorative damages.

Should the infringing goods be capable of being altered so that they may be used lawfully, the court may order a temporary recalling instead of ordering the recall or destruction of the goods, with the right to market the goods after adaptation to respect the IP right. The destruction or use of infringing goods cannot be ordered if they are owned by a party solely for personal use.

Alternatively, the goods manufactured, imported or sold in infringement of the IP right and the tools needed to manufacture them may be assigned to the rights holder by the court.

On the application of the rights holder, the court may order an infringer that knowingly engaged in an infringing activity to pay the rights holder damages appropriate to the prejudice suffered as a result of the infringement.

The recovery of damages may include any economic and any non-economic prejudice suffered by the rights holder. The damages may also compensate the moral prejudice caused to the rights holder by the infringement.

In calculating damages, the court takes into account all damage that the injured party has suffered, such as the negative economic consequences, including lost profits, and any unfair profits made by the infringer. The court may, in appropriate cases, set the damages as a lump sum. In this case the lost profits are quantified as a sum not lower than the amount of royalties or fees that would have been due if the infringer had requested authorisation to use the IP right in question.

The rights holder is entitled to ask for the profits obtained by the infringer as an alternative to damages or as far as such profits exceed the damages suffered by the rights holder.

The rights holder is not entitled to apply for punitive or indirect damages.

At the request of the applicant and at the expense of the infringer, the court may order that its decision be published in newspapers, magazines and so on, in full or in part.

The legal costs and other expenses incurred by the successful party are borne by the unsuccessful party, unless there are exceptional circumstances.

6.3 Invalidity action

A national design may be declared invalid if:

- it cannot be registered under the requirements of the law;
- it is contrary to public policy or to accepted principles of morality;
- by virtue of a court decision, the rights holder is not entitled to the design;
- it is in conflict with an earlier design that has been made available to the public after the date of filing of the application or, if priority is claimed, after the date of a priority, but which is protected from a date prior to this date through an earlier Community design, national design or international registration or by an application thereof;
- it constitutes an unauthorised use of a distinctive sign or of a work protected under copyright law; or
- it constitutes an improper use of any of the items listed in Article 6*ter* of the Paris Convention for the Protection of Industrial Property, or of badges, emblems and escutcheons other than those covered by this article and which are of particular public interest in the state.

In principle, the action on the merits aimed at obtaining a declaration of invalidity of a registered design may be filed by any interested party.

If the invalidity action is grounded on the existence of prior rights that represent an impediment to the valid registration of a design, or provided that the registration has been obtained by a subject different from the rights owner, the action should be filed by the rights holder.

The invalidity of a registered design is effective on the rights holder and on any third party once a decision on the merits becomes definitive.

7. Licensing and exploitation

The owner of a design may license to a third party all or a part of its exclusive rights. The licence may be conferred on an exclusive or non-exclusive basis and for a limited period of time or until the exclusive rights expire. The licensee may or may not be authorised by the licensor to enter into sub-licence agreements with third parties.

A licence usually involves the payment of a royalty by the licensee, based on the income of the licensee, and/or of a minimum sum per period.

A licence agreement may be registered before the ITPO, but this is not mandatory. The signatures of the parties must be properly authenticated by a public notary for the licence to be registered.

Without prejudice to any legal proceedings based on the law of contract, the licensor may invoke the exclusive IP rights conferred on the design against a licensee who contravenes any provision of the licence agreement with regard to the duration, the territory, the modalities in which the design may be used and the quality of products manufactured by the licensee.

There is no provision for the compulsory licensing of design-exclusive rights in Italy.

Japan

Takamitsu Shigetomi
Oh-Ebashi LPC & Partners

---

1. Summary of design protection

In Japan, industrial designs may be protected under the acts that govern intellectual property (IP):

- the Design Patent Act;
- the Trademark Act;
- the Copyright Act; and
- the Unfair Competition Prevention Act.

The usual approach is to obtain a design patent under the Design Patent Act. The other acts also provide for protection, depending on the nature of the design.

2. Registered design rights

Designs may enjoy protection under the design patent system or the trademark system.

2.1 Design patents

The best protection for a design is obtained by registering it as a design patent under the Design Patent Act. The system is as follows.

(a) Definition of design

Under Article 2 (1) of the Design Patent Act, 'design' means the shape, patterns or colours of an article, or part of an article, that creates a distinct visual impression. It may be achieved through any combination of these features. Industrial designs generally fall within the definition, and so may be protected under the act.

(b) Qualification

In order to be granted a design patent, an article must meet the requirements of Article 3 of the Design Patent Act. These are industrial applicability, novelty and creativity. In practice, the most important requirements are novelty and creativity.

The Patent Office will refuse an application on the ground that it lacks novelty if the design:

- was publicly known in Japan or another country before the application was filed (Article 3 (1) 1);
- was described in a circulated publication or was made publicly available through an electric telecommunication in Japan or another country before

the application was filed (Article 3 (1) 2); or
- is similar to one prescribed in the above two conditions (Article 3 (1) 3).

Even if a design patent application satisfies the novelty requirement, it will fail the creativity requirement if a person ordinarily skilled in the art of the design could have easily created the design based on the shape, patterns or colours, or any combination thereof, that were publicly known in Japan or another country before the application was filed (Article 3 (2)).

The Supreme Court explained the relationship between Article 3 (1) 3 and Article 3 (2) as follows: "While the similarity under Article 3 (1) 3 should be reviewed and determined from the perspective of general consumers, creativity under Article 3 (2) should be reviewed and determined from the perspective of a person ordinarily skilled in the art of the design."[1]

(c) ***Registration procedure***

Applications to register a design patent are filed with the Patent Office. Currently, most applications are filed online. The Patent Office will examine the application to ensure that all formal requirements are met, and then undertake a substantive examination. The process generally takes between six and seven months.

If the application is approved, a notice of allowance will be sent to the applicant and, after payment of the registration fee, the Patent Office will grant a registered design patent.

If the examiner finds any grounds for rejection, he will send a notice to the applicant setting out the reason(s) for refusal. The applicant may submit evidence to contest the finding and/or amend the application.

If on review the examiner still finds any reason for refusal, he will make a final decision of refusal. The applicant may file an appeal against a final refusal before the board of the Patent Office, which will review the application and make an appeal decision.

The decision of the board of the Patent Office may be appealed to the Intellectual Property High Court.

Over the last ten years, the average number of design patent applications each year has been between 30,000 and 40,000 and an average of between 27,000 and 33,000 design patents have been granted.

(d) ***Term of protection***

A design patent provides protection for 20 years from the date of registration (Article 21 (1) of the Design Patent Act).

(e) ***Infringement***

The rights holder has an exclusive right in the registered design and similar designs (Article 23 of the Design Patent Act). An identical or similar design will constitute an infringement.

---

1 Decision of March 19 1974 (Minshu 28-2-308).

Article 24 (2) provides that an identical or similar design is one that gives the same aesthetic impression to a consumer. The court[2] interprets Article 24 (2) to mean: 'whether or not both the registered design and the accused design are identical or similar enough for trader and/or consumer to be confused in an actual trading market as a result of observation of both designs' essential part which strongly captures traders' and/or consumers' attention'. The 'essential part' of a registered design is the part which:

- is novel in comparison with design(s) that were publicly known or distributed before the application was filed; and
- strongly captures traders' and/or consumers' attention.

The determination is based on the design stated in the design patent application and depicted in the drawing or represented in the photograph, model or specimen attached to the application (Article 24 (1)). Designs which were publicly known or distributed before the application was filed are considered in deciding the scope of design patent right.

(f) *Validity issues*

The validity of a design patent right may be challenged by filing a request for invalidation of the design registration before the Patent Office (Article 48). Any party may file an invalidation request, but only a design inventor, or its successor, may file a request if a design patent application is submitted by a copier that is not the inventor and does not have the authorisation of the inventor (Article 48 (2)). The major grounds for invalidity are lack of novelty and creativity. The Patent Office usually makes a decision within seven months of the request.

The accused infringer may submit an invalidity defence under Article 104 (3) of the Patent Act, which will be applied following Article 41 of the Design Patent Act.

(g) *Injunctive relief*

If design infringement is found, the rights holder is entitled under Article 37 (1) to seek injunctive relief to prevent the infringer from importing, making, selling, offering for sale, and using infringing products.

In addition to injunctive relief, the rights holder may seek remedy through measures necessary for the prevention of infringement under Article 37 (2), such as the disposal of infringing articles and the removal of the facilities used for the infringement.

(h) *Damages*

Design patent infringement is categorised as a tort under Article 709 of the Civil Act. The party committing the tort must compensate for any damage incurred by the injured party. Thus, a rights holder may seek compensation for damages arising out of a design patent infringement. Compensation may be awarded for lost profit and reasonable royalties for the duration of the infringement, and legal fees.

---

2 See the IP High Court Decisions of July 18 2006 (Heisei 18 (Gyo-ke) 10004), July 13 2006 (Heisei 18 (Gyo-ke) 10023) and October 31 2005 (Heisei 17 (Ne) 10079).

Articles 39 (1) and (2) of the Design Patent Act provide for the calculation of lost profit. Under Article 39 (1), the damage is calculated as the total number of infringing products sold multiplied by the profit per product that the rights holder would have made. Under Article 39 (2), the damage is calculated as the amount of profits earned by the infringer (the total number of infringing products sold multiplied by the profit per product earned by the infringer). The rights holder may choose whether Article 39 (1) or (2) is used to calculate the damages. The burden of proof lies with the infringer if the actual amount is less than that calculated under Article 39 (1) and/or (2).

If the rights holder does not sell its products in competition with the infringing products, it may seek compensation corresponding to the amount of reasonable royalty under Article 39 (3). 'Reasonable royalty' is calculated by multiplying the number of infringing products sold by a reasonable royalty rate. The rate is decided by the court, taking various factors into account.

In practice, the court allows about 10% of the total damages awarded to cover legal fees. For example, if lost-profit damages of ¥10 million are awarded, legal costs of ¥1 million are likely to be granted.

2.2 Trademarks

In addition to design patent protection, an industrial design may be protected under the Trademark Act. The trademark law regime is as follows.

(a) Definition of trademark

Under Article 2 (1) of the Trademark Act, the term 'trademark' includes character(s), figure(s), sign(s) or three-dimensional shape(s), or any combination thereof, or any combination thereof with colours. If a design falls into the definition of trademark, it is eligible to be protected under the Trademark Act.

In practice, trademark law protection is sought for:

- a design of characters (eg, characters representing a company name);
- a design of figures (eg, the logo for a corporate identity); and
- three-dimensional products (eg, the figure of Colonel Sanders of Kentucky Fried Chicken).

(b) Qualification of trademarks

A design holder must file a trademark application with the Patent Office to obtain trademark right.

The qualification criteria for a trademark are provided by the Trademark Act. Under Article 3, the mark applied should indicate the source of goods or services (eg, the manufacturer of the goods), and should be the mark by which consumers recognise the goods or services as those of a particular enterprise. The grounds for an unregistrable trademark are set out in Article 4 – for example:

- the mark applied must not be identical or similar to another registered trademark that had been filed before the application filing date, if such a trademark is used in connection with the designated goods or services relating to the registered trademark, or similar goods or services (Article 4 (1) 11);

- the mark applied must not be identical or similar to another trademark which is well known by consumers as indicating the goods or services of another enterprise, if the trademark is used in connection with such goods or services, or similar goods or services (Article 4 (1) 10).

(c) ***Registration procedure***

Trademark applications are filed with the Patent Office, designating the mark and the goods and/or services. The trademark registration procedure is similar to that of the design patent, but there are some differences:

- trademark applications are published in the *Official Gazette* by the Patent Office (Article 12 (2));
- there is an opposition proceeding in which any party can file an opposition to the trademark registration within two months of the date of publication in the *Official Gazette* (Article 43 (2)).

(d) ***Term of protection***

Trademark protection is granted for 10 years from the date of registration (Article 19 (1)). The trademark may be renewed by filing an application for registration of renewal (Article 19 (2)). There is no limit on the total term of protection, which may last indefinitely provided the trademark continues to be used.

(e) ***Infringement***

A trademark rights holder has an exclusive right to use the registered trademark in connection with the designated goods or designated services (Article 25). Use of the trademark in connection with the designated goods or services by a third party without authorisation will constitute an infringement. Acts of infringement are listed in Article 37 – for example, the use of a trademark similar to the registered trademark in connection with the designated goods or services, or the use of the registered trademark or a similar trademark in connection with goods or services similar to the designated goods or designated services, would constitute trademark infringement (Article 37 (1)).

In cases of infringement, the rights holder may seek injunctive relief, measures necessary for the prevention of infringement, and damages.

3. Unregistered design rights

Protection of unregistered designs is available under the copyright regime and under the Unfair Competition Prevention Act.

3.1 Copyright

(a) ***Definition of copyrighted work/qualification for copyright***

Under Article 2 (1) 1 of the Copyright Act, the term 'work', in relation to copyright, means a product in which thoughts or sentiments are expressed in a creative way and which falls within the literary, scientific, artistic or musical domain.

Article 10 provides examples of 'works', including paintings, engravings, sculptures and other artistic works. The term 'artistic works' should include fine art, and so fine art may be protected by copyright.

The legal issue may arise whether applied art, including industrial design, may be also protected as an artistic work under the copyright protection system. Under Article 2 (2), 'artistic work' includes a work of crafts of artistic value, which is one category of applied arts. The main issues are whether and to what extent any applied arts other than works categorised as a work of crafts of artistic value can be protected as artistic works under the Copyright Act. Case law[3] tends to adopt the legal standard that applied art is protected as copyright only when the art itself has a high degree of aesthetic creativity – enough to be the subject matter of aesthetic appreciation. For example, the Hakata doll, a Buddhist altar sculpture and a T-shirt design were found to be protected under the copyright regime, since they had a high degree of aesthetic creativity. However, the courts have refused to grant copyright protection to many applied arts and it must be concluded that copyright protection of industrial designs under the Copyright Act is not easy to obtain.

It is not necessary to file any application in order to seek copyright protection.

(b) *Term of protection*

If a copyrighted applied art is made public, it is protected for 50 years from the date of publication.

(c) *Infringement*

A copyright allows the rights holder the exclusive right to reproduce the design, to transfer its ownership and to exploit a derivative work. Any such action by a third party without the authorisation of the rights holder will constitute an infringement.

The rights holder may seek injunctive relief, any measures necessary for the prevention of further infringement, and damages.

3.2 Protection under the Unfair Competition Prevention Act

Design protection may be available under the Unfair Competition Prevention Act.

(a) *Protection under Article 2 (1) 1*

Under Article 2 (1) 1, the following acts constitute unfair competition: acts of creating confusion with another person's goods or business by using an indication of goods or business (which means a name, trade name, trademark, mark, or container or package of goods used in relation to a person's business, or any other indication of a person's goods or business; the same shall apply hereinafter) that is identical or similar to said person's indication of goods or business that is well-known among consumers or other purchasers, or by assigning, delivering, displaying for the purpose of assignment or delivery, exporting, importing or providing through an electric telecommunication line the goods using such an indication.

---

3 See the Osaka High Court Decision of July 28 2005 (Hanrei-Jiho 1928-116), the Osaka District Court Decision of November 25 2004 (Hanrei-Jiho 1901-106) and the Tokyo District Court Decision of July 11 2003 (Heisei 14 (Wa) 12640).

The purpose of Article 2 (1) 1 is to protect an enterprise's credibility with consumers against a third party's use without authorisation.

In order to seek a protection under Article 2 (1) 1, the rights holder needs to prove that:

- the design falls under the term 'indication of goods or business';
- the design is well known among consumers;
- the defendant's design is identical or similar to the design; and
- there is a confusion between the plaintiff's goods or business and the defendant's goods and business based upon the identity or similarity.

In practice, the holder of a well-known design (eg, a company logo) may seek legal protection of its design under Article 2 (1) 1. The protection lasts for an unlimited time provided the design remains well known among consumers.

(b) *Protection under Article 2 (1) 3*

Under Article 2 (1) 3, the following acts constitute unfair competition: acts of assigning, leasing, displaying for the purpose of assignment or leasing, exporting or importing goods which imitate the configuration (excluding configuration that is indispensable for ensuring the function of said goods) of another person's goods.

The purpose of Article 2 (1) 3 is to protect the configuration of goods, which an enterprise has developed with cost and effort, from a third party's copying without incurring substantive cost and effort.

The configuration does not need to satisfy the novelty and creativity requirements of the Design Patent Act in order to seek protection under Article 2 (1) 3.

However, legal protection under Article 2 (1) 3 lasts only for three years from the date the goods are first sold in Japan (Article 19 (1) 5-I). Thus, protection under Article 2 (1) 3 is most appropriate when the rights holder intends to seek protection for only a relatively short period.

(c) *Remedies for unfair competition*

If a court finds that a defendant's acts constitute unfair competition under Article 2 (1) 1 and/or 2 (1) 3, the plaintiff may seek an injunctive relief to prevent any further such acts by the defendant (Article 3 (1)). As well as injunctive relief, the plaintiff may also require the infringer to take measures to prevent unfair competition, such as the disposal of infringing products and the removal of facilities used under Article 3 (2).

The plaintiff may seek compensation for damages arising out of the unfair competition, comprising lost profit or reasonable royalty, and legal fees (Articles 4 and 5).

4. Design infringement litigation

In Japan, the main legal procedures to remedy infringement are litigation towards permanent or preliminary injunctions, and seizure.

4.1 Infringement litigation seeking permanent injunction

An average of 600 IP litigations are filed each year.

(a) *Jurisdiction*

A rights holder may file a design infringement action before the court where either the defendant's principal place of business is located or the alleged infringing products are manufactured, sold or used (Articles 4 (4) and 5 (9) of the Civil Procedure Act). Alternatively, the action may be filed before the Tokyo district court for cases in eastern Japan (Hokkaido, Tohoku, Kanto and Chubu) or the Osaka district court for cases in western Japan (Kansai, Chugoku, Shikoku, Kyushyu).[4] Since the Tokyo and Osaka district courts have specialised divisions to hear IP-related cases, they are more commonly used.

(b) *Proceeding*

In the IP-specialised divisions of the Tokyo and Osaka district courts, proceedings are generally divided into two phases: a proceeding to decide the issues of infringement and validity, and a proceeding to decide the amount of damages if infringement is found.

Cases are usually decided within one year of filing. A rapid hearing procedure has recently been introduced.

From April 2005, a defendant (accused infringer) has been permitted to submit an invalidity defence under Article 104 (3) of the Patent Act, which will be applied following Article 41 of the Design Patent Act. Previously, a defendant had to file a request for invalidation trial with the Patent Office. The Supreme Court has changed its case law and the court may now decide the validity issue in infringement litigation.[5] This change was introduced to provide a single track for IP dispute resolution (ie, infringement litigation) and to prevent a rights holder from enforcing its rights when there is a ground for invalidation by the Patent Office. As a result, the defendant now usually raises the invalidity defence in infringement proceedings. The court may only dismiss the rights holder's claim if it finds that there are grounds for invalidation – that is, the court is still unable to invalidate a right; only the Patent Office has this power.

4.2 Infringement litigation seeking preliminary injunction

A rights holder may file a motion for preliminary injunction before the court in order to seek injunctive relief as soon as possible.

In a preliminary injunction hearing:

- the only remedy available is injunctive relief – remedy for damages is not available;
- the rights holder files a separate action to obtain formal injunctive relief; and
- the rights holder must prove the need for a preliminary injunction (ie, it must show that it would incur irreparable harm without a preliminary injunction).

The court will review the issues of infringement and validity before granting injunctive relief. It will allow the defendant time to investigate the evidence (ie,

---

4 Article 6 (2) of the Civil Procedure Act.
5 Decision of April 11 2000 (Minsyu 54-4-1368).

design(s) which were publicly known or distributed before the filing of the patent application) and prepare an invalidity defence. Thus, it generally takes several months for the case to be decided and it is difficult for a rights holder to obtain rapid injunctive relief.

4.3 Custom seizures

If the infringing products are imported into Japan, the most effective action available is to file a motion for customs seizure with the Customs Office. Under the Customs Act, the holder of design patent, trademark or copyright may file a motion for customs seizure to prevent the import of infringing products.

A rights holder needs to prove that:

- it holds the relevant IP right (design patent, trademark or copyright);
- the IP right is valid; and
- the accused's products infringe that right.

A rights holder must provide the Customs Office with enough information to identify the infringing product during the customs clearance procedure. The office may be consulted during the preparation of necessary documentation.

If a request for customs seizure is granted, it will be effective throughout Japan. The office will start a so-called 'identification of infringing products proceeding' if it identifies any suspected infringing products during customs clearance. The rights holder will be informed and asked to investigate the products and submit a legal opinion on the issue of infringement for review by the office. If infringement is found, the products will be seized and disposed of.

5. Licensing and exploitation

A rights holder may exploit its design through a licensing arrangement.

The Design Patent Act provides for two types of licence: the exclusive licence and the non-exclusive licence.

Under Article 27 (1), a rights holder may grant an exclusive licence on the design right. If an exclusive licence is granted, the licensee has an exclusive right on the registered design and similar designs. Even the rights holder (licensor) may not use the design without the authorisation of the exclusive licensee (Article 23). An exclusive licence is effective only if it is registered with the Patent Office under Article 98 (2) of the Patent Act, which will be applied following Article 36 of the Design Patent Act.

Under Article 28 (1), a rights holder may grant a non-exclusive licence on the design right. The parties may choose and agree whether or not the rights holder may grant a further non-exclusive licence to a third party other than the licensee. A design rights holder may use the licensed design even after granting a non-exclusive licence. A non-exclusive licence does not need to be registered with the Patent Office in order to be effective.

The rights conferred by a non-exclusive licence are effective against not only the rights holder but also its successor, under the Patent Act, which applies following Article 36 of the Design Patent Act. This provision came into effect on April 1 2012.

Netherlands

Marc de Kemp
Wolter Wefers Bettink
Houthoff Buruma

1. Summary of design protection

Design rights protection in the Netherlands is regulated by a treaty that also applies to Belgium and Luxembourg. Under the treaty, a design is protected if it has been registered in the Benelux nations (ie, Belgium, the Netherlands and Luxembourg). Community designs and unregistered designs are protected in accordance with the applicable European regulations and directives. Dutch copyright law provides protection to a design which meets the originality threshold. The manufacturer of products that are an imitation of another's design may face legal action on slavish imitation, a form of tort.

Until 1975, industrial designs were not protected as such in the Netherlands. Although the Netherlands was a party to the Hague Agreement Concerning the International Registration of Industrial Designs 1925[1] (the Hague Agreement), it did not introduce specific legislation to protect industrial designs. Successive Dutch governments felt that the Hague Agreement did not provide for adequate protection in addition to the existing copyright protection. For instance, it did not require publication of applications for designs in a regularly published magazine, so that companies had no way of knowing of designs for which protection was sought. It was felt that this would unnecessarily hamper trade and create legal uncertainty.

However, some protection was available. Under the Copyright Act[2] the appearance of a product could be protected if it met the originality threshold for protected works; and the slavish imitation of designs was unlawful under the Civil Code.[3]

On January 1 1975 the Uniform Benelux Act on Designs and Models[4] (the Uniform Act) entered into force. The act was an annex to the 1966 Benelux Treaty on Designs and Models.[5] This treaty governed protection of design rights in Belgium, Luxembourg and the Netherlands.

The Uniform Act was amended several times and finally replaced by the Benelux Treaty on Intellectual Property Rights (the Benelux Treaty),[6] which entered into force on September 1 2006. The treaty concerns the protection of designs and trademarks

1 Bulletin of Acts and Decrees 1928, 196.
2 Act of September 23 1912, Bulletin of Acts and Decrees 1912, 308.
3 Bulletin of Acts and Decrees 1991, 600.
4 Bulletin of Acts and Decrees 1966, 292.
5 Bulletin of Acts and Decrees 1974, 66.
6 Bulletin of Acts and Decrees 2005, 96.

in the Benelux region. The material rules of the Uniform Act have not been changed by the treaty.

The Benelux Treaty also implements Directive 98/71/EC of the European Parliament and the Council of October 13 1998 on the legal protection of designs[7] (the Design Directive) and, to the extent necessary, Council Regulation 6/2002/EC of December 12 2001 on Community designs[8] (the Regulation on Community designs), which entered into force on March 6 2002. The designs regulation introduces the Community design right, which applies across the European Union and may be obtained with a single registration. The majority of the material rules in the regulation are the same as the rules laid down in the Design Directive. The system of protection of Community designs complements the system of protection provided by the Benelux Treaty.

The Hague Agreement entered into force in the Netherlands on August 1 1984 as a result of the Geneva Act of the Hague Agreement concerning the international registration of industrial designs.[9] Based on the Hague Agreement, Dutch persons and entities are entitled to file an international application for the protection of a design. If and when the Benelux region is designated as an area where protection is required (and if all relevant requirements are met), international designs will be protected in the Netherlands according to the rules and regulations of the Benelux Treaty.

2. Registered design rights

2.1 Nature of rights and qualification

Designs may be registered with the Benelux Office for Intellectual Property in The Hague. The office also has national offices in Belgium and Luxembourg. As of September 1 2011, some 16,000 designs were registered with the office.[10]

A 'design' is defined by the Benelux Treaty as the appearance of the whole or the part of a product resulting from the features of, in particular, the lines, contours, shape, texture and/or materials of the product itself and/or its ornamentation. A product is defined as any industrial or handicraft item, including parts intended to be assembled into a complex product, packaging, get-up, graphic symbols and typographic typefaces. The definitions are in line with Article 1 of the Design Directive.

Following the Software Directive,[11] computer programs are not protectable, but their look and feel may be protected by copyright. It may be argued that separate icons used in the graphical user interface of a computer program can be protected as a graphic design, since such protection does not interfere with the Software Directive.

A design can be two- or three-dimensional. An example of a two-dimensional design is the pattern on an item of clothing.[12] Until the implementation of the

---

7 Pb L289/28.
8 PbEG 2002, L31.
9 Bulletin of Acts and Decrees 1976, 32.
10 Source: Benelux Office for Intellectual Property, brochure "Protecting designs in the Benelux region".
11 Council Directive 91/250/EEC of May 14 1991 on the legal protection of computer programs.
12 In the official languages of the office, two-dimensional forms are called drawings and three-dimensional forms are called designs.

Design Directive in the Dutch legislation on December 1 2003, the Uniform Act required that a design must have a utility function in order to be granted design rights protection. Since then, products with a decorative function only may also be registered for protection. As a consequence of this strict utility-function requirement, design right protection had been limited to a product with a single function. A product with the same design but a different function was considered to be a different design, and could be registered by a third party. For example, a registered design used on towels could not form the basis of an action against wallpaper decorated with the same design, since the two have different utility functions. The Benelux Treaty now offers protection to the appearance of several products which have a different utility function but are based on the same design.

2.2 Registration procedure

Designs can be registered by natural persons, companies and organisations. A design may also be registered in the name of more than one person and/or entity.

The procedure for registering a design right in the Benelux nations is straightforward. An application form is available on the registry office's website[13] to print out, complete and send to the office by regular post. A Benelux application may be for a single design (single filing) or include several designs (multiple filing).

If the requirements of the implementing regulations of the office are met, it will set the filing date as the date the application was received. The applicant will be informed in writing of the filing date or the grounds for rejection if the application is not successful. The office may allow the applicant to correct its application, for example by filing new or additional documents. The office will not register an application that does not provide sufficient detail of the characteristics of the design.

The filing date determines the ranking order of design right applications and, if the application is accepted, the starting date of the term of protection. Unlike Benelux trademarks, which are also regulated in the Benelux Treaty, there is no opposition procedure for third parties to object to a design application, for example on the basis that it is identical to an older registered design. However, a rights holder may demand nullification of a registered design on that ground.

The office does not judge whether a design meets the requirements of novelty and individual character, but it does examine whether the design is contrary to morality or public policy in any of the Benelux countries.

The office will publish the registration of a Benelux design as soon as it has established that all the relevant application requirements are met. Applicants may ask the office to postpone publication for a not more than 12 months from the filing date or the priority date. The delay allows the applicant to ensure that the design remains unknown to the public while it prepares for the manufacture and launch of the product.

Once the design is registered, it may be invoked in legal action against infringing products, as discussed more in detail below.

13 www.boip.int.

3. Unregistered design rights

Unregistered designs are not protected by the Benelux Treaty. However, unregistered Community design rights are protected in the Netherlands under the Regulation on Community designs. Article 11(1) of the regulation provides that an unregistered design which meets the requirements under Article 1[14] may be protected as an unregistered Community design for three years from the date on which the design was first made available to the public within the European Union. This is the date on which it was published, exhibited, used in trade or otherwise disclosed in the European Union in such a way that, in the normal course of business, these events could reasonably have become known to the circles specialised in the relevant sector operating within the European Union. However, the design will not be deemed to have been made available to the public for the sole reason that it has been disclosed to a third person under conditions of confidentiality.

3.1 Copyright protection of designs

As set out above, designs may also be protected under the Copyright Act. This also applies to designs which do not meet all legal requirements and so cannot be considered a design within the meaning of the Benelux Treaty. Protection under both the Copyright Act and the treaty is possible if and when the requirements of both the Copyright Act and the treaty are met.

Article 1 of the Copyright Act defines copyright as "the exclusive right of the author of a literary, scientific or artistic work or his successors in title to communicate that work to the public and to reproduce it, subject to the limitations laid down by law". Article 10 of the act provides a non-exhaustive list of works eligible for copyright protection. Article 10, paragraph 1 at list item 11 specifically mentions "works of applied art and industrial designs and models". A wide range of products falls within this definition, such as bicycles, shoes, chairs, water drains, clothing, lamps, mobile phones and tablet PCs.

The basic rule of Dutch copyright law is that ideas are not protectable but the specific expression of an idea is. The threshold for copyright protection is relatively low. In the *Screenoprints* decision,[15] the Supreme Court decided that in order to be protected by copyright, a work should have its own, original character and show the personal choices of the author. The usual question to determine whether a work has its own character is whether it is reasonably possible that two authors have created the same work independently from one another.

In making this assessment a distinction should be made between the subjective and objective characteristics of a work. Existing material (facts, style, usual form) is not protected, but subjective elements (determined by the author's taste, preference or habit) usually are. However, copyright will only be infringed if the subjective aspects have replicated and have the same character, in themselves or in combination.

The Supreme Court elaborated on the notion of the personal choices of the

14 See, amongst others, Article 5(1) regarding novelty and Article 6(1) regarding individual character.

15 Dutch Supreme Court, November 29 1985, NJ 1987/880 (*Screenoprints/Citroën*).

author in its *Van Dale/Romme* decision.[16] The work should be the result of human creation and the personal choices should be apparent from the work itself, not from circumstances outside of the work.

The court clarified these requirements in its *Endstra* decision.[17] For a work to attract copyright protection, two criteria must be distinguished: a work must possess its own original character and bear the personal stamp of its author. According to the court the first requirement implies "that its form is not copied from another work". The second requirement means "that there must be a form that is the result of human creativity and of creative choices, and thus is a product of the human mind. This excludes, in any case, all forms that are so banal or trivial as to not demonstrate any creative labour whatsoever". The court said that this feature (personal stamp) should be "cognizable from the product itself". Copyright law does not require: "that the author consciously creates a work and makes deliberate creative choices, because this would burden parties with insurmountable problems of evidence".[18]

These requirements apply one-on-one to works of applied art and industrial designs. Some judgments of the Supreme Court[19] state that the eligibility of an industrial design for copyright protection may be determined by the way in which the technical aspects determine its appearance. If a design is (primarily) shaped in a specific way to obtain certain technical effects, limiting the creative choices of the author, it may be excluded from copyright protection – copyright will not be granted to designs which are (predominantly) created to obtain a technical effect.

In the *Una voce particolare* case, concerning an alleged copyright infringement in a TV format,[20] the Supreme Court ruled that in determining whether a product infringes the copyright in another product, the assessment should be based on whether the allegedly infringing product contains copyrightable elements of the original product to such an extent that the overall impression of the two products differs too little to consider the allegedly infringing product to be an independent work.

3.2 Slavish imitation

The rights holder may take legal action against an alleged infringer on the basis of the general tort provision in the Civil Code (Article 162 of Book 6).

As a rule, in commerce a party is allowed to profit from the achievements of others, even if the party thereby competes with them and creates a disadvantage for them.[21] Therefore, imitating a product is in itself not unlawful unless it constitutes design right or copyright infringement. In the case of an imitation of a product, a tort can only be based on facts which in themselves (ie, apart from the alleged design right or copyright infringement) can be considered unlawful. For instance, if a

---

16 Dutch Supreme Court, January 4 1991, NJ 1991/608 (*Van Dale/Romme*).
17 Dutch Supreme Court, May 30 2008, NJ 2008/556 (*Endstra*).
18 From: P Bernt Hugenholtz, "Chronicle of the Netherlands Dutch copyright law, 2001-2010", published at www.ivir.nl.
19 Dutch Supreme Court, January 29 2010, RVDW 2010/223 (*Gavita*) and Dutch Supreme Court, June 16 2006, NJ 2006/585 (*Kecofa/Lancome*).
20 Dutch Supreme Court, November 29 2002, NJ 2003/17 (*Una voce particolare*).
21 Dutch Supreme Court, June 23 1961, NJ 1961/423 (*Bolhoeve*).

manufacturer of a certain product deliberately and without need causes confusion among the public by imitating non-copyrightable elements of the (alleged) original product, this may constitute an unlawful act.[22] The imitator has an obligation to do all that is reasonably possible and necessary to prevent the likelihood of confusion arising because the appearance of its product is similar to the original product. The imitator must change the similar appearance of its product if this is possible without interfering with its reliability and usefulness. The public preference for standardisation of products is an element which needs to be taken into consideration when judging whether an imitation is a slavish imitation of the original product.[23] If the imitating product resembles the original on standardisation elements, it is less likely that it will be considered to be unlawful.

4. Qualification for protection

4.1 Registration requirements

Article 3.1 of the Benelux Treaty stipulates that a design will be granted protection only insofar as it is novel and has individual character. Article 3.3 of the treaty further elaborates on these requirements.

A design will be regarded as novel if, on the filing date (or the priority date, if the priority of an earlier registration is invoked), no identical design has been disclosed to the public. Designs are considered to be identical when their characteristics differ only in insignificant details. A design is regarded as disclosed to the public if before the filing date or priority date a similar design was made publicly available. This applies if the design was shown in a publication such as a magazine or on the internet, in an exhibition or in any other medium or location open to the public. Under the Uniform Act, the novelty requirement had a time limit of 50 years before registration of the design. The time limit was dropped in the Benelux Treaty: each and every design that has ever been disclosed to the public will harm the novelty of a design.

A design will have individual character if its overall impression on the informed user differs from that of all other designs disclosed to the public before the filing or priority date. The informed user is not an expert, but has more knowledge than the average user. He is deemed to have some knowledge of the relevant market and to be able to detect differences between two designs which the average user would not detect. It is possible that the informed user recognises individual character where the average user would not. The creator's degree of freedom in preparing the design is taken into account during the evaluation.

If and when the characteristics of the appearance of a product are exclusively imposed by its technical function, the design will not be granted design rights protection.[24] In general it is assumed that a technical function exists if and when the

---

22 Dutch Supreme Court, June 26 1953, NJ 1954/90 (*Hyster Krane*).

23 See also Dutch Supreme Court, January 8 1960, NJ 1960/415 (*Scrabble*), Dutch Supreme Court, June 12 1970, NJ 1970/434 (*Klerenhanger*), Dutch Supreme Court, May 31 1991, NJ 1992/391 (*Borsumij/Stenman*), Dutch Supreme Court, June 7 1991, NJ 1992/392 (*Rummikub*) and Dutch Supreme Court, April 2 2004, NJ 2004/388 (*Caravanvoortenten*).

24 Article 3.2, paragraph 1 under part a of the treaty.

specific appearance of a product makes it better qualified for its function.[25]

Article 7 of the Design Directive left it to member states whether to protect component parts of complex products, such as spare parts for cars. The Benelux Treaty excludes from protection the appearance of components which must necessarily be reproduced in their exact form and dimensions to be connected with and form a part of the product in which the design is incorporated. The exclusion of these connection pieces or coupling units encourages the standardisation of such products, which is beneficial for consumers: they are not forced to buy spare parts from the original manufacturer as other manufacturers may market an identical part; and the competition may result in a lower price.

4.2 Term of protection and rights granted

The registration of a design is valid for five years, and it may be renewed up to four times, providing protection for up to 25 years. The registry office sends a notice of the expiry date to the rights holder six months before a five-year period expires and, if applicable, informs it of the possibility to renew the registration for another five years.

The scope of protection is determined by Article 3.16 of the Benelux Treaty. The exclusive right in a design allows the rights holder to challenge the use of a product in which the design is incorporated or to which the design is applied, if the product has an identical appearance to the design as filed, or does not produce a different overall impression on an informed user, having regard to the creator's degree of freedom in preparing the design. The use includes in particular the making, offering, putting on the market, importing, exporting or using of a product or stocking the product for any of those purposes.

When deciding whether a certain product produces a different overall impression on an informed user, the courts must compare the design as it is registered with the office with the actual appearance of the product of the alleged infringer. None of the Design Directive, the Regulation on Community designs or the Benelux Treaty provides guidance on how to assess the overall impression, which has resulted in different approaches by the courts. The Supreme Court has ruled that the same overall impression is created if and when the alleged infringing product "only shows minor differences" from the protected design. 'Minor differences' are present if, when looking at both products, "there is a likelihood of confusion on the part of the public".[26] It may be questioned whether this criterion of likelihood of confusion, which appears to have been derived from trademark law, is entirely correct. It would appear to broaden the protection since it does not require evidence of actual confusion, leaving it to the court to determine in an abstract manner whether there is a likelihood of confusion.

---

25 See, for example, Court of Appeal Hertogenbosch, November 4 2003, *Intellectual Property Supplement* (BIE) 2004/267 (*Synergis/Geba*), Court of Appeal Arnhem, August 17 2004, *Intellectual Property Supplement* (BIE) 2005/263 (*Foodcontainers*) and President of The Hague District Court, April 26 2011, published at www.iept.nl, 2011/0426.

26 Hoge Raad, December 29 1995, NJ 1996, 546 (*Decaux/Mediamax*).

4.3 Validity issues

The exclusive right in a design may end in two ways: because the right is nullified or because the right lapses. Nullification has retroactive effect (the design right never existed), whereas when the right has lapsed the right no longer exists.

Since the office checks only whether a design is contrary to morality or public policy in one of the Benelux countries when it receives an application and does not assess the validity in relation to other designs, it is possible for a design that does not meet the legal requirements to be registered. The Benelux Treaty provides a right for interested parties (including the public prosecutor) to invoke the nullity of such designs after their registration. Article 3.23 of the Benelux Treaty contains a limited list of grounds to invoke the nullity:

- the design does not comply with the definition given under Article 3.1(2) and (3) – that is, the appearance of the whole or a part of a product is not regarded as a design;
- the design is not novel or does not have individual character(Articles 3.1(1), 3.3 and 3.4);
- the characteristics of the appearance of the product are exclusively imposed by its technical function (Article 3.2); and
- the design is contrary to morality or public policy or the filing does not sufficiently reveal the characteristics of the design (Article 3.6 under (e) or (f)).

A claim to invoke the nullity of a registered design is often filed as a counterclaim by the counterparty in infringement proceedings. The Benelux Treaty does not provide a time limit for invoking the nullity of a registered design.

The exclusive right in a design may lapse as a result of:

- voluntary cancellation or expiry of the registration of a Benelux filing;
- expiry of the registration of the international filing;
- renunciation of the rights for Benelux territory deriving from an international filing; or
- *ex officio* cancellation of an international filing when the registration fees have not been paid in time.

Annulment, voluntary cancellation and renunciation apply to a design in its entirety and to the entire Benelux region and can therefore not be limited to one of the filings (in the case of multiple filings) or to the Netherlands or another Benelux country only.

5. Infringement, damages and other relief

A rights holder can only invoke its design right against products which are marketed, sold, imported, stocked etc in the Benelux region. Acts done privately for non-commercial purposes do not constitute infringement.

If an alleged infringing product is offered on a website, it must be determined whether the website is directed at the Benelux region – by examining the language used on the website, the currency in which payments can be made, provision of telephone numbers with an international code, the top-level domain name used for the website, whether an advertisement with a link to the website features in a Google search conducted from the Benelux region, and, of course, whether products can be ordered by and are delivered to customers in the Benelux region.[27]

Generally, if a design right is infringed the rights holder will ask the court to prohibit the infringing party from making further use of its design. If granted, the injunction is usually combined with a penalty, which the infringer will forfeit for each day the infringement continues or for each infringing product which is marketed, sold, imported etc in the Benelux nations.

The rights holder may request compensation for damage sustained as a consequence of the infringement. Article 3.17(1) of the Benelux Treaty provides that the rights holder may claim compensation only for infringing acts[28] which have taken place after the publication of the design by the registry office. This is a logical consequence of the requirement that the characteristics of a design must be adequately disclosed and known to the public, so that others may be aware of the rights in the design.

In setting the compensation, the court must take into account the negative economic consequences, including lost profits, which the injured party has suffered, any profits unlawfully made by the infringer and, in appropriate cases, elements other than economic factors such as the moral prejudice caused to the rights holder as a result of the infringement. In appropriate cases, the court may set the damages at a lump sum of at least the amount of royalties which would have been due if the infringer had requested (and received) prior authorisation to use the design.

An infringer deliberately or knowingly using a design without the rights holder's consent will constitute bad faith infringement. Article 3.17(4) of the Benelux Treaty provides that in cases of bad-faith infringement, in addition to or instead of the action for compensation the rights holder may ask for the transfer of the profits made from the infringing use of its design, to be accounted for by the infringer in the manner established by the court (eg, through an auditor's certificate).

Although the text of this provision appears to suggest that the rights holder may demand both compensation and the transfer of profits, it is likely that the courts will award only one of the claims. Article 27a of the Copyright Act contains a similar provision and the Supreme Court has ruled[29] that a reasonable explanation of that provision does not allow a cumulative award of both compensation for damages and transfer of profits.

A licensee of a design right may intervene in proceedings instituted by the rights holder in order to obtain compensation for damages it has incurred or to receive a

27 See the Decision of the European Court of Justice of December 7 2010 in cases C-585/08 and C-144/09 (*Pammer* and *Hotel Alpenhof*). Although the cases concerned the question of a website directed at a consumer's country of residence in the context of the interpretation of Article 15 (1)(c) and (3) of the Brussels I Regulation (Council Regulation 44/2001/EC of December 22 2000 on jurisdiction and the recognition and enforcement of judgments in civil and commercial matters) in order to determine jurisdiction over a consumer contract, the criteria are similar to the ones applied by Dutch courts when determining whether, in the context of an infringement action, a website is directed at the Benelux region.

28 That is, manufacturing, offering, marketing, sale, delivery, hire, importing, exporting, exhibiting, use or holding for one of those purposes.

29 Dutch Supreme Court, April 14 2000, NJ 2000/489 (*HBS/Danestyle*).

proportion of the profit made by the infringer (see Article 3.26(4) of the Benelux Treaty). The licensee may institute independent action only with authorisation from the rights holder.

Article 3.17(3) of the Benelux Treaty provides that, at the request of the rights holder, the court may order that ownership of infringing products and the materials and implements principally used to manufacture them be transferred to the rights holder. The rationale behind this option is to prevent further damage to the interests of the rights holder. The court may make the order conditional upon payment by the claimant of compensation fixed by the court.

Article 3.18 of the Benelux Treaty specifies additional claims available to the rights holder. Paragraph 1 stipulates that, without prejudice to any damages due to the rights holder by reason of the infringement, the court may, at the request of the rights holder, order the recall or the definitive removal of the infringing goods from the channels of commerce, or their destruction. These measures implement Article 10 of the Enforcement Directive, which harmonises the way intellectual property rights are enforced in the European Union.[30] In addition, under the Benelux Treaty the rights holder may demand the destruction of materials and implements principally used in the manufacture of the infringing products. As a rule, the costs of these measures are borne by the infringer. In considering a request for any of these measures, the court will take into account whether the remedy requested is proportional to the seriousness of the infringement and whether the interests of third parties are affected.

Article 3.18 of the Benelux Treaty further provides for the possibility for rights holders to take provisional measures to preserve their rights, such as seizing infringing products or the means used to produce the infringing products. In addition, the rights holder may request the court to order the infringer to provide all available information on the origin and distribution of the infringing products, supported by documentary evidence such as copies of invoices and orders.

6. Design infringement litigation

If a product protected by a design right is infringed, it is common for the rights holder to initiate legal action primarily on the basis of its design right. Alternatively the action may be based on copyright protection or, as a final alternative, on tort (slavish imitation; see section 3.2 above). Each year, there are about 20 or 30 (published) cases in the Netherlands where a claim is based on a (registered) design right. The majority of the cases concerning the imitation of products are based on copyright law (due to the relatively low threshold for protection), invariably with tort (slavish imitation) as the alternative legal basis. However, claiming parties regularly use an unregistered Community design right as an alternative basis for their claims.

6.1 Remedies

A rights holder intending to take legal action against an infringing party has two

30 Directive 2004/48/EC of the European Parliament and of the Council of April 29 2004 on the enforcement of intellectual property rights, PB L195/16 of June 2 2004.

main options: proceedings on the merits or interim injunction (summary) proceedings.

Proceedings on the merits usually take between eight and 18 months from the date of serving the writ on the (alleged) infringing party to the court rendering its decision. Interim injunction proceedings are much quicker, and a decision is usually available within six weeks of serving the writ of summons. The vast majority of intellectual-property-related court proceedings are dealt with in interim injunction proceedings.

The Enforcement Directive was implemented in Dutch law on May 1 2007. Since that date it is also possible for rights holders to initiate *ex parte* provisional and precautionary measures where the defendant is not being heard (as mentioned in Article 9, paragraphs 1, 2 and 4 of the directive).[31] The defendant may then initiate summary proceedings to have the order lifted.

With respect to these legal remedies, the competent court is the court of the place of residence of the defendant. If the rights holder is able to prove that the infringement is also taking place within the jurisdictions of other courts, it may also choose to file its claims with such other courts.[32]

Proceedings in first instance must always be started in the district court.[33] Each party has the right to appeal a judgment in first instance with the Court of Appeal. The Court of Appeal decision may be appealed before the Supreme Court.

Since the implementation of the Enforcement Directive, in conformity with Article 14 of the directive, the courts have the right to award reasonable and proportionate legal costs and other expenses incurred by the successful party. As a general rule these are borne by the unsuccessful party, unless equity does not allow this. The courts have published a guideline[34] on the amounts the courts deem reasonable and proportionate. For relatively simple injunction proceedings, legal costs amounting to €6,000 are deemed reasonable and proportionate. In more complex injunction proceedings an amount of €15,000 is deemed reasonable and proportionate. In proceedings on the merits the amounts are €8,000 (simple proceedings on the merits) and €20,000 (more complex proceedings on the merits).

7. Licensing and exploitation

The exclusive right in a design may be licensed to a third party (Article 3.26(1) of the Benelux Treaty). The treaty does not contain any formal requirements with respect to licences. Consequently oral licences are valid, although nearly all licences will, for obvious reasons, be in the written form.

Licences can be exclusive or non-exclusive. Usually licences will contain certain limitations, which are also common in trademark and copyright licences, such as the term of the licence, the territory, the goods which the licensee is allowed to produce and the distribution channel.

---

31 The other remedies provided by the Enforcement Directive are also implemented in Dutch law, but are not discussed here.

32 Dutch Supreme Court, November 23 1917, NJ 1917, page 6 (*Oudenhoven/Brass*).

33 Interim injunction proceedings must be initiated with the president of the district court and proceedings on the merits with the regular chambers of the district court.

34 The guideline does not apply to legal proceedings regarding patent infringement.

Using a design beyond the restrictions of the licence agreement constitutes not only breach of contract but also design right infringement. Under Article 3.26(2) of the treaty, the rights holder may invoke this exclusive right against a licensee that infringes provisions on the term of the licence agreement, the form in which the design may be used, the goods for which the licence has been granted and/or the quality of the goods marketed by the licensee. This provision implies that the rights of the rights holder with respect to products sold in violation of the restrictions have not yet been exhausted. The rights holder can still take action against third parties who bought the products from the infringing licensee in order to market those products further.

Under Article 3.26(3) of the Benelux Treaty, entry of a licence in the registry office may be cancelled only at the joint request of the rights holder and the licensee.

The assignment, transfer or licence of a design can be invoked against third parties only after the parties involved have filed a copy of the document establishing the assignment, transfer or licence with the office (Article 3.27 of the Benelux Treaty).

The Benelux Treaty does not provide for compulsory licences.

New Zealand

Paul Sumpter
Chapman Tripp

1. Summary of design protection

Industrial designs in New Zealand are protected in two ways – by registration under either the Designs Act 1953 or the Copyright Act 1994.

The first method involves a formal process of application and registration (described below), in which a specific industrial design applied to an article is examined against novelty and other technical requirements by the New Zealand Intellectual Property Office (IPONZ). If the design is accepted for registration, the rights last, potentially, for 15 years from the date of application. A true monopoly right is granted – that is, even an independently produced design will infringe if it falls within the scope of the registration.

The New Zealand Designs Act 1953 is closely modelled on the UK Registered Designs Act 1949, before it was amended by the UK Copyright, Designs and Patents Act 1988. Case law in that jurisdiction will therefore be relevant, at least pertaining to the 1949 legislation. Any industrial drawing or design is likely to be a graphic work and fall within the category of an 'artistic' work as defined in the Copyright Act. Any original drawing will automatically qualify for copyright protection. The threshold for originality is low. Infringement arises if someone else, without permission, produces a drawing or design which is a copy or a copy of a substantial part of the first drawing/design. However, an independently produced drawing will not infringe: there is a requirement that the second drawing be derived from the first. In that sense, copyright protection does not give rise to a true monopoly.

A party qualifies for protection under the Designs Act 1953 by making an application and having that application accepted. A party qualifies for protection under the Copyright Act by being the creator of the design in New Zealand or in any other country that is a signatory to the Agreement on Trade-Related Aspects of Intellectual Property Rights (TRIPs).

2. Registered design rights

These are rights that arise from registration under the Designs Act 1953. Anyone claiming to be the owner of a design may apply for registration to IPONZ. The author or creator of a design will initially be the owner, but if it is created for 'good consideration' the ownership may be transferred.

A 'design' is defined in Section 2(1) of the legislation as the "features of shape, configuration, pattern, or ornament applied to an article by any industrial process or means, being features which in the finished article appeal to and are judged solely by the eye; it does not include a method or principle of construction or features of shape or configuration which are dictated solely by the function which the article to be made in that shape or configuration has to perform".

Therefore, to qualify for registration, a design must be applied to an article. The design is not the article itself, but is rather the concept of a shape, form or ornament applied to that article. An 'article' is defined in Section 2(1) of the Designs Act as "any article of manufacture; and includes any part of an article if that part is made and sold separately".

The features of design must be included in the finished article. A design may also be applied to a 'set of articles', defined in the legislation as "a number of articles of the same general character ordinarily on sale and intended to be used together, to each of which the same design, or the same design with modifications or variations not sufficient to alter the character or substantially to affect the identity thereof, is applied".

A design feature must be applied to an article by any "industrial process or means". Designs which are primarily literary or artistic in character may be excluded. The features protected are those of "shape, configuration", which will be three dimensional; "pattern, or ornament" refer to two-dimensional aspects applied to an article. Designs that are primarily literary or artistic in character also cannot be registered. Regulations stipulate that a design is not registrable in relation to certain items, including works of sculpture not intended to be used in an industrial process, wall plaques and medals, and printed matter primarily of a literary or artistic character (eg, calendars, dress-making patterns, greeting cards, maps and trade advertisements).

A key aspect of registration as a design is that the features in the finished article "appeal to and are judged solely by the eye". This is important both in the registrability/novelty context and in relation to infringement and the comparison necessary to decide whether a competitor has infringed the registered design.

A registered design must not be a method or principle of construction and must not be dictated solely by function. The latter requirement was explained in the Privy Council in *Interlego AG v Tyco Industries Inc.*[1] In a New Zealand example, a registration for a fence post in the shape of a Z was removed from the designs register (following a successful counterclaim by the defendants to an infringement action) on the basis that this fence post was simply a principle of construction and was also dictated solely by its function.[2]

To register a design, photographs or drawings, together with a statement of novelty and a simple application form, must be filed (attracting a fee) at IPONZ. The design must be applied to an article or a set of articles. Examination is primarily for novelty – that is, local novelty in New Zealand – generally judged when the examiner at IPONZ searches a database to consider existing registered designs and designs applied for.

The criterion is "new or original" – that is, the design must be sufficiently

1 [1988] 3 WLR 678.
2 *Sutton v Bay Masonry Ltd* (unrep, HC Tauranga, CIV-2003-470-000260, May 28 2004, Williams J).

different from the existing state of the art. The precise requirement, in Section 5(2) of the Designs Act, is that a design will not be registered "unless it is new or original and in particular shall not be so registered in respect of any article if it is the same as a design which before the date of the application for registration has been registered or published in New Zealand in respect of the same or any other article or differs from such a design only in immaterial details or in features which are variants, commonly used in the trade".

In an Australian decision, *Control Pty Ltd v Meco McCallum Pty Ltd*,[3] the court said:

The words 'new or original' involve the idea of novelty either in the pattern, shape or ornament itself or in the way in which an old patter, shape or ornament is to be applied to some special subject matter. There must be the exercise of intellectual activity so as to originate, that is to say, suggest for the first time, something which had not occurred to anyone before as to apply, by some manual, mechanical, or chemical means, some pattern, shape, or ornament to some special subject matter to which it had not been applied before.

If the design application is accepted, the certificate is issued to the applicant and the design is registered as of the date on which the application was made. There is no chance to oppose a design application for registration, but after registration anyone can apply to cancel it on any of the grounds that would have justified refusal of a registration in the first place (especially novelty).

The registration takes effect from the date of application. The maximum period of protection is 15 years. Renewal fees are payable every five years.

The rights granted are the exclusive right to prevent others from making, selling, hiring, importing for sale or using for business purposes any article (of the kind registered) featuring the design. It will also be an infringement to make anything or enable any such article to be made, whether in New Zealand or overseas.

The leading decision on registered design infringement in New Zealand is *UPL Group Ltd v Dux Engineers Ltd*.[4] In the New Zealand Court of Appeal, the test for whether a subsequent design is infringing is stated as follows:

The test is whether the article alleged to be an infringement has substantially the same appearance as a registered design. This involves a comparison between the article complained of and the representations of the article contained in the application for registration. It is not always easy to compare a two dimensional design with a three dimensional object. That difficulty and the fact that a design means features of shape, etc applied to an article by industrial processes makes it evident, and it has been so held (see Dunlop Row & Co Ltd v Golfball Developments Ltd *(1931) 48 RPC 268, 277, 280 and* Venchairs Ltd v Chair Centre Ltd *[1974] RPC 429, 441 and 442) that articles manufactured by the plaintiff which embody the design may be compared with the artefact set to have infringed.*

When comparing a registered design with a competitor's product, the relevant eye is that of the consumer or customer, although this may embrace trade customers. Sometimes the eye needs to be instructed by expert testimony.

3 (1996) 34 IPR 517, at 528.
4 1989] 3 NZLR 135.

There is a relationship between the degree of novelty or originality of a registered design and infringement. A high level of novelty will mean that small variations in the allegedly infringing article will be unlikely to save a defendant.

The remedies available upon a successful registered design infringement case are outlined in section 6 below.

If a rights holder brings a claim for infringement, a defendant might choose to apply to rectify the register and remove the registered design, usually on the grounds that it is not novel. Alternatively, at any time during the life of the registered design, anyone may seek to cancel the registered design on application to IPONZ, again usually on the grounds of lack of novelty.

Registered designs may be the subject of licence agreements. These may be exclusive, sole or non-exclusive. The usual rules of contract apply.

There are compulsory licensing provisions in the Registered Designs Act, but no reported cases on the procedure. The grounds for a compulsory licence are set out in Section 14 of the act and apply where "the design is not applied in New Zealand by any industrial process or means to the article in respect of which it is registered to such an extent as is reasonable in the circumstances of the case; and the Commissioner may make such order or application as he thinks fit."

3. Copyright protection

There is no law in New Zealand giving rise to unregistered design rights. However, the Copyright Act, which is very similar to the 1988 UK legislation, also protects industrial designs automatically upon creation.

Among the categories of works protected by copyright are those known as 'artistic works', a common sub-category of which is 'graphic works'. These will extend to a wide variety of industrial designs, including manufacturing drawings, sketch plans, production drawings and other types of commercial design.

Such designs must be original. This does not mean novel or new in the sense required under the designs legislation, but means merely that the creator must have expended a sufficient amount of "skill, judgement and/or labour". The precise parameters of the test have never been established under the common law – as in the United Kingdom and, generally speaking, other Commonwealth countries such as Australia. Very simple drawings will qualify, such as logos, sketch plans for women's dresses, parts of commercial articles (eg, a window frame) and so on.

There have been many cases involving industrial designs protected by copyright in New Zealand. The level of originality required has been described as "more than minimal" or "more than negligible".[5] The leading New Zealand authority on the matter, and the only copyright case to have reached the Supreme Court, is *Henkel KGaA v Holdfast New Zealand Limited*,[6] which concerned the packaging for a type of glue.

Authorship is separate from ownership. Ownership will initially lie with the author, unless that person is employed and the work is made in the course of his employment, in which case ownership will reside in the employer. For works that are

---

5 *Land Transport Safety Authority of New Zealand v Glogau* [1999] 1 NZLR 261 (NZ CA).
6 [2007] 1 NZLR 577 (SC).

commissioned, ownership will rest with the commissioner, provided that the commission was made in return for the promise of payment. The rules on commissioning are not exact but do not require a contractual relationship. Only the rights holder or, in certain circumstances, an exclusive licensee may bring an infringement action.

The term of protection for an artistic work is the lifetime of the author plus 50 years. However, there are important exceptions to the term of protection for industrial designs. The first arises if the work, or a copy thereof, forms part of a New Zealand patent specification that has been open to public inspection but has ceased to have effect, and the work is used for the purpose of making three-dimensional objects. The patent may have ceased to have effect for any reason. Similarly, it will not be an infringement to make a three-dimensional object (or in some circumstances a copy in two dimensions reasonably required for making the object) of the copyright of a literary or artistic work if the work or a copy thereof forms part of a representation or specimen of a design which has ceased and the representation or specimen is used for the purpose of making the object.

The second major exception relates to artistic works that have been applied industrially. Essentially, this limits protection against copyright infringement for design drawings to 16 years, beginning from the time that the objects based on the drawings are mass-produced for sale in New Zealand or anywhere in the world. The term 'applied industrially' is explained and means, for instance, where more than 50 three-dimensional copies have been made of the design for the purposes of sale or hire.

Restricted acts under the Copyright Act include the right to prevent copying without permission and issuing to the public (by sale or otherwise). Therefore, infringement will primarily arise if someone else copies the design or a substantial part of the design. There must be a causal connection between the defendant's creation and the allegedly infringed copyright design work; the former must have been derived from the latter. The question of substantiality can be difficult. A court will take into account the degree of originality in the copyright work in deciding whether a substantial part has been taken. Anyone is free to copy the idea or concept of the design, but this situation (the so-called 'idea/expression dichotomy') can sometimes be difficult.

Copying is one of the restricted acts known as primary infringements. It is no defence to such an infringement to have been unaware of the copyright protection in the design. There are also secondary infringing acts, which include importing an infringing copy (as defined) and possessing or dealing with such infringing copies. These activities require knowledge on the part of the defendant that it knew or ought reasonably to have known that it was dealing with infringing copies.

For artistic works, including industrial designs, it is an infringement to copy into a two-dimensional version and to make a three-dimensional version. This has the effect that someone may produce a product that is found to infringe an industrial drawing. For copying, the test for deciding whether infringement is made out involves determining whether there is objective similarity or sufficient resemblance, which assists with the second step – proof of a causal connection. In this regard, it has been held that unconscious copying is possible; the Copyright Act also makes clear that a defendant can copy indirectly. This occurred in a well-known New Zealand case, *Frank M Winstone (Merchants) Ltd v Plix Products Ltd.*[7] The defendant employed a designer to produce packaging drawings based on official specifications for such packaging (in the kiwi fruit industry). Unfortunately, the specifications were based upon the claimant's drawings, which were found to have been infringed.

Another form of infringement is authorising infringement. An example of this occurred when a manufacturer in New Zealand used building plans produced by one firm to employ another firm to build the same structure "as per the plans".[8] Remedies for a successful claimant in a copyright infringement are described below.

It is common to grant licences for copyright works, including designs. These can be implied from conduct or words, or may be the subject of formal agreements granting exclusive, sole or non-exclusive rights. The usual rules of contract apply. There is no system of compulsory licences under the Copyright Act.

4. Qualification for protection

Anyone who legitimately claims to be the owner may apply for a registered design in New Zealand under the Designs Act 1953. This includes a party that is resident overseas. Pursuant to international conventions, an overseas party may apply in New Zealand within six months of the date of initial filing and obtain a priority date in New Zealand equivalent to the foreign filing date. This can be important for questions of novelty, since novelty is judged at the priority date (either the actual filing date or the convention priority date).

The owners of designs created in overseas countries will receive automatic protection, pursuant to the Berne Convention (incorporated into TRIPs), in New Zealand under the Copyright Act. Under Article 5(2) of the Berne Convention, the substantive copyright laws of New Zealand (as well as remedies) may apply to works produced in foreign countries for which protection is sought to be enforced in New Zealand. This is known as the national treatment rule. Since TRIPs was signed in 1994, the number of countries to which reciprocal protection is extended has grown and it would now perhaps be unusual for a work to have been produced in a non-convention country.

5. Infringement

See section 6 below.

6. Design infringement litigation

There are differences in the level of proof required for an infringement action under the Designs Act and under the Copyright Act.

Under the Designs Act, there is a presumption of validity. The registered design will be clear from the representation as filed and accepted at IPONZ. Under copyright legislation, in contrast, it will be necessary to produce the actual, original design

---

7 [2007] 1 NZLR 577 (SC),

8 *Heinz Watties' Limited v Spantech Pty Ltd* (2006) 8 NZBLC 101, 679 (NZ CA).

drawing (or sufficient proof of its existence), and then to argue that the defendant has made a copy or a substantial copy of that drawing.

Whether for registered design infringement or copyright infringement, it is usual to send a cease-and-desist letter before action. This can be important for costs and for dealing with any claim of innocence (which can be taken into account in terms of damages).

This form of litigation is usually commenced in the High Court.[9] The usual papers are required – in particular, a statement of claim.

For infringements of copyright or registered designs, an interim injunction is often sought for reasons of urgency. Such an application is supported by affidavit evidence, a specific application and the usual statement of claim and supporting papers (one of which is an undertaking by the plaintiff to pay any damages should an interim injunction be granted, but at trial be found to have been unwarranted).

Interim injunctions are considered on the grounds first established in the UK case of *American Cyanamid v Ethicon*.[10] The main authority in New Zealand for these principles is *Klissers Farmhouse Bakeries Ltd v Harvest Bakeries Ltd*.[11] This latter decision provides that a claimant must prove that it has a serious question to be tried (sometimes referred to as an 'arguable case'), and that the balance of convenience is in its favour. Typical balance-of-convenience factors include:

- the adequacy of damages to the claimant if an interim injunction were not granted;
- the relative harm to the defendant if granted;
- the status quo; and
- in general, the overall justice of the situation.

Sometimes the courts may take into account the relative merits. For a registered design action, if a counterclaim for invalidity is brought, this might be taken into account. Any delay by a claimant in seeking an interim injunction will count against it. Frequently, an interim injunction will end the litigation (this is a matter that courts sometimes consider in deciding whether to grant such an injunction).

A number of other discretionary remedies may be relevant, including an Anton Piller order (made without notice to a defendant and allowing a search of premises for evidence).[12] It may also be possible to seek summary judgment for copyright and registered design infringement if the case is clear-cut and there is no proper defence.

The remedies for a successful copyright infringement action include damages, injunctions (interim and permanent), an account of profits and any other remedy that would be available for the infringement of a property right. Where two or more persons have a common purpose to infringe and do so, they will be liable as joint tortfeasors. There is no single measure of damages for copyright infringement. In

---

9 The hierarchy of courts in New Zealand comprises the district courts, the High Court, the Court of Appeal and the Supreme Court.

10 [1975] AC 396.

11 [1988] 1 NZLR 16.

12 These orders were first made in the United Kingdom in *Anton Piller KG v Manufacturing Processes Ltd* [1976] 1 All ER 779 (UK CA). The jurisdiction was recognised in New Zealand in *Busby v Form EMI Video Programmes Ltd* [1984] NZLR 461 (NZ CA).

several cases a notional licence fee has been held to be the most appropriate measure. It is also possible to obtain additional damages on the basis of the flagrancy of the infringement and any benefit accruing to the defendant. An account of profits, instead of compensatory damages, may also be available. If a defendant is truly innocent, the claimant is not entitled to damages, but to an account of profits only. Company directors may be personally liable if they have procured or directed the company to infringe.

A plaintiff whose allegations of copyright infringement turn out to be unjustified under Section 130 of the Copyright Act may be ordered to pay the defendant damages for any losses suffered as a result. If a plaintiff has brought proceedings in the genuine belief, held on reasonable grounds and after taking legal advice, that there had been or might have been an infringement of copyright, this will come within the meaning of 'justified'.

Under the Designs Act, a successful litigant can obtain damages, account of profits, interim and permanent injunctions and so on. A notional licence fee is often applicable. Innocence can be an exception from liability for damages and account of profits. Provision is also made for a remedy for groundless threats of registered design infringement proceedings. However, mere notification of a potential defendant that a design is registered does not constitute a threat.

The winner in litigation which is heard at full trial will be granted an award of costs according to a court scale. Actual solicitor–client costs are rarely awarded. Because of the pressures on the court system in New Zealand, there can be significant delays in obtaining hearing time for a full trial, particularly if this will last more than a week. Interim remedies are therefore popular, as are forms of alternative dispute resolution such as mediation and arbitration. However, in relation to registered design and copyright infringement, these alternatives are rare.

7. Licensing and exploitation

Both copyright-protected designs and those registered under the Designs Act are commonly licensed.

To prevent the possible abuse of a monopoly in a registered design, an application may be made for a compulsory licence under the Designs Act.

Typical contractual provisions in a normal industrial design licence (assuming the manufacture of products from the drawings) may include:

- the grant clause (ie, the right to make, use and/or sell; whether the rights are exclusive, sole or non-exclusive; territory; duration);
- the licensor's obligations (eg, to provide technical assistance);
- the licensee's obligations (perhaps minimum sales or at least to use best endeavours to sell);
- financial matters (eg, calculation of royalties);
- confidentiality provisions;
- improvements and grant-backs;
- warranties;
- acknowledgements of intellectual property ownership;
- the term of the agreement and any right of renewal;

- responsibility for infringement proceedings;
- rights of and reasons for termination, and consequences;
- indemnities;
- alternative dispute-resolution mechanisms;
- *force majeure*;
- sub-licensing/assignment;
- record keeping, auditing and reporting requirements;
- governing law and jurisdiction; and
- other general boilerplate clauses.

There is no requirement to register a licence, whether under the Copyright Act or the Designs Act.

Norway

Kaia Bugge Fougner
Ida Gjessing
Grette

---

1. Summary of design protection

In Norway, a design may be protected in a number of ways. The usual method is registration as a design with the Industrial Property Office. Registered designs are governed by the Act relating to design protection of March 14 2003 (the Design Act). The act implements EU Directive 98/71/EC into Norwegian law.

Norway has no legislation specifically governing unregistered design rights. However, a design's aesthetic properties may qualify it for protection as applied art under the Copyright Act of May 12 1961. The copying of a design may, depending on the circumstances, be prohibited as an act of unfair competition under Act 2 of January 9 2009 relating to the control of marketing and contract terms and conditions (the Marketing Control Act). The distinct shape of a product or a distinct graphical mark may also be protected as a trademark under the Trademarks Act of March 26 2010.

Under the Design Act it is possible for a designer, or his successor, to enjoy protection for the appearance of a product or part of a product for up to 25 years by registration with the Industrial Property Office. It is not possible to obtain protection by applying to the Office for the Harmonisation in the Internal Market (OHIM) for a Community trademark because Norway is not a member of the European Union. However, Norwegian persons and entities may apply for registration with OHIM to obtain protection within the Community. Norway may also be designated in an international design registration through the World Intellectual Property Organization (WIPO).

In order to obtain protection by registration with the Industrial Property Office, a design must be new and have individual character. Once registered, no other party may use the design, or part of the design that gives the informed user the same overall impression, without the consent of the rights holder.

2. Registered design rights

2.1 Nature of rights

Design registrations are processed by the Industrial Property Office. Since the Design Act implements into Norwegian law EU Directive 98/71/EC, European case law is relevant when interpreting the nature of the rights, the qualifications for registration and the scope of protection under the Design Act.

A design protection grants the rights holder an exclusive right to commercial exploitation of the appearance of a product. The protection does not include exploitation of technical solutions. More particularly, even if registered, a 'design' does not include purely functional features.

2.2 Qualification

The qualification for registration of a design is based on the appearance of a product or part of a product. It is the lines, contours, colours, shape, texture or materials of the product itself or its ornamentation that will be subject to design protection.

A product may be any industrial or handicraft item as, for example, packaging, get-up, graphic symbols and typographic typefaces. Thus, under the Design Act, a greater variety of products may enjoy protection, such as parts of products, web design and visual displays – even the visual representation of interior decorations. Computer programs are not considered to be a product under the Design Act.

A design must be new and have individual character. A design is considered new if no identical design has been made available to the public before the filing date of the application for registration or before priority date. Immaterial differences in details will not be enough to prevent designs from being identical. Under the Design Act, a design is not considered to have been made publicly available if it has been disclosed within a 'grace period' of 12 months before the application was submitted to the Industrial Property Office.

A design is considered to have individual character if the overall impression for the informed user differs from the overall impression he gets from other publicly available designs before the relevant date. When assessing whether the design has individual character, the degree of freedom of the designer in developing the design will be taken into consideration.

The concept of the 'informed user' is not defined in the Design Act. However, the informed user must be understood as a particularly observant user on account of his personal experience or his extensive knowledge of the sector in question.

2.3 Term of protection

A design registration is valid for five years from the application date. The registration may be filed for five consecutive five-year periods, allowing a total of 25 years' protection.

The registration of a design of spare parts for the repair of a complex product so as to restore its original appearance is only valid for a maximum of five years and may not be renewed.

2.4 Rights granted

A design registration grants the rights holder an exclusive right to the design such that no other party may use any design that gives the informed user the same overall impression without the consent of the rights holder. Under the Design Act, 'use' of a design means the making, offering, putting on the market, importing, exporting or using of a product in which the design is incorporated or to which it is applied, or stocking such a product for those purposes.

However, private and non-commercial use and use for experimental and educational purposes is permitted and will not be considered an infringement.

A design right does not exclude the use and resale of design-protected products that are put on the market in the European Economic Area (EEA) by the rights holder or with his consent (exhaustion of rights).

2.5 Damages and other relief

The usual remedies for infringement are restraining orders and compensation for damages. A party that wilfully or negligently uses a registered design will be liable to pay the rights holder a sum equivalent to a reasonable licence fee and compensation for any damages caused by the infringement. A party that infringes a design in good faith may be liable to pay remuneration and compensation. However, such remuneration and compensation may not exceed the estimated profit of the infringer.

A wilful infringer may also be liable to fines or imprisonment for up to three months. Public prosecution will only be initiated if it is requested by the aggrieved party. To date no public prosecutions for design infringement have been decided by the courts.

The rights holder may ask for the infringing products to be amended, destroyed or confiscated for the remainder of the protected period.

Proposals for more severe sanctions against design infringement have been put forward in a recent green paper and are under consideration.[1] The proposals include charging a double licence fee in the case of wilful or grossly negligent infringement and a maximum imprisonment term of one year, which may be increased to three years in aggravating circumstances.

2.6 Registration procedure

Applications for design registration are filed with the Industrial Property Office.

It is also possible to apply for an international design registration through the WIPO, as Norway acceded on March 17 2010 to the Geneva Act of the Hague Agreement concerning the International Registration of Industrial Designs 1999. The application may be filed directly with the WIPO or through the Industrial Property Office, and will in any event be examined by that office, following the same requirements as for national registrations.

An application for registration must be in Norwegian and must include illustrations that provide an accurate picture of the design. Both photographs and drawings are accepted. The application must include a short and precise description of the type of product the design applies to and the product must be classified in accordance with the Locarno Classification system. Such classification is a formal requirement, and has no bearing on the scope of protection.

A single design application may include several designs if all the products are within the same Locarno class.

A registered design is valid from the date of application. It is possible to claim

1 Green paper on the strengthening of the enforcement of intellectual property rights, Ministry of Justice, April 2011.

priority from an earlier application filed within six months after the filing of an application for design protection in a state that is party to the Paris Convention of March 20 1883 or the Agreement of April 15 1994 establishing the World Trade Organization.

The Industrial Property Office does not examine novelty and individual character *ex officio*, and will limit its examination to certain qualifications of public rights, such as the design not being contrary to moral standards. However, it is possible to ask for a separate examination.

Following registration, any third party may file an opposition to the registration. Grounds for opposition include lack of novelty and individual character. The office will undertake a full post-grant examination subject to the allegations of the parties.

2.7 Licensing and assignment

The designer has the right to apply for a design registration. The right may be transferred to another party, but the designer's name must be stated in the application.

There is no statutory law in Norway under which the right of an employed designer automatically passes to his employer. Such a transfer of the rights to the design should be addressed in the employment contract or when the design is created.

Under the Design Act, a rights holder may transfer (license) the right to exploit the design. A licensee may not transfer the licence to a design without the consent of the rights holder; thus, any sublicensing rights should be agreed explicitly in the licensing agreement. If a licence is granted to an enterprise, the general rule is that the licence may be transferred together with the enterprise if it is later sold.

2.8 Validity issues

If a design fails to meet the material requirements specified by the Design Act, that is, novelty and individual character, the design registration may be wholly or partly cancelled by the Industrial Property Office or be invalidated by a court of law. Any third party may file a request for administrative revocation or invalidity proceedings with the court. If the design has been registered in the name of a party that is not entitled to obtain registration, the registration will be cancelled or transferred to the rightful holder, if claimed.

3. Unregistered design rights

3.1 Introduction

Unregistered design rights under EU Regulation 6/2002/EC on Community designs are not implemented in Norway. Unregistered designs may enjoy protection as copyright-protected applied arts. The copying of design may also be prohibited as an act of unfair competition.

3.2 Copyright protection of applied art

Traditionally, the threshold for applied arts to be regarded as copyright-protected has been quite high. A refined piece of art in the form of a combined coffee and working table was regarded as a copyright-protected work by the Supreme Court in 1962,[2] but since then very few artefacts have qualified in this way. Although the Munkegaard lamp, designed by the well-known Danish designer Arne Jacobsen, was deemed copyright-protected by the Danish courts in 2010, in April 2011 the Oslo District Court was reluctant to classify it as such, and stated that the scope of protection was in any event limited and did not extend to the alleged infringing product.[3] The well-known Tripp Trapp® children's chair, designed by the well-known Norwegian designer Peter Opsvik, has been regarded as a copyright-protected work, and this was confirmed by the Borgarting Court of Appeals in August 2011. The court granted a quite wide scope of protection, stating that the alleged infringing chair "desires to be Tripp Trapp".[4] The decision has been appealed to the Supreme Court.

The reasoning behind the high threshold is that applied art serves a function, and that the granting of exclusive rights for 70 years following the year of death of the author is not suitable for such products. The threshold for copyright protection is not harmonised, even among the Nordic countries, as Norway is more reluctant to grant such protection than its neighbouring countries.

3.3 The Marketing Control Act

The general prohibition against acts of unfair competition under Section 25 of the Marketing Control Act extends to a variety of acts among business entities. Under Section 30, the copying of products is prohibited if it causes a risk of confusion in the marketplace and otherwise is considered to be unfair exploitation of another party's efforts or results.

Unlike many other jurisdictions, not only slavish copying is prohibited but also products whose appearance is deemed to be unnecessarily close to the original. The question is often whether there is a risk of confusion, especially when products are purchased following careful consideration. There are examples where the copying of products has been prohibited under the general provision of Section 25 of the Marketing Control Act against acts of unfair competition even where no risk of confusion has been demonstrated.[5] However, the Supreme Court has stated that there should be a threshold for applying the general rule when the conditions of the special rules of the Marketing Control Act are not met.

Overall, the Marketing Control Act provides a good basis for protecting an unregistered design against copying.

4. Qualifications for protection

Under the Design Act, a 'design' is defined as: "the appearance of a product or part of a product resulting from the features of, in particular, the lines, contours, colours, shape, texture or materials of the product itself or its ornamentation". 'Part of a product' means both separable and non-separable parts. It is not only the visual

---

2 Supreme Court decision, Rt 1962 p. 964.
3 Oslo District Court decision of April 26 2011.
4 Borgarting Courts of Appeal decision of August 23 2011.
5 Supreme Court decision, Rt 1995 p. 1908.

impression of a product that has significance for design: tactile characteristics such as those perceived by touching may have significance, although in general only if they are visible in the final product to which the design is applied.[6]

There are no requirements for quality or function. Thus, design protection is not limited to products that have aesthetic qualities.

A product is defined in the Design Act as: "any industrial or handicraft item, including *inter alia* parts intended to be assembled into a complex product, packaging, get-up, graphic symbols and typographic typefaces, but excluding computer programs". The product must be man-made or machined, so plants, animals, fruits, stones and other natural products are not protectable under the act. There is no requirement for any creativity in producing a design: the only requirement in addition to novelty is that the design has individual character for the informed user.

A design is considered to be new if no identical design has been publicly available before the filing date of the registration application or before the priority date. The deciding factor is whether the design has been made available to the public, not whether the design has been seen by the public. Immaterial differences in detail will not be sufficient to prevent designs from being identical.

The novelty requirement is not absolute, as it is under patent law, insofar as publications beyond the reasonable reach of the relevant professional group in the EEA will not destroy the novelty of a design.

Under the Design Act, the disclosure of a design by its rights holder within a grace period of 12 months before filing the registration application will not destroy its novelty.

A design is considered to have individual character if the overall impression for the informed user differs from the overall impression he gets from other publicly available designs before the relevant date. It is the design specification as it is registered that is relevant for the assessment – not, for example, how the prototype looks. A prototype will only be relevant for the assessment if it looks the same as the registered design.[7] When assessing whether the design has individual character, the degree of freedom of the designer in developing the design will be taken into consideration.

The concept of 'informed user' is not defined in the Design Act. However, the Court of Justice of the European Union has recently elaborated on the term.[8] The informed user must be understood as lying between the 'average consumer' (an expression used in trademark law), who is reasonably well informed and circumspect, and the 'sectoral expert' (an expression used in patent law), who is an expert with detailed technical expertise. Thus the informed user may be understood as a particularly observant user with experience or extensive knowledge of the sector in question. The same understanding will be taken into account in Norway.

Spare parts of complex products will be considered to be new and have individual

---

6 Are Stenvik, *Designrett*, 2006, p. 35.
7 See *Grupo Promer Mon Graphic SA v PepsiCo Inc*, Case C-281/10.
8 *Ibid.*

character only if they are visible during normal use and they fulfil the requirements for novelty and individual character. A 'complex product' is defined as a product that consists of multiple components which can be replaced, permitting disassembly and reassembly of the product. By normal use, the Design Act means use by the end user.

A design may not be registered if it:

- is contrary to public policy or morality;
- includes a coat of arms or other insignia without authorisation, a national flag, or an official control or guarantee mark for products of the same or a similar type as the products to which the design applies or which may be perceived as such a symbol, flag or mark; or
- infringes other intellectual property rights.

A design right will not be granted for technical features of a product or design that must be reproduced in its exact form and dimension in order to permit the product to be mechanically affixed to another product, so that either product may perform its function.

5. Infringement

A rights holder is granted the exclusive commercial use of its registered design. Infringing activities include the manufacturing, marketing, importing, exporting, distribution and sale of copied products. The use of products incorporating the protected design is illegal. Storage of infringing products is regarded as prohibited commercial exploitation, insofar as the storage is for the purpose of any of the above-listed activities. The handling of goods in a transfer not intended for import to Norway is not an act of infringement.

There are certain exceptions to the exclusive rights. Most importantly, acts done for private use may be freely undertaken. The distinction between commercial and private use with respect to design rights has not yet been decided by the courts, but importing more than one or two products may be regarded as beyond private use, depending on the circumstances.

There are exceptions relating to the use of a design for research and educational purposes, and special provisions apply to spare parts and equipment for vessels and aircrafts temporarily in Norway.

The scope of protection granted to a registered design mirrors the required variation from known designs. The protection extends to products that do not offer the informed user the same overall impression as the registered design. The freedom of variation will be considered when deciding the scope of protection.

6. Design infringement and litigation

Norwegian case law on the infringement of registered designs is scarce, most probably because design registration is not widely used. However, extensive case law on the copying of products under the Marketing Control Act is available.

A preliminary injunction against the import of counterfeiting products by way of a standing order to customs to seek and seize certain products may be granted. The order must be sought through the courts but is easy to acquire. It is usually limited to a duration of one year. The customs authorities are entitled to seek and seize goods *ex officio*, and will then inform the rights holder, who must reach an agreement or request a preliminary injunction within five days.

Design registrations may be enforced by claiming an injunction and other sanctions through the ordinary courts. Proceedings should be filed in the domicile of the infringer or where the infringing activities have occurred. Under a current green paper on the enforcement of intellectual property rights,[9] it is proposed that the Oslo District Court will be the mandatory court for deciding design infringement, as it is today with respect to validity cases.

The invalidity of a registration may not be used as a defence in ordinary infringement proceedings. If a plaintiff relies on invalidity, a separate invalidity action must be filed with the Oslo District Court. The cases may subsequently be joined.

Design infringement cases in ordinary proceedings will be heard quickly, at least in the court of first instance. Cases are normally heard within six to nine months, and a decision is rendered within a few weeks. There is a written preparatory phase requiring the submission of proceedings presenting the claim, the allegations and the evidence to be produced. The court will generally consider only allegations and evidence that have been presented during oral proceedings, so a design infringement case will normally last only a few days. The hearing is administered by a single professional judge. It is possible to appoint expert judges, although this is not usual in design infringement cases. The evidence of expert witnesses on the design may be useful. Expert witnesses may also be appointed by the court.

The procedure for appeals is often more time-consuming. The Courts of Appeals have a heavy workload and may take as long as two years to reach a decision. Appeals are heard by three professional judges, and there is an option to appoint two additional expert judges.

The possibility of an appeal to the Supreme Court is limited. If an appeal is accepted, the Supreme Court will reach a final decision within six months.

Cases involving intellectual property are often urgent, so enforcement requests may be started by filing a request for a preliminary injunction. In order to obtain an injunction, the applicant must prove that the design registration is valid, that it has been infringed and that there is a need for a quick decision. This will often be the case in design infringement proceedings as any decision to the contrary will undermine the exclusive rights granted by the registration.

If a preliminary injunction is obtained, its enforcement will normally be conditional on the filing of an action in ordinary proceedings. If the ordinary courts later decide that no valid design rights were infringed, the applicant will be liable for all costs and for the damages incurred by the competitor in being wrongly excluded from the marketplace. The strength of the design registration and the likelihood of a favourable decision in ordinary proceedings should be considered before filing a request for a preliminary injunction.

---

9 Green paper on the strengthening of the enforcement of intellectual property rights, Ministry of Justice, April 2011.

7. Licensing and exploitation

There are no statutory barriers in Norway to the licensing and exploitation of design rights. A licensing agreement may be made by a mutual understanding between the parties without requiring any written document, although this is not recommended.

Licensing agreements may be registered with the Industrial Property Office, although this is not a prerequisite for the validity of the licence. It is advisable to register a licence since registration in good faith will give priority over any conflicting licences that are not recorded.

Licensing agreements on registered designs are most common between a designer and an enterprise wishing to exploit the design. They are used less frequently between larger commercial companies in franchising structures or similar arrangements. Licensing fees may be agreed in any way – usually based on a percentage of net sales or a fixed amount per item, although annual fees or a lump sum may be agreed.

Under the Design Act, a licensee may only grant sub-licences with the consent of the licensor. The statutory provision is not mandatory, so it is advisable for a licensee to require a special provision in the licensing agreement if sub-licensing is anticipated.

Poland

Justyna Rasiewicz
LDS Łazewski Depo & Partners

1. Summary of design protection

Over the last six to seven years the number of disputes involving design rights has increased significantly and design protection has attracted the interest of Polish jurisprudence and legal writing.

Unlike other intellectual property (IP) rights, designs may be protected in a variety of ways, depending on their character, originality and the formal requirements met by their owners. Under the legal regime, the outer appearance of a product may be protected as a registered design under the Industrial Property Law or as an unregistered design under the Law on Combating Unfair Competition (the Unfair Competition Law), or even as a work of art under the Act on Copyright and Neighbouring Rights (the Copyright Act). The scope of the available remedies depends on the characteristics of a particular design – that is, whether it qualifies under all three systems of protection or under only some of them. The regime allows cumulative protection of one design, so it may be protected simultaneously under all three systems, provided it meets the criteria of all relevant provisions. In this case, the rights holder may benefit from the furthest-reaching remedies granted under each of the three laws.

The three methods of design protection have different qualification criteria. The Industrial Property Law protects only industrial designs registered at the Patent Office and only to the extent that an infringing design does not produce a different overall impression on an informed user. The Unfair Competition Law protects the outer appearance of a finished product against copying to the extent that an infringing product may cause confusion over the manufacturer or the product itself with consumers. Protection under the Unfair Competition Law is granted to the first like product to be made available to the relevant public in Poland. Designs that are individual and represent a "manifestation of creativity" may be protected under the Copyright Law.

2. Registered design rights

2.1 Nature of rights

Registered design rights are regulated by the Industrial Property Law. Registered design rights belong to the group of exclusive rights enabling their owners to prohibit any third party from using a design which does not produce a different overall impression in the whole territory of Poland. The exclusive rights are effective not only against those who have copied the design but also against those who have come up with the same/similar design after the priority date totally independently (unintentional infringement). To a certain extent, the exclusive right can also be pursued against those who had created an identical/similar design before the priority date as a result of independent work. In the latter case Polish law provides for a limitation of the exclusive right to the benefit of a person who used the design on the priority date or before in good faith in the territory of Poland ('right of the prior user'), which will be discussed in more detail in section 2.7 below.

When a design is registered, the Patent Office will issue a certificate of registration and provide a current copy of the entry in the register of industrial designs. Together, these documents provide the necessary evidence of rights granted to the rights holder.

2.2 Qualification for protection

A design qualifies for registration to the extent that it is novel and has an individual character.

Regulation of novelty under the Industrial Property Law is largely consistent with Articles 4 and 6 of Directive 98/71/EC of the European Parliament and of the Council of 13 October 1998 on the legal protection of designs (the Design Directive). The novelty may be destroyed by any public disclosure of an identical design. An 'identical design' includes designs that have features which differ only in immaterial details.

There is one significant exception from the principles of disclosure provided by the Polish legal regime in comparison with the Design Directive. Polish law requires a so-called global novelty – that is, the disclosure which destroys novelty is not limited to a disclosure that could reasonably have become known in the normal course of business to the circles specialised in the relevant sector concerned, operating within the European Union (Article 6.1 of the Design Directive). Evidence of the disclosure may be gathered from anywhere in the world and it is not necessary to prove that the information could have been reasonably available to specialists in the sector concerned, operating within the European Union.

The following events will not destroy the novelty of the design:

- disclosure to a third person under explicit or implicit conditions of confidentiality;
- disclosure by the designer, his successor in title or a third person acting with the consent of designer during the 12 months preceding the priority date; and
- disclosure resulting from an abuse in relation to the designer or his successor in title.

Regulation of the individual character of a design is to some extent inconsistent with Articles 5 and 6 of the Design Directive, but this has been reduced by the administrative courts' interpretation of the provisions of the Industrial Property Law. The law does not require that the overall impression produced by a later design is clearly different from the impression produced by existing designs (point 13 of the Preamble to the Design Directive). The regime is an exact implementation of Article

5 of the Design Directive. Unlike the Design Directive, the Industrial Property Law does not regulate the conditions of a relevant disclosure in relation to the individual character of the design. The regulation of disclosure has been specifically linked to only novelty.

The provisions in Articles 7 and 8 of the Design Directive, dealing with the invalidation of a registered design, have been fully implemented in the Industrial Property Law. Protection will not be granted to designs:

- that are contrary to public policy or morality;
- in which the appearance of a product is solely dictated by its technical function; or
- that must be reproduced in their exact form and dimensions to enable the product to be mechanically connected to or co-function with another product.

2.3 Registration procedure

Design rights are granted through a formal registration system, based on correctly submitted application forms. The Patent Office was granted authority to examine design registration applications in 2007. It will reject an application if it is obvious that the appearance of the product or its part is not novel or does not present individual character, or if the design does not meet the criteria of a product. In recent years, the number of applications refused by the office as a result of the examination has increased.

2.4 Term of protection and rights conferred

Registered design rights are granted for five-year terms, with a maximum aggregate of 25 years.

A registered design grants the rights holder an exclusive right to use the design in a professional or commercial capacity within Poland and to prevent any third party from using the design. The monopoly of the rights holder encompasses: production, offering, putting on the market, importing, exporting or using a product in which the design is incorporated or to which it is applied, or stocking such a product for these purposes.

However, the design right is limited to the category of products that was stated in the application.

2.5 Infringement

The protection granted by a registered design right is regulated by the Industrial Property Law, under the same terms provided by Article 9 of the Design Directive. Protection may be enjoyed by any design which does not produce on the informed user a different overall impression, taking into account the degree of freedom of the designer in developing his design.

Many of the courts' rulings on registered design infringement are based on the jurisprudence of the Office of Harmonisation for the Internal Market, the Board of Appeal and the European Court of Justice. Most of these decisions are based on the Regulation on Community designs.[1]

The term 'informed user' is interpreted by the courts in accordance with the prevailing view in the European jurisprudence – that is, a person being "somewhere between" a well-informed and reasonably observant and circumspect average consumer and an expert or specialist capable of observing in detail the minimal differences that may exist between conflicting designs.[2] However, as the informed user must possess certain knowledge of current designs in the sector and features which those designs normally include, the Supreme Court has accepted that in some cases the similarity of the overall impression produced by the designs in question should be assessed by a court-appointed expert.[3] Although the view adopted by the Supreme Court should be applied in all matters concerning designs in specialist sectors (as the judge may not have enough information accurately to assess the scope of the designer's freedom in the sector), the Supreme Court ruling has caused some discrepancy in the jurisprudence of the lower courts, some of which tend to order a court-appointed expert's opinion in every design case, while others do not, irrespective of the complexity of the design concerned.

A registered design right protects only the type of products listed in the application, and so only the same type of product may infringe the design. The interpretation of 'type' of product is controversial and it is not clear whether such a limitation is consistent with European law.

2.6 Available reliefs

The reliefs available to the rights holder in cases of infringement are:

- preventing further infringement;
- release of undue benefits;
- payment of compensation;
- an order to publicise the judgment, in full or in part, or information about the judgment in the manner and in the scope prescribed by the court; and
- an order to destroy, remove from trade or transfer the counterfeited goods to the rights holder.

In practice, the majority of rights holders pursue only the claim for discontinuance of infringement and an order to publicise the judgment. Although the order does not provide financial compensation for the rights holder, it is frequently applied in order to punish the infringer. Publication is ordered at the infringer's cost, and this cost may exceed the monetary compensation which would be due to the rights holder. Publication will be ordered irrespective of whether the infringement was intentional or unintentional.

Unlike claims for discontinuance and for publication, monetary claims are rarely pursued because of the legal and practical difficulties in enforcing them. A claim for release of undue benefits may be pursued even for unintentional infringement and will usually encompass the net profit resulting from the infringement. It has been

1 EU Regulation 6/2002/EC of December 12 2001 on Community designs.
2 Judgment of the Court of Justice of October 20 2011, Case C-281/10.
3 Judgment of the Supreme Court of Poland of October 23 2007, II CSK 302/07.

suggested that the net profit may also include the fictional licence fee which the infringer would have paid had he exploited the design right with the rights holder's consent.

Compensation is available only when the owner can prove intentional infringement. It can be claimed either in the form of actual damages and lost profit or in the form of a licence fee. In practice, compensation is rarely claimed and awarded owing to restrictions of the civil procedure.

In exceptional cases of unintentional infringement the court may award from the infringer an appropriate monetary amount instead of ordering it to discontinue the infringement or to destroy, remove from trade or transfer the counterfeited goods to the rights holder.

2.7 Limitations of registered design rights

Registered design rights can be subject to compulsory licensing, in particular but not limited to cases of an abuse of the design right. The scope, term and conditions of the licence, including the amount of the licence fee, are determined by the Patent Office. Decisions on the grant of a compulsory licence can be appealed to the administrative courts.

Unlike compulsory licensing, which has little practical application to the design right, a more effective limitation is available – the so-called 'pre-user exception'. A party that used the design in good faith or that had the equipment necessary to use the design ready at the priority date will be allowed to use the design free of charge in the same way as if it had used (or had been prepared to use) it previously.

2.8 Validity

Validity issues are assessed separately from an alleged infringement. The validity of a design is always assessed by the Patent Office. The prevailing view of the Supreme Court is that design infringement proceedings cannot be suspended based on a motion for invalidation of the design.

Two procedures are available to challenge the validity of a design. Any natural or legal person may file an opposition to the design's registration within six months of its official publication. After the six-month period, only natural or legal persons who can prove a legitimate interest in invalidating the design may file a motion for invalidation. Examples of a legitimate interest are where the rights holder has taken legal steps against the applicant based on the design (where a cease-and-desist letter represents a sufficient legal step) and where the applicant declares that it intends to use the design in its business activity.

Patent Office decisions on the validity of a design may be appealed to the Voivodeship Administrative Court in Warsaw. The judgment of this court may be appealed to the Supreme Administrative Court. In practice, invalidation proceedings may take several years to reach a final ruling. The (common) Supreme Court accepts that the invalidation of an exclusive right by the Patent Office cannot be enforced if the decision can be (or even has been) appealed to the administrative court.

3. Unregistered design rights

3.1 Nature of rights

Unregistered designs can be protected by an exclusive right (a copyright) or based on the Unfair Competition Law against slavish copying. Copyrights and rights granted by the latter law cannot be registered.

3.2 Qualification for protection

(a) Copyright

Copyright offers the broadest scope of protection, but also has the strictest requirements to qualify for protection. There is no separate regulation of copyright protection of designs – they are treated in the same way as any other work of art.

Designs ("works of art in the field of industrial designs") are explicitly listed in the Copyright Act as having the potential to be granted copyright protection. To qualify for copyright protection, the design must be created by a human, be creative (ie, subjectively novel) and have individual character. The 'individual character' requirement is not the same as the individual character of registered designs but, rather, is that it is one of a kind or unique.

(b) Unfair Competition Law

The Unfair Competition Law protects the outer appearance of a finished product. The protection is granted on the basis of the priority of use, it is narrowed only to copying and it requires the likelihood of confusion with the product or its manufacturer. The Supreme Court has stated that the likelihood of confusion will not exist if the disputed product and its packaging are visibly, clearly and permanently marked with a producer's name or logo.

In very rare cases, unregistered designs with a reputation may benefit from a broader protection against copying even if the likelihood of confusion does not exist.

3.3 Term of protection and rights granted

Copyright protection lasts for 70 years after the author's death.

There is no set term of protection under the Unfair Competition Law, but it is of some practical importance since in most cases the alleged infringers begin marking their products appropriately before the litigation ends.

Copyright is divided into personal copyright and economic copyright. Personal copyright cannot be limited in time or renounced by the author, although it is commonly accepted (especially in the field of designs) that the author may agree not to exercise his personal copyright within a certain period of time.

Personal copyright includes, for example, the right to be acknowledged as the author on each copy of the work, the right of the work's integrity and the right to supervise the exploitation of the work.

Economic copyright offers the exclusivity to exploit the design, to make it available to the public and to collect remuneration for its exploitation by third parties.

The Unfair Competition Law does not grant any protection rights but establishes the prerequisites for protection, civil law claims and principles of criminal liability for any infringement.

3.4 Infringement

Almost any unauthorised use of the design protected by copyright qualifies as infringement, especially if done for a commercial purpose.

Rights to designs protected under the Unfair Competition Law can only be infringed by copying the design using a technical method of reproduction in a commercial setting. The Supreme Court has extended the liability to entities which do not copy the design themselves but knowingly benefit from the infringement.

3.5 Available reliefs

Unregistered rights holders protected by a copyright may claim the following reliefs:

- discontinuance of the infringement;
- release of undue benefits;
- payment of compensation;
- an order to distribute a retraction statement in public;
- an order to destroy the counterfeited goods, remove them from trade or transfer them or the means and materials used to commit the infringement to the rights holder; and
- payment of an appropriate amount to a public fund defined in the Copyright Act, if the infringement is both intentional and committed within a business activity.

Compensation can be claimed either in accordance with the general principles of civil law or as a remuneration which would have been paid for the legal exploitation of the infringed copyright. In the first scenario, the copyright holder must prove the intentional nature of the infringement and is entitled to compensation which covers actual damage and lost profit. The latter scenario is unique among the IP protection regulations. It provides for a double remuneration in cases of unintentional infringement and for a triple remuneration in cases of intentional copyright infringement. In practice, the most frequently awarded compensation in IP disputes is compensation for copyright infringement.

The following reliefs are available to an unregistered rights holder protected by/under the Unfair Competition Law:

- discontinuance of the infringement;
- release of undue benefits;
- payment of compensation in accordance with the general principles of the civil law;
- an order to distribute in public the retraction statement;
- an order to destroy, remove from trade or transfer counterfeited goods or the means and materials used to commit the infringement to the rights holder; and
- in the case of an intentional infringement, payment of an appropriate amount to an organisation protecting Polish culture or heritage.

3.6 Limitations of copyright

Polish copyright law does not provide for a compulsory licence. It may only be considered on the basis of the *acqui communautaire* in view of European competition law.

The scope of limitations of copyright defined under the legal regime is determined by fair use.

4. Qualification for protection

The criteria that a given design must meet in order to qualify for protection depend on the system of protection which the design is eligible for, and they have been described in the preceding sections. A design may meet the conditions required under two or even all three of the systems of protection simultaneously. In this case the rights holder may enjoy the benefit of the furthest-reaching claims provided in all the applicable systems.

4.1 International obligations

National regulations on the principles of qualification for protection of designs are in general consistent with international obligations, as discussed above. However, there are some controversial Polish regulations on international obligations.

(a) Disclosure relevant for eliminating individual character of the design

The 'individual character' requirement for qualifying as a registered design is an exact implementation of Article 5 of the Design Directive. However, unlike the Design Directive, Poland's legal regime does not regulate the conditions of a relevant disclosure in relation to the individual character of the design (Article 6 of the Design Directive has been included in the provision concerning novelty of the design). In the current author's opinion, this discrepancy could be eliminated by using a pro-European interpretation of Polish provisions.

(b) Restriction of protection of the registered design to the kind of products which the design was applied for

The registered design's protection encompasses only the kind of products which the design was applied for. Although so far this restriction has not caused any controversy in litigation, legal writers have suggested that potentially it is inconsistent with the Design Directive. The directive does not mention the possibility of limiting the protection of the design to a certain type of goods.

(c) Expiry of copyright protection for a registered design

The Court of Justice's judgment in the *FLOS* case[4] clarified another controversy in the national system, namely a provision of the Industrial Property Law according to which: "economic copyright protection does not apply to products manufactured according to the design and put on the market after the expiry of the registered design right". This must be interpreted strictly – that is, the refusal of copyright

4 Case C-168/09.

protection may only apply to the two listed forms of exploitation: manufacturing and putting on the market.

These two forms of exploitation are the most important ones for the rights holder's economic interest, and the majority of legal writers agree that the national system deprives the copyright owner of some protection (and may be inconsistent with Article 17 of the Design Directive), or at least shortens the period of protection (and may be inconsistent with Article 7.4 of the Berne Convention for the Protection of Literary and Artistic Works and Council Directive 93/98/EEC of October 29 1993 harmonising the term of protection of copyright and certain related rights).

5. Infringement

Any infringement of registered design rights may be pursued in civil litigation.

Infringement of an unregistered design may be pursued in civil litigation or before criminal authorities as both the Copyright Act and the Unfair Competition Law provide for criminal liability of the infringer. Under the Copyright Act, acts by parties that knowingly benefit from the infringement may be penalised to some extent.

6. Design infringement litigation

6.1 Procedure and courts

Civil procedure in commercial matters (to which most IP litigations belong) is complex, and may be complicated further by a major amendment to the Code on Civil Proceedings which comes into force in the middle of 2012. The new rules will need to be interpreted by the Supreme Court.

Unlike other European procedural systems, the Polish civil procedure regime employs a system of preclusion of evidence, requiring both parties to submit all their statements and evidence within tight deadlines. Currently the time limits (usually of 14 days) are specified in legal provisions, but this system will change during 2012 when judges are given the discretion to set the deadlines for each party.

All civil IP litigations must be initiated before the regional (ie, higher) courts. Appeals and complaints from rulings issued by those courts are heard by the Courts of Appeal. There are restrictions in filing cassations to the Supreme Court and not every IP case will qualify to be heard by the Supreme Court.

6.2 Right to act in the capacity of plaintiff

Claims resulting from infringement of a registered design may be pursued by the rights holder or an exclusive licensee whose rights have been recorded in the Register of Designs.

Claims resulting from infringement of a copyright-protected unregistered design may be pursued by the rights holder (the author or his successor) or the exclusive licensee within the scope of the granted licence. Parties to the licence agreement may exclude the licensee's right.

Claims resulting from the infringement of an unregistered design protected under the Unfair Competition Law may be pursued by any party whose interests have been infringed (eg, the manufacturer of the protected product, its distributor or licensee). A claim must be relevant to the interest of the plaintiff.

6.3 Interim remedies

Interim remedies are readily available to the rights holder provided that the infringing product is very similar to the protected design. There are two material conditions for granting interim remedies: corroboration of the claim (ie, proving that the infringement is probable) and corroboration of a legitimate interest in requesting the remedy. In most IP cases the legitimate interest is accepted without controversy provided that only a reasonable time has elapsed between the rights holder learning of the alleged infringement and the filing of the motion for interim remedies.

Interim remedies may comprise any order appropriate to protect the legitimate interest of the rights holder, but in practice two types are usually requested and granted:

- interim injunction; and
- seizure of disputed products.

Interim remedies are granted at closed hearings in *ex parte* proceedings, but if an alleged infringer becomes aware of the pending case, it is allowed to file statements of defence and the court may even schedule a hearing to assess the arguments of the parties. Motions for interim remedies should be assessed within three days of filing and are usually assessed within a few days. In some courts the procedure may last longer – up to several weeks. Interim remedies may be granted against a plaintiff's deposit, the amount of which is determined at the discretion of the judge (generally in the five- to six-figure PLN range, ie, tens of thousands of US dollars).

Each party has the right to appeal a decision on the interim remedies. An appeal does not automatically cancel the enforceability of the remedies granted.

Depending on the character of the remedy granted to the rights holder, the decision may be enforced by a lower court (eg, injunctive measures) or by a bailiff (eg, seizure of products). If the injunction has to be enforced by a court (ie, when the defendant refuses to comply with the decision), enforcement proceedings may be time-consuming and therefore ineffective.

A rights holder that has enforced interim remedies is liable for damages caused to the defendant if it finally loses the case on formal or material grounds.

6.4 Right to information

The right to information is recognised in the IP protection system, but until 2007 it encompassed only cases of copyright infringement (including copyright-protected designs). As a result of the implementation of Directive 2004/48/EC of the European Parliament and of the Council of April 29 2004 on the enforcement of IP rights (the Enforcement Directive), the right to information was extended to industrial property rights, including registered designs, in 2007. The right to information cannot be exercised on the basis of the Unfair Competition Law – that is, it does not cover unregistered designs which are not protected by copyright.

The scope of the right to information in copyright infringement is different from that under registered designs protection, although both regimes allow the right to be exercised against the infringer and third parties under the conditions specified in Article 8.1 (a) to (d) of the Enforcement Directive.

The procedure for applying for information is based on interim remedies proceedings but, unlike those proceedings, the motion for information in registered designs cases must be assessed in an open hearing.

Decisions concerning the right to information are issued by the regional (ie, higher) courts and may be appealed.

6.5 Preserving evidence

A request for preserving evidence in design infringement proceedings may be pursued irrespective of the basis on which a design is protected. However, there are three different procedures:

- for registered designs, the procedure is regulated by the Industrial Property Law and, in principle, is an *ex parte* procedure in which the right of appeal is expressly provided by the law;
- for unregistered designs protected under Unfair Competition Law, the procedure is regulated by the Code on Civil Proceedings. In principle, it is not an *ex parte* procedure and, according to a controversial ruling of the Supreme Court, there is no right of appeal against the decision concerning preservation of evidence; and
- for unregistered designs protected by the Copyright Act, the procedure is regulated by the Copyright Act and, in principle, it is an *ex parte* procedure in which the right of appeal is expressly provided by the law.

6.6 Costs

(a) Court costs

Court costs include a court entry fee and expenses which occur during the litigation.

All design protection proceedings are in principle assumed to have an economic value for the rights holder. The rights holder must estimate the value of its interest in pursuing each of the claims put forward in the statement of claim, and a 5% court entry fee will be charged on the basis of the estimate. If it is not possible or it is too difficult to estimate the said value, the court may apply an interim court entry fee of between PLN30 (about €7.50) and PLN1,000 (about €250).

The amount of expenses varies depending on the actual amounts which the court pays in consideration for particular services (eg, a witness testimony by a foreigner may require fare and accommodation expenses, reimbursement of the witness's remuneration and costs of certified interpretation of his testimony).

All court costs will be charged to the losing party. If both parties lose a part of the case, costs will be shared proportionally.

(b) Legal fees

Legal fees of the successful party are reimbursed by the losing party. However, calculation of the amount awarded is based on legal provisions, not the actual costs borne by the successful party.

The statutory levels of legal fees are low:[5]

- for registered design protection, the minimum fee (usually awarded by courts) is PLN840 (about €210) and the maximum fee is PLN5,040 (about €1,260);
- for unregistered designs protected under Unfair Competition Law, the fee is calculated on the basis of the value of the claims and may range from PLN180 (about €45) to PLN43,200 (about €10,800);
- for unregistered designs protected by the Copyright Act, the minimum fee (usually awarded by courts) is PLN360 (about €90) and the maximum fee is PLN2,160 (about €540).

6.7 Validity

The validity of a registered design is assessed by the Patent Office, separately from the infringement proceedings. The prevailing view is that a motion for invalidation of the registered design should not result in suspension of the infringement proceedings. Invalidation of the design by the Patent Office leads to a dismissal of infringement claims, despite the fact that the decision of the Patent Office may be appealed to the administrative courts.

7. Licensing and exploitation

The licensing and exploitation of a design right will depend on which system of protection the design falls under.

Statutory rules on licensing and exploitation apply only to registered designs and copyright-protected unregistered designs. It is possible to grant a licence to use the unregistered design which can be only protected under the Unfair Competition Law. Such an agreement is not regulated by Polish law and so all terms and conditions of the licence must be defined with care.

7.1 Registered designs

A licence agreement must be in writing; otherwise it will be declared void.

Unless the scope of exploitation of the design has been restricted in the agreement, the licensee is entitled to use the design in the same scope as the licensor.

The types of licence available comprise exclusive licences and non-exclusive licences. An exclusive licence may be granted on two bases: the licensor may agree not to grant a licence to any other party within the scope of exclusivity (eg, territorial) or may agree not exploit the design itself (a full exclusive licence). Any licence may be entered into the Register of Designs maintained by the Patent Office. Registration of an exclusive licence allows the licensee to pursue claims against infringement of the design within the scope of the authorisation granted to it under the licence agreement.

A sub-licence may be granted only with the consent of the rights holder. Further sub-licensing is not allowed.

Unlike the copyright licensor, the registered design licensor does not benefit from a presumption that the licence has been granted in consideration for remuneration.

---

5 The figures quoted are for the first-instance proceedings. Generally amounts awarded for the second instance and proceedings before the Supreme Court are lower.

7.2 Unregistered designs protected by copyright

A copyright licence agreement does not require any special form. Only an exclusive licence must be concluded in writing under pain of nullity. As the transfer of copyright must also be recorded in writing, quite often in practice agreements on the transfer of copyright which do not meet this condition are validated as non-exclusive licence agreements.

A licence agreement covers exploitation of the design only in the fields of exploitation expressly stated in the agreement.

The statutory term of a licence agreement is five years and encompasses the territory of a state in which the licensee has its seat. Both of those conditions may be altered by agreement between the parties.

There are two types of copyright licence agreements: as an exclusive licence and a non-exclusive licence (the latter being presumed unless the parties agree differently). A sub-licence may be granted only if the licence agreement allows it or if the rights holder agrees at a later date.

An exclusive licensee is entitled to pursue claims for protection of the economic copyright within the scope of the licence, provided the licence agreement does not state otherwise.

Unlike other types of licence, copyright licences carry a risk in provisions relating to the remuneration for exploitation of the design. There is a presumption that a licence will be granted in consideration for remuneration and this may be expressly changed only by parties. Unless the remuneration has been specified in the agreement, it will be determined based on the scope of the exploitation and profits made on using the design. The author is entitled to request a judicial correction (increase) of the agreed remuneration if there is a gross discrepancy between the amount specified and the profits generated by the licensee.

The Copyright Act provides for a unique right to information and access to documents relevant to the determination of the amount of remuneration due to the author (or economic copyright owner) if the amount of remuneration has been specified on the basis of an income on the exploitation of the design. In practice, this right, together with procedural measures on preserving evidence and the general right of information, is often exercised by authors and the economic copyright owner and awarded by courts without respecting the trade secrets of the licensee.

Russia

David Aylen
Gowlings Russia/CIS

1. Summary of design protection

Intellectual property rights in Russia are provided for in Part IV of the Civil Code of the Russian Federation,[1] which came in to force in January 2008. Part IV consolidated and revised the various individual intellectual property laws that had been first implemented in 1992 following the break-up of the Soviet Union. The 1992 laws, like the Soviet Union laws of 1991, which did not fully enter into force, gave back to citizens the right of private ownership of intellectual property that, during communist times, had been mainly designated as being property of the state. The 2008 consolidation into Part IV included the Patent Law 1992 (amended in 2003), which is the law that had provided for design protection. Administrative procedures relating to designs are further covered in Order 325 by the Ministry of Education and Science, dated October 29 2008, entitled Administrative Regulations on the Federal Service on Intellectual Property Patents and Trademarks Performing the State Function of Organising Acceptance, Consideration and Examination of Applications for Industrial Design and the Issuance in the Established Procedure of Design Patents of the Russian Federation. These will be referred to simply as 'the Regulations'.

Part IV acknowledges, in Article 1225, that the results of intellectual activity of legal persons and legal enterprises, including designs, are granted legal protection.

In Russia today, the term 'patents' is a collective term that means inventions, utility models and designs. In particular, Article 1345 in Chapter 72 of Part IV of the Civil Code, provides as follows: "Intellectual rights to inventions, utility models, and designs are patent rights."

Article 1346 stipulates that registration is a requirement for there to be any property rights in favour of the owner. The rights that are accorded are simply expressed as the "exclusive right" and the "right of authorship" along with any other incidental rights. Accordingly, in the case of patents, including designs, there are no unregistered design rights that accrue to an author upon creation or commercialisation of his design, and registration is a strict requirement.

Rights of authorship are provided for under Articles 1228 and 1345. The right to apply for protection first accrues to the author. The author is the person by whose creative labour the intellectual activity has been created. The person indicated as the

1 The governing language under the Civil Code, Part IV is the official Russian version. There are a few English translations available, including one on the ROSPATENT website, which is identified as being "unofficial". Perhaps this one is nonetheless the most reliable. It is available at: www.rupto.ru/en_site/policy_law/policy_law.html.

author in any application is presumed to be such unless it is proven otherwise.

Despite the right-of-authorship attribution, which is unalienable, there are provisions that stipulate that the author may not be the first owner in certain employment and contractor situations. These provisions are reviewed in section 2.3 below.

The exclusive right begins with Article 1229, which provides that the right may be jointly held by one or more persons and he or they:

- will have the right to use protectable rights of intellectual activity at his/their discretion;
- may dispose of that right;
- may permit others to use that right; and
- may prohibit others from using that right.

Those to whom such rights may accrue include citizens and enterprises of the Russian Federation, and foreign persons or entities.

2. Registered design rights

2.1 The regulatory authority

In Russia, the Federal Service for Intellectual Property Patents and Trademarks (ROSPATENT) is responsible for intellectual property. ROSPATENT operates under the Ministry of Education and Science of the Russian Federation. Within ROSPATENT, the Federal Institute of Industrial Property, known as FGU or FIPS, is the central authority for receiving applications for patents for designs (in addition to trademarks), for examination and for the issuance of certificates of registration.

The Chamber of Patent Disputes is the quasi-judicial and administrative body within FIPS that reviews, among other things, appeals from final rejections of applications as well as invalidity proceedings at the first instance. The chamber itself has a staff of about 60 examiners in addition to the 600 regular patent examiners attending to the day-to-day prosecution of applications.

Comprehensive information concerning both ROSPATENT and FIPS, as well as an electronic database of prior art and legislation, can be found at both: www.rupto.ru and www.fips.ru.

2.2 Entitlement

Article 1352 of the Civil Code stipulates the conditions of patentability of a design in five paragraphs:

- *Paragraph 1, Subject-matter, novelty and originality:* to be registrable, the proposed design must be an artistic design presentation of a manufacture of industrial or handicraft production defining its outward appearance.

The focus is always on the essential characteristics as defined in words in the application. The design must be artistic and define external appearance. Appearance includes shape, configuration, ornamentation and combinations of colours. Under Item 9.4 of the Regulations, articles may be two- or three-dimensional. They include labels, emblems, prints, compound articles, components to be assembled as compound articles, independent parts of articles, and so on. Independent parts of articles include functional parts that are visible in the process of the article's operation. Components to be assembled as compound articles are functionally independent parts of a compound article intended for assembly that may be dismantled without disturbing its integrity – for example a car headlight or bumper. Designs also include patterns, graphics and fonts as examples, as well as overall shape or external form. There is no stated requirement of the number of commercial products that must be manufactured in order for the process to be classified as manufacture – presumably it would include subject matter of one single handicraft production.

The essential characteristics of the design must also be new and original:

- *Paragraph 2, Novelty:* a design is deemed to be new if the sum of its essential features is not known from information generally available anywhere in the world before the priority date of the application. Item 22.5.4 of the Regulations sets out in detail the test for novelty that is to be applied during substantive examination.
- *Paragraph 3, Originality:* a design must be not only new but also original. Paragraph 3 states that a design is deemed to be original if its essential features are determined by the creative nature of the special aspects of the article. It is probable that originality, as distinguished from novelty, does not mean that the totality of the essential features are new but that the design in addition to being new was also conceived independently by the author. Item 22.5.5 of the Regulations expands on this by stating that a design should be regarded as original if its essential features are defined by the creative character of the article's peculiarities.

Notwithstanding an absolute novelty requirement, there is a six-month grace period. The applicant has six months to file an application with ROSPATENT (where the filing date must be the actual filing date with the patent office and not the convention priority date) from the date that the author, applicant or other person who may have received information from them made public the information on the essence of the design. If there has been such a publication or disclosure, the burden of proof rests on the applicant to prove that it nonetheless qualifies for the grace period.

Under Item 9.5 of the Regulations, protection is not given to designs reproducing trademarks for which an earlier application was filed, or for which there is already a registration or in respect of which well-known status has been declared.

In relation to subject matter that is excluded from legal protection:

- *Paragraph 4* sets out how legal protection is not available for designs that are determined exclusively by the technical functionality of the article. The word 'exclusively' is noteworthy as designs that are not determined exclusively by functionality would qualify. The scope and meaning of 'exclusively' has been the subject of judicial scrutiny in other countries, but the Supreme Court in Russia (the only court empowered to ascribe constructions and interpretations to the code in a binding way) has not yet considered the scope and meaning of this term.

Works of architecture, industrial, hydro-technical and other stationary structures are also excluded, apart from "minor architectural forms", for example kiosks or booths, which do qualify as subject matter.

- *Paragraph 5* excludes objects of unstable shape such as liquids, gases, dry substances and the like.

2.3 Authorship and ownership

(a) Authorship

Russia provides some unique laws as regards ownership rights to patents. These provisions may be derived from quasi-communist principles despite the fact that the legislation was enacted after the communist era had ended and significantly revised in 2008.

The author of a design is the person whose creative labour led to the result. One or more persons can be authors and co-authors. Those who have not made a creative contribution to the design, but rather made a merely technical, organisational or financial one, are not authors.[2] Attribution of authorship is an unalienable right that arises upon creation.

There is an initial presumption that the author of the work is the owner of the work. The exceptions arise either by operation of statute, for example with employees, or by reason of contract.[3]

If there is more than one author then each co-author has the right to use the design at his discretion, unless they have agreed otherwise in writing.[4] None of the co-authors are entitled to dispose of the right unless the disposition is made jointly or is otherwise provided for in a contract between them.[5] This means that a co-author cannot dispose of or license his share without the consent of the other co-authors.

Under Article 1348, each of the co-authors has the right independently to take measures to protect his rights. Article 1229 states that the income from the joint use of a right is to be divided equally amongst the rights holders. If the rights holders jointly agree to a licence or jointly pursue an infringer, it would seem that they share the proceeds equally. But the rights of other co-authors when only one co-author takes action for infringement are not elaborated in detail.

(b) Ownership: employees

If an author is an employee and either created the design in connection with the performance of his employment or as a result of a specific task, then the design is regarded as an 'employment design'.[6]

The exclusive right to an employment design, including the right to a patent, belongs to the employer unless there is a written labour contract that provides otherwise.[7]

---

2 Articles 1228 and 1347 of the Civil Code.
3 Article 1228, paragraph 4.
4 Article 1348.
5 Article 1229, paragraph 3.
6 Article1370.
7 Article 1370 of the Civil Code.

These principles accord more or less with the laws in common-law countries. However, Article 1370 is more unique and stipulates as follows:

- An employee must notify his employer in writing of a creation made in connection with the performance of the employment. There is no stipulated time limit within which the author must give such notice.
- The employer has four months from receiving the notice either to file an application in Russia for a design patent, to transfer the rights to a third party or to advise the employee that the design will be maintained as a secret.
- If the employer fails to do so, the right to obtain a design patent flows by operation of law to the employee/author.
- In this case the employer retains a 'shop right' to use the design in the employer's own production. The parties are obliged to enter into a licence agreement between them to define the terms of their understanding, failing which the court may do so upon request.
- If the employer obtains a patent on the design, transfers it to a third party or declares that it will be kept secret, the employee is entitled to compensation for the invention above and beyond his normal salary (unless an agreement between them provides otherwise).
- Not unlike the law in many other countries, if an employee develops a patentable design with the use of monetary, technical or other material assets of his employer but not in connection with his employment, the rights are retained by the author/employee and not by the employer. Again, the employer has a limited shop right in the form of a simple, non-exclusive licence to use the design.

(c) ***Ownership: contractors***

Article 1371 envisages two scenarios as regards ownership rights between a contractor (performer) and customer: designs incidentally developed and designs made on order.

Incidentally developed designs: when a design is developed in the course of a contract where it was not envisaged that the design would be created, the rights belong to the contractor (performer), unless the contract provides otherwise. In this case the customer has a shop right to use the design for the purposes in respect of which the contract was made. No compensation is provided for what is a simple, non-exclusive licence granted to the customer. Any person who takes over ownership of the design rights by way of transfer from the contractor takes on the condition that the customer's shop right is not assignable. Conversely, if the performer under contract has agreed that the design rights would belong to the customer, unless otherwise provided in that contract the performer retains his own shop right by way of non-exclusive licence to use the design for his own needs.

If the author of the design is not the ultimate holder of the patent, he is entitled to additional compensation as an employee of the contractor (performer).

Designs made on order: in the case where a design is made under contract 'on order', Article 1372 stipulates that the right to the receipt of the design patent belongs to the customer. The contractor (performer) has a shop right to use the design for his own needs under a simple, non-exclusive royalty-free licence. If the written contract stipulated otherwise, namely that the performer retained the rights notwithstanding that the design was developed on order, then the customer has, by operation of law, the right to use the design for his own needs under a simple, non-exclusive licence. Such a right is not transferable.

Employers, employees and contractors are strongly advised to eliminate uncertainty at the beginning of the relationship. The relationship should be defined in detail in a written contract that accords with the dictates of the Civil Code. In most cases they can be relatively standard-form contracts. The contract may be an employment contract or a services contract that sets out the basic terms of the relationship and also provides additional terms as regards respective rights and obligations relating to knowledge-based rights, including inventions, designs and trade secrets. Consideration should be given to ownership, right of attribution, rights upon termination and derivative rights, to name a few.

(d) Joint ownership

It is often the case that an invention or a design will be developed by two or more people together or in succession. The authors may be any combination of joint employees working together in the same company, or employees, each from the contractor and the customer companies, or individuals working independently as entrepreneurs. When designs are involved, there is often an outside creative person/artist who is a freelance entrepreneur working in conjunction with a design agency or directly on contract with a customer company and its employees.

It is therefore important to record in writing as much as possible in advance – for example, who the respective owners will be of any design or other rights that emerge as a by-product of the relationship.

To the extent that those rights are not predetermined in a written contract, the following basic principles apply:

- Under the general provisions as regards intellectual property rights:
  - An author is any person who, by the result of intellectual activity, has made a creative result. Those who have not made a creative contribution but merely a clerical, consulting or organisational one are not authors or co-authors.[8]
  - As between co-authors, the rights to a result of intellectual activity created by the creative labour of two or more persons belong to them jointly as co-authors.[9] If the co-authors are themselves employees or contractors, then their respective individual ownership rights will be governed by the rules of ownership outlined above.
  - As with single authors, the exclusive right to use intellectual property protected under the Civil Code is initially recognised as being in favour of the author or, in this case, co-authors under Article 1229, paragraph 2.

---

8 Article 1228, paragraph 1.
9 Article 1228, paragraph 4.

  - Article 1229, paragraph 3 is a substantive provision that states that joint owners of a right have the right to use the intellectual property at their discretion, income from the joint use is to be shared equally and disposition of the right is to be made jointly, and the co-owners are to govern their relations by way of agreement, failing which a court can be asked to resolve the dispute.[10]
- Under the provisions specific to patents, including those for designs:
  - Co-authors are those who have made a design by joint creative labour;[11]
  - Each co-author has the right to use the design at his discretion unless provided otherwise;[12]
  - The obligation to share income and the right of disposition of designs are cross-referenced back to Article 1229, paragraph 3; and
  - Each co-author may independently take measures to enforce his rights.[13]

It would seem that these provisions prevent co-authors and co-owners from independently assigning away their own equal but undivided interests; however, it appears that they can each use the rights for their own use; they can also license those rights to others and enforce those rights against others so long as the licence fees and damages are shared amongst them equally.

It is advisable to stipulate the respective rights amongst co-authors and co-owners at the outset by way of written agreement in order to avoid uncertainty and to facilitate monetisation and commercialisation.

(e) *Assignment*

The Civil Code allows for the assignment of the intellectual property associated with an unregistered design as well as the assignment of a registered design. Design rights may also be licensed, either on an exclusive or a non-exclusive basis.

There is no express provision stipulating that a person can separate off some of the design variants in a design registration by way of partial assignment, nor is there any provision for an assignment limited to geographic territory. However, this could be done by way of a non-exclusive licence.

In terms of assignments, the following provisions apply:

- Article 1228, paragraph 3 grants to the author of an intellectual property right, which would include both a registered right and the right to apply for such a right, the further right to transfer the right to another person by contract (or by devolution upon death). Article 1357, paragraph 2, as well as Items 5.1 and 14 of the Regulations, affirms this specifically for designs.
- Article 1233, paragraph 1 further provides that not only the author but also the rights holder (eg, an employer) may dispose of an exclusive right by way of contract, in any manner not contrary to statute. Article 1365 specifically confirms that designs may be assigned.

---

10 Article 1406 of the Civil Code.
11 Article1348, paragraph 1.
12 Article1348, paragraph 2.
13 Article1348, paragraph 4.

- Under Article 1233, paragraph 4, no contract of assignment can stipulate any form of restrictive covenant to the effect that either of the parties is in any way restricted from engaging in an area of intellectual activity or is restricted in respect of the right to transfer the rights to others.
- An assignment must be in writing[14] and must be duly recorded with the patent office. Until the assignment is recorded it is of no effect.[15] However, in the case of inheritance a written contract is not necessary.[16]

For an assignment to be accepted by the patent office, it must specifically identify the design registration or application being assigned. Both parties must sign it.[17] The assignment must be filed along with the requisite fee and a power of attorney authorising a patent attorney to act on behalf of the assignor and/or assignee.

2.4 Nature and scope of rights

(a) *Official registration*

Article 1353 of the Civil Code stipulates that the exclusive right to a design patent is recognised when the patent is issued.

The issue of a design patent serves as a certification by the state of the priority of the design, the authorship and the grant of the exclusive right. Under paragraph 3 of Article 1353, the scope of protection accorded by the grant is defined by the totality of its essential features expressed both in the illustrations forming part of the registration and the attached written description of essential characteristics.

(b) *Patent rights*

The following fundamental rights are acknowledged in Articles 1356 to 1358:

- *Right of authorship:* the author of the design has the inalienable, non-transferable right to attribution as the author. This is the case no matter that the right may be transferred and no matter that the author may have intentionally waived the right to be so attributed with authorship.
- The author has the first right of ownership and, save for circumstances involving employer/employee and contractor relationships where there may be an exception, the right to receive a patent belongs to the author. This right may be transferred either before or after grant, either by way of succession or by written contract. Alienation contracts that are not in writing are void.
- *Exclusive rights:* the exclusive right to use an issued design patent is granted to the rights holder, who may be the author, the employer of an assignee.
- *'Use':* in the context of the exclusive right, the right to use includes the right to:
  - import, manufacture, exploit, offer for sale, sale, or other introduction into circulation, or the storage for such purposes, any product that incorporates the design; and

---

14 Article 1234 and Article1357, paragraph 3 of the Civil Code.
15 Article 1369.
16 Article 1241.
17 Regulations, Item 14.

- deemed use of the protected design if the article in dispute contains all of the essential features both shown in the illustrations and stated in the list of essential features.

2.5 Registration procedure

(a) *Application formalities*

In order to obtain a filing date for a design, Article 1377 of the Civil Code and Item 9 of the Regulations stipulate that the following documents must be filed.

Request for issuance: the request must be filed in the Russian language and be signed by the applicant or its representative.

Certified copy of priority application: see section 4.1 below on Convention priority.

Power of attorney: Item 5.2 of the Regulations stipulates that foreign entities must be represented by a registered Russian patent attorney. Normally, no power of attorney is required[18] unless the prosecution of the application becomes contentious or intervening steps are required during prosecution, such as the filing of an assignment, or revisions to the application. In that case, a power of attorney is required so that the designated attorney may communicate with the patent office.

Set of representations of the article: representations of the article must provide a full and detailed illustration of the outward appearance – at least one and possibly more than one view of the article is required in order to give a detailed idea of the article's visual appearance. If colour is an aspect of the design, the representation must show that colour. The drawings/photographs must be sharp, clear-cut and presented against a neutral background. Dotted lines may be used to show non-essential features or features whose legal protection is not claimed.[19]

Drawing(s): a drawing of the general view of the article[20] is also required if it is essential for disclosing the essence of the design.

Description: Item 9.2 of the Regulations specifies that the description must disclose verbally the features of the visual appearance of the article. It must consist of the following sections.

Title: the title is to state the purpose of the article and should be singular unless it is a collective term such as 'shoes' or 'scissors'.[21]

---

18 Articles 1376 to 1377.
19 Regulations, Item 9.8.2.
20 Article 1377 and Regulations, Item 9.2.

Purpose and field of application: this part sets out the purpose of the article and is to indicate the primary fields of the article's application.[22]

Analogues: the author must give information on known analogues (ie, prior art), making a special note of the features of the analogues that coincide with those of the subject design. Bibliographic data is also required. In addition the 'nearest analogue' must be identified in terms of its essential features.[23]

List of pictures/drawings: the list of pictures and drawings must identify them by number and provide a concise description of what is depicted in each.[24]

Disclosure of the essential elements: the most critical aspect regarding both formalities and substance is the requirement to provide a list of the essential features of the design.[25] The essential-features listing will be the primary consideration during both the substantive examination as to novelty and originality and in connection with an infringement analysis. Additional characteristics in the list of essential features cannot be added as supplementary material after the initial filing date.[26]

Item 9.9.4.4 sets out the regulatory requirements in this regard:

- the essence of the design is to be set out in the totality of essential features;
- those features are to include features determining the aesthetic or ergonomic peculiarities of an article's visual appearance, form, configuration, ornament, colours and so on;
- a design may include the article's lines, contours, decor, texture or pattern and the essential features must produce a visual impression;
- non-essential features are those whose exclusion does not change the visual impression;
- in the list of essential features, those which are distinctive over the nearest prior art must be specifically identified;
- reference to the drawings, photographs, etc is to be made in the list of essential features so as to identify those features in the drawings, etc;
- the description must set out the peculiarities of the article that are an embodiment of the design;
- further details concerning the style and approach to describing the essential features are provided in the Regulations at Items 9.9.4.4.1 and 9.9.4.4.2;
- the list of essential features must be in a single claim for each design, expressed as a "logically connected and consistent statement of ... features in one sentence".[27]

If the required documents are not all filed at once and satisfactorily, the filing

21 Regulations, Item 9.9.3.
22 Regulations, Item 9.9.4.1.
23 Regulations, Item 9.9.4.2.
24 Regulations, Item 9.9.4.3.
25 Article 1377 and Regulations, Item 9.2.
26 Article 1378 of the Civil Code.
27 Regulations, Item 9.10.3.1.

date will be the date upon which the application is completed.[28]

See Appendix 1 to this chapter, where a design registration document from Russia, in the public domain since July 2011, is shown (translated into English) as an example of what information needs to be supplied.

(b) *Examination*

The examination takes place in two distinct stages, namely formal and substantive.

Upon filing, the application undergoes a formal examination to ensure the minimum compliance with the filing requirements for documentation. If the application passes the formal examination, the applicant is notified and an official filing date is assigned. If the formal requirements have not been met, the applicant will be notified and allowed two months to rectify the shortcomings. Under Article 1377, the filing date of the application will be the date on which the application has been amended to satisfy all requirements.

Although in the case of patents for inventions, a notice of patent application is published and laid open for public inspection after 18 months, this is not the case for design applications. Nor is there any requirement to request a substantive examination, which is automatic.

The substantive examination primarily focuses on assessing whether the design meets the requirements of novelty and originality. In the case of prosecution, the examiner may request supplementary materials, an amended list of essential elements and corrections to any shortcomings of the application.[29] Time limits are extendable and missed deadlines can be reinstated for up to 12 months.[30]

Further details on the steps in formal and substantive examination are set out in the Regulations in Items 21 to 24.

Once a positive decision has been reached, the design registration will be issued upon payment of the final fee.[31] The registration is then published in the *Official Gazette*.[32]

On publication, the application documents and the search reports are available for public inspection.[33] This does not include any correspondence after filing.

If the examiner issues a negative decision on patentability, that decision may be reviewed by the Chamber for Patent Disputes. The chamber may, in turn, confirm the rejection of the application or allow it.[34]

(c) *Term of protection and maintenance*

Protection for a design begins on registration and may last for up to 25 years, beginning with an initial term of 15 years from the filing date. One ten-year extension is available on payment of a renewal fee, in addition to annual maintenance fees.[35]

---

28 Article 1377, paragraph 2.3.
29 Article 1386, paragraph 5 and Article 1391, paragraph 2.
30 Article 1389.
31 Article 1393.
32 Article 1394.
33 Article 1394, paragraph 2.
34 Article 1248, paragraph 2 and Article 1406, paragraph 2.
35 Article 1363.

The annual maintenance fees increase from year to year. For design registrations, the first payment is due at the end of the second anniversary of the registration date. There is a six-month grace period within which to make an overdue payment of an additional fee.

(d) *Early termination and reinstatement*

If the deadline date for payment of an annual maintenance fee is not met, the registration is deemed to be terminated under Article 1399 of the Civil Code. However, the design registration may be reinstated upon payment of additional fees within three years of the initial payment deadline. Notice of the reinstatement is published in the *Official Gazette*. The registration is of no effect as regards infringement during the period of early termination and reinstatement.

A person who, in the period of early termination, began to use the design or made preparations necessary for using it retains the right to use it even after the design has been reinstated. This exceptional provision is not available to anyone who had begun to use the design before the initial early termination of its registration; it is only available to those who began use or preparations for use after termination and before reinstatement. The user only has a limited right to continue using, without broadening the scope of such use. However, it is not entirely clear what 'scope of use' and 'without broadening the scope of such use' mean, for example in the case of a manufacturing scenario where a production line may have been constructed in order to make a design with line production capabilities that could be substantially varied based on demand. This exception is provided for in Article 1400, paragraph 3.

3. Unregistered design rights

If a design defines the outward appearance of an article and the author created it as a result of his intellectual activity, it is protectable as a registered design provided that the work product is also new and original. However, Article 1353 stipulates that a design is only protectable as a design if it is duly registered on the basis of a grant from the patent office.

Accordingly, a third party is free to use and copy the subject matter of a design created by someone else provided that no other collateral intellectual property rights such as patents or copyright are infringed at the same time (see section 4.2 below).

An unregistered design that qualifies for registration still has value as a form of unregistered intellectual property right in the sense that it can be the subject of an application for registration. In that context the unregistered right has value until the grace period has expired or another party has filed its own application.

4. Qualification for protection

In addition to previously outlined formal and substantive requirements for registrability of designs, such as subject matter, novelty and originality, there are a few additional aspects to protection. These include convention priority, the interface between copyright, trademarks and design, and marking requirements.

4.1 Convention priority

The priority date for an application first filed in Russia is the filing date.

Russia is a member of the Paris Convention for the Protection of Industrial Property. Accordingly, under Article 1382 of the Civil Code, the priority date of a design may be established as the date of filing of the first application in another state that is also a member of the Paris Convention, provided that the filing of the application in Russia is made within six months of the first filing date. This period may be extended for up to two months if, for circumstances not dependent on the applicant, it could not have been filed in a timely manner.[36]

In order to claim priority, a certified copy of the priority application must be filed with the patent office within three months of the filing in Russia. Multiple priority claims are permitted and all priority applications must be filed within the three-month period.[37]

4.2 The design, copyright and trademark interface

In the Russian Federation, there is no express provision to the effect that copyright, design and trademarks are mutually exclusive. Accordingly, it is possible that a single design, whether it is two- or three-dimensional, could be protectable simultaneously as design and trademark subject matter. It is an open issue whether it can also be protected by copyright at the same time. Of course, in each case the article or design would have to independently qualify for each right.

This may be distinguished in some countries, for example Canada, where a design that would qualify as a protectable design, and otherwise as copyright subject matter, would be statutorily excluded from protection as copyright subject matter if more than 50 articles were commercially produced. Further, the use of the design that is protectable as copyright and design subject matter may be also be a registrable trademark provided that it has become distinctive as an indication serving to individualise goods or services of legal persons and entrepreneurs.

The issue of functionality may be a factor in the registrability of trademarks and designs but not of copyright.

4.3 Marking requirements

There is no statutory requirement to mark designs that are registered in Russia as designs. There is also no prohibition from doing so. Properly marking a product with information concerning a patent registration is advisable to ward off infringers and strategically to bolster the owner's (and to diminish the infringer's) credibility at trial. However, it would not be advisable incorrectly to mark a design as being registered when it is not, as this could form the basis of a possible anti-monopoly proceeding against the manufacturer and the distributor.

---

36 Article 1382, paragraph 1.
37 Regulations, Item 9.3.

5. Infringement and validity

5.1 Infringement

Article 1229 falls under Chapter 69 of the General Provisions of Part IV of the Code. In acknowledging the exclusive right to intellectual activity protected under the Civil Code, paragraph 1 stipulates that:

> *The rightholder may at his discretion permit or prohibit other persons to use the result of intellectual activity ... Absence of prohibition shall not be considered to be consent (or permission).*
>
> *Other persons may not use the corresponding result of intellectual activity ... without the consent of the right holder, with the exception of cases provided under the present Code. The use of a result of intellectual activity ... if such use is conducted without the consent of the right holder is unlawful and shall entail the liability established by the present Code and other statutes with the exception [where it] is allowed by the present Code.*

Further guidance is given by Article 1250, paragraph 1, which states that intellectual property rights will be protected by the means provided by the Code, taking into consideration the essence of the infringed right and the consequence of the infringement of this right.

As regards the rights in question, Article 1358 grants the rights holder the exclusive right to use a design by any means. In terms of exclusivity, the right of 'use' includes:

- *exclusive rights:* the exclusive right to use an issued design patent is accorded to the rights holder, who may be the author or the employer of an assignee;
- *'use':* in the context of the exclusive right, the right to use includes the right to:
  - import, manufacture, exploit, offer for sale, sale, or other introduction into circulation, or the storage for such purposes, any product that incorporates the design; and
  - deemed use of the protected design if the article in dispute contains all of the essential features shown on the application both in the illustrations and stated in the list of essential features.[38]

Article 1252 sets out the remedies that are available generally, such as injunctions, damages and so on (see section 6.3 below).

Exclusive licensees enjoy the right to sue and claim infringement just as the rights holder does. The exclusive licensee may file an action for infringement and claim the same remedies that the rights holder can. Such an action may be filed with the rights holder as a co-plaintiff or independently of the rights holder.

In addition to other subjects of jurisdiction, the courts are exclusively empowered to hear and rule upon disputes at the first instance which are associated with infringement of registered design rights. The courts also have exclusive jurisdiction under Article 1406 of the Civil Code to consider issues relating to:

38 Article 1358, paragraph 3.

- disputes on assignment contracts;
- disputes on licence agreements;
- findings as to rights of prior and later use; and
- assessment of compensation.

A person accused of infringement of a design in a court proceeding may assert the following defences in the proceeding:

- *non-infringement/essential elements:* that on a construction of the registered design illustrations and in the list of essential features, the article does not take all of the essential characteristics;
- *licence:* that the acts complained of are the subject of a licence;
- *prior use:* that the defendant has rights of prior use under Article 1361;
- *state use:* that the use is a use of a design by the state under Article 1360;
- *compulsory licence:* that the use is under compulsory licence obtained under Article 1362 by reason of failure to use a design;
- *non-ownership:* that the plaintiff is not the owner of the design by reason of assignment;
- *exhaustion of rights:* that the use is of a design originating from the rights holder or one of the rights holder's authorised licensees such that exhaustion of rights applies;
- *abandonment:* that the design was previously revoked for non-payment of maintenance fees;
- *limitation period:* that there is an expired limitation date to file a claim; or
- *special exemption:* that the actions are exempt from infringement under Article 1359, namely experimentation, use in extraordinary circumstances (such as natural disasters), personal, non-commercial use, one-time preparation of pharmaceutical preparations, importation with the consent of the rights holder and so on.

5.2 Invalidity and cancellation

While a determination of infringement at the first instance is determined by the court (usually a commercial court if the dispute is between legal entities and/or registered entrepreneurs), the assessment of invalidity is independently determined at the first instance by the Chamber for Patent Disputes. Even if there is a pending action for infringement in the court, that court is not competent to hear and determine assertions of invalidity at the first instance as this is reserved to the Chamber for Patent Disputes. Unlike the case in many other countries, invalidity is not a defence that can be put forward as a defence in an infringement action. Ultimately, but not necessarily, the two proceedings might come together at higher appellate levels.

Article 1363, paragraph 5 stipulates that a design right may be found to be invalid and certified as such under the procedure set out in Articles 1398 and 1399. Under Article 1398 the grounds of invalidity are set out next.

(a) *Unpatentable design*

As mentioned in section 2.2 above, Article 1352 stipulates the conditions of patentability of a design, namely subject matter, novelty and originality.

Subject-matter: to be registrable, the proposed design must be an artistic design presentation of a manufacture of industrial or handicraft production defining its outward appearance.

The focus is always on the essential characteristics as they are defined in words in the application. The design must be artistic and define external appearance. Appearance includes shape, configuration, ornamentation and combinations of colours. This would probably include patterns, graphics and fonts as examples, as well as overall shape or external form. There is no stated requirement that the commercialised product be manufactured in a specified amount, so as to be regarded as a solution of a manufacture – presumably it would include subject matter of one single handicraft production.

The essential characteristics of the design must also be new and original.

Excluded subject matter: legal protection is not available for designs that are determined exclusively by the technical function of the article. The word 'exclusively' is noteworthy as designs that are not determined exclusively by functionality would qualify. The scope and meaning of 'exclusively' has been the subject of judicial scrutiny in other countries, but the Supreme Court in Russia (the only court empowered to ascribe constructions and interpretations to the Code in a binding way) has not yet considered the scope and meaning of this term.

Works of architecture, industrial, hydro-technical and other stationary structures are also excluded save from "minor architectural forms, which do qualify as subject matter", such as gargoyles, railings and doors.

Paragraph 5 of Article 1352 excludes objects of unstable shape, such as liquids, gases and dry substances.

Novelty: a design is deemed to be new if the sum of its essential features is not known from information generally available anywhere in the world before the priority date of the application.

Absolute novelty and grace period: notwithstanding an absolute novelty requirement, there is a six-month grace period. The applicant has six months to file an application with ROSPATENT (where the filing date must be the actual filing date with the Russian patent office and not the convention priority date) from the date the author, applicant or other person who may have received information from them, made the information on the essence of the design public. Should there have been such a publication or disclosure, the burden of proof rests on the applicant to prove that the applicant nonetheless qualifies for the grace period.

Originality: a design must not only be new but it must also be original. Paragraph 3 of Article 1352 states that a design is deemed to be original if its essential features are determined by the creative nature of the special aspects of the article. It is probable that originality, as distinguished from novelty, does not mean that the totality of the essential features are new but that the design in addition to being new was also conceived independently by the author.

(b) Improperly included essential features

The registration will be invalid if any essential features listed for the registered design were not included in the original list filed with the application or were not present in the illustrations submitted on the filing date.

(c) Same priority date

It is not legally possible to have two patents for identical designs with the same priority dates. A patent issued despite this prohibition will be invalid. In that case, Article 1383 should have been applied and will be if one of the applications is still pending. In any case, the issued patent(s) can be declared invalid. If one patent is still the subject of an application and the other has been issued, the issued patent can be invalidated. As regards the pending application, it is likely that the owner of the issued and now invalidated patent could request the patent office to implement Article 1383. In that case, the owner of the issued and invalidated patent could require that the author of the invalidated patent be indicated as a co-author in the pending application which is about to issue.

(d) Misnaming of author

A registered design can be invalidated if either the registration wrongly identifies as an author a person who is not the author (even if the correct authors are also named) or the registration fails to include a person who is the author, such as a co-inventor.

An interested party may initiate proceedings to cancel a registered design under Articles 1248 and 1406 of the Code and also in accordance with the governing patent office regulations.

5.3 Limitation period

There is a three-year general limitation period for intellectual property and other commercial claims under the Civil Code. The applicable provision is contained in Chapter 12 of the Code.

The limitation is triggered on the day when the rights holder learned or should have learned about the violation of its right – in this case the alleged infringing act. However, the Civil Code and other laws establish certain exceptions to this rule.

6. Design infringement litigation

A rights holder has three options available to enforce registered rights, namely civil proceedings, administrative proceedings (such as border measures and anti-monopoly proceedings) and criminal enforcement.

6.1 Civil proceedings

Under Article 1248, disputes on the infringement of intellectual property (IP) rights must be considered by a court.

There are two possible courts for such disputes, namely the courts of general jurisdiction and the commercial courts. As a general rule, an action must be brought in the courts of general jurisdiction if at least one party to the dispute is a natural person not registered as an entrepreneur. When only legal entities and/or entrepreneurs are involved, the commercial courts have jurisdiction. The court of principal and preferred jurisdiction is the commercial court, which hears the greatest number of intellectual property cases and thus has the commensurate experience. However, the commercial court is not an intellectual property specialist court and it hears cases of all kinds regarding disputes between legal entities. The formation of a specialist patent court is currently being discussed, but the timing of this is uncertain.

The commercial courts have three levels. The fourth level is an appeal to the Supreme Commercial Court. The courts of first instance are the commercial courts of the federal districts, of which there are about 80. At this level, matters are heard by a single judge. Decisions of the commercial courts may be appealed to the Commercial Courts of Appeal, where the appeal is heard by three judges. A further right of appeal is to the Federal Commercial Courts of Cassation Appeals. The final level of appeal is to the Supreme Commercial Court. This structure is illustrated in Appendix 2 at the end of the chapter.

The formation of a specialist IP court is currently planned for February 2013. The IP court would hear appeals from the Chamber for Patent Disputes (such as decisions on validity and patentability) and appeals from the Commercial Courts of Appeal (such as those dealing with infringement).

6.2 General procedure and evidentiary requirements

In an infringement action filed in the commercial court, the initiating document is a statement of claim. Once the claim has been reviewed by the court authorities for its compliance with formalities, the claim is accepted and the proceedings are officially initiated. As it is a court system associated with a Civil Code country, the evidence in the proceedings focuses mainly on a review of documents in conjunction with submissions of counsel and, in many cases, the input of a court-appointed expert. Oral evidence from live witnesses is rare, as is cross-examination.

In infringement cases, both the rights holder and an exclusive licensee, if any, may institute proceedings.

Liability for infringement is assessed objectively and it is a strict liability offence. Article 1250 provides that: "the absence of fault of an infringer shall not free him from the obligation to stop infringement … and shall not exclude the application to the infringer of measures directed to the protection of such rights".

The time taken to get to trial and to obtain a ruling is relatively short, usually between one and two years.

6.3 Remedies

A rights holder enjoys the exclusive right to the design patent. Under Article 1229 of the Civil Code, a rights holder has the right to prohibit others from using that right. Any unauthorised use of the right is deemed to be unlawful. Protection of the exclusive right entitles the owner to request one or more of the following forms of relief in the courts:

- *recognition of rights:* in effect a declaration, this remedy entitles the rights holder to recognition that the rights in question have been infringed by the defending party;
- *termination of the activities:* the rights holder is entitled to claim injunctive relief, both interim and permanent, to enjoin the infringing activities or the threat of infringing activities; in cases of interim relief the rights holder may be required to post security with the court;
- *compensation:* the infringer may be obliged to pay compensation to the rights holder, either in the form of damages or alternative relief in the form of compensation for infringement – for example, an accounting of profits or a reasonable royalty. In that case the rights holder does not need to prove actual damage and can turn to the court for compensation from the infringer for each case of unlawful use;[39]
- *seizure:* equipment and physical carriers associated with an infringement may be ordered removed from circulation and destroyed;
- *publication of decision:* the rights holder may request publication of the decision declaring him to be the owner and the defendant the infringer; and
- *bad faith:* in cases where the court recognises the infringement as having been in bad faith, protection may be available under anti-monopoly legislation as well as under Part IV of the Civil Code.

Under Article 1253, if a legal person repeatedly violates intellectual property rights, including design rights, the court may direct that the legal entity be dissolved. In the case of an individual, the court may direct that his activity as an individual entrepreneur be terminated.

6.4 How courts have assessed infringement in practice

There is no doctrine of *stare decisis* under the Civil Code. With the exception of guidance given by the Supreme Commercial Court on the subject of interpreting and applying the provisions of Part IV, the courts are free to interpret the legal provisions applying to design protection according to the circumstances. The decisions concerning design are generally brief, providing a simple declaration of the court's conclusions. Thus, little guidance can be taken from earlier case law to assess the possible outcome of a future case. However, for cases on design infringement, the courts consistently have regard to the list of essential elements, with reference to the drawings or images. Should an accused infringing product not have each and every essential element, it is probable that the court will find no infringement.

6.5 Cancellation proceedings

A request to cancel a registered design may be instituted in the Chamber for Patent Disputes on the statutory grounds mentioned above. Any third party may bring a cancellation request.

---

39 Article 1252, paragraphs 1(2) and 3.

There is no official procedure to oppose or to protest a pending design application. However, any party can send an informal letter to the examiner before application is allowed, which may be considered. No substantive correspondence will be entered into and the examiner is free to consider all or none of the submissions made.

6.6 Costs

No costs awards associated with the outcome of the decision are given in cancellation proceedings before the Chamber for Patent Disputes. Each party bears its own costs.

Under Article 110 of the Commercial Procedural Code, the basic rule is that the unsuccessful party will bear the burden of court costs. Under Article 106, costs include the amounts payable to experts, witnesses and interpreters, expenses associated with on-site inspections, lawyers' fees and so on.

However, the fees paid to court-appointed experts, for example, are very low and the amounts payable for legal fees are also very low. Thus, the court costs payable by the unsuccessful party are low and usually do not represent a significant amount when compared with the amount or significance of the claim itself.

7. Licensing and exploitation

Under Part IV of the Civil Code, a rights holder may permit others to use that right.[40] The licence agreement must be signed by both parties, it must clearly identify the right that is being licensed and it must be registered in the patent office. If the licence is not recorded, the code stipulates that it is invalid. As is the case with assignments, under Article 1233, paragraph 4, no licence may provide any form of restrictive covenant to the effect that either of the parties are in any way restricted from engaging in an area of intellectual activity or are restricted in the respect of the right to transfer rights to others. A licence can be exclusive or non-exclusive, can be territorial and can provide for carve-outs of specific rights forming part of a greater whole.

The main provisions relating to licensing are contained in Article 1235, which relates to all forms of intellectual property rights. The key points are as follows:

- a licence grant must be in writing and extends only so far as the grant provided for in the written contract;
- a licence grant must be registered in the patent office;
- a licence is presumed to cover the whole of the Russian Federation unless it expressly provides otherwise;
- the licence can be for any length of time provided that the term does not extend beyond the life of the intellectual property right being licensed – in this case a design registration;
- if no time period is stipulated, the term of the licence is deemed to be five years;
- if the intellectual property right that was licensed is terminated, for example by way of cancellation or non-renewal, the licence is also terminated;

---

40 Article 1229.

- there is no minimum consideration requirement – the consideration may be nil if the parties so choose. However, if the contract stipulates that it is made for consideration but fails to state the consideration, then it is void;
- the contract itself must identify the design registration which is licensed by giving the number and date of issue;
- the licence must indicate the permitted uses; and
- if the licensor assigns the design right to a new assignee, the assignee takes that right subject to the previously granted and recorded licence.

Licenses can be non-exclusive or exclusive. Unless provided otherwise, a licence is deemed to be non-exclusive.[41]

It is legally possible for a licensee to sub-license rights relating to a design, provided that the licensor has consented to this in the licence contract. Such consent could be provided in the master licence between the licensor and the licensee. As with any licence, it must be registered in the patent office or it will have no effect. The licensee can only receive a sub-licence that is as broad as the terms set out in the master licence and for a term not exceeding that of the master licence. If there is a sub-licence, then the licensee under the master licence/sub-licensor is liable for the actions for the sub-licensee unless the contract provides otherwise.

Unless the licence contract provides otherwise, Article 1237 of the Civil Code stipulates performance obligations on the licensee that will be read into the contract. For example, the licensee must present reports on the use of the licensed design on the demand of the licensor. The licensor in turn must refrain from doing anything that might hinder the realisation by the licensee of the rights that were licensed. To the extent that a licensee carries out an activity that is not covered by the terms of the licence, or in the event that the licence has expired or been otherwise terminated and the licensee is continuing the previously licensed activity, such unlicensed use is actionable as infringement.

The rights holder also has an opportunity to offer an open licence. In that case the owner submits to the patent office a statement offering the licence, which is on a non-exclusive basis and the maintenance fees otherwise payable are reduced by 50% from the time the offer of an open licence has been published in the *Official Gazette*. The rights holder retains the right to stipulate the licence terms, which are also published.[42]

7.1 Compulsory licences

Article 1362 contains two compulsory licence provisions, namely non-use compulsory licences and dependent invention licences. Non-use compulsory licences are available for inventions, utility models and designs. Dependent invention licences are not available for designs but are available for inventions and utility models.

41 Article 1236.
42 Article 1368.

(a) ***Non-use compulsory licences***

If the rights holder does not use a registered design for four years from the date of issue, a third party may apply for a licence. The third party must first ask the patentee for a licence. If the request is rejected, the third party has a right to seek a licence by way of court order. The rights holder then has an opportunity to justify its non-use. If a licence is then granted, it is a non-exclusive one on terms that are intended to reflect industry standards.

(b) ***Dependent invention licences***

In circumstances where a rights holder in either an invention or a design cannot use the invention or design without infringing the rights of another rights holder, the court may grant a licence, and even a cross-licence. As mentioned above, this further provision does not apply to designs.

To date, there is no record of any compulsory licences having been issued.

7.2 Pledge and security interest

Paragraph 5 of Article 1233 of the Civil Code allows for rights holder to pledge the right as a security interest. During the subsistence of the pledge agreement, the pledgor has the right to continue using the right, and even to transfer the exclusive right to use it without the consent of the pledgee. However, the transferee would in such a case take ownership of the right subject to the pre-existing pledge.

The contract granting the security interest must be in writing and must be registered. As with licences and assignments, the pledge agreement will be null and void if it is not properly registered.

Appendix 1: Sample design registration (English translation)

RUSSIAN FEDERATION	**(19) RU (11) 78947 (51) ICID 9 09-03**
	(15) Registration date: 16.07.2011
	(21) Application number: 2010501102
	(22) Filing date: 22.04.2010
	(24) Valid from: 22.04.2010
FEDFERAL SERVICE FOR INTELLECTUAL PROPERTY, PATENTS AND TRADEMARKS	(45) Publication date: 16.07.2011

(12) DETAILS OF INDUSTRIAL DESIGN PATENT

Priority:	
(30) Convention priority: **19.03.2010 US 29/357,978**	(72) Inventor(s): **Dudek, Jason Charles (US)** **Coble, Justin Allen (US)**
(73) Patent holder(s): **Mars Incorporated, a Delaware corporation (US)**	(74) Representative of the patent holder: **Sinitsyna A Yu, reg no 856**
	Address for service: **Gowlings International Inc.** **Gogolevsky Boulevard, 11,** **Moscow 119019, Russia** **Attention: Sinitsyna A Yu**
(54) CONTAINER (COMBINED), CONTAINER BOX (2 options, separate unit of the article) and INSERT (3 options, separate unit of the article)	
(55) (57)	

1. Combined container for confectionery

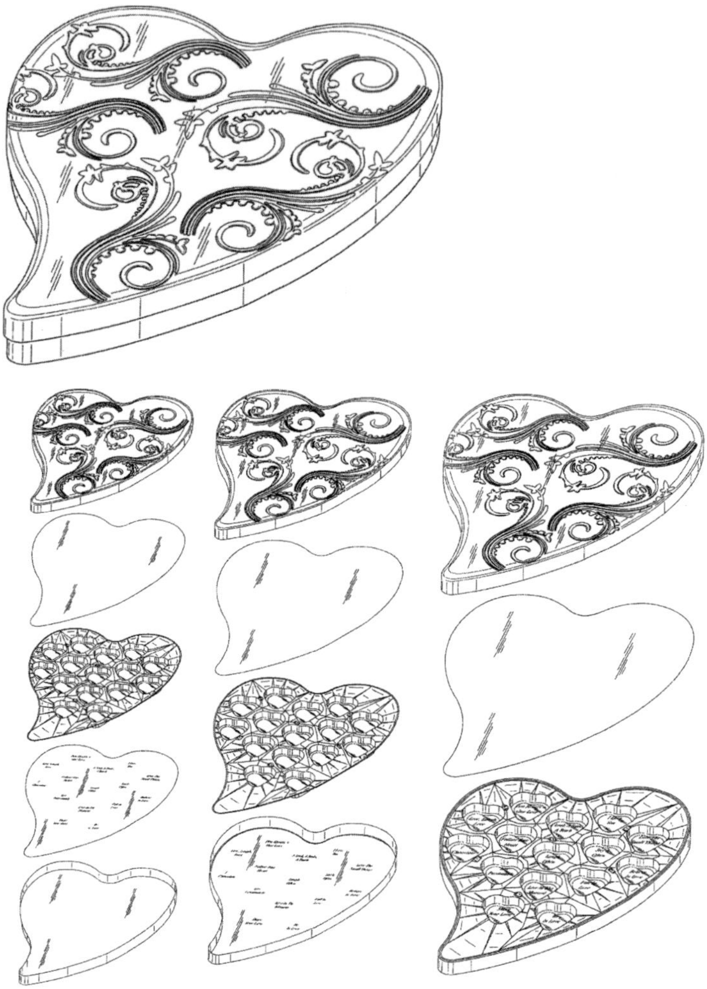

Characterised by:

- a composition comprising a box consisting of a pallet, a removable cover and an insert with shaped cavities;
- a shape on the basis of a triangular prism with curved sides;
- pictorial design of the box cover;
- rhythmic arrangement of cavities in the insert;
- heart-shaped article with asymmetric sidewalls – convex right sidewall and wave-like left sidewall;
- coupling of sidewalls rounded off at the front;
- coupling of the box cover with the pallet and formation of a step-like lateral area;
- design of the upper side of the cover having bevelled edges;

- decoration of the cover top with flower ornament on the basis of the linear representation of a stylised shamrock with lateral elements in the form of oppositely oriented vignettes;
- heart-shaped cavities of the insert arranged in chess-board fashion;
- folded pattern of the insert intervals between cavities, contour border of the cavity bottom;
- upper surface of the insert decorated with arrow-shaped elements outwardly radiating from the outer edges of the sidelong cavities;
- arrangement of the peripheral section of the insert, wherein said peripheral section is bent up relative to the cavities area.

2. **A container box (option 1, separate unit),**

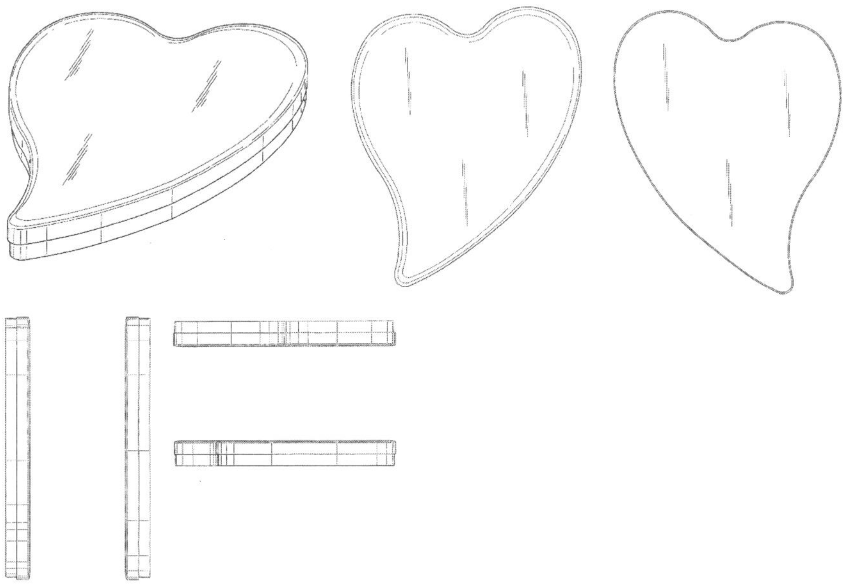

Characterised by:

- a composition comprising the insert and the removable cover;
- a shape on the basis of a triangular prism with curved sides;
- heart-shaped article with asymmetric sidewalls – convex right sidewall and wave-like left sidewall;
- coupling of sidewalls rounded off at the front;
- coupling of the box cover with the pallet and formation of a step-like lateral area;
- design of the upper side of the cover having bevelled edges.

3. A container box (option 2, separate unit):

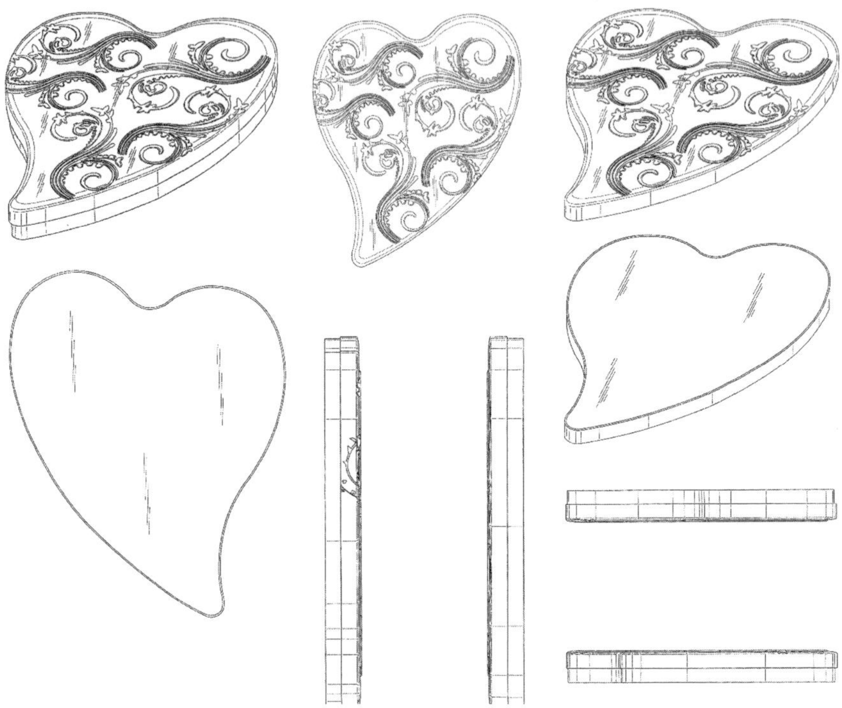

Characterised by:

- a composition comprising the insert and the removable cover;
- a shape on the basis of a triangular prism with curved sides;
- pictorial design of the box cover;
- heart-shaped article with asymmetric sidewalls – convex right sidewall and wave-like left sidewall;
- coupling of sidewalls rounded off at the front;
- coupling of the box cover with the pallet and formation of a step-like lateral area;
- design of the upper side of the cover having bevelled edges.

4. An insert (option 1, separate unit):

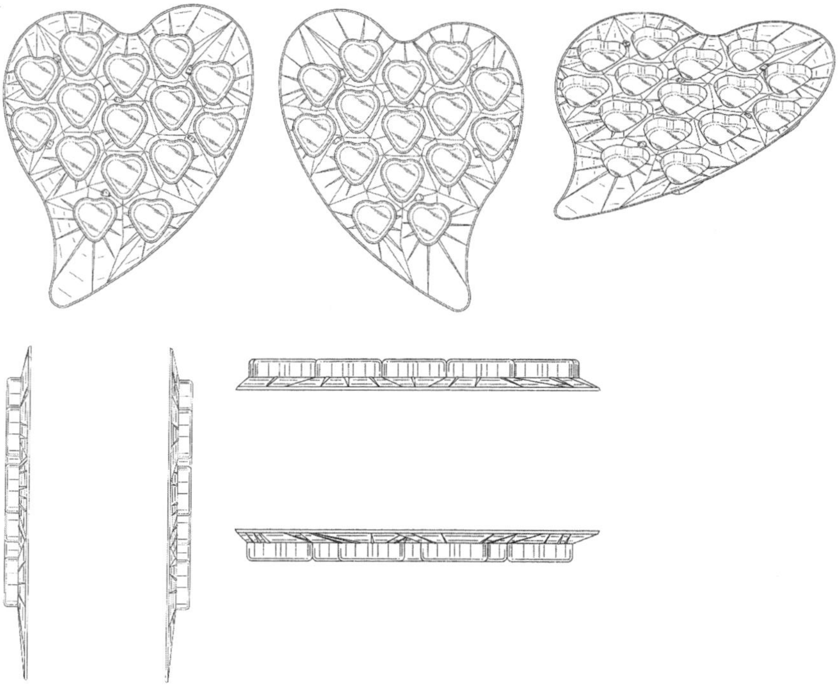

Characterised by:

- an embossed plate with shaped cavities;
- rhythmic arrangement of cavities over the insert;
- folded pattern of the insert intervals between cavities, contour border of the cavity bottom;
- upper surface of the insert decorated with arrow-shaped elements outwardly radiating from the outer edges of the sidelong cavities;
- arrangement of the peripheral section of the insert, wherein said peripheral section is bent up relative to the cavities area;
- heart-shaped cavities of the insert arranged in chess-board fashion.

5. An insert (option 2, separate unit):

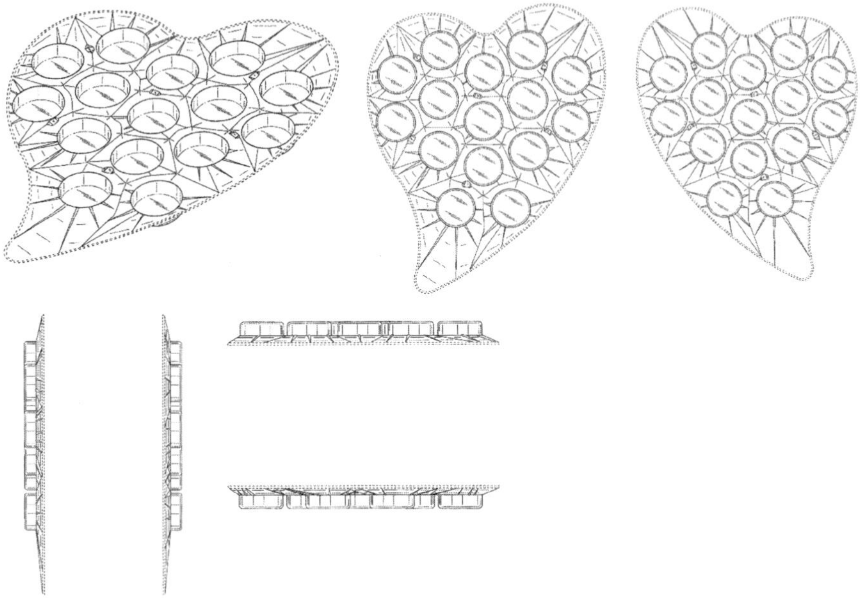

Characterised by:

- an embossed plate with round cavities;
- rhythmic arrangement of cavities over the insert;
- folded pattern of the insert intervals between cavities, contour border of the cavity bottom;
- upper surface of the insert decorated with arrow-shaped elements outwardly radiating from the outer edges of the sidelong cavities;
- arrangement of the peripheral section of the insert, wherein said peripheral section is bent up relative to the cavities area;
- heart-shaped cavities of the insert arranged in chess-board fashion.

6. **An insert (option 3, separate unit):**

Characterised by:

- an embossed plate with rectangular cavities;
- rhythmic arrangement of cavities over the insert;
- folded pattern of the insert intervals between cavities, contour border of the cavity bottom;
- upper surface of the insert decorated with arrow-shaped elements outwardly radiating from the outer edges of the sidelong cavities;
- arrangement of the peripheral section of the insert, wherein said peripheral section is bent up relative to the cavities area;
- heart-shaped cavities of the insert arranged in chess-board fashion.

Appendix 2: The Russian commercial court system

The organisational structure of the Russian commercial (arbitration) courts system is based on four levels, as follows.

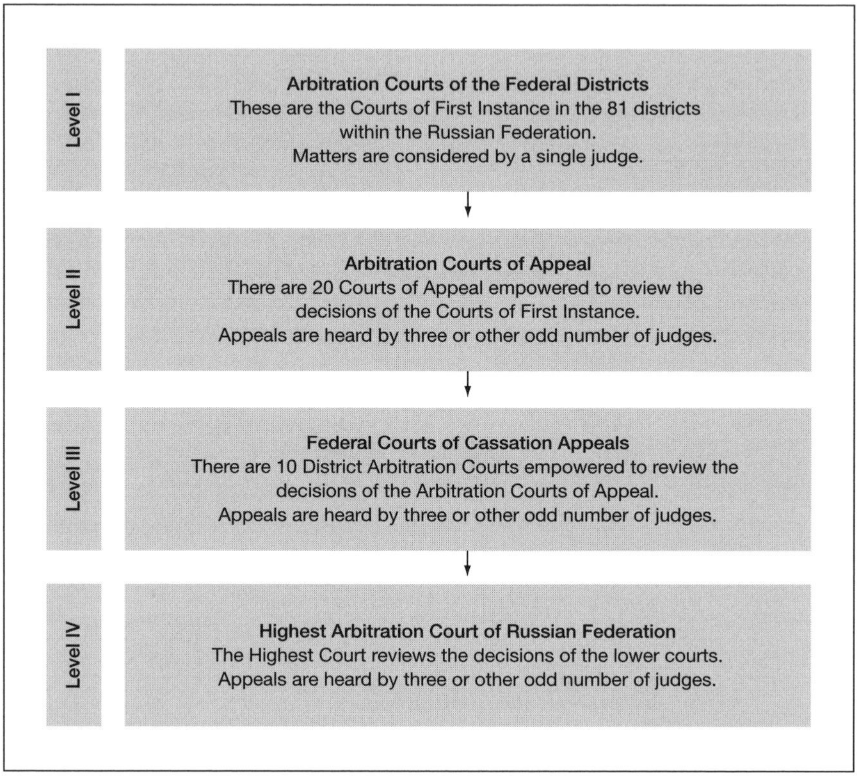

Singapore

Alban Kang
ATMD Bird & Bird LLP

1. Summary of design protection

In Singapore, the protection of industrial designs is governed by the Registered Designs Act 2000.[1] The act came into force on November 13 2000. Before that, the registered designs regime was governed by the UK Designs (Protection) Act.[2]

Under the UK act, a design had to be registered in the United Kingdom. It would then enjoy the same rights and benefits in Singapore as it did in the United Kingdom for as long as the UK protection remained valid. Design infringement actions filed in the Singapore courts relied on the UK-registered designs, and in determining infringement the court would look at the relevant UK statute. The reliance on UK legislation for the protection of industrial designs in Singapore was unsatisfactory.

The UK act was repealed by the Registered Designs Act. Provisions were made for the protection of existing registered UK designs. The act established a registration system for industrial designs, very similar to that of the United Kingdom. Thus UK case law on the UK registered design statutes together with local decisions on the UK act became relevant and of persuasive authority before the Singapore court.

Singapore became a member to the Hague Convention[3] on April 17 2005, which allowed for the protection of industrial designs in member jurisdictions through an international registration filed through the Singapore Designs Registry.[4] Convention priority could also be claimed, which gave foreign owners of industrial designs up to six months from the date of obtaining the foreign design registration to file a design registration in Singapore. With the coming into force of the Registered Designs Act in 2000, Singapore set up its own industrial designs registration system.

The act established a Singapore Designs Registry,[5] where all new industrial designs may be registered.[6] The registry conducts a formality check on a design application but does not examine the design.[7] Once registered, a design is protected for five years, and the registration can be renewed for two further five-year terms.[8]

Registered designs enjoy protection against infringement. If a design is not registrable, it may still enjoy protection under copyright law.[9]

1 Cap 266, Singapore Statutes 2005 Ed.
2 Cap 339, Singapore Statutes 1985 Ed.
3 The Hague Agreement Concerning the International Registration of Industrial Designs and the Geneva Act of the Hague Agreement.
4 The Singapore Designs Registry is part of the Intellectual Property Office of Singapore (IPOS).
5 Registered Designs Act, Part V.
6 *Ibid*, Section 5.
7 *Ibid*, Section 19.

2. Registered designs rights

The Registered Designs Act governs the registration and protection of industrial designs. Registration is a straightforward process and takes only a month or two from filing the application.

An application for registration of a design is filed with the Registry of Designs.[10] The design must be new or novel.[11] The application should state the features of the design which the applicant claims to be new and is seeking to protect. A two-dimensional drawing or picture of the design or article must be submitted with the application. However, it is not necessary to submit the actual article itself.

The priority date of the registration will be the date of the application[12] unless priority is claimed in respect of a prior application in a Convention country filed not more than six months before the Singapore application.[13]

The application should be filed by the person claiming to be owner of the design. Generally, the designer of a design is considered to be the owner of the design.[14] However, subject to any agreement to the contrary, in the case of a commissioned work for money or money's worth, the person commissioning the design will be treated as the owner of the design.[15] In the case of designs created by employees, the employer is treated as the owner of a design subject to any agreement to the contrary.[16] In the case of a computer-generated design such that there is no human designer, the person by whom arrangements necessary for the creation of the design are made will be deemed to be the designer.[17]

There is no substantial examination of the design proper. An application will be examined only to ensure that it satisfies the formal requirements for filing an application.[18] The applicant will be given an opportunity to correct any defects,[19] and an application may be rejected if any defects are not corrected.[20] An application may also be refused if, on the face of the application, the design is not new or registrable for any reason.[21]

If the formal requirements are found to have been satisfied, the design will be registered and notice of the registration will be published.[22] Unlike a patent or trademark application, no opposition can be filed against a design registration. Anyone wishing to challenge the design would need to bring revocation proceedings against the design registration.

A registration is valid for five years from the date of registration of the design,

---

8 *Ibid*, Section 21.
9 Copyright Act (cap 63), Section 74.
10 Registered Designs Act, Section 11.
11 See section 4 below.
12 Registered Designs Act, Section 20.
13 *Ibid*, Sections 12 and 13.
14 *Ibid*, Section 4(1).
15 *Ibid*, Section 4(2).
16 *Ibid*, Section 4(3).
17 *Ibid*, Section 4(6).
18 *Ibid*, Section 16.
19 *Ibid*, Section 16(2).
20 *Ibid*, Section 17.
21 *Ibid*, Section17(2).
22 *Ibid*, Section 18.

which is the date of the application.[23] The registration may be extended for a further two terms of five years upon payment of the prescribed fees. A six-month grace period is given for late extension of the registration.[24]

A registration may be voluntarily surrendered by the rights holder.[25] The only other way to cancel the registration is to have it revoked. An application for revocation may be made to the registrar or to the court, but if there is a pending proceeding in the court in respect of the design, the revocation proceedings must be started in the court.[26] The revocation of a design will take effect from the date of registration or from the date on which the right in the registered design expired.[27]

3. Unregistered design rights

Unregistered designs or designs which are unregistrable may enjoy protection under copyright law.[28] An unregistered design will be protected as an artistic work under the Copyright Act.[29] Both forms of protection grant to the owner a statutory monopoly to exploit the rights granted. However, there are differences between the protection offered by copyright and the protection granted by the Registered Designs Act for a registered design.

Under the Registered Designs Act a design must be new in order to be registrable, while under the Copyright Act, an artistic work must be original.[30] The test for originality is different from the test for novelty under the Registered Designs Act. Copyright exists by virtue of creation of the work and no form of registration is required. The term of protection granted to an artistic work is life of the author plus 70 years,[31] which is much longer than the 15 years of protection available for a registered design.

The copyright monopoly grants to the owner the right to prevent others from reproducing the work or a substantially similar work,[32] even if such reproduction is in a three-dimensional form.[33] This is different from the registered designs monopoly, which is limited to the reproduction of the specific article which is covered by the design. Given the difference in protection, there are limitations imposed in the Copyright Act to artistic works which are registered or capable of being registered as a design.

Under the Copyright Act, an artistic work will not be infringed if a corresponding design has been registered under the Registered Designs Act.[34] Even if the design registration has expired, the artistic work will not enjoy any copyright protection under the Copyright Act.[35] A 'corresponding design' of an artistic work means "a

---

23 *Ibid*, Section 20.
24 *Ibid*, Section 21(5).
25 *Ibid*, Section 26.
26 *Ibid*, Section 27.
27 *Ibid*, Section 27(6).
28 Copyright law is governed by the Copyright Act.
29 Section 7 of the Copyright Act defines an artistic work as including "a painting, sculpture, drawing, engraving or photograph whether the work is of artistic quality or not".
30 Copyright Act, Section 27.
31 *Ibid*, Section 28(2).
32 *Ibid*, Section 26t.
33 *Ibid*, Section 15.
34 *Ibid*, Section 74.
35 *Ibid*, Section 74(1)(b).

design which when applied to an article, results in a reproduction of the work".[36] Therefore, once a design has been registered, the design or the artistic work in the design loses copyright protection. The rationale for this is to ensure that there is no overlap of the protection granted.

In addition to registration, there are other circumstances when a design will be denied protection under the Copyright Act. If a design or the artistic work has been applied industrially by the copyright owner or sold, let for hire, or offered for sale or hire, whether in Singapore or elsewhere, the term of copyright protection in the design or artistic work will be reduced to 15 years[37] – the same period of protection granted under the Registered Designs Act. The protection is also limited to what would have been available under the Registered Designs Act. 'Industrial application' of an artistic work means more than 50 articles are made or, if reproduced on a plate, to make more than 50 reproductions of an object in three dimensions for the purpose of sale or hire.[38] This dichotomy between copyright and registered design protection is to ensure that owners of registrable designs register their designs.

If a design is unregistrable, the prevalent view is that copyright protection will be extended to the underlying artistic work, provided the design has not been applied industrially.

4. Qualification for protection

4.1 Definition of 'a design'

Not all industrial designs qualify for protection under the Registered Designs Act. The act defines a design as: "features of shape, configuration, pattern or ornament applied to an article by an industrial process".[39] An 'article' has been defined to mean any article of manufacture and includes:

- any part of an article if that part is made and sold separately; and
- any set of articles.[40]

However, the following are not considered to be registrable as a design:

- a method or principle of construction; or
- features of shape or configuration of an article that:
  - are dictated solely by the function which the article has to perform;
  - are dependent on the appearance of another article of which the article is intended by the designer to form an integral part; or
  - enable the article to be connected to, or placed in, around or against, another article so that either article may perform its function.

A design must therefore have an 'eye appeal'.[41] It is the aesthetic characteristics

36 *Ibid*, Section 73(1).
37 *Ibid*, Section 74.
38 *Ibid*, Section 70.
39 Definition of 'design': Section 2(1).
40 Definition of 'article': Section 2(1).
41 See *Amp Inc v Utilux Pty Ltd* [1972] RPC 103.

of a design that are registrable, and purely functional designs would be deemed unregistrable. Registrable designs may be three-dimensional (ie, features of shape or configuration) or two-dimensional (ie, patterns or ornaments). Designs printed on textiles or wallpapers are also registrable.

Complex articles with component parts may be registered as designs if they are made and sold separately. The courts have given a rather purposive interpretation of the meaning of 'made and sold separately'.[42] Exclusions to registrability are based on public policy reasons.

The exclusion against a method or principle of construction is to prevent the design registration system from being used to gain a monopoly over a manufacturing process or a principle of construction.[43]

Designs which are dictated solely by function are also not registrable. This is to ensure that a monopoly over functional design features is not granted, since the registration system is to protect the aesthetic aspect of an article's feature. The design must be "dictated solely by function", which the courts have interpreted to mean "attributable to or caused or prompted by" function-related considerations.[44] The functionality bar applies so long as the designer was motivated by functional objectives.

The Registered Designs Act also excludes designs which are "dependent upon the appearance of another article to which the article is intended by the designer to form an integral part". This is known as the 'must match' exclusion or the 'spare parts' exclusion. The rationale behind this exclusion is to prevent a monopoly in the after-sales market of complex articles which require replacement parts, such as spare parts for motor cars.[45]

Similar to the must-match exclusion is the 'must fit' exclusion, where the article to be connected to, or placed in, around or against, another article so that either article may perform its function. The rationale for this exclusion is that design rights should not be granted to an article that is to be interconnected or interfaced with another article.[46]

Other exclusions include designs the publication or use of which would be contrary to public order or morality,[47] and computer program and layout designs,[48] which enjoy specific protection under the Copyright Act and the Layout-Designs of Integrated Circuits Act.[49] Designs of works of sculpture, designs applied to wall plaques, medals and medallions, and designs applied to printed matter primarily of a literary or artistic character[50] are not registrable as they would generally be protected under copyright law.

---

42 See *Ford Motor Co Ltd's Design Application* [1995] RPC 167.

43 See *Pugh v Riley Cycle Co Ltd* (1912) 29 RPC 196.

44 See *Amp Inc Utilux Proprietary Ltd* [1972] RPC 103, which was followed in *Sebel Furniture Ltd v Tiong Hin Engineering Pte Ltd* [1998] 3 SLR(R) 690.

45 See *British Leyland Motor Corp v Amstrong Patent Co Ltd* [1986] AC 577.

46 See *Nagasima Electronic Engineering Pte Ltd v APH Trading Pte Ltd* [2005] 2 SLR(R) 641.

47 Registered Designs Act, Section 6.

48 *Ibid*, Section 7.

49 Cap 159A.

50 Registered Designs Rules, Rule 9.

4.2 Novelty requirement

The most important qualification for registering a design is that it must be new. A design will not be new if it is the same design:

- registered in respect of the same or any other article in pursuance of a prior application; or
- published in Singapore or elsewhere in respect of the same or any other article before the date of the first application.[51]

The priority date of an application on which novelty of the design is to be determined is usually the date of application for registration of the design.[52] An earlier priority date of up to six months can be claimed if there is a corresponding earlier application filed in a member country of the Paris Convention or the World Trade Organization.[53] Thus an earlier priority date will be the date on which the determination of novelty of the registered design is made, notwithstanding a later filing date in Singapore.[54]

The novelty of a design will be destroyed by an identical design registered earlier in respect of the same or any other article, or where the same design was published in Singapore or elsewhere before the priority date.[55] The test for publication is similar to the test under patent law. Any form of disclosure, whether written or oral, will constitute publication of the design. Advertisement of the design by a foreign designs registry also constitutes publication, notwithstanding that the design may not proceed to registration. For the publication or disclosure to destroy novelty, there must be clear and unmistakable directions to make the article with the same design.[56] As with patent law, the disclosure should be contained in a single document and mosaic or derived from a collection of documents.

Not all forms of disclosure will affect the novelty requirement of a design. The following types of disclosure will not be a ground for refusal of registration or a ground for revocation of the registration:

- the disclosure of the design by the owner to any other person in circumstances that would make it contrary to good faith for that other person to use or publish the design;
- the disclosure of the design in breach of good faith by any person other than the owner of the design;
- in the case of a new or original textile design intended for registration, the acceptance of a first and confidential order for goods bearing the design; or
- the communication of the design by the owner to a government department or the registry or to any person authorised by a government department or the registry to consider the merits of the design, or of anything done in consequence of such a communication.[57]

---

51 Registered Designs Act, Section 5.
52 Registered Designs Rules, Rule 16.
53 Registered Designs Act, Section 12.
54 *Ibid*, Section 12(2).
55 See *Nagasima Electronic Engineering Pte Ltd v APH Trading Pte Ltd* [2005] 2 SLR(R) 64, where the Court took into consideration the existing designs that were already in the market.
56 See *Hunter Manufacturing Pte Ltd v Soundtex Switchgear & Engineering Plc Ltd* [2000] 1 SLR(R) 50.

The first two categories cover disclosures made in confidence or made in breach of a duty of confidence. A special exception is allowed for textiles where a first order of the textiles is made in confidence. The last category protects disclosure to government agencies only if the disclosure is for the purpose of determining the merits of the design.

Any disclosure at an international exhibition and any unauthorised disclosure from that exhibition will not be a ground for refusing or revoking a design registration, provided the application is made no more than six months after the exhibition opens.[58]

There are other exceptions to the prior publication exclusion of new designs. If an artistic work has been exploited in public and the registration of the design is with the consent of the copyright owner in the artistic work, the design will be treated as new.[59] However, this special novelty-saving provision will not apply if the prior use or publication of the artistic work consisted of or included the sale, letting for hire, or offer or exposure for sale or hire of articles which had applied the design industrially or a design differing from it only in immaterial details or in features which are variants commonly used in the article, and this use was with the consent of the copyright owner.[60] Once the copyright owner has exploited the artistic work by applying the corresponding design industrially, the design will not be considered novel.

The Registered Designs Act also allows the owner of a registered design to file, in respect of the same or other articles, additional designs consisting of the earlier registered design with modifications or variations to alter the character or substantially to affect the identity of the registered design.[61] This allows the rights holder to file variations of the design without the later designs being denied novelty. However, the duration of protection granted to the later designs will not exceed the length of protection of the original design.[62]

5. Infringement

Registration of a design grants the rights holder exclusive rights to exploit or apply the design to commercial use. A rights holder has the exclusive right to:

- make in Singapore or import into Singapore
  - for sale or hire; or
  - for use for the purpose of trade or business; or
- sell, hire, or offer or expose for sale or hire, in Singapore,

any article in respect of which the design is registered and to which that design or a design not substantially different from it has been applied.[63]

Thus, a registered design is infringed if another party, without the consent of the

57 Registered Designs Act, Section 8(1).
58 *Ibid*, Section 8(2).
59 *Ibid*, Section 9.
60 *Ibid*, Section 9(2).
61 *Ibid*, Section 10.
62 *Ibid*, Section 10(2).
63 *Ibid*, Section 30(1).

rights holder, does any act that is an exclusive right granted to the rights holder under the Registered Designs Act or makes anything for enabling any article to which an infringing design has been applied to be made in Singapore or elsewhere.[64] The design is also infringed if any party does in relation to a kit anything that would constitute an infringement of the design if it had been done in relation to the assembled article, or makes anything for enabling such a kit to be made or assembled in Singapore.[65]

Liability for infringement is strict; and if the infringing design is not substantially different from the registered design, infringement will be found. Unlike copyright infringement, it is not necessary to show that the infringer was aware of the registered design rights. Ignorance of the design rights will count towards avoiding a claim for damages or an account of profits,[66] but not towards avoiding liability.

There are exceptions to what constitutes an act of infringement. A registered design is not infringed by:

- the doing of any act for a private non-commercial purpose; or
- the doing of any act for the purpose of evaluation, analysis, research or teaching.[67]

A design is not infringed by the reproduction of a functional feature or such other features that are excluded when determining if the design is registrable.[68] The Registered Designs Act also provides that any article that is made, imported, sold, or offered for sale or hire in Singapore and which was placed in the market in Singapore or elsewhere with the consent of the rights holder is not an infringement of the registered design.[69] This essentially protects grey-market or parallel-imported goods and is in line with the policy to allow free movement or exports of goods.

Any party that, before the date of registration, has in good faith used or applied a design or made preparations to use or apply the design will have the right to continue without being liable for infringement.[70] This right is personal and the right to use may not be licensed to third parties.[71] However, where an article is disposed to another party in exercise of that right, the other party may deal with the article in the same way as though it was disposed by the rights holder.[72]

If a registered design is jointly owned, an action for infringement can be brought by any one of the co-owners.[73] The other co-owners should be made party to the proceedings, but if any co-owner is made a defendant to the proceedings, he will not be liable for any costs or expenses unless he takes part in the proceedings.[74] Similarly an exclusive licensee may bring an action for infringement in its own name and the

64 *Ibid*, Section 30 (2).
65 *Ibid*, Section 30 (2).
66 *Ibid*, Section 39(2).
67 *Ibid*, Section 30(5).
68 *Ibid*, Section 30(6).
69 *Ibid*, Section 30(7).
70 *Ibid*, Section 31(1).
71 *Ibid*, Section 31(3).
72 *Ibid*, Section 31(4).
73 *Ibid*, Section 37(1).
74 *Ibid*, Section 37(2).

rights holder need not be added as a party to the proceeding. However, in awarding damages or an account of profits to an exclusive licensee, the court will take into consideration only the losses suffered or the profits derived from the infringement which are attributable to the infringement of the exclusive licensee's rights.[75]

Infringement is determined by a visual comparison of the registered design and the infringing article. The registered design features are compared with those of the alleged infringing article and if they are similar or not substantially different, infringement will be established.[76] The court will make the comparison through the eyes of an average consumer;[77] no expert witness is required. If a product is purchased by trade, the comparison should be in the eyes of the trade consumer and not the average consumer.[78] If a design is in respect of a common article, there will be no infringement if there are slight differences "even in comparatively small aspects" between the registered design and the article.[79]

If infringement is found, the rights holder will be entitled to reliefs including an injunction, damages or an account of profits, and delivery-up of the infringing articles.[80] The rights holder can also request a certificate of contested validity.[81] If no infringement is found, the defendant may seek a declaration of non-infringement.

A declaration of non-infringement can also be sought independently of any infringement action if it can be shown that:

- the party concerned had applied in writing to the rights holder, furnishing full particulars of the acts committed and seeking a declaration that there is no infringement; and
- the rights holder has refused to give any such acknowledgement.[82]

In this situation, the party may bring proceedings seeking a declaration of non-infringement.

6. Design infringement litigation

An action for design infringement is the same as those to enforce other types of intellectual property rights. An action for infringement of a registered design must be brought in the High Court,[83] either by the rights holder,[84] by an assignee or by an exclusive licensee.[85] In the case of an exclusive licensee, the infringement must take place after the exclusive licence has been granted.[86]

If there is more than one rights holder, each is entitled to commence an action for infringement of the design, subject to any agreement to the contrary.[87] The other

---

75 *Ibid*, Section 38.
76 See *Hunter Manufacturing Pte Ltd v Soundtex Switchgear & Engineering Plc Ltd* [2000] 1 SLR 401.
77 See *Risis Pte Ltd v Polar Gems Pte Ltd* [1995] 1 SLR 88.
78 See *Essen System Builders Plc Ltd v Essential Roofing Systems Plc Ltd* [1997] SGHC 280.
79 See *Risis Pte Ltd v Polar Gems Ltd* [1994] 2 SLR ® 1091.
80 See section 6 below.
81 Registered Designs Act, Section 43.
82 *Ibid*, Section 42.
83 *Ibid*, Section 2(1) defines 'court' as "High Court".
84 *Ibid*, Section 36(1).
85 *Ibid*, Section 38.
86 *Ibid*, Section 38(1).
87 *Ibid*, Section 37(1).

rights holders should be made party to the proceedings.[88]

An action is started by filing a writ of summons in the High Court, together with a statement of claim. Both the writ and the statement of claim should be served on the defendants. The statement of claim should clearly set out the details of the registered design and the particulars of infringement. The defendant must file a defence, which may deny the infringement and/or counterclaim that the design is invalid and should therefore be revoked. A design may be revoked on the grounds that at the date of registration of the design, it was not new or on any other ground on which the Registrar of Designs could have refused the registration.[89] Once the defence has been filed, a reply may also be filed, and once the pleadings are closed, the action will proceed like any other civil trial – that is, discovery, interrogatories, preparing of evidence and eventually a hearing before a judge, who will determine the issues. Expert witnesses are not usually called in design infringement actions, but witnesses can be called and cross-examined. At the end of proceedings the court will decide if the registered design has been infringed.

The following relief is available to a successful rights holder:

- an injunction (subject to such terms as the court thinks fit); or
- damages or an account of profits.[90]

A claim for damages will be compensatory, while an account of profits will be restitutionary. A rights holder can choose which of the two remedies will be awarded. In the case of an exclusive licensee, the court may take into consideration only the losses suffered or likely to be suffered by the exclusive licensee or the profits derived from the infringement which are attributable to the exclusive licensee's rights.[91]

However, the court will not award damages or make an order for an account of profits against a defendant who proves that at the date of the infringement it was not aware and had no reasonable grounds for believing that the design in question was registered.[92] The mere fact that the word 'registered' is on the article is not sufficient to give notice of the design registration unless it is followed by the registration number.[93]

In addition to an award for damages or an order to account for profits, the court may order the delivering up[94] or an order for disposal[95] of all infringing articles. Interim injunctions are also available as a relief and may be obtained fairly quickly before the court.

A successful rights holder can apply to the court for a certificate of contested validity of registration.[96] If the validity of the design is challenged and the court has found the design to be valid, it may certify the finding along with the fact that the

---

88 *Ibid*, Section 37(2).
89 *Ibid*, Section 27.
90 *Ibid*, Section 36(2).
91 *Ibid*, Section 38(2) and (3).
92 *Ibid*, Section 39.
93 *Ibid*, Section 39(2).
94 *Ibid*, Section 40.
95 *Ibid*, Section 41.
96 *Ibid*, Section 43.

validity of the registration has been contested. When such a certificate is issued and in subsequent infringement or revocation proceedings:

- the validity of the registration is again challenged; and
- the rights holder obtains a final order or judgment in his favour,

the rights holder will be entitled to claim his legal costs from the other party.

It is fairly common practice to issue a 'cease and desist' letter before starting litigation for design infringement, although there is no legal requirement to do so. However, care should be taken to ensure that the letter does not become a groundless threat if the infringement cannot be proved.[97] If a party is threatened with proceedings for infringement of a registered design, it may bring an action for groundless threats of infringement proceedings, and seek the following reliefs:

- a declaration that the threats are unjustified;
- an injunction against the continuance of the threats; and
- damages in respect of any loss it has sustained as a result of the threats.

The defendant in a groundless threats action can avoid liability only if it proves that the acts in respect of which proceedings were brought constitute, or if done would constitute, an infringement and the plaintiff fails to show that the design registration is invalid.

A groundless threat action is not available for threats made in respect of an alleged infringement that involves the making or importing of anything.[98] However, a notification that a design is registered does not constitute a threat of proceedings.[99]

Revocation proceedings against the validity of a design registration may be brought before the registrar or the court.[100] However, if there are proceedings concerning the design pending in the court, the application for revocation must be made to the court.[101]

7. Licensing and exploitation

A registered design and any rights in the registration may be assigned or transmitted in the same way as other personal property.[102] The rights may also be licensed or sub-licensed.[103] An exclusive licensee has the right to bring proceedings for infringement of a registered design.[104]

The government and any person authorised in writing by the government may use any article to which a registered design is applied, for any purpose which appears to the government necessary or expedient:

- to avoid prejudice to the security or defence of Singapore;
- to assist in the exercise of powers and the implementation of civil defence

97 *Ibid*, Section 44.
98 *Ibid*, Section 44(3).
99 *Ibid*, Section 44(4).
100 *Ibid*, Section 27(1).
101 *Ibid*, Section 27(3).
102 *Ibid*, Section 32.
103 *Ibid*, Section 32(3).
104 *Ibid*, Section 38.

during a state of emergency; or

- for public non-commercial use.[105]

The supply of an article to another country for the defence of that country or to the United Nations will also be deemed to be use of the design for the services of the government.[106]

Any government use of an article before the date of registration will be free of royalty, but any use after the date of registration will be made on terms agreed between the government and the rights holder[107] or, in default of an agreement, as determined by the court.[108] There is no other form of compulsory acquisition of the registered design.

105 *Ibid*, Section 45(4).
106 *Ibid*, Section 45(3).
107 *Ibid*, Section 46.
108 *Ibid*, Section 48.

South Africa

Lodewyk Cilliers
Owen Dean
Spoor & Fisher

---

1. Summary of design protection

The South African Designs Act provides for the registration of designs for articles that are produced by industrial processes. In contrast to patent rights, which protect an invention (ie, the principle underlying a process or product), registered design rights protect only the physical form of a manufactured article. South African law is unique in that it recognises two types of registered design – aesthetic and functional. In both cases the focus is on the appearance of the article rather than the underlying concept. However, the appearance of functional designs results from the function of the relevant article. Functional designs should not be confused with utility models, which are available in many other jurisdictions, because the ambit of a functional design is appearance. Integrated circuits in the form of mask works qualify for registration as functional designs.

Rights holders in South Africa may exclude others from making, importing, using or disposing of any article which embodies the registered design, or a design that is not substantially different from the registered design. An article can infringe a registered design only if it is in the same class as the registered design, so correct classification is important.

2. Registered design rights

2.1 Nature of rights

South African law provides for the registration of both aesthetic and functional designs. These are referred to as Part A and Part F registrations, respectively, according to the part of the official Designs Register in which their details are recorded at the South African Designs Office.

An aesthetic design has features that appeal to and are judged solely by the eye – that is, features that persuade a purchaser to select it over another article that performs the same function but that has a different appearance. Aesthetic design registration protects shape and configuration, as well patterns and ornamentation. The fact that an article performs a particular function does not mean that the design should be a functional design rather than an aesthetic design. For example, even though a bottle has a function – to contain a liquid – its design is usually based on aesthetic considerations, not the function that the bottle is to perform.

A functional design has features which are dictated by the function of the article to which the design is applied. These features may be the shape or configuration of the article, or a pattern applied to the article. For example, a metal extrusion may have a particular profile based on the need to include a seal and a pane of glass, while also meeting particular structural requirements. Such a profile would be irrelevant insofar as classical aesthetic considerations were concerned, and might not even be perceivable by an end user. However, the profile is still important and would thus be protectable as a functional design. The nature of a functional design means that the feature of ornamentation is not applicable. However, a pattern applied to an article may still be protectable if it has a functional purpose – for example, to improve the grip on a handle. As previously mentioned in section 1, integrated circuits can constitute functional designs and can be registered as such.

Both functional and aesthetic design applications may be made for the same article. However, an aesthetic design registration affords the rights holder no rights in the purely functional features of the registered article, or in its method of construction. If it is important that a functional feature of an article also be protected, it may be necessary to file applications for design protection in both Parts A and F of the Designs Register.

In addition to the selection of the correct part (Part A or Part F), the choice of an appropriate class is important, as the rights afforded by a registered design in South Africa are limited to the class in which the design has been registered. For example, a registration for a motor vehicle in Class 12 would not prevent another person from selling a toy car of the same design, as the toy car would fall within Class 21. It is possible to file applications in more than one class, but they will be separate and independent applications. The Locarno Classification (ninth edition) is applicable in South Africa.

2.2 Qualification

To be registrable, an aesthetic design must be new and original, whereas a functional design must be new and not commonplace. In addition, an article to which the design is to be applied must be intended to be produced by an industrial process and must not be only a spare part.

Multiple designs are not protectable in a single application – separate applications must be filed for different designs. Separate applications are also required to protect one design in different classes. It is possible to protect a set of articles in a single design, but specific criteria must be met (discussed in more detail below).

2.3 Registration procedure

The proprietor of a design may apply for its registration. The proprietor of a design is:

- the author (creator) of the design;
- a person for whom the author has executed the design;
- the employer of an employee who, in the course of his employment, makes the design; or
- a person to whom the ownership of the design has passed – for example, by assignment from the author.

An application for the registration of a design must be accompanied by the following information and/or documentation:

- Form D3 – a declaration by the applicant that he is the proprietor of the design and the grant of a power of attorney (so that an attorney can file the application);
- Form D6 – indicating, among other things, the classification, the article to which the design is to be applied, the release date (if applicable), the type of design (ie, aesthetic or functional), a definitive statement setting out the features for which protection is claimed and, optionally, an explanatory statement that describes the article to which the design is applied and/or the design applied to the article in more detail;
- representations of the article that is the subject of the design registration; and
- other formal documentation (Forms D1 and D3, which are administrative documents). and do not require further explanation here.

When filing a convention design application that claims priority over an earlier application in terms of the Paris Convention, the following documents must also be filed:

- a certified copy of the first filed application in support of the claim of convention priority; and
- an assignment of priority rights if the South African applicant is not the same as the applicant in the first filed application.

Applications are examined by the registrar only for their compliance with the formal requirements for registration. If the registrar is satisfied that all requirements have been met, a notice of registration is issued and the registration is advertised in the *Patents and Designs Journal*. It is then open for public inspection. The process from filing to grant usually takes between nine and 12 months.

There is no substantive examination, and there are no opposition proceedings in the design registration process. If a third party wishes to challenge a design registration on a substantive basis, it must submit an application for revocation of the registration.

2.4 Rights granted

Once a design application been registered, the rights holder is granted, for the duration of the registration, the exclusive right in South Africa to exclude others from making, importing, using or disposing of any article embodying the registered design (or a design that is not substantially different from the registered design).

Aesthetic design registrations last for 15 years and functional design registrations last for 10 years. In both cases renewal fees are payable from the third year calculated from the date of filing of the application, the priority date or the release date, whichever is earliest, and annually thereafter.

2.5 Infringement

In cases of infringement of a registered design, the rights holder is entitled to the following reliefs:

- an interdict;
- surrender of any infringing product or any article or product of which the infringing product forms an inseparable part; and
- damages or, in place of damages, a reasonable royalty which would have been payable by a licensee in respect of the registered design.

Infringement proceedings may be instituted only by the rights holder. The rights holder must give notice to every recorded licensee before proceedings are instituted. The recorded licensee(s) may then elect to intervene as co-plaintiff(s).

Infringement proceedings are discussed in more detail in section 6.

2.6 Licensing/assignment

A rights holder may assign or license its rights in a design registration to another person.

2.7 Compulsory licences

Any interested person that can show that the rights in a registered design are being abused may apply to the court for the grant of a compulsory licence in respect of the registered design. The rights in a design shall be deemed to be abused if:

- articles embodying the registered design are not available to the public in South Africa on a commercial scale or to an adequate extent after the registration date and there is, in the opinion of the court, no satisfactory reason for this;
- the availability of articles embodying the registered design in South Africa on a commercial scale or to an adequate extent is being prevented or hindered by the importation of such articles;
- the demand for the articles embodying the registered design in South Africa is not being met to an adequate extent and on reasonable terms;
- by reason of the rights holder's refusal to grant a licence or licences upon reasonable terms, the trade, industry or agriculture of South Africa, or the trade of any person or class of persons trading in South Africa, or the establishment of any new trade or industry in South Africa, is being prejudiced and it is in the public interest that a licence or licences be granted; or
- demand for articles embodying the registered design is being met in South Africa by importation, and the price charged by the rights holder, its licensee or agent for the articles is excessive in relation to the price charged in countries where those articles are manufactured by or under licence from the rights holder or its predecessor or successor in title.

3. Unregistered design rights

No provision is made in South African design law for the protection of unregistered designs. A design that is applied to an article and for which no design has been filed will enjoy no protection under the Designs Act.

The Copyright Act provides for limited design-like protection, in that technical drawings used to manufacture articles are subject to copyright as artistic works. Under the Copyright Act, another person is not permitted, without authorisation, to reproduce the drawings or to make a three-dimensional article from the drawings. However, the act specifically allows the reproduction of three-dimensional articles themselves (even if they are derived from protected drawings) if:

- those articles have been made available to the public by or with the consent of the rights holder;
- the reproductions primarily have a utilitarian purpose and are made by an industrial process; and
- the derivative three-dimensional articles are made from authorised articles, and not from the protected drawings themselves.

The Copyright Act therefore allows for reverse engineering if the three-dimensional article is used as a departure point, which emphasises the importance of obtaining design protection.

4 Qualification for protection

4.1 Novelty, originality, commonplaceness

In order to be registrable, an aesthetic design must be new and original, while a functional design must be new and not commonplace. The primary requirement for registrability is therefore that the design as applied to the article concerned be novel in the absolute sense – that is, not yet disclosed publicly in any manner, anywhere in the world, prior to filing the application for design protection. Notwithstanding this requirement, where a design has already been disclosed, valid design protection may still be obtained on the basis of an application filed no more than six months after the date of the disclosure (called the 'release date'). In this case the exact date of disclosure must be declared in the application. In the case of an integrated circuit topography, a mask work or a series of mask works, a functional design can be filed within two years of the release date. Priority can also be claimed in terms of the Paris Convention if the South African design application is filed within six months of the filing of a priority application in another convention country.

The South African courts have interpreted the meaning of 'original' in design law as similar to 'original' in copyright law. The design for which protection is claimed must, therefore, not have been copied from the design of an earlier article and must have been created by the designer in order to be protectable under design law. While the concept 'not commonplace' is not defined, it may be argued that the meaning is similar to the inventiveness requirement in patent law. This is, however, conjecture, and until the courts have issued guidance in this regard, 'not commonplace' should be given the dictionary definition of a design that is not ordinary, everyday, usual or hackneyed.

4.2 Produced by industrial process

A further requirement for registrability is that the article to which a design is applied be intended to be produced by an industrial process. This excludes one-off works of art (which would be protected by copyright), but the term 'industrial process' allows room for an interpretation that extends beyond mechanised processes. In a copyright judgment dealing with the same wording (*Bress Designs (Pty) Ltd v GY Lounge Suite M'fers (Pty) Ltd and anr* 1991 (2) SA 455 (W), it was held that the concept of an industrial process must not be limited to manufacture by a mechanised process. It is submitted that a similar interpretation should be given to 'industrial process' in the design law context, and the question should thus be whether the intention is to mass-produce the product, even if the process is manual and unsophisticated.

4.3 Specific functional design exclusion – spare parts

Functional design rights cannot be enforced in respect of spare parts for machinery and equipment. However, this exclusion does not prevent the obtaining of valid aesthetic design protection for spare parts in the event that the spare part also has aesthetic features. There is unfortunately no definition in the Designs Act of exactly what constitutes a 'spare part'; nor have the courts had an opportunity to rule on this matter. One interpretation is that a spare part is a part expected to wear or to be consumed – that is, one expected to require regular replacement during the lifetime of a machine or piece of equipment, such as a spark plug in an engine. A stricter interpretation is that any replaceable part of a machine or piece of equipment would constitute a spare part – for example, the cylinder head of an engine.

4.4 Specific aesthetic design exclusions

The Designs Act also stipulates that no feature of an article, insofar as it is necessitated solely by the function which the article is intended to perform, shall afford the rights holder of an aesthetic design any rights in terms of the act in respect of such feature, method or principle. This also applies to the method or principle of construction.

4.5 Sets of articles

A set of articles may be filed in a single design application, provided that it meets the criteria defined in the Designs Act. A 'set of articles' means any number of articles of the same general character that are ordinarily sold together or intended to be used together, and in respect of which the same design is applied to each article. The applied design need not be identical, as long as variations and modifications of the design applied to the different articles are not sufficient to alter the character of the articles or substantially alter their identity. Examples of sets of articles that may be registered as single designs are sets of cutlery and crockery. However, sets of articles should not be confused with the requirement of unity of design, which is discussed in more detail in section 4.6 next.

4.6 Unity of design

Multiple designs are not allowable in terms of the Designs Act, and registration is granted for a single design only. However, the act also precludes any person from applying for the revocation of a design registration on the ground that it comprises more than one design, which is somewhat perplexing. In practice, the registrar will not review a design application for unity of design, and a design application including more than one embodiment will likely be granted. However, once granted, there may be a risk – albeit small – that the rights holder may be forced to amend the design by excising additional embodiments should it be challenged on the ground that the application was not made in the prescribed manner. It is also arguable that the registrar may be challenged by recourse to common-law review proceedings on the basis that the design application should not have been granted in the first place. These approaches have never been tested in the courts; the authors' view is that the prudent approach is to file multiple design applications should there be more than one embodiment of a design.

5. Infringement

The rights holder is granted, for the duration of the registration, the exclusive right in South Africa to prevent others from making, importing, using or disposing of any article embodying the registered design, or a design not substantially different from the registered design. If another person performs a protected act without authorisation, the rights holder can institute infringement proceedings against the offending party.

The first step is therefore to establish whether an offending design does in fact infringe a registered design, because it embodies the registered design or (somewhat more problematic) because it embodies a design which it not substantially different from the registered design. The assessment takes the form of a direct visual comparison of the allegedly infringing article and the representation in the registered design, along with consideration of the scope of protection claimed in the definitive statement. A doctrine such as imperfect recollection plays no part, and the allegedly infringing article is said to be viewed "through the eyes of the court wearing the glasses of the likely consumer".

A test that has been distilled by the South African courts, and which is helpful when giving meaning to the term 'substantially', is one that is informally referred to as the 'step test'. This test is based on the principle that the scope of protection is determined by the difference of the registered design over the prior art. If the registered design constituted only a small change over that which formed part of the prior art at the time, the scope of the registered design will also be reasonably narrow – that is, 'substantially' will be given a narrow interpretation. If the registered design constituted a major advance over that which formed part of the prior art at the time, the scope of the registered design will also be reasonably broad – that is, 'substantially' will be given a broad interpretation.

Once it is clear that there is at least a reasonable chance that the court may find that there is infringement, and that further action taken against the alleged infringer will therefore not be unjustifiable, legal proceedings can commence.

6. Design infringement litigation

6.1 Place of standing

An infringement action may be instituted in the High Court against any person who, without the authority of the rights holder, performs any of the protected acts. Only the rights holder is entitled to institute an action for infringement. A licensee has no independent right to institute such an action as the sole claimant. If there are registered licensees, the rights holder as claimant in the proceedings must give notice to these licensees, which will then be entitled to intervene as co-claimants.

6.2 Procedure

The Uniform Rules of Court provide for two forms of procedure: actions and applications.

Actions are commenced by summons. In design matters, the summons is accompanied by a statement known as the claimant's particulars of claim. The issues between the claimant and the defendant are defined by an exchange of pleadings. The hearing of an action is called a trial and, at the trial, oral evidence is heard.

Applications are commenced by notice of motion supported by evidence on affidavit setting out the facts and the basis of the relief claimed. A party defending the proceedings, called a respondent, may file answering evidence on affidavit, and the originating party, the applicant, has a right of reply on affidavit. Applications are normally determined at a hearing 'on paper' and oral evidence is not heard. Unlike in action proceedings, damages cannot be awarded in application proceedings.

6.3 Remedies and nature of court order

A successful claimant in an action for infringement is usually entitled to the following reliefs:

- an interdict (ie, an injunction) ordering the defendant to refrain from further infringement. If the defendant continues to infringe the registered design and ignores the interdict, it may be committed for contempt of court;
- an order for the delivery-up of any infringing product or any article or product of which the infringing product forms an inseparable part;
- damages for infringement. A defendant is liable for damages in the same way that it would be for committing any other type of wrong. In other words, the defendant must compensate the claimant for its patrimonial loss, actual or prospective, sustained through the infringement. It is sometimes difficult to prove the exact quantum of damages suffered, but the quantum can include any loss of profits that the rights holder has sustained in respect of those infringing articles that would have been made and sold by the rights holder were it not for the sales of infringing articles carried out by the infringer. In view of the difficulty in calculating and proving damages, and in order to keep the issues before the trial judge clear, it is not unusual to ask the court initially only for an enquiry into damages so that complex questions such as loss of profits can be left to be considered once the questions of design infringement and validity have been adjudicated upon. Such a request can be made without abandoning any rights to claim damages;
- in lieu of damages, and on the claimant's request, an amount calculated on the basis of a reasonable royalty that would have been payable by a licensee in respect of the design concerned; and
- costs of suit.

Save for an award of damages or payment of a reasonable royalty, the same relief is available to a rights holder in application proceedings.

6.4 Defences and counterclaims

A defendant being sued for infringement can plead non-infringement of the design and/or invalidity of the design. In addition, the defendant may counterclaim to apply for revocation of the design on any one or more of the grounds for revocation set out in the Designs Act. Any ground for revocation can be relied upon by way of defence.

6.5 Appeal

A judgment of the High Court is subject to an appeal to the Appeal Court or full bench of the particular division of the High Court, or directly to the Supreme Court of Appeal. A decision of the appeal bench of the court of first instance is also subject to an appeal to the Supreme Court of Appeal. Leave to appeal must be given by the court that made it. If leave to appeal is refused, a special application for leave to appeal can be made to the Supreme Court of Appeal, which can override the initial refusal.

7. Licensing and exploitation

The rights holder may exploit a registered design in its own capacity, or may assign or license its rights in the registration to another person or entity.

It is not compulsory to record the assignment or licensing of a design registration at the Designs Office, but there are advantages in doing so. Most importantly, an assignment which is not recorded has no validity except as between the parties to the assignment. One possible consequence of this is that a third party with no knowledge of the assignment can deal with the original rights holder as if that person were still the rights holder. This could be detrimental for the new rights holder, which would have only a contractual claim against the original rights holder. Also, in the case of infringement, only the rights holder may institute proceedings. Thus, if an assignment is unrecorded there will be a delay in taking action until the assignment is recorded.

Except in very limited circumstances, a licensee may not sue for infringement. Where the rights holder of a design registration institutes infringement proceedings, it is obliged to give notice of this to all recorded licensees.

Sweden

Michael Plogell
Erik Ullberg
Wistrand

1. Summary of design protection[1]

In Sweden, any physical person (and legal entities by way of transfer of rights) may obtain enforceable legal rights for a design that they have created. Designs may be protected under the following acts:

- as a registered design right under the Design Protection Act (1970:485), as amended (the Designs Act);
- as an unregistered work of art under the Act on Copyright to Artistic and Literary Works (1960:729), as amended (the Copyrights Act); or
- as a registered or unregistered mark under the Trademarks Act (2010:1877).

Although not an exclusive right as such, it is also possible to obtain protection against the marketing of misleading copies under the Swedish Market Practices Act (2008:486).

The Patents Act (1967:837) may provide an indirect protection for designs. Since patents are primarily used as means of protecting technical innovations, they are not discussed in this chapter.

Sweden is a member of the European Union and so registered and unregistered Community designs enjoy protection under Council Regulation 6/2002/EC on Community Designs and Council Regulation 207/2009/EC on Community Trade Marks.

2. Registered design rights

2.1 The Designs Act

(a) General

The creator of a design may obtain an exclusive right (design right) to exploit the design through registration (Section 1a of the Designs Act). A design right can only be obtained if the design is new and has individual character (see section 4.1 below).

For the purposes of the Designs Act a 'design' is defined as "the appearance of the whole or a part of a product resulting from the features of the details of the product

1 There are no official English versions of the acts discussed in this chapter. Non-official translations are available on the World Intellectual Property Organization's website at www.wipo.int/wipolex/en/profile.jsp?code=SE.

or of the details of the ornamentation of the product, in particular as regards the lines, contours, colours, shapes, textures or materials" (Section 1(1)).

(b) ***Registration***

Applications for design rights are filed with the Swedish Patents and Registrations Office (the Registry). An administration fee is payable. The Registry only checks whether there are any formal obstacles to the design application – similarity searches and so on must be carried out by the applicant before filing his application.

Any interested party may file an opposition to the registration. This must be submitted in writing to the Registry within two months of publication. Registry decisions in opposition proceedings may be appealed to the Patents Appeals Court, and then to the Supreme Administrative Court, subject to leave to appeal.

Certain designs cannot be registered, such as designs that are contrary to morality or public order, or designs that include another person's trade name or trade symbol already protected in Sweden, or anything that can be perceived as a sign that has been established on the market in Sweden by another person in the course of business or trade activities (Section 4 of the Designs Act).

(c) ***Term of protection***

Design rights are valid for one or more five-year terms, starting on the date of filing the application. However, the total term of protection cannot exceed 25 years. Applications for renewal must be filed in writing to the Registry within one year before and six months after the right expires (Sections 24 to 25 of the Designs Act).

(d) ***Rights granted***

A design right means that no other person may exploit the design without the authorisation of the rights holder. In particular, this includes the manufacture, offering for sale, marketing, importation into and exportation from Sweden, and the use of any product of which the design forms part or to which it is applied, or to keep in stock such a product for these purposes (Section 5 of the Designs Act).

There are some exceptions, such as exploitation that is carried out privately or for non-commercial purposes.

The design is not protected if another person uses it for goods that have been put on the market within the European Economic Area (EEA) with the rights holder's consent (Section 7b of the Designs Act).

(e) ***Infringement***

Civil remedies are available to the rights holder in cases of infringement. These include injunctions to stop the infringement (usually subject to conditional fines) and compensation (damages etc), and preliminary relief such as interim injunctions.

If an infringement has been committed intentionally or by gross negligence, the infringer and/or his accomplices could face criminal charges and be sentenced to fines or, in severe cases, imprisonment for up to two years (Section 35 of the Designs Act). Only physical persons have criminal liability in Sweden.

A rights holder may obtain information on an alleged infringement using infringement investigations and orders.

Remedies for infringement are discussed in sections 5 and 6 below.

(f) *Licensing*

A rights holder may grant licences to third parties. Assignments of registered intellectual property rights may be notified to the Registry to be legally effective, but this is not mandatory.

A licensee may assign his right to exploit a design only if there is an agreement to that effect with the rights holder. However, if the licence forms part of a business activity, it may be transferred together with the activity, unless there is an agreement to the contrary. In such a case, the transferor remains liable for the fulfilment of the licence agreement (Section 26 of the Designs Act).

A registered licensee may in certain circumstances enjoy a better position (see below).

(g) *Compulsory licences*

Anyone who has been deprived of a design registration but, in good faith, has started to exploit the design in the course of business activities, or has taken significant measures to do so, may continue the exploitation or start the intended exploitation while maintaining the design's essential features, against a fair payment to the rightful owner and on other conditions considered reasonable (Section 32(2) of the Designs Act). This right also applies to any licensee recorded in the register.

(h) *Validity and ownership issues*

A design right may be transferred freely, separately or in connection with a transfer of business activity (see further in section 7 below). If a business activity that includes a design right is transferred, the design right is usually deemed part of the transfer.

It is not mandatory to notify transfers of registered intellectual property rights to the Registry for the assignment to be legally effective. However, in litigation relating to the right, the person who was last recorded in the Design Register in this capacity is presumed to be the rights holder (Section 27(3) of the Designs Act).

An acquirer of a design right (transfer in title) has the right to transfer the design right further unless otherwise agreed.

If a design has been registered for a person who is not the true rights holder, then the person entitled to the design may bring an action in order to transfer the registration to him (Section 32(1) of the Designs Act). The action must be brought within one year of the plaintiff becoming aware of the registration and the other circumstances on which the action is based. If the rights holder was in good faith when the design was registered or when the design right was transferred to him, then an action may not be brought later than three years after the registration.

Anyone who is affected by a design right may file to a general court for an action for invalidation of the design right. An invalidation proceeding may also be initiated as a counterclaim by the defendant in an infringement proceeding, thus serving as a defence.

2.2 The Trademarks Act

(a) General

It is possible to acquire, through registration, an exclusive right to a trademark as a special symbol for the purpose of distinguishing goods made available in the course of a business activity (Chapter 1, Section 6 of the Trademarks Act).

A 'trademark' may consist of any sign capable of being represented graphically, in particular words, including personal names, as well as designs, letters, numerals or the shape or the ornamental aspects of goods or their packages, provided that such signs are capable of distinguishing goods (Chapter 1, Section 4 of the Trademarks Act). Hence, it is possible to acquire trademark protection for various designs, usually referred to as three-dimensional trademarks.

It is also possible to acquire an exclusive right to a trademark through establishment. This requires that a sufficient part of the relevant market recognises the trademark as a sign for a particular good or service and is an unregistered right (Chapter 1, Section 7 of the Trademarks Act).

(b) Registration

Applications for trademarks are filed with the Registry. A fee is payable. The Registry examines both formal and substantive obstacles (such as confusingly similar marks) to the application.

The Registry's examination is a preliminary one, and a registration may be challenged during the registration process through opposition proceedings, or even after registration through invalidity proceedings.

Anyone affected by a registration may file an opposition, asking for the registration to be cancelled or to be transferred to the opponent. Oppositions must be filed in writing to the Registry within two months of publication of the registration. Decisions by the Registry in opposition proceedings may be appealed to the Patents Appeals Court, then to the Supreme Administrative Court, subject to leave to appeal.

Certain trademarks cannot be registered. The main reasons for refusal are that a mark lacks distinctiveness or is confusingly similar to an older trademark (including Community trademarks) or trade symbol; other reasons include that a mark is contrary to morality or public order and so on (Chapter 2, Sections 7 to 11 of the Trademarks Act).

(c) Term of protection

Trademarks are valid from the application date, initially for 10 years (counting from the publication of the trademark registration). They may be renewed for an unlimited number of 10-year terms (Chapter 2, Section 32 of the Trademarks Act). Applications for the renewal of a trademark can be filed in writing with the Registry at the earliest one year before its expiration and at the latest six months after its expiry (Chapter 2, Section 33 of the Trademarks Act).

(d) Rights granted

The exclusive right to a trademark grants that no person other than the rights holder is entitled to use a symbol which is confusingly similar to the protected one for goods falling within the protective scope of the trademark in the course of business activities. This applies whether the symbol is on the goods or their packaging, in advertising, on business documents, or in any other form, including oral use. This applies regardless of whether the goods are offered, or intended to be offered, for sale in Sweden or abroad or are imported (Chapter 1, Section 10 of the Trademarks Act).

However, Chapter 1 Section 11 of the Trademarks Act states that:

provided that he uses them in accordance with honest practices in industrial or commercial matters, anyone is entitled to use, in the course of his business activity, as a symbol for his goods

- *his own family name, address or trade name,*
- *indications concerning the kind, quality, quantity, intended purpose, value, geographical origin, the time of their production, or other characteristics of the goods.*

The exclusive right to a trademark does not apply if a person other than the rights holder uses the trademark for goods that have been put on the market within the EEA with the rights holder's consent.

(e) ***Infringement***

A trademark rights holder enjoys the same protection as a design rights holder (see section 2.1(e) above). See also sections 5 and 6 below.

(f) ***Licensing***

A rights holder may grant licences to third parties.

Assignments of trademarks may be notified to the Registry for the assignment to be legally effective, but this is not mandatory.

A licensee may not assign his right further without the licensor's consent. However, if the licence forms part of a business activity, it may be transferred together with the activity, unless there is an agreement to the contrary. In such a case, the transferor remains liable for the fulfilment of the licence agreement (Chapter 6, Section 4 of the Trademarks Act).

(g) ***Compulsory licences***

There is no regulation of compulsory licences under Swedish trademarks law.

(h) ***Validity and ownership issues***

A trademark may be transferred freely, separately or in connection with a transfer of business activity (see further in section 7 below). In the transfer of a business activity, any trademark that forms part of that business activity will be deemed part of the transfer, unless there is an agreement to the contrary (Chapter 6, Section 2 of the Trademarks Act).

Normally, an acquirer of a trademark (transfer in title) may transfer the trademark further.

It is not mandatory to notify assignments of registered intellectual property rights to the Registry for the assignment to be legally effective. However, in litigation relating to a right, the person who was last recorded in the trademarks register in this capacity is presumed to be the rights holder (Chapter 6, Section 3 of the Trademarks Act).

A trademark may be cancelled, in whole or in part. The most common grounds for invalidity are lack of distinctiveness, confusingly similar marks or signs, registration in bad faith and cancellation due to non-use (Chapter 3, Sections 1 to 2 of the Trademarks Act).

3. Unregistered design rights

3.1 Designs

Unregistered community designs enjoy protection under Council Regulation 6/2001/EC on Community Designs, which may be invoked in Sweden.

3.2 The Copyrights Act

(a) General

Some designs are considered to be works of art. Protection under the Copyrights Act is granted by the mere creation of the work – there is no need to register a copyright, and indeed no register exists for this purpose.

In order to be protected as a work of art, the design must be original, have an individual character and have been created by a human being.

(b) Term of protection

Generally, copyright protection lasts until the end of the 70th year after the year of the creator's death (Section 43 of the Copyrights Act). Where there are joint creators, copyright will expire at the end of the 70th year after the death of the longest-surviving creator.

(c) Rights granted

A creator or his successor in title has both economic and moral rights to the work. The rights refer to the work both in its original form and when it is available in a revised form, such as an adaptation or other derivative work.

The economic rights grant the rights holder an exclusive right to make copies of the work and to make the work available to the general public – that is, to present the work publicly, to display it publicly or to distribute copies of it.

The moral rights provide:

- the right to be named in conjunction with the work being used, to the extent and in the way required by good practice; and
- the right to respect for the work – that is, that the work may not be altered or made available to the general public in a form or connection that is prejudicial to the creator's literary or artistic reputation or distinctive character.

The Copyrights Act prescribes certain limitations. For instance, it is possible in some cases to make copies of works for private purposes (Section 12 of the Copyrights Act).

As a general rule, when a sample of a work has been transferred with the consent of its rights holder, it may be further distributed (Section 19 of the Copyrights Act).

(d) *Infringement*

A copyright rights holder enjoys the same protection as a design rights holder (see section 2.1(e) above). See also sections 5 and 6 below.

(e) *Licensing*

A rights holder may grant licences for economic rights to third parties. Moral rights may be waived in relation to third parties.

A licensee may not alter the work or license the copyright to others, unless there is an agreement to the contrary. However, if the copyright forms part of a business activity, it may be assigned together with the business activity or of part thereof. In this case the transferor remains liable for the fulfilment of the agreement (Section 28 of the Copyrights Act). This also applies to a transfer in title of copyright (see section 3.2(g) below).

(f) *Compulsory licences*

There is no regulation of compulsory licences under Swedish copyright law.

(g) *Ownership issues*

The economic rights to copyright may be transferred freely, in their entirely or in part. However, the moral rights cannot be transferred. They can only be waived in relation to uses that are limited as to their character and scope (Section 3(3) of the Copyrights Act).

The transfer of a copy does not include a transfer of the copyright (Section 27 of the Copyrights Act).

In the absence of an agreement to the contrary, the person to whom a copyright has been transferred may not alter the work or transfer the copyright to others. However, if the copyright forms part of a business activity, it may be transferred together with the business activity or part thereof. In this case the transferor remains liable for the fulfilment of the agreement (Section 28 of the Copyrights Act).

3.3 The Market Practices Act

The Market Practices Act does not grant an exclusive right to a design or product.

However, the act provides that a trader may not, in the course of marketing, use copies that are misleading in that they can easily be confused with another trader's known and distinctive products. This does not apply to copies of the design which are primarily intended to render the product functional (Section 14 of the Market Practices Act).

This prohibition will only apply if the marketing is likely to affect the recipient's ability to make a well-founded transaction decision (Section 8 of the Market Practices Act).

Section 14 of the Market Practices Act is complemented by point 13 of the so-called 'blacklist' (Annex 1 to Directive 2005/29/EC on Unfair Commercial Practices), which bans: "promoting a product similar to a product made by a particular manufacturer in such a manner as deliberately to mislead the consumer into believing that the product is made by that same manufacturer when it is not". The act goes beyond the directive in that traders as well as consumers can rely on point 13 under the act.

In the event of a violation of the Market Practices Act, a claimant may request both an injunction (or interim injunction) against the challenged marketing and damages from the breaching trader.

4. Qualification for protection

As a member of the European Union, Sweden is subject to Community law and has implemented relevant EU directives and applies relevant EU regulations with regard to designs, copyright and other intellectual property and marketing law.

Sweden is also party to international treaties such as the Berne Convention for the Protection of Literary and Artistic Works, the Paris Convention for the Protection of Industrial Property, and the Agreement on Trade-Related Aspects of Intellectual Property Rights (TRIPs).

4.1 The Designs Act

As stated above, a design right can only be obtained if the design is new and has individual character.

Under Section 2 of the Designs Act, a design is considered to be new if no identical design has been made available to the public before the application for registration is filed or, if priority is claimed, before the date of priority. Designs will be considered identical if their features differ only in immaterial details.

Section 2 also provides that a design will be considered to have an individual character if the overall impression given to an informed user differs from the overall impression produced by any other design which has been made available to the public anywhere in the world. However, a design will not be deemed to have been made available to the public if the specialised sector concerned, operating within the EEA, could not reasonably have become knowledgeable of the publication in the normal course of business (Section 3 of the Designs Act).

A grace period is usually available to submit an application for registration of a design within 12 months of the design being made available to the public (Section 3a of the Designs Act).

In assessing whether the design has an individual character, the degree of freedom of the designer in developing the design is taken into consideration.

Section 2a of the Designs Act provides that a design relating to a part of a complex product (ie, a product which, by comprising multiple replaceable components, can be disassembled and then reassembled) will be considered new and having a individual character only if:

- the component part, or part thereof, remains visible during normal use of the product once it has been incorporated; and

- the design, to the extent that it remains visible, in itself fulfils the requirements of novelty and individual character.

The term 'normal use' means use by the end user, excluding maintenance, service and repair work.

4.2 The Copyrights Act

A design can also be afforded protection under the Copyrights Act as a work of art (applied art).

Protection is only granted for creations that display originality or individuality as a result of the creator's personal making. Thus, facts and ideas are not protected – it is only the creator's individual expression that is protected.

The threshold for designs to be protected as works of art has been set at a fairly low level by case law. However, in a judgment on copyright for the shape of a Mini Maglite flashlight, the Supreme Court held that the standard for protection must not be neglected (NJA 2009:18). The case established that the scope for protection will be in proportion to the originality of the work.

Applied art is often governed by functional features, and the scope of protection will usually be quite narrow.

A design deemed as applied art may be referred to the Svensk Form Copyright Panel (an impartial expert body within the Swedish Society of Crafts and Design) to determine whether a design can enjoy protection under the Copyrights Act. The panel's opinions on copyright protection for works of applied art are in general respected by the courts.

4.3 The Trademarks Act

A trademark may be registered only if it is distinctive (Chapter 2, Section 5 of the Trademarks Act). A mark that – exclusively or with only minor changes or additions – only indicates the kind, quality, quantity, use, price or geographical origin of the goods or the date of their production is not classed as distinctive. All circumstances, in particular the scale and time of the use of the mark, are considered when assessing whether a mark is distinctive.

A symbol consisting exclusively of a shape which results from the nature of the goods or of a shape which is necessary to obtain a technical result or of a sign which gives a substantial value to the goods may not be registered as a trademark (Chapter 2, Section 4 of the Trademarks Act).

In order for the shape or the ornamental aspects of goods (three-dimensional trademark) to be afforded protection under the Trademarks Act, they must have distinctive character. In practice this means that the three-dimensional trademark must be able to function as a symbol for the goods.

4.4 The Market Practices Act

The Market Practices Act protects only products that are known and distinctive (Section 14).

To be distinctive, the product must have a prime characteristic function that results in an aesthetic appearance which is different from other products (see MD 2009:23, MD 2010:3 and MD 2010:29). A product may be distinctive in itself or acquire distinctiveness through commercial use.

In order to fall under the protective scope of the act, a product must be known by a sufficient part of the relevant market.

The Market Court has established that in order for point 13 of the Directive 2005/29/EC on Unfair Commercial Practices blacklist to apply (see section 3.3 above), a product must be distinctive, but it does not necessarily need to be known on the market (MD 2009:23).

5. Infringement

Rights holders for designs, trademarks and copyrights may take action against infringing third parties.

In addition, under the Market Practices Act unauthorised marketing of known distinctive products may constitute to a breach of the act.

A rights holder may refer to the courts to seek legal remedies (see section 6 below). Generally, a 'cease and desist' letter or similar notification will be sent to the alleged infringer before starting proceedings, to establish whether the claim is disputed and to avoid unnecessary court proceedings where possible. Even a successful claimant in an unnecessary action may be liable for all or part of the losing party's legal costs. However, if there is danger in delaying proceedings (eg, when interim measures are sought), they may be started without the defendant being notified.

Cease-and-desist letters may lead to negotiations between the parties, and the dispute is often then settled out of court.

6. Design infringement litigation

6.1 The procedure

In the event of an infringement of the Copyrights Act, the Designs Act or the Trademarks Act, rights holders may bring proceedings against the infringer before a competent general court. Judgments of the first-instance (district) court may be appealed to the Court of Appeal and then to the Supreme Court, with both being subject to leave for appeal.

Proceedings under the Market Practices Act are referred to the District Court of Stockholm or another competent general court, provided that the action includes claims for damages. Appeals are made to the Market Court. If a case concerns only injunctions against marketing, the Market Court will be the first and final instance.

An administrative fee is usually payable for actions filed with the general courts, but not for those filed with the Market Court.

Generally, the losing party in both general and Market Court proceedings must bear its costs. The successful party is usually compensated by the losing party for reasonable legal costs (normally, the cost of the party's attorney plus its own costs).

The District Court of Stockholm is the competent court of first instance for actions on the infringement of Community designs and Community trademarks rights.

6.2 Legal remedies

The remedies available to rights holders are similar in all legislation on intellectual property rights (copyright, design rights, trademarks etc). They are based on Directive 2004/48/EC on the Enforcement of Intellectual Property Rights and offer the following to copyright, design and trademark holders:

- injunction (interim and final);
- order to provide information;
- infringement investigation;
- compensation (damages etc);
- destruction or other reasonable disposal of infringing samples;
- impounding of infringing samples; and
- order to publish the judgment.

Injunctions make it possible to stop an ongoing infringement. They may be either final or temporary (interim) until a final judgment is reached.

As a general rule, a party seeking an interim injunction must provide adequate security (normally a bank warranty) in favour of the defendant for any damages incurred by an incorrect interim decision.

Rights holders may gather information on an already established infringement using orders to provide information and infringement investigations. These may also be used to investigate a potential infringement, provided there are good reasons to believe that an infringement has occurred. A claimant is required to provide security when starting an infringement investigation, in the same manner as for interim injunctions.

A court will only grant interim injunctions, orders to provide information and infringement investigations if the justification for the measure outweighs the inconvenience or other harm that it would cause to the accused party.

It is possible to request the destruction or other reasonable disposal of infringing samples. A rights holder may also ask for alleged infringing samples to be impounded pending judgment. This will be subject to security being provided for the damages the defendant may incur as a result of the impounding if the claim is not upheld.

Compensation may be awarded for infringements in good faith, but this is normally restricted to the amount that would have been paid for a licence. A rights holder is entitled to compensation for damage caused if the infringement is a result of negligence or intent. Such damages are determined with particular consideration of loss of profit, any unfair profits made by the infringer and, in appropriate cases, elements other than economic factors, such as the moral prejudice caused to the rights holder by the infringement.

A rights holder may request that the court orders its judgment to be published in a relevant publication, at the infringer's expense, to bring the infringement to the public's attention.

Remedies under the Market Practices Act are more limited – for instance, it is not possible to request an order to provide information or an infringement investigation. However, injunctions and damages are available.

6.3 Validity issues

Anyone who is affected by a registered design right or trademark may file for an action for invalidation of the right in question in a competent general court.

An alleged infringer may file a counterclaim for invalidation during infringement proceedings.

7. Licensing and exploitation

Design rights, copyrights (the economic rights, see section 3.2(c) above) and other intellectual property rights to a design can be freely transferred or licensed by an oral or written agreement, and even through an implied contract. The general opinion among legal scholars and others is that a right *in rem* to intellectual property rights and licences to intellectual property rights are achieved by binding contracts. This view has some support in the case law.

Both non-exclusive and exclusive licences are commonly granted. Given the complexity of licensing, written agreements are preferred and more common.

It is not mandatory to register assignments of registered intellectual property rights in order for the assignment to be legally effective. However, in related litigation, the person who was last recorded in the Design Register or Trademarks Register in this capacity is presumed the rights holder (see sections 2.1(h) and 2.2(h) above).

A trademark application and registration may be pledged by registering the pledge agreement (Chapter 7, Section 2 of the Trademarks Act). An administration fee is payable. Copyrights and design rights cannot be pledged under the Copyrights Act and Designs Act respectively. However, they may be transferred as security for assets.

Under Article 29 of Council Regulation 6/2001/EC on Community Designs, Community designs may be given as security or be the subject of property rights. There is no legislation governing the pledge of Community designs under the Swedish legal regime.

Switzerland

Markus Wang
Bär & Karrer

1. Summary of design protection

In Switzerland, design protection is primarily governed by the Federal Act on the Protection of Designs of October 5 2001 (the Designs Act). Protection under the act is available for novel and original designs for up to 25 years, but only upon registration. Switzerland does not recognise the concept of unregistered design rights – unlike, for example, under the EU Regulation on Community Designs. This situation is mitigated in part by the Federal Act on Copyright and Neighbouring Rights of October 9 1992 (the Copyright Act), which protects individual designs as works of applied art for 70 years following the death of their creator.

These two acts form the basis of design protection in Switzerland. They are supplemented by the Federal Act on Trademarks and Indications of Origin of August 28 1992 (the Trademarks Act). Under this act, certain distinctive shapes of products or their packaging can be registered as trademarks and protected for an unlimited period. When the Trademarks Act was enacted, it was widely assumed that the regime would provide an easy-to-obtain and effective means of design protection. However, the last 20 years have shown that trademark protection for industrial designs – at least for objects of utility, equipment, apparatus and furniture – is rather limited. This is mainly because the Swiss Federal Institute of Intellectual Property (IPI) takes a strict approach to the required distinctiveness of a product's shape. It often registers industrial designs only if it can be proved (typically through consumer surveys) that they have acquired a secondary meaning. Similar problems exist under the Federal Act against Unfair Competition of December 19 1986. This act offers a basis to take action against the use of an identical or similar design, but in practice such use is considered unfairly competitive only if a distinctive design is involved. As the Trademarks Act and Unfair Competition Act have limited application to industrial designs, they are not examined further in this chapter.

Any Swiss or foreign individual, partnership or legal entity may avail itself of the means of protection described above. While design and copyright protection is available only to a party that either is the creator of a design (which by definition can only be an individual) or has acquired the right in the design from the creator, trademark protection is granted to whoever files the design for registration.

A design may enjoy protection under the Designs Act, the Copyright Act and the Trademarks Act simultaneously, provided that it meets the material and formal (registration) protection requirements under each of these acts.

2. Registered design rights

2.1 Nature of rights

As mentioned above, the main method for obtaining protection of an industrial design is registration under the Designs Act. Upon registration, the rights holder is granted a real monopoly right in the design, which may be enforced against any third party that uses an identical or similar design, irrespective of whether the third party has counterfeited the design or created it independently (Article 9 of the Designs Act). It is unclear whether this monopoly right is tied to the product type for which the design is registered. The question has been debated in academic circles, but a 2007 Swiss Federal Supreme Court judgment (4A_288/2007, Cons 6.2) suggests that the court views the design right under the Designs Act as not being tied to the product type for which it is registered. This means that the use of an identical or similar design for product types other than those claimed in the application may qualify as infringement of the registered design right.

Where a design meets the criteria for protection under the Designs Act, the rights therein vest in the individual or group that created it (Article 7 of the Designs Act). An exception exists for designs created by employees during the course of their work, whereby the rights vest in the employer (Article 332 of the Swiss Code of Obligations). The rights can be freely assigned by contract, even before their creation (Article 14 of the Designs Act).

2.2 Qualification

The appearance of products or parts of products – as characterised by the arrangement of lines, surfaces and contours, as well as by the colours or materials applied – can be protected as the object of a registered design right (Article 1 of the Designs Act). For the registration to be valid, the design must be novel and original (Article 2 of the Designs Act).

The Designs Act provides for a so-called 'relative novelty' requirement, whereby a design is not novel if an identical design disclosed to the (worldwide) public before the filing or priority date was or could have been seen by the relevant public (potential consumers and industrial circles) in Switzerland (Article 2, paragraph 2 of the Designs Act). It follows that any presentation of the registered design to the public prior to the filing or priority date may destroy its novelty. However, Article 3 of the Designs Act provides that any disclosure made in the 12 months preceding the filing or priority date, by the rights holder itself or by a third party acting abusively and to the detriment of the rights holder, will not compromise the novelty of the design.

The originality requirement is satisfied if the overall impression created by the design differs from that of other designs known by the relevant public in Switzerland as a result of the inclusion of features that are considered more than insignificant (Article 2, paragraph 3 of the Designs Act).

Irrespective of novelty and originality, a design cannot be protected if its features are wholly determined by the technical function of the product (Article 4(c) of the Designs Act). According to commentators, this ground for exclusion must be interpreted narrowly and excludes only designs that are an unavoidable consequence of the technical function of the product. Designs that violate international treaties or Swiss federal law (Article 4(d) of the Designs Act), or that are contrary to public policy or principles of morality (Article 4(e) of the Designs Act), are also excluded from protection. Unlike the EU Regulation on Community Designs, the Designs Act does not provide for an exclusion of must-fit and must-match parts. However, interconnections are regularly regarded as being exclusively determined by the technical function of the product and are therefore excluded under Article 4(c) of the Designs Act.

2.3 Registration procedure

The design right arises as soon as the design has been registered in the Design Register (Article 5 of the Designs Act). The registration process starts with the filing of a design application with the IPI. The application must be accompanied by reproducible illustrations of the design(s) (Article 19, paragraph 1 of the Designs Act). These may be filed in paper form (minimum size A7, maximum size A4) or electronically (admissible formats include .tif, .eps, .psd, .jpg, .pcd and .bmp, with a recommended resolution of 300 dpi). Standard application forms are available on the IPI's website at www.ipi.ch. The application must specify the applicant's details, the name of the creator of the design and the type of product for which the design is intended. Applicants domiciled outside Switzerland must either appoint a Swiss representative or, at minimum, have a Swiss domicile for service (Article 18 of the Designs Act).

It is possible to include several designs in the same application, provided that they all relate to goods within the same class of the Locarno Classification (Article 20 of the Designs Act). There is no limit to the number of designs that may be included in an application, but the total weight of illustrations must not exceed five kilograms and the package must not measure more than 0.3 metres in any dimension (Article 10 of the Ordinance on Design Protection of March 8 2002). Applications can be filed by post, fax or email to design@ipi.ch.

The IPI will examine the application to ensure that it is complete and complies with the requirements (Article 24, paragraph 2 of the Designs Act). It will further check whether the objects filed qualify as designs under Article 1 of the Designs Act and do not manifestly violate Swiss law, international treaties, public policy or principles of morality (Article 24, paragraph 3 of the Designs Act). However, it will not investigate whether the material protection requirements (novelty and originality) have been satisfied, or whether the design is determined by the technical function of the product. This means that registration gives little comfort regarding the validity and enforceability of the design right.

Once the IPI has approved the application and the registration and publication fees have been paid, the IPI will register the design and publish the registration at www.swissreg.ch. The current (2012) fees are as follows:

- applications – Sfr200 for the first design and Sfr100 for each additional design, with a cap of Sfr700 per application; and
- publication – Sfr20 per illustration.

Publication can be suspended upon written application for up to 30 months from the filing or priority date (Article 26 of the Designs Act). However, the design right is then not enforceable against any third party that has started in good faith to use the design before its publication (Article 12, paragraph 1(b) of the Designs Act).

The same rights as are granted to a design registered in Switzerland are likewise granted to designs registered under the Hague Convention on the International Registration of Industrial Designs and designating Switzerland (Article 29 of the Designs Act). Switzerland is a party to each version of the Hague Convention, including the Geneva Act of 1999.

2.4 Term of protection

Once registered, a design is protected for five years from the filing date. Protection may be extended for up to four additional five-year periods, giving a maximum term of protection of 25 years (Article 5 of the Designs Act). Renewal is effected by written application and/or payment of the renewal fees, which are the same as the registration fees, within six months of the expiry of the preceding term of protection (Article 21, paragraph 1 of the Designs Ordinance). If this deadline is missed, renewal is still possible if authorised by the IPI. Authorisation will be granted based on a related application, provided that the application is made and the renewal fees are paid within two months of becoming aware of the missed renewal deadline or, at the latest, within six months of its expiry (Article 31 of the Designs Act).

2.5 Rights granted

The holder of a registered design right can stop any third party from using the design for any commercial purpose (Article 9 of the Designs Act). Using a design within the meaning of Article 9 includes, in particular, manufacturing, stocking, offering, putting on the market, importing, exporting or transiting through Switzerland products that incorporate the design, or possessing such products for such purposes. Any use that has an economic basis in the widest sense – irrespective of whether for consideration or profit-oriented – qualifies as use for a commercial purpose. This means that the distribution of free goods (eg, as give-aways or samples), non-profit-oriented use by charitable organisations and use for experimental purposes also constitute infringements of a registered design right. Only purely private use is exempted. Private use includes use for an individual's own purposes or use for the benefit of his closest friends and family. Legal entities or other commercial undertakings may not claim private use. One exception is that the rights holder has the right to prohibit the import, export and transit of counterfeit goods through Switzerland, even if this is for private use (Article 9, paragraph 1*bis* of the Designs Act). This provision was introduced to provide a basis for taking action against the import of counterfeit goods, such as watches, that consumers purchase for their private use during holidays abroad.

Unlike the Copyright Act, the Designs Act does not afford any further rights in the design to the rights holder. In particular, it does not provide for moral rights. The creator of a design thus has no right to be named as such on or in connection with the design, and has no means to take action against any modification or distortion of the design.

A registered design right cannot be enforced against the continued use of the design by a third party that was already using it in good faith to the same extent before the filing or priority date, or, if a suspension of publication has been requested, during the period of suspension (Article 12 of the Designs Act). Article 13 of the Designs Act grants a similar right of continued use to parties that started to use a registered design in good faith between the end of the renewal deadline and a late renewal based on Article 31 of the Designs Act (see above).

2.6 Infringement

Any commercial use in Switzerland (within the meaning outlined above) of a product incorporating a design that is identical or similar to a registered design qualifies as infringement of the registered design. Protection extends to any design that has the same essential features and produces the same overall impression as the registered design (Article 8 of the Designs Act): an imitation that is distinguishable only upon close examination is likewise infringing. A change of colour or materials alone does not avoid an infringement.

Although one of the declared objectives of the last revision of the Designs Act was to extend its scope of protection, the Swiss Federal Supreme Court has shown that this is still relatively narrow (eg, ATF 129 III 545 (no infringement); ATF 130 III 636 (infringement); ATF 130 III 645 (no infringement)).

2.7 Remedies

The Designs Act provides for the standard civil-law remedies available under Swiss law in the event of infringement of intellectual property rights. These include injunctions (Article 35, paragraphs 1(a) and (b) of the Designs Act), and the seizure and destruction of infringing goods (Article 36 of the Designs Act). Further, the rights holder may request a declaratory judgment establishing infringement (Article 33 of the Designs Act), or an order obliging the infringer to disclose the origin and amount of infringing goods in its possession, as well as the number of goods transferred to commercial third parties and the addresses of the recipients (Article 35, paragraph 1(c) of the Designs Act). Financial remedies include damages and the surrender of profits earned through the infringement (Article 35, paragraph 2 of the Designs Act).

Design infringements are also subject to criminal sanctions. Large-scale infringements committed for professional purposes are prosecuted *ex officio* and are punishable by up to two years' imprisonment and/or a monetary penalty. Other infringements are prosecuted only upon application by the rights holder and are punishable on conviction by up to one year's imprisonment or a monetary penalty (Article 41 of the Designs Act).

2.8 Licensing

Design rights may be freely licensed by the rights holder on an exclusive or non-exclusive basis (Article 15, paragraph 1 of the Designs Act). Under Swiss law, a licence is a purely contractual relationship between the licensor and licensee. As such, a licence does not grant the licensee any rights that it can enforce against third parties. However, the Designs Act provides for two exceptions in this regard:

- under Article 35, paragraph 4 of the act, an exclusive licensee is deemed authorised to initiate a design infringement action in its own name, unless this is expressly excluded in the licence agreement. However, in such an action the licensee is enforcing not its own rights, but rather those of the licensor. As a consequence, the licensee cannot claim damages suffered through the infringement – these are reserved to the licensor; and
- if the licence is registered in the Design Register, it may also be enforced against a third-party acquirer of the registered design right (Article 15, paragraph 2 of the Designs Act).

With the exception of the licence-like rights for continued use conferred to third parties by Articles 12 and 13 of the Designs Act, the act does not provide for compulsory licences.

2.9 Validity issues

As mentioned above, the IPI's examination of the material protection requirements and grounds for exclusion during registration proceedings is very limited. The novelty and originality requirements, and whether the design is determined by the technical function of the product, are not examined. Although the novelty and originality requirements (as well as the right of the applicant in the design) are assumed to be fulfilled upon filing (Article 21 of the Designs Act), a Swiss registered design is thus regarded as a rather weak right. Its validity is typically tested only within the context of an infringement action, upon the filing of a nullity objection or even a nullity counterclaim by the defendant (which often takes place).

3. Unregistered design rights

3.1 Nature of rights

As set out above, the Designs Act protects only registered designs. In Switzerland, protection for unregistered designs is available only, if at all, under the Copyright Act.

Unlike the Designs Act, the Copyright Act does not grant a real monopoly right in the design to the creator or its legal successor, but only a right to prohibit third parties from using or otherwise exploiting an identical or similar design that copies, or at least was inspired by, the original design. In other words, the rights holder has no means under the Copyright Act to proceed against a third party that has created an identical or similar design independently (so-called 'parallel creations'). This weakness in enforcement is somewhat mitigated by the fairly high material protection requirements under the Copyright Act (see below). These reduce the probability of parallel creations occurring, leading to an assumption that the later design has been copied. As the copyright in a design is not product-type bound, the rights holder may also prevent a third party from applying its design to goods that are completely different from those for which the design was initially created.

Copyright vests exclusively in the individual or group that created the design (Article 6 of the Copyright Act). This also applies to designs made by employees in the course of their employment. However, unlike in some other jurisdictions, in Switzerland copyright may be freely transferred by assignment to any other party (Article 16 of the Copyright Act). Some limitations apply in respect of certain moral rights, such as the right of the creator to object to the distortion of its creation (see below).

3.2 Qualification

In order to enjoy copyright protection, a design must qualify as an intellectual artistic creation with individual character (Article 2, paragraph 1 of the Copyright Act). This requirement is met by any design created by a human being (resulting in the exclusion of purely machine-generated forms). The term 'art' is not understood in a qualitative sense; basically, every creation that the creator wants to be understood as art qualifies as an artistic creation within the meaning of the Copyright Act. The decisive requirement for protection is therefore individual character, and under the Copyright Act a creation must generally be unique. A design must therefore present itself as the individual result of an intellectual effort or the expression of a new, original idea (ATF 113 II 190, 196). As such, it must be obviously different from earlier designs; mere variations or combinations of known forms are not regarded as individual. The same applies to all forms that are essentially dictated by the purpose of the particular item or by technical requirements. However, this limitation is mitigated by the acknowledgment that where creative freedom is limited by technical or other constraints, a relatively small degree of individuality is sufficient for protection (ATF 113 II 190, 196).

In the past, the courts adopted a rather restrictive approach when assessing the individual character of designs, particularly in relation to objects of utility. However, in a landmark decision (ATF 113 II 190) the Swiss Federal Supreme Court affirmed that Le Corbusier seats and couches qualified as individual works of art; since then, it has been clear that designs of objects of utility can also be protected by copyright. In practice, copyright protection is significant for furniture and other home fixtures. For example, copyright protection has been affirmed for the Tizio table lamp (Zurich Supreme Court, SMI 1991, 88), various chair and sofa models by Charles and Ray Eames (Swiss Federal Supreme Court, 4C.72/1995) and the Tripp Trapp child's chair (Cantonal Court of St Gallen, 2001, 491).

3.3 Term of protection

Copyright protection for an individual design starts automatically upon its creation and lasts for 70 years following the death of its creator (Article 29 of the Copyright Act).

3.4 Rights granted

Under Swiss law, copyright confers two types of right:

- rights protecting the commercial interests of the rights holder in the work (Article 10 of the Copyright Act); and
- moral rights – that is, rights that protect the personal relationship of the creator with his design (Articles 9 and 11 of the Copyright Act).

The first category includes the right to prohibit any third party from copying the design – including by manufacturing objects incorporating the design or offering, selling or otherwise distributing copies thereof (Article 10, paragraphs 1(a) and (b) of the Copyright Act). The Copyright Act includes another set of rights that protect the commercial interests of an author in his works, although these have only limited relevance to industrial designs. Unlike for other types of work, here the copyright owner has no right to control the rent of objects incorporating the design which have been put onto the market by it or with its consent; it is also not entitled to royalties for such exploitation of the design (Article 13, paragraph 2 of the Copyright Act). As under the Designs Act (see above), purely private use – including for an individual's own purposes and for the benefit of his closest friends and family – is exempted.

Moral rights include the right:

- to be named as creator of the design (Article 9, paragraph 1 of the Copyright Act);
- to decide on its first publication (Article 9, paragraph 2 of the Copyright Act);
- to modify the design (Article 11, paragraph 1(a) of the Copyright Act); and
- to prohibit the creation of a derivative work or the inclusion of the design in a collection (Article 11, paragraph 1(b) of the Copyright Act).

However, the creator may waive these rights contractually. The right to modify the work and to decide on the creation of a derivative work or inclusion in a collection may even be transferred to an acquirer of the copyright. However, the creator has the inalienable right to object to a distortion of a design that affects its personality (Article 11, paragraph 2 of the Copyright Act).

3.5 Infringement

Subject to the private-use exemption, the manufacture, putting on the market, sale or other distribution in Switzerland of a product that incorporates the design qualifies as copyright infringement. However, as mentioned above, copyright is not infringed if the conflicting design is an independent parallel creation.

The scope of protection conferred by copyright extends beyond identical designs to derivative works (Article 3, paragraphs 1 and 4 of the Copyright Act). The copyright is therefore also infringed by a third-party design that, while obviously different from the original, incorporates the features on which the individual character of the original design is based.

3.6 Remedies

Like the Designs Act, the Copyright Act provides for the standard civil-law remedies available under Swiss law in the event of infringement of intellectual property rights. These include:

- injunctions (Article 62, paragraphs 1(a) and (b) of the Copyright Act);
- declaratory judgments (Article 61 of the Copyright Act);
- the seizure and destruction of infringing goods (Article 63, paragraph 1 of the Copyright Act);
- disclosure of the origin and amount of the infringing goods in the infringer's

possession, and of the number of goods transferred to commercial third parties and the addresses of the recipients (Article 62, paragraph 1(c) of the Copyright Act);
- damages (Article 62, paragraph 2 of the Copyright Act); and
- the surrender of profits gained through the infringement (Article 62, paragraph 2 of the Copyright Act).

Article 67 of the Copyright Act provides for the same criminal penalties as apply under the Designs Act (see section 2.7 above).

3.7 Licensing

The copyright in designs may be freely licensed by the rights holder on an exclusive or non-exclusive basis. Unlike under the Designs Act, it is not possible to register a copyright licence and thus make the licence enforceable against a third-party acquirer of the right. However, under the Copyright Act, an exclusive licensee is deemed authorised to initiate an infringement action in its own name, unless this is expressly excluded in the licence agreement (Article 62, paragraph 3 of the Copyright Act).

The Copyright Act does not provide for any of compulsory licences of relevance to designs.

4. Qualification for protection

Switzerland is a party to the latest versions of all international treaties covering the protection of industrial designs, including the Paris Convention for the Protection of Industrial Property, the Agreement on Trade-Related Aspects of Intellectual Property Rights (TRIPs) and the Berne Convention for the Protection of Literary and Artistic Works. It is also a party to the Hague Convention concerning the International Registration of Industrial Designs, including the Geneva Act of 1999.

Under Swiss law, foreigners (but not Swiss individuals or partnerships, or legal entities domiciled in Switzerland) may directly invoke the provisions of these treaties if those provisions are sufficiently concrete to form the basis of a decision. Therefore, foreigners can enforce industrial designs that qualify for protection under any of the treaties, as provided in the relevant treaty. This applies even if the design would not qualify for protection under Swiss law or if Swiss law would provide a less favourable level of protection than the relevant treaty.

However, in the design field, this advantage is somewhat theoretical. First, Swiss law generally grants foreigners both design and copyright protection under the same conditions as apply to Swiss rights holders. Switzerland does not make use of the exception of national treatment provided in Article 2, paragraph 7 of the Paris Convention. It will also grant copyright protection to foreigners' individual designs if these would be eligible for protection under the home country's design legislation. Secondly, Swiss law is generally regarded as compliant with these treaties. There was some discussion in academic circles before the enactment of the Designs Act as to whether its material protection requirements – novelty and originality – are TRIPs compliant, since TRIPs provides for the protection of designs that are either new or original; it does not require both novelty and originality, as the Designs Act does. However, the prevailing view is that TRIPs does not prevent a contracting state from requiring both novelty and originality. This is because the undefined terms 'new' and 'original', as used in Article 25, paragraph 1 of TRIPs, are understood only as a reference to the two classic categories of material protection requirements used in contracting states providing for special design protection legislation.

Swiss law also complies with the requirements under the Paris Convention. The protection of an industrial design depends neither on its use (Article 5(b) of the Paris Convention) nor on it being labelled with an indication of registration of the industrial design (Article 5(d) of the convention).

5. Infringement

Design infringement actions are relatively rare in Switzerland. Published court decisions indicate that only 10 to 20 actions are filed each year, a significant number of which are settled in court.

Before an action is launched, the infringer is usually served with a 'cease and desist' letter. Although this is not a legal requirement for taking court action, it is nonetheless recommended – particularly where the infringing goods have not already, or have only sporadically, been put on the market or otherwise commercially used. The courts regard the refusal of an alleged infringer to comply with a cease-and-desist letter as sufficient to establish the legal interest required to obtain an injunction.

An infringement action begins with the filing of a comprehensive written statement of claim with the competent court (Articles 220 and following of the Swiss Code on Civil Procedure). The statement of claim must contain, among other things, the detailed prayers for relief, the amount in dispute and the alleged facts, along with all available evidence. The evidence must be filed together with a detailed statement of claims, so that the defendant can file a detailed response (Article 222 of the Swiss Code of Civil Procedure). The defendant may file a nullity counterclaim along with its response (Article 224 of the Swiss Code of Civil Procedure). This will be dealt with by the court in the same proceedings. Depending on the complexity of the case, the court may order a second exchange of briefs and/or invite the parties to a direction hearing (Articles 225 and 226 of the Swiss Code of Civil Procedure). The proceedings end with the main hearing (Articles 228 and following of the Swiss Code of Civil Procedure), at which (if no second exchange of briefs has taken place) reply and rejoinder are presented, evidence is taken and each party's closing statement is delivered. The court then renders its decision. Depending on the complexity of the case, it usually takes between one and two years for the court to issue its decision.

In Switzerland, the judicial system is organised at a cantonal level. However, each canton must designate one court to hear actions under the Designs Act or Copyright Act (Article 5(a) of the Swiss Code of Civil Procedure). In most cantons this is the superior court or cantonal court, although in some it is the commercial court. Decisions of these courts are subject to appeal before the Swiss Federal Supreme Court.

Before or at the same time as filing an action, the claimant may request the court to order interim measures, such as a preliminary injunction, the seizure of goods and/or (other) measures required to secure evidence. The court will grant such measures if, based on the *prima facie* evidence presented and after hearing the defendant, it concludes that the infringement is probable and the rights holder is likely to suffer irreparable damage if interim measures are not granted (Article 261(c) of the Swiss Code of Civil Procedure). In urgent cases the court may order interim measures in *ex parte* proceedings (Article 265 of the Swiss Code of Civil Procedure). A party concerned that a request for an *ex parte* injunction will be filed against it may file a protective brief with the competent court in which it sets out its position (Article 270 of the Swiss Code of Civil Procedure).

The final remedies available under both the Copyright Act and the Designs Act include:

- permanent injunctions;
- the seizure and destruction of infringing goods;
- declaratory judgments;
- disclosure of the origin and amount of infringing goods in the infringer's possession, and of the number of goods transferred to commercial third parties and the addresses of the recipients; and
- damages or the surrender of profits earned by the infringer (see above).

Reasonable damages often cannot be recovered, since under Swiss law only damages actually suffered are recoverable and it is usually very difficult for the claimant to discharge the related burden of proof.

Court costs are borne by the losing party (Article 106 of the Swiss Code of Civil Procedure), which must also pay the other party compensation for its legal costs. These costs depend on the amount in dispute and are determined based on cantonal tariffs. The courts can, and regularly do, make the claimant pay a cost advance up to the amount of the estimated court costs (Article 98 of the Swiss Code of Civil Procedure). On the application of the defendant, the court may also stipulate an advance for the potential party compensation – in particular, if the claimant is not domiciled in Switzerland (Article 99 of the Swiss Code of Civil Procedure).

6. Licensing and exploitation

As set out above, design rights under both the Designs Act and the Copyright Act may be freely licensed by the rights holder on an exclusive or non-exclusive basis. Subject to some limitations in respect of moral rights under the Copyright Act, the rights under both acts can also be exploited through assignment. Unlike under the Designs Act, under the Copyright Act it is possible to assign only part(s) of the copyright, not just the copyright in its entirety. It is therefore possible for the copyright owner to assign, for example, the right to use a design for the manufacture of specific products only and to keep all other rights under its control. This means that exploitation of rights by way of assignment instead of licence plays a more important role under the Copyright Act than under the Designs Act.

Under the Designs Act, it is possible – on the application of either licensor or licensee, and at no cost – to register a licence granted under a registered design right (but not under a pending application) in the Swiss Design Register (Article 15, paragraph 1 of the Designs Act). Registration is not a requirement for the validity of the licence, but it allows the licence to be enforced against a third-party acquirer of the registered design right (Article 15, paragraph 2 of the Designs Act). It is not possible to register a licence under a design right protected in Switzerland based on a registration under the Hague Convention concerning the International Registration of Industrial Designs.

Thailand

Vorarit Karadist
Deissenberger & Partners Ltd

1. Summary of design protection

The development of Thailand's legal regime has been influenced by British legal tradition,[1] German civil law[2] and the French dual-court system.[3]

Intellectual property (IP) rights, particularly the rights in patent, were not recognised or enforceable[4] in Thailand until the first Patent Act came into force in 1979. Unlike the legal systems in some other countries, this act offers protection to both the invention and the design itself. The act contains a chapter (Patent for Designs) devoted to the protection of designs which are new and capable of industrial and handicraft application. Under this chapter, novel industrial designs may be protected by law within a defined time frame upon successful application and registration of the patent, taking into account that all predefined conditions are being satisfied.

One of the most important conditions that a design must meet in its application for and the granting of a patent is the quality of being new. The term 'new' is technically defined as not being widely known or used by any others in Thailand before the application for patent is filed; not being disclosed, described or published in any document or printed publication in Thailand or a foreign country before the application is filed; and not visually bearing a striking resemblance to any earlier designs so as to be seen as an imitation.[5] Other conditions include that the design must not contravene public order or morality and must not be forbidden by royal decree.[6]

Since Thailand is an active member and contracting party to the General Agreement on Tariffs and Trade (GATT), the Agreement on Trade Related Aspects of Intellectual Property Rights (TRIPs), the Berne Convention, the World Intellectual Property Organization, the Paris Convention for the Protection of Industrial Property and, most recently, the Patent Cooperation Treaty, it is obliged to comply with the rule of national treatment[7] to: "[a]ccord to the nationals of other Members treatment no less favourable than that it accords to its own nationals with regard to the

1 The courts are not legally obliged to honour past decisions in similar cases as the UK courts are, although they do refer to existing precedents as legal references in their adjudications.
2 See Civil Code of Federal Republic of Germany. The Thai Civil and Commercial Code has been codified based on the German code and Thailand's tradition of customary laws.
3 *Dualité de Juridiction*: the dual jurisdiction system of France, where disputes between governmental and non-governmental bodies (known as administrative cases) are brought before an administrative court rather than the civil or criminal courts.
4 See *Charles Pfizer & Co Ltd v Atlantic Trading Co Ltd*, Supreme Court decision 837/2507.
5 See Patent Act BE 2522, Office of the Council of State, Kingdom of Thailand, Sections 56 to 57.
6 Patent Act, Section 58. At present, no royal decree about this has been prescribed.
7 See Agreement On Trade-Related Aspect Of Intellectual Property Rights (TRIPs), Part I, Article III.

protection of intellectual property". Thus, applicants who are nationals of the member countries of any of these conventions or agreements are eligible for the same protection as enjoyed by Thai nationals (as also reflected in the domestic legislation[8]).

In general, a design patent is valid for 10 years from the date of filing the application for registration in Thailand. No party other than the rights holder will have the right to use a patented design in the manufacture of a product or to sell, have in possession for sale, offer for sale or import a product embodying the patented design, unless this use is for the purpose of study or research.

In 1997, a specialised court known as the Central Intellectual Property and International Trade Court was established under the Act for the Establishment of and Procedure for Intellectual Property and International Trade Court.[9] The court hears criminal and civil litigation cases concerning IP law, international trade and maritime law, which were previously brought before the criminal and civil courts. The court follows a customised legal procedure that differs from civil and criminal actions, which are heard under the Civil Procedural Code and Criminal Procedural Code. Unlike the typical three-tiered court (Court of First Instance, Court of Appeal and Supreme Court), appeals from the Central Intellectual Property and International Trade Court, which is considered as the Court of First Instance, are brought directly to the Supreme Court, where a division of IP cases gives the final rulings.

2. Registered design rights

2.1 Nature of rights

The right in a design is a form of IP right under the regime of patent protection. The law does not define the term 'design rights'. The protection of design rights is principally governed and administered by the Patent Act. A design right is established by the registration of a particular patent, known as a 'patent for designs'.

2.2 Qualification

(a) Design

Under Sections 56 and 57 of the Patent Act, there are two significant factors that determine the patentability of a design. The design must have an industrial or handicraft application and it must be new. The act does not define 'new', but provides the conditions which do not constitute novelty:

1) a design which was widely known or used by others in this country before the filing of the application for a patent;
2) a design which was disclosed or described in a document or a printed publication in Thailand or a foreign country before the filing of the application for a patent;
3) a design which was published under Section 65 and Section 28 before the filing of the application for a patent; or

8 See Patent Act, Section 14.
9 BE 2539.

4) any design so nearly resembling any of the designs prescribed in (1), (2) or (3) as to be an imitation.

This implies that a design which lacks either a practical industrial or handicraft application or novelty will not be granted a design patent. A design that meets both conditions may still not be patentable if it is contrary to public order or good morals or possesses an attribute specified by royal decree.

(b) *Applicant*

The Patent Act has been amended to comply with the TRIPs Agreement and the Paris Convention. It sets the categories of applicants eligible for the patent design registration as:

- being a Thai national or a juristic person having its headquarters in Thailand;
- being a national of a country party to a convention or an international agreement on patent protection to which Thailand is also a party;
- being a national of a country which allows Thai nationals or juristic persons having their headquarters to apply for patents in that country; or
- being domiciled or having a real and effective industrial or commercial establishment in Thailand or a country party to a convention or an international agreement on patent protection to which Thailand is also a party.[10]

A designer meeting one of these qualifications is entitled to file an application for patent. The right to apply for a patent may be assigned or transferred by succession,[11] and the assignee or legal successor will enjoy the same rights as the designer. The legal successor or heir of a designer must prove his succession in the application. An assignee must provide proof of assignment in writing, signed by both the assignor and assignee.[12]

If a designer is bound by a contractual relationship, such as an employee to his employment contract or a government official to the government agencies or state enterprises, the right to apply for a patent for an invention made in the execution of his employment contract or contract for performing certain work will belong to the employer or the commissioner of the work, unless otherwise provided in the contract. This also applies where an employment contract does not require an employee to exercise any inventive activity, but the employee has made the invention using any means, data or report that his employment has put at his disposal. The same also applies to government officials.

2.3 Registration procedure

The Department of Intellectual Property (DIP) is the principal administrative body responsible for administrating and regulating IP-related rights. Its official functions include administering public requests, processing applications, registration,

---

10 Patent Act, Section 14.
11 *Ibid*, Section 10.
12 *Ibid*, Section 10, paragraph 3.

examination, inspection and granting of patents and trademarks, etc.

A design registration application is filed with the patent division of the DIP (one of the departments of the Ministry of Commerce) or to the Provincial Commercial Office, on the application form provided. A ministerial regulation made under the Patent Act provides that the application form should include the following:

- the design;
- a statement specifying the product for which the design is to be used;
- the specific claims; and
- any other particulars prescribed by the ministerial regulation.

An officer of the DIP will examine the forms and accompanying documents filed with the application for preliminary consideration. The applicant will be notified of any missing information and asked to provide it. The officer may instruct[13] the applicant to appear before him to answer any questions or to produce any document or item requested. If an application for a patent has been filed in any foreign country, the applicant must submit a report of that examination in accordance with the rules and procedures prescribed by ministerial regulations. If any document is filed in a foreign language, it must be accompanied by a Thai translation. If the applicant does not comply with these instructions or fails to submit the examination report within 90 days, the application will be deemed to have been withdrawn. The 90-day period may be extended by the director general[14] of the DIP.

Once the application has been examined, a report on the design is sent to the director general,[15] and:

- if it the director general concludes that the design is not patentable, the application will be rejected and the applicant will be notified by registered mail or by any other method prescribed by the director general within 15 days from the date of rejection; or
- if the director general concludes that the design is patentable, he will order the application to be published in accordance with the rules and procedures in the ministerial regulations.

The applicant must pay a publication fee before the design is published. The DIP officer will notify the applicant that a publication fee is due, using any method prescribed by the director general or by registered mail. If the applicant does not pay the fee within 60 days of receiving the notice, a second notification will be sent by registered mail. If the publication fee is not paid within 60 days of receipt of that second notice, the applicant will be deemed to have withdrawn its application.

When an application is published,[16] but before the registration of and grant of a patent for the design, if it appears that the application does not comply with the requirements and eligibility set by the law, the director general will reject the

---

13 *Ibid*, Section 27, applied by Section 65.

14 Head of the department of intellectual property, under the Patent Act, Section 3, including a person who is officially assigned for the duty by the director general.

15 Patent Act, Section 28, applied by Section 65.

16 *Ibid*, Section 61, paragraph 1.

application. The DIP officer will notify the applicant and any opposing party of the decision, and a copy of the decision will be displayed at the place of filing.

(a) *Grant of patent*

If after considering the examination report the director general finds no reason to refuse the patent grant, and there has been no objection or there has been an objection but the director general has decided that the invention belongs to the applicant, he will order the design to be registered and granted to the applicant. The DIP officer will then notify the applicant that the fee must be paid, within 60 days of receipt of the notice. The design will be registered and a patent granted to the applicant within 15 days of payment of the fee, but not before any ongoing appeals have been decided.[17]

(b) *Objections and validity issues*

Objections to an application may be lodged by the public during the publication.[18] Any party that believes it is entitled to the patent, rather than the applicant, or that the application does not comply with one or more of the legal requirements, may submit a notice of objection to the DIP officer. The objection must be submitted within 90 days of publication of the application.

A copy of the notice will be sent to the applicant, who must file a counterstatement within 90 days of receipt. If the applicant does not file a counterstatement within 90 days, it will be deemed to have abandoned its application. The filing of the notice of objection and the counterstatement must be substantiated with supporting evidence to validate the objection.

If the director general rejects[19] the application and an objection is submitted, he will consider the objection. The objecting party and the applicant may introduce any evidence or make any additional statements to support the grounds they rely on in accordance with the procedures prescribed by the director general. The applicant and the objecting party will be notified of the director general's decision along with his reasoning. The decision can be appealed.

If an objection is submitted and the director general decides that the disputed design belongs to the objecting party, he will reject[20] the original application. If the applicant does not appeal the decision, or appeals it and the board of patents[21] or the court has made a final decision, and if the objecting party has filed an application for a patent within 180 days of the rejection by the director general or from the date on which the final decision is given, the objecting party will be deemed to have filed its application on the filing date of the applicant, and the publication of the application for a patent of the applicant shall be deemed to be the publication of the application of the objecting party. In this case, no one may object to the application

---

17 *Ibid*, Section 72.
18 *Ibid*, Section 31, applied by Section 65.
19 *Ibid*, Section 61, paragraph 2.
20 *Ibid*, Section 34, applied by Section 65.
21 The board of patents is appointed by the cabinet, with power to decide any appeal made against any order or decision of the director general on patents or petty patents according to the Patent Act.

of the objecting party on the ground that they have better rights in the design than the objecting party.

Any patent which is granted contrary to the requirements of the Patent Act will be invalid. The validity of a patent may be challenged[22] by any person who has an interest in the patent, or by the public prosecutor, by filing with the court a petition to cancel an invalid patent.

(c) *Dispute of priority*

Where two or more parties have separately and independently made the same design and each has submitted a patent application, the first applicant to file will be granted the patent. If the applications were filed on the same date, the parties must agree whether the patent should be granted to one of them or all of them jointly. If an agreement is not reached within a period prescribed by the director general, the parties must submit the case to the court within 90 days of the prescribed period. If they fail to do so, they will be deemed to have abandoned their applications.

2.4 Term of protection

A design patent provides protection for 10 years from the date of filing[23] the application in Thailand. There are some exceptions to the date deemed as the date of filing, for example:

- an eligible applicant[24] that has filed a patent application for a design in a foreign country may claim the first filing date in the foreign country as the filing date in Thailand if the application is filed within six months of the first filing date in the foreign country; and
- any person[25] who has exhibited his design in an exhibition which has been sponsored or authorised and held in Thailand and who applies for a patent for the design within 12 months of the opening date of that exhibition will be deemed to have filed his application on the opening date of the exhibition.

The term of a patent does not include any period of court proceedings.

The patent may not be renewed when its term of protection expires.

2.5 Infringement

The rights holder has an exclusive right to use the patented design in the manufacture of a product or to sell, have in possession for sale, offer for sale or import a product embodying the patented design. Any act in contravention of this right constitutes an infringement, except the use of the design for the purpose of study or research. Infringers[26] may be sentenced to imprisonment for up to two years, or a fine of up to Bt400,000 (approximately US$13,000) or both.

---

22 Patent Act, Section 64.
23 *Ibid*, Section 62.
24 *Ibid*, Section 60 bis, specifying persons pursuant to Section 14.
25 *Ibid*, Section 19, applied by Section 65.
26 *Ibid*, Section 85.

The rights holder has an exclusive right to use the words[27] 'Thai Patent', 'Thai Petty Patent', or its abbreviation or foreign words of the equivalent meaning, on any product, container or package of a product or in advertising any invention or design. Infringers[28] may be sentenced to imprisonment for up to one year, or a fine of up to Bt200,000 or both.

Unauthorised disclosure[29] of information contained in the detailed description of a design before publication of its patent application is an infringement, as is committing any act which is likely to cause damage to the applicant, unless it is authorised in writing by the applicant. Infringers[30] may be sentenced to up to six months' imprisonment, or a fine of up to Bt20,000 or both.

2.6 Licensing

A rights holder may grant a licence to exercise the rights conferred by the patent to any other party or may assign the patent to any other party. However, the licensing agreement must not impose any condition, restriction or royalty term which is unjustifiably anticompetitive on the licensee. A licensor may not demand payment of royalties for the use of an expired patented design. Any[31] prohibited terms or conditions imposed on the licensing agreement are null and void.

A licensing agreement and the assignment of a patent must be in writing and must be duly registered following the requirements and procedures prescribed by the ministerial regulations. A registration may be rejected totally or partly if it appears to be contrary to the legal provision, depending on severability clauses of such agreement. All registrations must be recorded at the DIP.

2.7 Compulsory licensing

The Patent Act does not provide any explicit provision on compulsory licensing in its Patent for Designs chapter, and the provision in the Patent for Inventions chapter is not applied to the design patent. Thus, in practice, unlike patents for inventions, compulsory licensing is not applicable for design patents.

3. Unregistered design rights

This chapter provides only a brief, generalised overview of the possible legal protection for unregistered designs, taking into account available legal provisions and examples set by decisions of the Supreme Court.

While registered design rights are clearly protected by the Patent Act, no specific legislation has been tailored for unregistered design rights. However, an unregistered design may enjoy some legal protection as a trade secret if it has not been published.

Section 3 of the Trade Secret Act[32] defines 'trade secrets' as follows:

'Trade Secrets' means trade information not yet publicly known or not yet accessible by

27 *Ibid*, Section 75.
28 *Ibid*, Section 84.
29 *Ibid*, Section 22, applied by Section 65.
30 *Ibid*, Section 82.
31 *Ibid*, Section 39.
32 Trade Secret Act BE 2545, Office of the Council of State, Kingdom of Thailand.

persons who are normally connected with the information, the commercial values of which derive from its secrecy and that the controller of the trade secrets has taken appropriate measures to maintain the secrecy.

'Trade Information' means any medium that conveys the meaning of a statement, facts, or other information irrespective of its method and forms. It shall also include formulas, patterns, compilations or assembled works, programs, methods, techniques, or processes.

A design may also be interpreted as a form of artistic expression or a rendition of visually discernible constructions of lines, shapes or colours under a copyright, particularly as an artistic work.

In spite of much debate among legal scholars and practitioners on the concept of the practical separation of protection of IP rights and the overlapping protection of each of the existing rights, many remain in existence. Unregistered designs are a good example. Since by its nature a design may be either a wholly individual construction of or a collective composition of lines, colours and shapes, it may also be construed as an artistic work, which is protectable as a copyright under the Copyright Act.[33]

Under Section 3 of the Copyright Act, an 'artistic work' is defined as being one or more of the following:

(1) work of painting or drawing, which means a creation of configuration consisting of lines, light, colours or any other element, or the composition thereof, upon one or more materials;
(2) work of sculpture, which means a creation of configuration with tangible volume;
(3) work of lithography, which means a creation of pictures by printing process and includes printing blocks or plates used in the printing;
(4) work of architecture, which means a design of buildings or constructions, a design of interior or exterior decoration as well as a landscape design or a creation of a model of buildings or constructions;
(5) photographic work, which means a creation of pictures with the use of image recording apparatus which allows the light to pass through a lens to a film or glass and developed with liquid chemical of specific formula or by any process that creates a picture or an image recorded by any other apparatus or method;
(6) work of illustration, which means a map, structure, sketch or three-dimensional work with respect to geography, topography or science; and
(7) work of applied art, which means a work which takes each or a composition of the works mentioned in items (1) to (6) for utility apart from the appreciation in the merit of the work such as for practical use of such work, decorating materials or appliances or using for commercial benefit,

whether with or without artistic merit, and shall include photographs and plans of such works.

Under these definitions, a design may be classified as an artistic work, particularly as a 'work of painting or drawing' and a 'work of applied art'.

33 Copyright Act BE 2537, Office of the Council of State, Kingdom of Thailand, Section 4.

A Supreme Court decision[34] on a dispute over the design of a pen provides an example. The court ruled in favour of the plaintiff, the owner of the design, which was not patented. In its final decision, the court stated that: "the plaintiff has made an effort in the creation of configuration of lines and shapes which contemplates for use the creation of a pen which is considered as the combination of 'the work of painting or drawing' and 'work of applied art' that is entitled to legal protection according to the Copyright Act as copyrighted work, without regard to the artistic merit of the work".

The decision was based on the ground that no legal provision forbids such protection. Some legal scholars take a different view – that the IP system is aimed at offering different protection that is specific to each class of characteristic right. Although the court is not obliged to follow past decisions, it will refer to existing precedents as legal references for its adjudication. Thus, it is possible that future disputes may receive similar adjudication.

If an unregistered design can be shown to have a copyright, the right is granted automatically on creation of the work and subsists[35] for the lifetime of its author plus 50 years after his death. Works of joint authorship enjoy copyright protection for the lifetime of the joint authors plus 50 years after the death of the last surviving joint author. If the author or all joint authors die before publication of a work, copyright subsists for 50 years as from first publication of the work. Where the author is a legal person, copyright subsists for 50 years as from authorship; if the work is published during this period, the copyright lasts for 50 years from first publication.

It is not possible legally to licence an unregistered design before a formal registration is made.

4. Qualification for protection

The requirements for qualification for protection are discussed at sections 2.2 and 3 above for registered and unregistered design rights respectively.

5. Infringement

Infringement of a patent for design constitutes both a criminal and a civil offence. For a criminal offence, infringers will face terms of imprisonment and fines. These will vary in duration and amount depending on the seriousness of the charges, but may not exceed the maximum rates specified by law. A criminal penalty does not interfere with the right of the rights holder to claim against infringers for civil damages in a separate civil action. Criminal charges and civil actions are brought before a specialised court, the Central Intellectual Property and International Trade Court.

6. Design infringement litigation

A rights holder or unregistered design owner may seek judicial remedies in criminal and civil actions against infringement of IP rights in the Central Intellectual Property and International Trade Court.

---

34 Supreme Court Decision 6379/2537.
35 Copyright Act, Section 19.

Criminal proceedings offer two alternatives. First, the damaged party may file a complaint about an alleged violation with the police, who will investigate the claim. If substantial grounds and evidence to support the claim are found, the case will be passed to the public prosecutor, who will file it as a criminal case with the court. The damaged party may file a motion to the court requesting permission to be the co-prosecutor in the case. The advantage of being a co-prosecutor is that if the public prosecutor decides not to appeal a decision of the court of first instance, as co-prosecutor the damaged party alone may file an appeal to the Supreme Court.

The Thai legal system follows an accusatorial/adversarial system in most court[36] proceedings, whereby any injured or damaged party may file a criminal charge without having to proceed through the police or public prosecutor (unlike common-law jurisdictions that use an inquisitorial system, whereby citizens could only file civil actions against one another, not criminal charges). Thus, the second alternative is to file a criminal case directly with the court as a prosecutor in the case.

In civil cases, local attorneys who have expertise in the IP and international trade area may be employed.

The Central Intellectual Property and International Trade Court offers legal steps that are different from the civil and criminal procedures in other courts. One of the most significant differences is the possibility for a plaintiff to file a motion requesting an injunction before filing an action with the court. In other courts, this may only be done after an action has been filed. An injunction before filing an action will ensure that the plaintiff receives immediate remedies for and assistance with minimising the damage caused by the infringement.

The court proceeding is considerably efficient. The quorum of judges in a trial comprises two professional judges and a lay judge who is specialised in the matters in dispute. Communication with the court can be conveniently established electronically via any available means of information technology, such as videoconferencing. Written affidavits of witness are acceptable as evidence in lieu of the taking of witness statements before the court. The decision of the court can be appealed directly to the Supreme Court, where a specialised division of intellectual property and international trade will adjudicate and make final a decision on the case. Upon the final court decision, the case can be enforced within a period of 10 years from the date of announcement of the decision.

The cost of litigation in IP-related matters varies according to the complexity the case.

An attorney may charge litigation fees based on a lump sum and/or an hourly rate. The basis used will depend on the estimated time for preparation of the case and the work to bring it to completion.

The cost of the court proceedings is relatively inexpensive in comparison with many other countries. Under an amendment to the law in 2008, the court fee is calculated at 2% of the capital not exceeding Bt50 million (approximately US$1.6 million), but limited to Bt200,000. Any amount over the Bt50 million threshold is

---

36 In some courts, such as the administrative court and the Supreme Court's Criminal Division for Political Office Holders, an inquisitorial system is adopted for all legal proceedings.

calculated at 0.1%. However, the court-ordered reimbursement of costs of the legal representation of each party is much lower than the actual costs – in effect, the parties are paying for their own representation costs.

7. Licensing and exploitation

Licensing and exploitation of registered and unregistered design rights are discussed at sections 2.2 and 3 above respectively.

Turkey

Dilek Ustun
Istanbul Patent & Trademark Consultancy Ltd

---

1. Summary of design protection

In Turkey, several forms of protection are available for designs, dependent on their character:

- copyright:
  - work of art;
  - originality; and
  - individual character;
- trademark:
  - distinctive character;
  - non-descriptive; and
  - specific goods and services;
- patent:
  - not solely dictated by technical function;
  - novelty; and
  - inventive character;
- unfair competition:
  - product established in the market;
  - competition situation; and
  - risk of confusion;
- designs:
  - the appearance of the whole or a part of a product;
  - novelty; and
  - individual character.

Industrial designs are governed by Decree-Law 554 Pertaining to the Protection of Industrial Designs, which came into force on June 27 1995, and the Implementing Regulations under Decree-Law 554 pertaining to the Protection of Industrial Designs, including the Amended Implementing Regulation of December 31 1997.

Turkey is also a party to:

- the Hague Agreement;
- the Locarno Agreement;
- the Paris Convention; and
- the WIPO Convention.

Decree-Law 554 governs the principles, rules and conditions for the protection of registered designs. For non-registered designs, the general provisions will prevail. The rights conferred by Decree-Law 554 do not invalidate the protection granted by the Literary and Artistic Works Law.

Copyrights are governed by Law 5846 of December 5 1951, on Intellectual and Artistic Works, as last amended on June 7 1995 by Law 4110.

Turkey is also a party to:

- the Berne Convention;
- the Rome Convention;
- the World Intellectual Property Organization (WIPO) Convention;
- the WIPO Copyright Treaty; and
- the WIPO Performances and Phonograms Treaty.

2. Registered design rights

Under Article 3 of Decree-Law 554:

- 'design' means the entirety of the various features such as lines, colour, texture, shape, sound, elasticity, material and other characteristics apparent to the human eye of the appearance of the whole or a part of a product or its ornamentation;
- 'product' means any industrial or handicraft item, parts of a complex system, sets, compositions of items, packaging, get-ups, graphic symbols and typographic typefaces, excluding computer programs and semiconductor products;
- 'designer' means the creator of the design to be protected; and
- 'Institute' means the Turkish Patent Institute, assigned to implement the rules of this legislation.

Protection under Decree-Law 554 is available to natural and legal persons who are domiciled or who have industrial or commercial establishments within the territory of the Turkish Republic, or to the persons who have application rights resulting from the terms of the Paris Convention, the Berne Convention or the Agreement Establishing the World Trade Organization.

Natural or legal persons, other than those referred to in the first paragraph of Article 3 of Decree Law 554, who are nationals of states which accord legal and *de facto* protection to Turkish nationals will enjoy reciprocal principal design protection in Turkey.

2.1 Articles 5 (General), 6 (Novelty) and 7 (Individual character)

Protection will be granted to a design that is new and has an individual character. Designs of products that are parts of complex items will be protected if the design of the part itself is new and has individual character.

A design will be considered new if before the date of reference no identical design has been made available to the public anywhere in the world. Designs differing only in immaterial details will be deemed to be identical. 'Making available to the public' covers sale, use, publication, publicity, exhibiting and similar activities.

A design will have individual character if the overall impression it creates on the informed user is significantly different from the overall impression created on the same user by any design referred to in paragraph 2 of Article 7, under which the design used for the comparison must have been:

- made public in Turkey or elsewhere in the world before the application date; and
- published by the Institute as a registered design, with some unexpired protection period on the application date of the design with which it is to be compared.

In the assessment of a design's individual character, emphasis is placed on the common features of the designs and the degree of freedom of the designer in developing the design.

2.2 Scope of protection

In determining the scope of protection, all designs which produce on the informed user a significantly similar overall impression in conformity with Article 7 will be taken into consideration. Common features are given more weight than differences, and the degree of freedom of the designer in the development of the design is taken into consideration.

2.3 Outside the scope of protection

(a) Disclosures that will not prejudice novelty or individual character

If a design for which protection is claimed has been made available to the public during the 12 months before the application is filed, or if a priority is claimed during the 12 months before the date of priority, by the designer, his successor in title or a third party (either with the approval the designer or his successor in title or in abuse of their relationship), the disclosure will not affect the novelty and individual character of the design.

(b) Designs contrary to public order and morality

Protection is not available for designs that are contrary to public order and general morality principles.

(c) Other situations

Designs resulting from a technical function which does not leave to the designer any freedom in the design characteristics and elements fall outside the scope of protection.

Designs fall outside the scope of protection when they must be produced in their exact form and dimensions in order to enable the product in which the design is incorporated or to which it is applied to be mechanically assembled or connected with other products.

However, designs whose purpose is to enable simultaneous and infinite or multiple assembly or connection of identical or mutually interchangeable products within a modular system are protectable, provided they meet the provisions of Articles 6 and 7.

2.4 Term of protection

A registered design enjoys protection for five years from the date of filing of the application. The protection is renewable in five-year terms, up to a total term of 25 years.

2.5 Registration procedure

The procedure for registering a design is outlined in the flow diagram below.

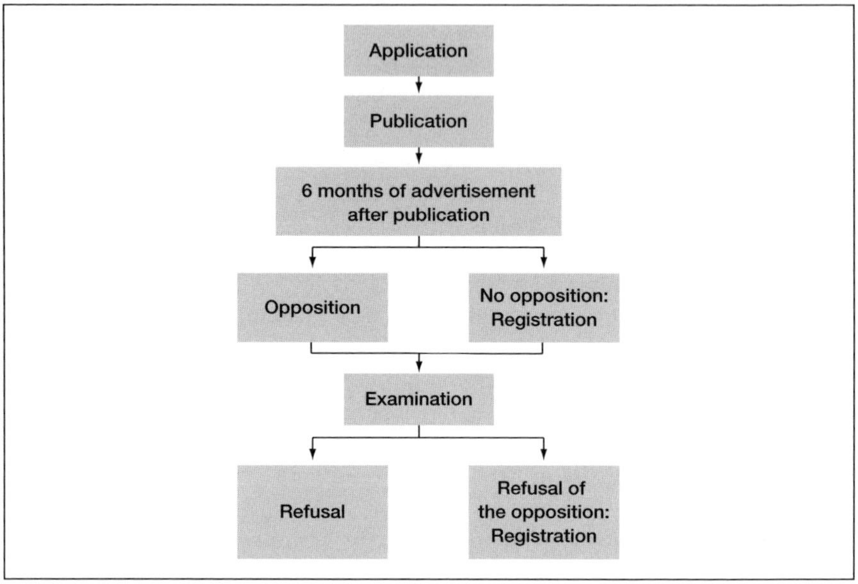

The application for registration of a design must include the following:

- a petition, the form and contents of which are specified in the Implementing Regulation, and information identifying the applicant; and
- a drawing, painting, graphic, photographic or similar representation of the design, suitable for reproduction and reflecting all of its specific features.

The application must contain a written description of the design and list the products in which the design is intended to be incorporated or to which it is intended to be applied.

An application fee must be paid and the receipt of payment submitted with the application, otherwise the application will be invalid.

The identity of the designer must be stated in the application. If the applicant is not the designer or not the sole designer, the ground for the right to apply for registration must be stated.

All documents filed with the application for registration of a design or submitted later to the Institute must comply with the Implementing Regulation.

2.6 Multiple applications

Two or more designs may be filed together in one application.

2.7 Right of priority

Natural or legal persons or their legal successors in title who are nationals of any state that is party to the Paris Convention or, if not nationals, who are domiciled or have an active business in these states enjoy a right of priority of six months from the date of filing a valid application with the authorised bodies of these states, to file an application for a Turkish registration for the same design.

2.8 Exhibition priority

Natural or legal persons specified in the first paragraph of Article 29 of Decree-Law 554 who have shown products in which the design is incorporated or to which it is applied at national or international exhibitions in Turkey or at official or officially recognised national or international exhibitions in the states party to the Paris Convention, may claim a right of priority for the registration of the design in Turkey if the application for priority is filed within six months of the date of the first display of the products.

2.9 Opposition

Natural or legal persons or related professional organisations may submit an application for the declaration of invalidity of a registered design, after its publication, to the Institute following the procedures prescribed in the Implementing Regulation.

An application for a declaration of invalidity must state the objections clearly and must be filed as a written statement within six months of publication. The fee prescribed in the Implementing Regulation must be paid before the application will be considered. The Institute may request additional documents, evidence and justification, which must be provided within a time limit set by the Institute.

2.10 Invalidity

A registered design will be declared invalid by the court if:

- it is proved that the design is not eligible for protection;
- it is proved that the entitlement to the design right belongs to another party or parties; or
- a conflicting design exists which has been made available to the public at a later date but has an earlier filing date.

Any party may request invalidity except in the cases specified in the second bullet item above.

Under paragraph (c) of Article 43 of Decree-Law 554, a declaration of invalidity can be requested only by the previous rights holder(s). Under Articles 13, 14, 15 and 16 of the same legislation, the rights holder(s) must request the declaration during the period of protection or within five years of the right terminating.

An action brought before the court for invalidity will be against the rights holder registered in the Design Register at the time the action is filed.

3. Unregistered design rights

3.1 Copyright

Intellectual and artistic works are defined and classified in the Copyright Act (Law 5846) as follows:

- Works of science and literature:
  - (amended: 7.6.1995-4110/Article 1) works expressed in language and writing in any way and computer programs expressed in any form and their preliminary designs, provided that these lead to a program in the next stage;
  - (amended: 1.11.1983-2936/Article 1) all kinds of dances, written choreography works and similar unworded stage works; and
  - (amended: 7.6.1995-4110/Article 1) all kinds of technical and scientific photographic works that do not have rhetorical character; all kinds of maps, plans, projects, sketches, pictures, geographical and topographical models and the like; and all kinds of architectural and civil designs and projects, architectural models, industrial, environmental and stage designs and projects.

  Ideas and principles constituting a basis for any element of a computer program, including the ideas and principles constituting a basis for its interface, are not considered works.
- Works of music:
  - all types of worded and unworded compositions;
- Works of fine art (amended: 7.6.1995-4110/Article 2):
  - oil and watercolour paintings, all types of pictures, designs, pastels, engravings, manuscripts and gilding, works drawn or fixed with mineral, stone, wood or other substances by scratching, engraving, tapping or similar methods, calligraphy and screen printing;
  - statues, reliefs and carvings;
  - works of architecture;
  - handicrafts and minor works of art, miniatures and products of decorative art, and textile and fashion designs;
  - photographic works and slides;
  - graphic works;
  - cartoon works; and
  - all kinds of typing, with aesthetic value.

The use of sketches, pictures, models, designs and similar works as industrial models and pictures does not affect their classification as intellectual and artistic works.

The rule of pre-emption that bars technical and functional creations from obtaining exclusive intellectual property rights other than through the patent system does not apply in respect of non-technical creations. Therefore, cumulative protection by copyright and industrial design rights is possible for the non-functional features of a product configuration.

3.2 Owner of the work

The 'owner' of a work is the person who creates it.

Unless otherwise agreed by special contract or the nature of the work, the owner of the financial rights of works created by employees in the course of their employment will be the person(s) employing or assigning them. The same applies to corporate entities.

The owner of an adaptation is the adapter, provided that the rights of the original owner are reserved.

The producer or publisher of a work can exercise financial rights only under a contract concluded with the owner of the work.

In cinematographic works, the director, the composer of the original soundtrack and the author of the script are the collective owners of the work. The collective owners of a work can transfer the financial rights to the producer under a contract and against a suitable cost.

If the collective owners of a cinematographic work transfer their financial rights, they cannot object to the duplication, distribution, supply to the public, cable transmission, broadcast by means of television or other media, subscription or dubbing of the work by the producer, unless there is an agreement to the contrary.

3.3 Intellectual rights

(a) Rights of the owner of the work

The financial and moral interests of the owners of intellectual and artistic works are governed by the Copyright Act.

The rights and authorities granted to the owner of the work cover the whole and parts of the work.

(b) Moral rights

Moral rights comprise:

- authority to present the work to the public;
- the authority to state the name of the owner of the work; and
- prohibition of any changes to the work.

Abridgements, additions or other changes to the work or to the name of the owner of the work cannot be made without the owner's permission.

4. Qualification for protection

4.1 Unfair competition

Unfair competition applies to a product established in a market, where the product is in a competition situation and where there is a risk of confusion. It is defined more fully in Section 56 of the Commercial Code. An action will be considered unfair competition if the criteria of economic competition, breach of good faith and misuse are all met.

The first criterion is the existence of competition in an economic system. The second criterion, breach of good faith/honesty, is the essence of the unfair-competition law. Section 56 describes it as "a deceptive action or an action against principles of good faith".

The criterion of breach of the principles of good faith, which is needed for enforcing the unfair-competition rules of the Commercial Law, is based on the principle of honesty defined in Section 2 of the Civil Law. A misuse of economic competition is a breach of good faith. Section 57 of the Commercial Law states that:

> *Trying to plagiarise or taking steps to plagiarise somebody else's products, works, activities or commercial operations, using such distinguishing marks as a name, title, trademark or mark rightly used by somebody else, or making plagiarising goods available for sale in a deliberate or non-deliberate way, or keeping such goods in stock for any reasons other than personal need shall be considered a breach of good faith.*

5. Infringement

5.1 Infringement of a design right

Under Article 48 of Decree-Law 554, the following acts constitute an infringement of a design right:

(a) without the consent of the design rights holder, to make, produce, put on the market, offer, sell, put to use, import or keep in stock for these purposes an identical or significantly similar design;
(b) to transfer to third parties or to expand the rights acquired by a licensing contract;
(c) to participate in, to assist, to encourage or to facilitate in whatever form the acts referred to in sub-paragraphs (a) and (b);
(d) to abstain from explaining where and how an illegally produced and marketed product has been obtained when found in possession; and
(e) seizure of entitlement.

If the application for a design has been published, the rights holder has the right to institute civil and penal proceedings against the infringing party. If the infringing party has been informed of the application and its scope, infringement will be considered to exist before publication when the court rules that the infringing party was acting in bad faith.

5.2 Criminal infringement

A decision of the Constitutional Court regarding some of the provisions of Decree-Laws 554 and 551 has clarified the position in connection with criminal infringement on or after January 1 2009.

On the basis of Laws 5349 and 5560 amending and adding thereto transitional Article 1 of Law 5252 concerning "the modality of enforcement and application of the Turkish Criminal Code" (Law 5237 of June 1 2005), the court found that the criminal provisions and sanctions provided in the above-mentioned Decree-Laws that were deemed as "specific criminal acts/provisions" were to be applicable only until December 31 2008 in the absence of any further legislation voted through Parliament up to that date. In fact, no legislation has been voted through Parliament for any of the above-mentioned Decree-Laws in that period.

The want of legislation has left the criminal route and associated sanctions baseless, and therefore Impracticable, as from January 1 2009 for all intellectual property rights protected in Turkey on the basis of the above-mentioned Decree-Laws.

6. Design infringement litigation

6.1 Procedure

A rights holder whose rights have been infringed may request the following of the court:

- a ruling that an infringement has taken place;
- the prohibition and prevention of the acts of infringement;
- remedies for the infringement and compensation for damages incurred;
- that the products produced or imported and the equipment used directly to produce them be confiscated;
- transfer of confiscated products to the rights holder. The value of the products will be deducted from any compensation awarded, and if the value of the products is greater than the compensation value awarded, the rights holder will repay the balance to the infringing party;
- enforcement measures to prevent continued infringement, in particular the destruction of the infringing products and equipment, if this is necessary to stop further infringement or the prevention of any alteration of the products and equipment confiscated under the fourth point above;
- disclosure to the public and to the involved parties of the court's decision by means of publication, the cost of which is to be met by the offending party.

The court will rule in accordance with the applicable provisions of the Civil Procedures Code on precautionary measures.

The competent court for a rights holder to bring civil proceedings against infringers is the court of the domicile of the plaintiff, the court of the place where the act was committed or the court of the place where the act had effect.

If a plaintiff is not a citizen of Turkey, the competent court is the court of the domicile of the authorised agent registered in the registry. If the agent's registration has been cancelled, the competent court is the court of the domicile of the Institute.

The competent court for third parties to bring an action against a rights holder is the court of the domicile of the defendant. If the rights holder is not domiciled in Turkey, the provisions above prevail.

Where there are several competent courts, the court at which the proceedings are first instituted will be the competent court.

The damage suffered by the rights holder includes the loss of income incurred because of the infringement, as well as the value of the actual loss.

The loss of income is calculated using one of the following evaluation methods, chosen by the infringed rights holder:

- the possible income that the rights holder would have generated if the competition of the infringing party did not exist;
- the income generated by the infringing party from the use of the design; or
- a licence fee that would have been paid if the party infringing the design right had used the design under a legal licensing contract.

The calculation of lost profits will include the economic value of the design, the term of protection remaining at the time of infringement, the type and number of licences outstanding and similar factors.

6.2 Publication of the court's decision

When a court judgment becomes final, the successful party may request its publication, in full or in summary, in a daily newspaper, on the radio, television or other media, the costs of which will be met by the losing party.

The nature and extent of the publication will be determined in the judgment. Publication must be made within three months of the final judgment.

7. Licensing and exploitation

7.1 Registered design

The application right or the design right may be licensed to be effective within all or part of the territory of national boundaries. A licence may be exclusive or non-exclusive.

The application or the rights holder may institute legal action against the licensee in the event of any of the contract conditions by the licensee.

Unless otherwise specified in the contract:

- the licence will be understood to be non-exclusive. The rights holder may itself make use of the design rights while also granting licences to third parties;
- if an exclusive licence is granted, the licensor may not grant licences to other parties and cannot itself make use of the design right;
- a licensee cannot transfer the rights arising from the licence and cannot grant a sub-licence; and
- a licensee will have exclusive rights in the use of the design within the whole of the national boundaries during the period of protection.

Licensing contracts must be in writing and may be entered in the designs register and published at the request of one of the parties.

Unless provided otherwise by the contract, the holder of an exclusive licence may, in the case of an infringement of the design rights, institute in its own name all legal proceedings which have been made available to the rights holder by Decree-Law 554. Holders of non-exclusive licences do not have the right to institute legal proceedings.

In the case of an infringement, the holder of a non-exclusive licence may give notice, through a notary public, requesting the rights holder to institute such proceedings as required. If the rights holder refuses to initiate proceedings, or fails to institute proceedings within three months of receiving notice, the non-exclusive licence holder will have the right to institute proceedings.

A licensee may request the court to issue an injunction for interim measures if facing serious damage where time is of the essence. The licensee who has instituted proceedings in this respect must notify the rights holder that the proceedings have been instituted.

If an application right or a design right has been licensed or transferred by an unauthorised person, that person will be liable for his acts against the parties involved.

7.2 Copyright

(a) Contract and disposals

The owner of a work or his successors in title may transfer the financial rights legally granted to them to others in a restricted or unrestricted manner in terms of duration, place and contents, with or without any return.

The authority merely to exercise the financial rights (licence) can also be assigned to another person.

Acts of disposal specified in the preceeding paragraphs shall be null and void if they relate to a work that has not yet been created or has yet to be completed at some future date.

(b) Acquisition by transfer

Any person who has acquired a financial right or a licence to exercise such a right from the owner of the work or his successors in title may transfer such rights or a licence to exercise such rights to someone else only through the written consent of the owner or his successors.

In the transfer of the right to adapt, the consent of the owner of the work or his successors is also required for the person acquiring these by transfer in the same manner.

(c) Licence

A licence is a 'simple licence' if it does not prevent the granting by the owner of the financial right of the same licence to others and a 'full licence' if it is exclusive to only one person. Unless otherwise understood from the law or the contract, every copyright licence is considered to be a simple licence.

The provisions on revenue lease are applied for simple licences and the provisions on right of benefit are applied for full licences.

(d) Transfer of property

The transfer of the property right on original or duplicated copies does not include the transfer of intellectual rights unless otherwise decided.

United Arab Emirates

Stephen Jiew
Al Tamimi & Company

---

1. Summary of design protection

1.1 Introduction

The protection of industrial designs and models in the United Arab Emirates is regulated by Chapter 3 of Federal Law 17/2002 Regulating and Protecting Patents and Property Rights in Industrial Designs and Models.

Design rights protect the novel visual aspects of a product or its packaging. To qualify for protection, a design must display aesthetic features and must not be predated by a known identical or similar design.

Designs can be expressed in two-dimensional (drawing) or three-dimensional (model) formats. Designs contribute significantly to the marketability of goods and are crucial assets in many industries, such as textiles, fashion, mobile consumer devices, computer software (interfaces), automobiles, and furnishing and decoration.

The Patent Office, under the Ministry of Economy, is responsible for the registration of designs in the United Arab Emirates.

1.2 Paris Convention

The United Arab Emirates is a member of the Paris Convention for the Protection of Industrial Property and priority claims under the Paris Convention, within six months of the priority date, are allowed.

1.3 Hague Agreement

The United Arab Emirates is not a member of the Hague System on the International Registration of Industrial Designs.

2. Registered design rights

2.1 Nature of rights

Design rights protect the novel or innovative visual aspects of a product or its packaging.

2.2 Qualification

Under the design protection regime, 'design' refers to the features of shape, configuration, pattern or ornamentation which give a product a unique appearance.

Designs and models must be innovative or novel and must serve as a pattern for an industrial product or handicraft and must not be contrary to the public order or morality. The applicable standard of novelty is absolute novelty.

2.3 Registration procedure

An application to register a design or model must be in Arabic and include an English translation of the description (statement of novelty) and representations. A power of attorney, a deed of assignment, a certificate of incorporation of the applicant (where applicable) and a certified copy of any priority document(s) must be filed in support of the application within three months of the application's filing date.

The application is then examined for formalities only. If all formalities are complied with, the application for registration will be granted.

The Patent Office no longer undertakes a substantive examination of applications to register an industrial designs and models.

2.4 Term of protection

A registered design or model enjoys protection for 10 years, provided that the annual fees are paid on time. There are currently no provisions for the restoration of lapsed designs or models. This is so even if the design or model (or application) were to lapse through no fault of the applicant or rights holder.

2.5 Infringement

Upon registration, a rights holder is vested with the power to prevent third parties from:

- using the design or model in the manufacture of any product; and
- importing any product relating to the design or model or possessing with the intent of using, offering to sell or selling such a product.

2.6 Licensing

A rights holder may authorise a third party (natural person or corporate entity) to use the protected design or model, subject to the terms of the licence granted. The terms of such a licence must not exceed the protection provided to the rights holder under the legal regime. The licence must be in writing and be signed by all parties.

The licence must be recorded on the Designs Register, upon payment of the required fee, and published in the *Bulletin* in order to be enforceable against third parties.

The licence contract will not prevent the rights holder itself from using or working the subject matter of the design or model or granting other licences to third parties, unless otherwise provided in the licence contract.

The licensee is entitled to use and work the design rights granted under the licence throughout the United Arab Emirates during the period of legal protection, unless otherwise provided by the licence contract.

Except where the ownership of a business is assigned or transferred as a whole or with respect to the part which uses the licence, the licensee may not assign the licence to a third party or grant sub-licenses, unless otherwise provided by the licence contract.

3. Unregistered design rights

3.1 Nature of rights

Unregistered designs are protectable as copyright in the form of a literary work. Copyright may protect documents detailing the design as well as any artistic or literary work incorporated within the finished product, whereas a pure design right focuses on the shape, configuration and construction of a product.

The first ever Copyright Law and its Implementing Regulations came into force on April 12 1993 and September 1 1994, respectively. In 2002, the United Arab Emirates promulgated a new copyright law entitled Federal Law No. 7/2002 (UAE) concerning Copyrights and Neighbouring Rights.

As the United Arab Emirates is a signatory to the World Trade Organization, the provisions relating to intellectual property in the Agreement on Trade-Related Aspects of Intellectual Property Rights (TRIPs), including reciprocity, are applicable.

The Copyright Law is a federal law and protects original intellectual works created in the fields of literature, arts and science, whatever the value, nature, purpose or mode of expression of the work.

It is not necessary to register a design for it to enjoy protection. Designs may be registered through an application to the Ministry of Information and Culture, but it is not a prerequisite for the work to be protected.

Designs are often registered in order to establish proof of the date and content of the work for any potential later dispute or legal claim.

3.2 Qualification

Unregistered design rights are automatic and are treated in a similar manner to copyright.

Copyright protects a broad range of intellectual creations, more specifically literary works (including computer software), artistic works, musical works and broadcasts – for example, copyright in a book, a photo or software.

3.3 Term of protection

Copyright protection is limited typically to the life of the author plus 50 years.

3.4 Rights granted

The author of the copyrighted work enjoys both moral and economic rights. Moral rights comprise the continuing personal and legal connection that authors hold in their literary and artistic works. An author's moral rights include the right to determine when, where and in what form the work is made public, including the first publication of the work, the right to be identified as the author of the work, the right to object to any distortions, mutilations or other modifications that cause harm to the author's honour or reputation, and the right to withdraw the work from circulation.

Economic rights include the exclusive right to license the use of the work through any means, in particular through reproduction, any form of representation, broadcasting or re-broadcasting, public performance, translation, modification, alteration, leasing, rental, lending, and any form of publication by any means, including through computers and communication networks.

3.5 Infringement

Copyright infringement occurs when any party without the written permission of the author or rights holder makes any work subject to copyright available to the public through the computer, Internet, communication networks or any other means, or sells, rents or otherwise puts it in circulation to the public.

3.6 Damages and other relief

Penalties for copyright infringement include imprisonment for not less than two months and/or a fine of between Dh 10,000 (approximately $2,700) and Dh50,000 (approximately $13,700). Repeat offenders may be punished by imprisonment for at least six months and fined not less than Dh50,000 (approximately $13,700).

3.7 Licensing

Rights holders are expressly empowered to grant licences for exploitation of the copyrighted work by any means, in particular for copying, including electronic loading or storing, acting a play by any means, broadcasting, re-broadcasting, transmission, performance, public communication, translation, modification, alteration, rental, lending, and publication by any means.

3.7 Compulsory licences

Compulsory licences may be granted by the Ministry of Economy to any party that applies to the ministry for the purposes of reproduction or translation of a protected work. Conditions on the time and place of the exploitation will be imposed and a fair compensation will be granted to the rights holder. The grant of a compulsory licence is limited to educational needs and the needs of public libraries and archives.

4. International treaties

The United Arab Emirates acceded to both the Berne Convention for Literary and Artistic Works and the World Intellectual Property Office Copyright Treaty in 2004, and to the World Intellectual Property Office Performance and Phonographs Treaty in 2005.

5. Infringement

The copyright in any work is infringed when any act to which the rights holder has an exclusive right is done by any party in the United Arab Emirates that is not the rights holder (or a licensee). Examples include when a work is published, reproduced or performed in public without the rights holder's permission.

For a copyright to be infringed, a substantial portion of the protected work must have been reproduced or another copyright use made of it (eg, it is communicated to the public). The test for what is a 'substantial portion' is often a qualitative rather than a quantitative test. It is the quality or essence of what has been taken rather than the amount that is taken that will determine whether the portion taken is substantial.

6. Design infringement litigation

6.1 The court system

The United Arab Emirates is governed by the UAE Constitution, which was signed in 1971 by the rulers of the seven Emirates of Abu Dhabi, Dubai, Sharjah, Fujairah, Umm Al Quwain, Ras Al Khaimah and Ajman.

The UAE Constitution allows each Emirate to have its own legislative body and judicial authority. As such, there are federal courts and local courts within the United Arab Emirates. All Emirates other than Dubai and Ras Al Khaimah have transferred their judicial systems to the UAE Federal Judicial Authority. Dubai and Ras Al Khaimah have retained their own judicial systems, so they have no federal courts and all matters are adjudicated by their local courts.

The local courts and the federal courts apply UAE federal law, which is enacted by the Supreme Council, as well as the laws and regulations enacted by the rulers of the individual Emirates. In the event of a conflict between federal law and the local law, the federal law will supersede the local law.

Judgments delivered by the Federal Courts of Appeal, as applicable in Abu Dhabi, Sharjah, Fujairah, Umm Al Quwain and Ajman, are subject to an appeal to the Federal Supreme Court of Cassation based in Abu Dhabi. Judgments delivered by the Dubai Court of Appeal are subject to an appeal by the Dubai Court of Cassation. There is no Court of Cassation in Ras al Khaimah and as such the final appellate court is the Court of Appeal.

6.2 Procedure

A claim for infringement is filed at the applicable court of first instance governing the jurisdiction where the defendant is domiciled.

Arguments are mainly presented to court through written submissions. The case is usually managed through a series of adjournments while pleadings and supporting evidence are exchanged between the parties, before the case is reserved for judgment. When technical features are examined, the civil courts are likely to refer the matter to one or more experts for an expert opinion on the matter.

6.3 Courts

An infringement case is filed before the applicable court of first instance. Any judgment delivered by a civil court may be the subject of an appeal to the Court of Appeal. The grounds of appeal may be based on either factual or legal matters and either party may submit further evidence or submit a request to hear witnesses. Arguments are presented through written submissions.

Appeals are heard by the courts described in section 6.1 above.

The Court of Cassation is the highest appellate court in the United Arab Emirates. No further evidence is admissible and the parties are usually given the opportunity to make one written submission before arguing the case in a single hearing, whereupon the case is reserved for judgment.

6.4 Interim remedies

The courts do not recognise the system of preliminary injunction.

A rights holder may seek an order from a competent court – a federal court or local court, depending on where the defendant is domiciled – for the provisional attachment of an infringing product. An attachment order will only be granted against assets which can be located and are actually physically available for attachment by the court.

The applicant for an attachment order must provide a guarantee in an amount determined by the court prior to the grant of the attachment order, and the attaching party must file a substantive case within eight days of the issue of the order, failing which the attachment will be revoked.

A respondent may file a claim for damages within 90 days of the end of that period or from the date of issue of a final judgment dismissing the substantive case filed by the attaching party.

The law also provides a punishment of imprisonment or a fine of between Dh5,000 (approximately $1,370) and Dh100,000 (approximately $26,700), or both, for submitting false documents or using wrong information or misrepresentation to design protection. These penalties also apply to infringers of registered designs under the law. The court may order the items attached to be confiscated and forfeited.

6.5 Damages

Rights holders may claim damages. The actual tort and damages must be proved in order to claim compensation. There are no statutory or punitive damages. Damages are commonly sought by claimants to exert pressure on the defendants to cease the infringing action(s).

United Kingdom

Clive Thorne
Reynolds Porter Chamberlain LLP

1. Summary of design protection

In the United Kingdom, designs created after August 1 1989 are governed by the Copyright, Designs and Patents Act 1988, which introduced a new code for design protection consisting of:

- a strengthened Registered Designs Act 1949, which is set out in its entirety in Schedule 4 to the Copyright, Designs and Patents Act 1988;
- a new UK national unregistered design right which is set out in Part III of the 1988 act; and
- limited copyright protection for designs derived from artistic works.

The regime has been supplemented by an amended Registered Designs Act 1949 stemming from Directive 98/71/EC on the legal protection of designs (which was intended to harmonise registered design rights within member states of the European Union) and by the introduction of Community registered and unregistered design rights under EU Regulation 6/2002/EC, which has direct effect within member states.

The differences between registered design protection under the 1949 act and unregistered design protection are summarised in the table on the next page.

2. Registered design rights

2.1 Nature of rights

The scheme of the Copyright, Designs and Patents Act 1988 was:

- to extend the period of protection for aesthetic designs registered under the Registered Designs Act 1949 to a maximum of 25 years from the existing 15-year maximum;
- for a new unregistered design right to have no more than a 15-year period of protection; and
- for industrially exploited artistic works to have copyright protection for 25 years.

Under the transitional provision of the Copyright, Designs and Patents Act 1988 existing design copyright for designs created before August 1 1989 could extend for a maximum of 10 years until August 1 1999.

Registered design	Unregistered design right
Subject to official examination at Designs Registry.	Arises automatically subject to qualification.
Registrable at Designs Registry.	Not registrable.
Must be novel.	Need not be novel but a requirement exists of 'original' creation; must be created independently and not be commonplace.
Infringement does not require copying.	Infringement requires copying.
Maximum term 25 years.	Maximum term 15 years.
Governed by Registered Designs Act 1949, as amended.	Governed by Part III of the Copyright, Designs and Patents Act 1988.
In general, rights granted can overlap with unregistered rights.	

2.2 The harmonised registered design system

(a) Definition of 'design'

The definition of 'design' was amended by the Registered Designs Regulations 2001.

Under the old law – before the 2001 regulations came into force – 'a design' was defined by Section 1(1) of the Registered Designs Act 1949 as:

> *Features of shape, configuration, pattern or ornament applied to an article by any industrial process, being features which in the finished article appeal to and are judged by the eye.*

What is registered is not the design itself but the article incorporating the design. Therefore a design must be registered separately for each article incorporating the same design. In *Sifam v Sangamo*[1] 'an article' was held to be "anything intended to be sold separately".

The meaning of the phrase 'appeal to and are judged by the eye' was considered in *Amp Inc v Utilux Pty Ltd*,[2] where the House of Lords held that an electrical terminal clip for use inside a washing machine was a (solely) functional design which did not 'appeal to' nor was 'judged by the eye'. The House of Lords set out a number of general propositions, including the following:

1 [1973] RPC 899.
2 [1972] RPC 103.

- the eye to be considered is the eye of the customer and not the eye of the judge;
- an article may still appeal to the eye even though it is not of aesthetic quality or a work of art;
- the intention of the designer is of value but it is not conclusive; and
- a solely functional article does not possess features judged solely by the eye since the only issue of interest to purchasers is whether the article will meet its intended function.

The issue of registrability was considered further by the Privy Council in *Interlego AG v Tyco Industries Inc.*[3] The case involved the design of children's building blocks. It was argued by Interlego that the block design was dictated (solely) by function, which, under the Copyright Act 1956, would have entitled the design to copyright protection for life plus 50 years rather than the shorter 15-year period from the date of first marketing if it could be shown that the design of the bricks was capable of registration under the Registered Designs Act 1949. The Privy Council held that an article qualified as a design under the 1949 act if its features or configurations, taken as a whole, had eye appeal even though there were some features which were dictated by purely functional requirements. The shape of the bricks was found to have not only eye appeal but also significant features of outline and proportion which were not dictated by any mechanical function which the bricks had to perform as part of the construction set. Unless every feature of the design is dictated by the function which the article is to perform, the design of the article is in principle capable of registration as a registered design under the 1949 act.

An amendment to Section 1(3) of the 1949 act was made by the Copyright, Designs and Patents Act 1988 to the effect that a design is not registrable if the "appearance of the article is not material, that is, if aesthetic considerations are not normally taken into account to a material extent by persons acquiring or using articles of that description, and would not be so taken into account if the designs were applied to the article". This amendment removes many household articles from protection under the 1949 act which might otherwise be registrable on the basis that their design is not dictated by function. For example, the case of *Gardex v Sorata*,[4] where the design of the underside of a shower tray was held to be registrable, would now be decided differently.

(b) The new law after the 2001 regulations

The definition of a design has been broadened through the 2001 regulations to cover:

> *the appearance of the whole or a part of a product resulting from the features of, in particular, the lines, contours, colours, shapes, texture or materials of the product or its ornamentation.*[5]

A 'product' is defined as:

---

3 [1989] AC 217.
4 [1986] RPC 623.
5 Registered Designs Act 1949, Section 1(2).

any industrial or handicraft item other than a computer program; and, in particular, includes packaging, get-up, graphic symbols, typographic type-faces and parts intended to be assembled into a complex product.[6]

A 'complex product' is defined as:

a product which is composed of at least two replaceable component parts permitting disassembly and reassembly of the product.[7]

Under the new law:

- spare and replacement parts can generally now be registered, provided that the parts remain visible during normal use by the end user of the complex product comprised of the assembled parts, provided that the parts themselves satisfy the criteria for registrability;[8]
- the concept of 'dictated solely by function' is reintroduced. In general, a design can now be registered irrespective of any aesthetic merit – that is, designs with an element of functionality may be registrable, but designs dictated solely by the product's technical function may not be registered.[9] This resurrects the reasoning of the House of Lords in *Amp v Utilux*;[10]
- there is a 'must fit' exception in respect of features which must necessarily be reproduced in their exact form and dimensions to permit the product incorporating the design, or to which the design is applied, to be mechanically connected to another product so either can perform its function – for example, auditorium seating with interlocking features which provide for multiple assembly;[11] and
- there is an exclusion for designs which are contrary to public policy or to accepted principles of morality.[12]

2.3 Exceptions to registrability

Before the 2001 regulations, the 1949 act expressly excluded the following from registration:[13]

- methods or principles of construction – that is, the process which gives the article its appearance. For example, the weaving of a basket has been held to be a method of construction, whilst the surface ribbing on a hot-water bottle has been held to be a design feature rather than a production feature;
- features dictated by function (see above);
- features of shape that are dependent on the appearance of the product which the article is intended by the author of the design to form an integral part of. The effect of this exception is that designs for spare parts, such as car body panels which must fit with both the rest of the body structure and the design of the car body as a whole, are not normally registrable. This should be

---

6 *Ibid*, Section 1(3).
7 *Ibid*, Section 1(3).
8 *Ibid*, Section 1B(8).
9 *Ibid*, Section 1C(1).
10 [1972] RPC 103.
11 Registered Designs Act 1949, Section 1C(2) and (3).
12 *Ibid*, Section 1D.
13 At Section 1.

contrasted with car accessories such as mirrors or alloy wheels, which are likely to be sold separately and registrable in their own right. This so-called 'must match' exception was therefore introduced to prevent the registration of a design whose purpose is to enable the product to which the design has been applied to fit with some other article. This section was considered by the House of Lords in *Re Ford Motors Designs*,[14] where their Lordships excluded from registration articles which had "no independent life as an article of commerce";
- designs contrary to law or morality. Section 4(1) of the 1949 act excludes from registration all designs which in the opinion of the registrar would be contrary to law or morality. This section was considered in *Masterman's Design*,[15] where on appeal from the registrar the court held that the design of an obscene model doll of a Scotsman wearing a kilt did not offend against morality; and
- designs excluded under rule 26 of the Registered Design Rules 1989, including sculptures, wall plaques, medallions and printed matter primarily of a literary or artistic character.

(a) *Novelty*

Under the law before the 2001 regulations, a design could only be registered if it was 'new' under Section 1(2) of the 1949 act:

a design shall not be regarded as new for the purposes of this Act if it is the same as a design –

(a) registered in respect of the same or any other article in pursuance of a prior application, or

(b) published in the UK in respect of the same or any other article before the date of the application, or if it differs from such a design only in material details or in features which are variants commonly used in the trade.

For registered design purposes, the word 'published' means disclosed to the public. This can be distinguished from copyright law, which uses the word in a number of different defined ways.

It has been held that the whole design need not be new to qualify for registration. The concept of 'new' is not the same concept as 'originality' in copyright. The design will not be new if it differs only in immaterial respects or by way of common trade variants from a prior design.

A consequence of the requirement of novelty is that registration may be the subject of attack because the design is not new. Because prior publication of the design would defeat novelty, provision is made so that prior publication does not arise in certain circumstances, including:

- disclosure in breach of a duty of confidentiality or in breach of good faith;
- disclosure with the rights holder's consent at an exhibition certified by the Secretary of State for Trade and Industry; or
- communication of the design to a government department to allow its merits to be assessed.

---

14 [1995] RPC 167.
15 [1991] RPC 89.

Under the 2001 regulations applicable to registrations applied for on or after December 9 2001:

- the design must be new and have individual character;[16]
- the novelty of a design will now be defeated by prior disclosure anywhere in the world, not as formerly just in the United Kingdom;[17]
- the prior disclosure need not be of an identical design. A similar design differing in immaterial details may be effective prior art, destroying the novelty;[18]
- as a defence, a 12-month grace period has been introduced to allow a designer to market a design and ascertain its commercial value, before incurring the cost of registration;[19]
- it may nevertheless be prudent to apply for registration as soon as the design is in a state capable of registration in order to obtain priority against a possible third-party application for registration of a conflicting design; and
- in considering whether a design has individual character, it is necessary to consider the overall impression it produces on the informed user and show that it differs from the overall impression produced on the user by any design which has been made available to the public before the date of application for the registration. It is expressly provided that the degree of freedom of the designer in creating the design will be taken into account.[20]

A number of these requirements were addressed in the recent case of *Dyson v Vax*,[21] where Arnold J confirmed that:

- whilst the statement of novelty defines the scope of the protection for the registered design, it does not necessarily preclude aspects of the design which are not contained in the statement from being taken into consideration when looking at the design features that contribute to the product's aesthetic appeal;
- the informed user was "reasonably discriminatory" with "a relatively high degree of attention", albeit one to distinguish between the aspects of a design that are purely the result of a product's technical function and those that are not; and
- the technical specification of a product should be the reference point when assessing the designer's degree of freedom. Thus, a product with a high technical specification would impose a greater constraint on the designer that a less technical one. The Court of Appeal confirmed this principle to be correct, although it clarified that it applied to the designer of the registered design, rather than to the allegedly infringing design.[22]

---

16 Registered Designs Act 1949, Section 18(1).
17 *Ibid*, Section 1B(5).
18 *Ibid*, Section 1B(2).
19 *Ibid*, Section 1B(6)(c).
20 *Ibid*, Section 1B(3) and (4).
21 [2010] EWHC 1923 (Pat).
22 [2011] EWCA Civ 1206.

2.4 **Proprietorship**

Only a party claiming to be the original proprietor may apply for registration of a design under the Registered Designs Act 1949. Section 2(1) of the act provides that the author of the design will be treated as the original proprietor save that, where a design is created under a commission, the party commissioning the design will be treated as the original proprietor. If a design is created by an employee in the course of his employment, his employer is treated as the original proprietor. The author of the design is defined as the person who creates it. Provision is made for computer-generated designs (where there is no human author) so that the person who makes the arrangements necessary for the creation of the design is the author. Registered designs and the rights to apply for registration are capable of assignment.[23]

2.5 **Registration procedure**

An application for registration of a design must be made by the proprietor or by an agent acting on his behalf, on forms published under the Design Rules. Details of the design are normally provided by drawings, samples or photographs. A statement of novelty must be signed. On receiving the application, the registrar must be satisfied that the design is new. The searches are not conclusive and are not undertaken in great depth. Even if at the time of application the registrar considers the design to be new, it may later be attacked in separate revocation proceedings in the courts, or in the Designs Registry or through a counterclaim in an infringement action.

Appeals from the registrar's decisions lie to the Registered Designs Appeal Tribunal.

2.6 **Term of protection**

A design registration lasts initially for five years from the date of application and may be renewed for a maximum of four further five-year terms, to a maximum term of 25 years.[24]

2.7 **Infringement**

Under Section 7 of Registered Designs Act 1949, the rights holder is granted an exclusive right to use the design and any design which does not produce on the informed user a different overall impression. It is expressly provided that in considering the "different overall impression on the informed user the degree of freedom of the author in creating the design shall be taken into consideration".

Use of the design is taken to include a reference to:

- the making, offering, putting on the market, importing, exporting or using of a product in which the design is incorporated or to which it is applied; or
- stocking such a product for these purposes.

The rights created are exclusive, so that under Section 7A acts which offend against the exclusive right of the rights holder constitute an infringement. It is also

23 Registered Designs Act 1949, Section 2.
24 *Ibid*, Section 8.

an infringement to make anything, such as a drawing or a mould, which could enable an article to be made which infringes the design. It is not an infringement to do acts privately and for non-commercial purposes or for experimental or teaching purposes.

Proceedings may not be brought for infringement before the certificate of registration is granted.

2.8 Damages and other relief

(a) *Remedies for registered design infringement*

Actions may be brought in the High Court (Patents Court) or the Patents County Court. A successful claimant would normally be entitled to:

- damages for infringement (which would probably be assessed at a separate damages inquiry); or
- an account of the profits made by the infringing defendant;
- an injunction restraining further infringement; and
- an order for the delivery-up or destruction of articles which infringe the design.

(b) *Defences to an action for infringement*

A defendant to a claim for infringement would normally defend the action:

- on the basis that the articles complained of did not infringe the design; and
- counterclaim that the registered design was invalid because it lacked novelty and that the register should be rectified by removal of the design and marked with an indication of its invalidity.

A limited defence is available for innocent infringement.

(c) *Unjustified threats*

Section 26 of the Registered Designs Act 1949 provides remedies for groundless threats of registered design infringement. Extreme care should be taken to ensure that an action for infringement is not threatened. Mere notification of the design does not constitute a threat. A person threatened can:

- claim against the rights holder or any party (including professional advisers) making the threat, that the threats are unjustified;
- seek an injunction to restrain continued threats; and
- seek damages to compensate for any loss suffered.

The courts have construed widely what constitutes a threat. The writer of a letter, even if acting in a professional capacity (eg, a solicitor), may have a personal liability in addition to the client. Therefore, it is normally prudent to do no more in open correspondence addressed to the infringer than notify of the existence of the registration.

2.9 Licensing

Under Section 222 of the Copyright, Designs and Patents Act 1988, registered design rights may be assigned, disposed of or licensed as they are considered personal moveable property. Any licence of a registered design right will bind every successor in title of the right unless a purchaser has had no actual or constructive knowledge of the licence and has provided valuable consideration in good faith for the right.

Licensing allows the rights owner to obtain an income from the design right. If the rights owner is unable commercially to exploit its registered design right, the right of licensing can be very lucrative.

2.10 Compulsory licensing

Licences of right have been available from August 1 1994 through the harmonisation of laws on registered design rights.

A licence of right is available in the final five-year term of the maximum outstanding period of copyright protection. Effectively, a party that wishes to use the registered design in the final five years of copyright protection may approach the rights holder requesting a licence to use registered design right. If the rights holder refuses to grant such a licence, the party can apply to a comptroller for the enforcement of a licence of right.

2.11 Validity issues

The system of design registration established in the Registered Designs Act 1949 was generally continued by the Copyright, Designs and Patents Act 1988. Schedule 4 to the 1988 act incorporates an amended Registered Designs Act 1949 in its entirety. The main change introduced by the 1988 act was the extension of the maximum period of protection for registered designs to 25 years from the previous 15 years, which is consistent with the 25-year term of copyright protection for artistic works applied industrially under Section 52 of the 1988 act.

The original purpose of the registered design system was to provide a system of registration for aesthetic designs applied industrially.

The 1949 act was amended by the Registered Designs Regulations 2001, which came into force on December 9 2001. The 2001 regulations were intended to implement the EU Registered Design Harmonisation Directive 98/71/EC and amend the 1949 act on a line-by-line basis. However, the regulations have been criticised as being "like a sculptor crafting a cat out of a dog".

In *Oakley Inc v Animal Ltd*[25] the validity of the 2001 regulations was attacked on the basis that in implementing them the Secretary of State had acted *ultra vires* in relation to the European Communities Act 1972. In a judgment of constitutional importance, Mr Peter Prescott QC (sitting as a deputy High Court judge) rejected this contention in respect of the 2001 regulations in their entirety, but nevertheless found that Regulation 12(2) and (3) were *ultra vires*, so that the amended law did not apply in respect of applications for registration after October 28 2001 and before December 9 2001. Thus, the law before the 2001 regulations in respect of validity and rights given by registration, the period of protection and the terms of pre-existing times was judged to apply to applications for registration made before December 9 2001.

---

25 [2005] EWHC 210 Ch.

2.12 Community registered and unregistered design rights

These new rights are governed by EU Regulation 2245/2002/EC, implementing EU Regulation 6/2002/EC. This is binding in its entirety and directly applicable in all member states, so there is no national implementing legislation. The regulation creates directly enforceable rights and is in key aspects identically worded to the EU Registered Design Harmonisation Directive 98/71/EEC.

In order to be protected as a Community design, as design must satisfy the following requirements:

- it must meet the definition of a design;[26]
- it must relate to a product;[27]
- it must not relate to functional features;[28]
- it must be new;[29]
- it must have individual character;[30] and
- it must not be contrary to public policy or morality.[31]

(a) Definition of 'design'

Under Article 3(a) 'design' is defined as "the appearance of the whole or part of a product resulting from the features of, in particular, the lines, contours, colours, shape, texture and/or materials of the product itself and/or its ornamentation".

(b) Definition of 'product'

Under Article 3(b) 'product' is defined as meaning:

> *any industrial or handicraft item, including inter alia parts intended to be assembled into a complex product, packaging, get-up, graphic symbols and typographic typefaces, but excluding computer programs.*

It should be noted that:

- the definition is widely worded and includes parts intended to be assembled into a complex product, such as packaged self-assembly kitchen units; and
- the inclusion of typographic typefaces reflects old-style printing plates, even though typefaces are now generally electronic.

(c) Exclusion of technically functional features

This exclusion contained in Article 8 encompasses features of the appearance of a product which are "solely dictated by its technical function". This is a similar exclusion to that arising in pre-1988 design copyright law. Thus, the electric terminal considered in *Amp v Utilux*[32] would not attract protection. A similar interpretation was accorded by the European Court of Justice (ECJ) in the trademark case of *Philips v Remington*,[33] where the court held that:

---

26 Article 3a.
27 Article 3b.
28 Article 8.
29 Article 5.
30 Article 6.
31 Article 9.
32 [1972] RPC 103.
33 [2003] RPC 14.

the grounds for refusal of [trademark] registration …is to prevent trade mark protection from granting its proprietor a monopoly on technical solutions or characteristics of a product …

(d) Novelty

The requirement of novelty in Article 5 – that is, "that it is new", applies to both registered and unregistered Community designs. The requirement of novelty for UK national design rights is discussed at section 2.3(a) above.

The operative date for establishing novelty in respect of registered Community designs is the date the application is filed. For unregistered Community designs, it is the date on which the design "has first been made available to the public".

(e) Individual character

This is an additional requirement to that of novelty.

Article 6 of the regulation provides that a design will be considered to have individual character:

if the overall impression it produces on the informed user differs from the overall impression produced on such a user by any design which has been made available to the public.

It is expressly provided that the "degree of freedom of the designer in developing the design" will be taken into consideration.

The overall impression of a design is the key issue to be decided by an informed user. This latter is akin to the patent law concept of a 'person skilled in the art' and suggests that the court, in considering the validity of the design, should rely upon expert evidence rather than reaching its own conclusion.

The date at which novelty and individual character is to be assessed will be either the date at which the unregistered Community design was first made available to the public or, in the case of registered Community designs, the date when the application is filed.

The 'degree of freedom' and 'informed user' concepts were considered in the case of *PepsiCo v Grupo Promer Mon Graphic SA*,[34] both in the first-instance decision by the EU General Court and on appeal to the ECJ.

Whilst the General Court confirmed that minor differences between designs may be enough to produce a different overall impression on the informed user where the designer has a low degree of freedom, the ECJ confirmed that the informed user is a person in between the average consumer that is reasonably well-informed in trademark matters and the specialist or technical expert, a person of "average attention" who is "particularly observant" due to his personal experience and extensive knowledge of the sector.

The importance of the overall impression cannot be understated in the context of potential design infringements. This was underlined by the Court of Appeal in *Dyson v Vax*,[35] where the court recognised that, even if a design is afforded a broadened degree of protection due to its "great departure" from the existing design

34 Case C-281/10 P, October 20 2011.
35 [2010] EWHC 1923 (Pat).

corpus, another design that contains many similar features will not infringe if it produces a different overall impression.

Similarly, in *Kwang Yang Motor Co Ltd v OHIM*,[36] the court confirmed that the overall impression of the informed user is based on a design's basic structure rather than its detail, and therefore minor differences in the designs will not necessarily result in a different overall impression if they would not be considered different by the informed user.

(f) *Term of protection*

An unregistered Community design enjoys protection for three years, starting on the date when it was first made available to the public within the European Union.[37]

A registered Community design is protected for up to 25 years from its filing date, based on five-year terms.[38]

(g) *Infringement – Article 19*

A registered Community design right grants exclusive rights in the design. Infringement arises in respect of the use of a design or any design "which does not produce a different overall impression on the informed user". In the case of an unregistered Community design, there is an additional requirement of 'copying' – that is, that "the contested use results from copying the protected design". Copying will not arise if the contested use results "from an independent work of creation by a designer who may be reasonably thought not to be familiar with the design".

This suggests that the courts will approach infringement of an unregistered Community design in similar terms to their approach to copyright and unregistered (national) design rights – that is, independent creation will provide a defence. Some assistance is given by Laddie J in *Mattel Inc v Woolbro (Distributors) Ltd*,[39] where in a case of unregistered Community design infringement the court admitted evidence of 'similar fact' evidence of copying.

(h) *Application for a registered Community design*

Application for a registered Community design is made to the Office for the Harmonisation in the Internal Market (OHIM) in Alicante, Spain, or at the UK Designs Registry. The application must be in a prescribed form and include details of the identity of the applicant and a representation of the design to be registered. There is no substantive examination of the design applied for. There is a possible appeal to the OHIM board of appeal.

3. UK unregistered design rights

The unregistered design right, or 'design right' as it is more commonly known, was introduced by the Copyright, Designs and Patents Act 1988 as a means of providing residual protection for purely functional designs such as toys, furniture, pottery,

36 Cases T-10/08 and T-11/08, September 9 2011.
37 Article 11.
38 Article 12.
39 [2004] FSR 12.

cutlery and industrial gadgets which would not qualify for protection under the Registered Designs Act 1949. However, the scope of design right is sufficiently wide to encompass aesthetic designs which might also be registered under the 1949 act. The right is something of a hybrid, incorporating elements from copyright, registered designs and patent law. Overall, a registered design confers stronger rights. The differences between a registered design right and an unregistered design right include the following:

- The protection granted by a design right applies automatically to qualifying designs without the need for action by the design owner – an unregistered design comes into effect automatically. By contrast, a registered design requires action by the design owner.
- The main purpose of the design right is to give relatively short-term protection (generally 10 years from the date of first marketing) to industrial designs, as opposed to a registered design, which gives a relatively long-term protection to artistic designs.
- Registered design protection is an exclusive right, whilst unregistered design protection requires copying to establish infringement.

3.1 Definition of design right

Section 213 of the Copyright, Designs and Patents Act 1988 provides that design right is a property right subsisting in an original design. For this purpose, 'design' is expressed to be the design of "any aspect of the shape or configuration (whether internal or external) of the whole or part of an article". The rights holder may choose to assert design right in the whole of or in any part of its product. A recent case used the analogy of a teapot so that the right vests in the teapot as a whole or in parts such as the spout, handle or lid, or even part of the lid. It would appear that even if the part lacked visual significance, it would still be protected.

3.2 Exceptions to design rights

An unregistered design right does not subsist in the following:

- a method or principle of construction – see *A Fulton Co Ltd v Grant Barnett,*[40] where Park J considered that the design (of an umbrella case) was based on the shape or configuration produced by methods of construction of the design;
- the features, shape or configuration of an article which enable the article to be connected to or placed in, around or against another article so that either article may perform its function or which are dependent upon the appearance of another article of which the article is intended by the designer to form an integral part. These exceptions constitute the well-known must-fit and must-match exceptions;
- surface decoration – see, for example, *Cow & Co v Cannon*[41] in respect of hot-water bottle surface ribbing, but contrast that with *A Fulton Co Ltd v Grant*

40 [2001] RPC 257.
41 [1959] RPC 240.

Barnett,[42] where Park J found that the raised edges of an umbrella case were not surface decoration but features of shape and configuration; or

- a juxtaposition of colours – in *Lambretta Clothing Co Ltd v Teddy Smith (UK) Ltd*[43] the Court of Appeal held that a juxtaposition of colourways for the design of a track top could not be "an aspect of shape or configuration" under Section 213(2). The court also held that the juxtaposition of colours did not enjoy protection as a registered design or under artistic copyright.

(a) ***The must-fit and much-match exceptions***

Features of articles that are dictated by the need to fit or interface with each other so that the two together can perform their intended function – for example, mechanical parts of a car such as an exhaust pipe – or which are dictated by the appearance of another part with which it is required to form an integral whole, such as car body parts, are excluded from design right protection. These exceptions are influenced by the *British Leyland* spare-parts exception. In *Ocular Sciences Ltd v Aspect Vision Care Ltd*[44] the court held that the design of contact lenses was excluded from protection because the lenses were designed to fit with the eyeball, which was an 'article', albeit a living one.

The exceptions were considered in depth by Mann J in *Dyson Ltd v Qualtex (UK) Ltd*,[45] a case involving duplicate spare parts and accessories for Dyson vacuum cleaners. The judge appears to have rejected the applicability of a general right to repair based upon *British Leyland* and concluded that spare parts should not be subject to some special regime, but are to be treated like other commercial articles.

In considering the must-match test, he held that the test to be applied was:

whether there is dependency of the kind, or to the extent, which would make the overall article in question radically different in appearance if [the substitute article] were not the shape it is ...The saleability of the item can be used as a sort of guide to assessment or a cross-check in any particular case.

In considering the must-fit exception (which the judge pointed out was a shorthand which did not form part of the wording of Section 213 of the Copyright, Designs and Patents Act 1988), the judge approved and applied *Ocular Sciences*. Thus, interconnecting elements of the design will be excluded from protection even if they have another functional role in the design.

3.3 Originality

Although Section 213 of the Copyright, Designs and Patents Act 1988 refers to design rights subsisting in an "original" design, 'original' is not defined. Section 213(4) states that a design is not original if it is "commonplace in the design field in question at the time of its creation". The concept of 'commonplace' was considered in *Ocular Sciences Ltd v Aspect Vision Care Ltd*,[46] where it was suggested that "any design which

42 [2001] RPC 257.
43 [2005[RPC 6.
44 [1997] RPC 289.
45 [2004] EWHC 2981.
46 [1997] RPC 289.

is trite, trivial, common-or-garden, hackneyed or of the type which would excite no peculiar attention in those in the relevant art is likely to be commonplace".

This was considered further by the Court of Appeal in *Farmers Build Ltd v Carrier Bulk Materials Handling Ltd*.[47] The court held that 'originality' should be considered in the "copyright sense" (ie, not copied visibly from an earlier design). If the court is satisfied that the design has not been copied from an earlier design, then it is original in the copyright sense. The court then has to decide whether it is commonplace. For that purpose it is necessary to ascertain how similar the design is to the design of similar articles in the same field of design made by persons other than the parties or persons unconnected with the parties.

It has not been established whether prior art necessary to establish the design field in question should be limited to the United Kingdom or applied worldwide. The current leading authority was provided by Fysh J in the Patents County Court in *A Fulton v Totes Isotoner*,[48] who took the view that it was limited to the United Kingdom, even though the designs in dispute were created in the Far East. Moreover, unregistered design right protection is granted to designs created by designers outside the United Kingdom.

3.4 Qualifications for design right protection

The qualifications for design right protection are governed by the complicated provisions contained in Sections 217 to 221 of the Copyright, Designs and Patents Act 1988. Generally, only designs created in the United Kingdom, the European Union and certain limited designated countries (mainly British dependent territories) are entitled to protection. In particular, designs created in countries such as the United States and Japan, and European Economic Area countries such as Norway, would not normally qualify for design right protection.

For a design to be protected:

- the designer must be a qualifying person; or
- the design must have been created by an employee of or commissioned by persons who were qualifying persons.

If neither of these tests applies, the first marketing of articles made to the design must have been undertaken by a qualifying person and in a qualifying country.

(a) Qualifying person

A person will qualify if he is:

- a citizen, or subject of or habitually resident in a qualifying country; or
- a company or other legal entity:
  - formed under the law of any part of the United Kingdom or a qualifying country; and
  - having in any qualifying country a place of business where a substantial business activity is carried out.

---

47 [1999] RPC 461.
48 [2004] RPC 16.

(b) ***Recording of the design***

The right does not subsist until the design has been recorded in a design document or an article has been made to the design.

3.5 Duration of the design rights

Design rights last for 15 years from the creation of the design document or 10 years from the date on which articles made to the design were placed on the market in the United Kingdom.

3.6 Ownership of design rights

Generally, the designer is the first owner of a design right and is defined as the "person who creates it". In the case of a computer-generated design, the person who makes the arrangements necessary for the creation of the design is the designer. If the design has been created in the course of employment or by commission, the employer or the commissioning party will be the first owner. If a design qualifies for protection on the basis of having been first marketed in the United Kingdom, the person (provided he is a qualifying person) first marketing the articles is regarded as the first owner of the design right.

3.7 Rights granted by design right

A rights holder is granted the exclusive right (without territorial limitation) to reproduce the design for commercial purposes by making articles to the design or by making a design document recording the design for the purpose of enabling such articles to be made.

3.8 Infringement

The right is infringed by a party that does or authorises another to do anything which is within the exclusive right of the rights holder. The infringement may be direct or indirect and it is immaterial whether or not any intervening acts lead to the infringement. Provision exists for secondary infringement of design right by the import or dealing in articles in which a design right exists with the knowledge of the infringer that the article is an infringing article.

An unfortunate side-effect, which was approved by the Court of Appeal in *A Fulton v Totes Isotoner (UK) Ltd*,[49] is that infringement may be established in only part of a design, even though the infringing article, when looked at as a whole, could not be regarded as a reproduction of the protected design when looked at as a whole. The Patents County Court had already found that the alleged infringing article (an umbrella case) when taken as a whole did not infringe the claimant's registered design of the whole umbrella case. The practice has grown up of pleading unregistered design infringement not merely in the design as a whole but in 'cropped' parts of the design. It has the somewhat unjust effect of a defendant not being able to evaluate the merits of the claim against it, nor of establishing whether its design infringes, until the claim against it is properly pleaded.

49 [2004] RPC 16.

3.9 **Remedies for infringement**

The usual remedies for infringement of intellectual property rights are available, including damages, injunctions and accounts of profits. In addition, in cases of flagrant infringement and taking into account any benefit accruing to the defendant, the court has jurisdiction to award additional damages. This is a similar concept to additional damages under Section 97 of the Copyright, Designs and Patents Act 1988 in relation to flagrant infringement of copyright. There is provision for delivery-up of infringing articles and for the disposal of infringing articles.

3.10 **Licensing**

As with registered design rights, in the last five years of a design right term, licences of right are available, which, in default of agreement, are settled by the comptroller (see the analysis at section 2.10 above).

3.11 **Protection under copyright**

Articles which are themselves artistic works may still acquire copyright protection if they are original and can be brought within the definition of artistic works in Section 4 of the Copyright, Designs and Patents Act 1988.

Section 4(1) of the act provides:

In this Part "artistic work" means –

(a) a graphic work, photograph, sculpture or collage, irrespective of artistic quality,

(b) a work of architecture being a building or a model for a building, or

(c) a work of artistic craftsmanship.

Section 4(2) defines further the concept of a 'graphic work', which is expressed to include paintings, drawings, diagrams, maps, charts and plans as well as engravings and etchings, whilst a sculpture is expressed to include a cast or model made for the purposes of sculpture.

Of most practical importance are works of artistic craftsmanship and sculptures manufactured industrially in three-dimensional form ('industrial' in this context means mass-produced).

Examples include jewellery, designer clothes, designer crockery, cutlery and furniture. The scope of works of 'artistic craftsmanship' was construed narrowly by the House of Lords in *Hensher v Restawile*,[50] where the subject matter was a suite of furniture. A level of artistic intent or attainment by the designer is necessary for protection to be available in this category of copyright. In a subsequent case,[51] where a rain cape was held not to be a work of artistic craftsmanship, the test was interpreted as to whether the designer possessed the conscious purpose of creating a work of art.

The issue of sculpture was considered in *Lucasfilm Ltd v Ainsworth*.[52] The case considered the helmets and armour of the stormtroopers from the film *Star Wars*. It

50 [1976] AC 64.
51 *Merlet v Mothercare plc* [1986] RPC 115, CA.
52 [2008] EWHC 1878 (Ch), [2009] FSR 2.

was held that they were not sculptures but a mixture of costume and prop, the primary focus being utilitarian. The concept of sculpture should not go far beyond what an ordinary member of the public would think it meant. There had to be something which "of its nature is capable of appealing to artistic sensibilities", which must to some extent be the purpose of the article. Mann J, whose views were largely approved by the Court of Appeal,[53] gave the following example:

If the pile of bricks sat in the Tate Modern for two weeks on display as an exhibit, it could be a sculpture. However, if it was left outside a part of a building project, it would clearly not be a sculpture. The difference lay in the purpose of the creator of the pile.

In dismissing the second appeal over the definition of sculpture, the Supreme Court upheld Mann J's decision that the designs should be viewed as utilitarian rather than artistic, citing that there were clear policy reasons why the court should not seek to widen the category of works that are entitled to full copyright protection.[54]

The nature of a work produced industrially appears not to matter provided that it constitutes a reproduction of a substantial part of the artistic work. Thus in *Oakley Inc v Animal Ltd*[55] Peter Prescott QC (sitting as a deputy High Court judge) referred to the example of the author of a sculpture (an artistic work) licensing the reproduction of the sculpture as mass-produced garden gnomes. The gnomes would be subject to copyright protection for a 25-year term.

Under Section 52(2) of the Copyright, Designs and Patents Act 1988, the period of protection for artistic works manufactured by an industrial process is limited to 25 years from the date of marketing such articles in the United Kingdom or elsewhere.

3.12 Community registered and unregistered design rights

See section 2.12 above.

4. Qualification for protection

The qualification requirements for registration of registered design rights and design rights differs broadly. To qualify for a registered design right, the design must be novel. The concept of 'new with individual character' is used as the threshold for qualification. The judgment of Arnold J in *Dyson v Vax*[56] has provided certainty in this area, which is something that is lacking in the current unregistered design right scheme.

The qualification requirements for unregistered design rights are subject to Sections 271 to 221 of the Copyright, Designs and Patents Act 1988, provided a qualifying person has designed the design (whether or not employed or commissioned) or has undertaken the first marketing of the articles to which the design right relates.

The key difference between the two protections are the international repercussions.

Under the Copyright, Designs and Patents Act 1988, only designs created in the

---

53 [2009] EWCA Civ 1328.
54 [2011] UKSC 39
55 [2005] EWHC 210 (Ch).
56 [2010] EWHC 1923 (Pat).

United Kingdom, the European Union and other limited designated countries are entitled to protection under the unregistered design right scheme. Contrast this with registered design rights, where for a design right to be granted protection in the European Community an application for a registered Community design must be made.

Regardless of whether a right is registered, if the rights holder requires protection outside the European Union it must apply directly to each jurisdiction it wishes the design to be protected in.

5. Infringement

Both Community and UK-registered designs grant exclusive rights to the use of the design in the territory it has been registered in. Infringement is essentially the production of a design which does not produce a different overall impression on the informed user.

This differs for unregistered designs. Section 226(2) of the Copyright, Designs and Patents Act 1988 defines 'infringement' as "copying the design so as to reproduce articles exactly or substantially to the design". Infringement was considered in *C & H Engineering v Klucznik*,[57] a case involving pig-fenders. The court compared the alleged infringing article in its entirety with the design and held that, because the article embodied other features, there was no infringement. There must be a copying of the design that reproduces articles exactly or substantially similar to that design. The test is therefore objective as seen through the eyes of the overall consumer of the product, bringing both the registered design right and the unregistered design right tests closer together than they originally appear.

6. Design infringement litigation

Intellectual property rights are governed under special Civil Procedure Rules (CPR) as enshrined in Rule 63. Under Rule 63.2, any claim arising from a registered design right must be started in the Patents Courts. Unregistered design rights are also dealt with under Rule 63, but claims must be started in either the Chancery Division of the High Court, the Patents County Court or a county court that has a Chancery District Registry.

To start a claim, the same procedures must be followed as for starting a claim that does not involve intellectual property rights in the English courts. The only exception is that if a claim is to be dealt with in the High Court and not the Patents Courts, the claim form must include the words "intellectual property claim" and include the registered design number, if applicable, to allow it to receive the appropriate consideration.

As there are numerous remedies for both design right and registered design rights infringement, any claim must state in its particulars the remedy which is sought and the justifications for that being the most appropriate remedy.

The final remedies for infringement are the same for both design right and registered design rights. They are damages, injunctions and accounts of profits.

---

57 [1992] FSR 421.

Double recovery is not permitted in design right infringement litigation: a claimant may only recover either damages or accounts of profits, not both.

Design right litigation is expensive and, depending on the court where the claim is started, certain costs rules must be considered. Costs can be capped depending on which track the claim has been allocated to, or the court that the claim has been started in. In the Patents County Court, costs are capped at £50,000 and in the High Court, if a claim is allocated to the fast track, costs are capped to the value of the claim.

Once the judgment has been granted, the claimant can enforce the costs on the infringer through the usual methods employed in the English courts.

7. Licensing and exploitation

Under the Copyright, Designs and Patents Act 1988, a design right may be licensed or assigned since it is a personal right. Under the same act, any licence granted by the rights holder will bind successors in title, provided no notice has been given but valuable consideration has.

There can be two different types of licensees: exclusive licensees and non-exclusive licensees. An exclusive licensee enjoys the right to exercise all rights of the design as if they were the rights holder, to the exclusion of the licensor or any other party. This gives the licensor no rights over the design, and any rights that the licensor may require at a later date will need to be granted by the licensee under a sub-licence. An exclusive licence agreement must be in writing; this is not a requirement for non-exclusive licences.

Any licences granted do not need to be registered.

United States

Jared C Bunker
Lynda Zadra-Symes
Knobbe Martens Olson & Bear LLP

1. Summary of design protection

There is no single body of law in the United States dedicated to protecting industrial designs. Rather, designers must look to a combination of three distinct protection regimes: design patents, trade dress and unfair competition claims, and copyrights. This chapter discusses how to obtain and enforce industrial design rights within each of these legal regimes.

2. Design patent protection for industrial designs

2.1 Nature of rights

In addition to the common utility patents granted to protect functional aspects of inventions, the US Patent Act also allows for patents protecting the design of articles of manufacture. This design patent protection is meant to fill a gap between copyright protection for non-useful items and utility patent protection for useful items.[1]

2.2 Requirements for design patent protection

There are five elements necessary for obtaining a design patent: the design must be new, original, non-obvious, ornamental and for an article of manufacture.[2] The design must also satisfy the requirements of a design: it must be a definite, preconceived visual entity which is inseparable from the article to which it is applied.[3] Thus, the design cannot be merely a random by-product of the manufacturing process.[4]

(a) *Novelty*

As with utility patents, designs must be new before they can be patented.[5] A novel design claim must not be identical in material respects to any earlier art.[6] The point of reference for what is novel in a design claim is an 'ordinary observer', which differs from the 'person having ordinary skill in the art' of a utility patent. Thus, a design

1 Donald S Chisum, *Chisum On Patents,* Section 23.02[1] (2011).
2 35 USC 171 (2010); 35 USC 103 (2010).
3 Patent and Trademark Office, *Manual of Patent Examining Procedure,* Section 1504 (8th edn 2001 rev, October 2005).
4 Patent and Trademark Office, note 3 above, Section 1502.
5 35 USC Section 102 (2010).
6 *Door-Master Corp v Yorktowne, Inc,* 256 F.3d 1308, 1451 (Fed Cir 2001).

patent is novel when the "average observer takes the new design for a different, and not a modified already existing design".[7]

(b) *Originality*

A patented design must be original to the named inventors – it cannot be derived from any other person or source. Thus, the design of naturally occurring objects or persons cannot be patented.[8]

(c) *Non-obviousness*

A design must also be non-obvious.[9] This means that a patent will not be granted for a design that would have been obvious to a designer of ordinary skill in the pertinent art.[10] This requirement is comparable to that for utility patents. As with utility patents, evidence of secondary considerations, such as commercial success, can support design non-obviousness.[11] It must be clear, however, that the commercial success is due to the design rather than the functional aspects of the article.[12]

(d) *Ornamentality*

Ornamentality requires that patented design features be visually appealing, rather than simple, insignificant physical details.[13] However, the ornament does not need to be fine art, and design patents for ornaments such as the appearance of a concrete mixer have been upheld.[14] Moreover, the ornament need not be visible in the finished product.[15] An ornamental design may be patented if the design would affect a consumer or user at some point during the object's commercial life. Thus, the ornamental design of a grooved femoral hip stem prosthesis was patentable despite obscurity in its final use, because doctors selecting which prosthesis to use might base their decision partly on the ornamental and non-functional aspects of the product.[16]

(e) *Article of manufacture*

A patentable design must be for an "article of manufacture". Such articles have been defined as man-made, tangible objects.[17] This has been interpreted fairly broadly, and includes articles such as the water design for a water fountain and computer-generated icons.[18]

---

7 *Rains v Cascade Indus., Inc*, 402 F.2d 241,247 (3d Cir 1968); see also *Int'l Seaway Trading Corp. v. Walgreens Corp.*, 589 F.3d 1233, 1240 (Fed. Cir. 2009).
8 Patent and Trademark Office, note 3 above, Section 1504.01(d).
9 35 USC Section 103.
10 *Durling v Spectrum Furniture Co*, 101 F.3d 100, 103 (Fed Cir 1996).
11 *Litton Sys, Inc v Whirlpool Corp*, 728 F.2d 1423 (Fed Cir 1984).
12 *Ibid.*
13 *Bliss v Gotham Indus, Inc*, 316 F.2d 848, 851 (9th Cir 1963); *Metrokane, Inc v Wine Enthusiast*, 185 F.Supp.2d 321,328 (SDNY 2002).
14 *In re Koehring*, 37 F.2d 421 (CCPA 1930).
15 *In re Webb*, 916 F.2d 1553 (Fed Cir 1990). See also *Franklin Knitting Mills, Inc v Gropper Knitting Mills, Inc*, 15 F.2d 375 (2d Cir 1926) (elements of a necktie that were hidden when worn were considered ornamental because they may still be pleasing to a purchaser in the box).
16 *Ibid.*
17 *In re Hruby*, 373 F.2d 997, 1000-01 (CCPA 1967); Chisum, note 1 above, Section 23.02[2].
18 *Ibid*, at 1001-01; Patent and Trademark Office, note 3 above, Section 1504.01(a).

2.3 Registration procedure for design patents

A design patent application and fee must be filed with the Patent and Trademark Office. The application must include drawings of the design and a single-sentence description of the design. An examiner reviews the application, performs a prior-art search and assesses whether the design meets the requirements of novelty, originality, non-obviousness, ornamentality and article of manufacture. The prior art used to evaluate novelty and non-obviousness is defined by 35 USC Section 102.

Once the application is allowed, the applicant must pay an issue fee. The office issues the patent shortly after receiving the issue fee. The average time between filing an application and the issue of a design patent is nine to 12 months, which is significantly shorter than that for utility patent applications. Moreover, on average, the office allows about 90% of all design patent applications.

2.4 Term of protection and rights granted for design patents

A design patent is valid for 14 years from the date the patent is issued.[19] This is in contrast to the term for utility patents, which is 20 years from the earliest filing date of the utility patent application.[20]

2.5 Infringement of design patents

The federal district courts have exclusive jurisdiction over litigation relating to infringement of design patents. To prove infringement, a rights holder must prove that an ordinary purchaser or consumer would consider the accused article's design to be substantially the same as the patented design.[21] In addition, the accused design must imitate the ornamental aspects of the patented design rather than functional aspects.[22]

2.6 Damages and other relief

If the court finds infringement, the rights holder may demand compensatory damages.[23] Typically, compensatory damages correspond to a reasonable royalty or the rights holder's lost profits. The court may increase the damages owed to the rights holder by three times the amount of compensatory damages if the infringement is found to be wilful.[24]

Alternatively, the rights holder may demand damages equal to the infringer's total profits.[25] Seeking the infringer's lost profits is often advantageous because these profits are typically higher than a reasonable royalty (although lost profits awards generally may not be increased for wilful infringement).[26]

The rights holder may also seek preliminary and permanent injunctive relief

---

19 35 USC Section 173.
20 *Ibid*, Section 154(a)(2).
21 *Egyptian Goddess, Inc v Swisa, Inc*, 543 F.3d 665, 671-672 (Fed Cir 2008).
22 *OddzOn Products, Inc v Just Toys, Inc*, 122 F.3d 1396 (Fed Cir 2007).
23 35 USC Section 284.
24 *Ibid*, Section 284.
25 *Ibid*, Section 289.
26 *Braun, Inc v Dynamics Corp of Am.*, 975 F.2d 815, 824 (Fed Cir 1992).

against accused infringers.[27] In deciding whether to grant preliminary injunctions, courts consider four factors:

- the rights holder's reasonable likelihood of success;
- the irreparable harm the rights holder will suffer if a preliminary injunction is not granted;
- the balance of the hardship to the parties; and
- the adverse impact on the public interest.[28]

2.7 Licensing of design patents

Initially, design patents are owned by the individual inventor(s).[29] However, patents and patent applications are treated as personal property and may be assigned to other individuals or companies.[30] A design patent assignment must be in writing.[31] Rather than assigning the entire interest in the design patent, a rights holder may convey to a third party or company a licence, granting only some of the rights in the design patent.[32] For example, a rights holder may grant a licence to sell only specific products embodying the patented design or a licence to sell a patented design only in a specified geographic location. A licence may be 'exclusive', meaning the licensee is the only party permitted to sell the specified products or in the specified location, or 'non-exclusive', meaning other people or companies may be granted the same right to sell the specified products or sell in the specified location. Only assignees and exclusive licensees are permitted to sue for infringement.[33]

2.8 Compulsory licensing of design patents

There is no compulsory licensing regime in the United States for design patents. However, some courts in cases involving utility patents have included a compulsory licence as a remedy for patent misuse or anti-trust violations.[34] In addition, 28 USC Section 1498(a) allows the government and government contractors to use an invention covered by a US patent without a licence. Under 28 USC Section 1498, the rights holder's remedy is an action in the Court of Federal Claims against the United States for recovery of reasonable compensation. Injunctive relief is not available.[35]

(a) Validity issues

Design patents are presumed valid by law and the accused infringer has the burden of proving by clear and convincing evidence that the design patent is not novel, is not ornamental or would have been obvious to a designer of ordinary skill in the art.

---

27 35 USC Section 283.
28 *Reebok International Ltd v J Baker, Inc.*, 32 F.3d 1552, 1555 (Fed Cir 1994).
29 *Arachnid, Inc v Merit Indust, Inc*, 939 F.2d 1574 (Fed Cir 1991).
30 *Ibid*; see also 35 USC Section 261.
31 *GAIA Tech, Inc v Reconversion Tech, Inc*, 93 F.3d 774 (Fed Cir 1996).
32 *Intellectual Property Development, Inc v TCI Cablevision of California, Inc*, 248 F.3d 1333 (Fed Cir 2001).
33 *Ibid.*
34 See *Rite-Hite Corp v Kelley Co, Inc*, 56 F.3d 1538, 1547-48 (Fed Cir 1995) for discussion of such cases.
35 *Severson Environmental Services, Inc v Shaw Environmental, Inc*, 477 F.3d 1361 (Fed Cir 2007); *Zoltek Corp v United States*, 442 F.3d 1345 (Fed Cir 2006); *Crater Corporation v Lucent Technologies*, 255 F.3d 1361 (Fed Cir 2001).

3. Trade dress protection for industrial designs

3.1 Nature of rights

Industrial designs can also be protected under trademark and unfair competition laws where it can be established that the design or product configuration is non-functional and has achieved distinctiveness as a protectable trade dress. 'Trade dress' is a product's total image and overall appearance, and has been explicitly defined to "encompass the design of a product".[36]

3.2 Requirements for trade dress protection

In order for an industrial design to be protectable trade dress under the legal regime, it cannot be functional and must be distinctive so as to serve as a source indicator.

(a) Non-functionality

Trade dress is functional if it affects the cost or quality of a product or is essential to the product's purpose or use. In determining whether trade dress is functional, factors considered include:

- advertising that touts its utilitarian advantages;
- the availability of alternative designs;
- whether it results from a comparatively simple or inexpensive method of manufacture; and
- the existence of a utility patent that discloses its utilitarian advantages.[37]

While a utility patent can be strong evidence that the features claimed are functional,[38] a design patent covering an industrial design weighs against a finding of functionality, because a design patent only covers ornamental and non-functional features.[39]

(b) Distinctiveness

An industrial design in a product configuration must also be distinctive in order to be afforded trade dress protection. Under the legal regime, product designs can never be inherently distinctive.[40]

As a result, it must be proven that an industrial design has acquired distinctiveness through use in the marketplace. 'Acquired distinctiveness', also called 'secondary meaning', means that, through extensive use of the design in the marketplace, the public has come to associate the trade dress with a single source or producer (even if the actual producer is unknown), rather than just as the product itself.[41] Secondary meaning can be shown through length and exclusivity of use, sales

---

36 *Wal-Mart Stores, Inc v Samara Brothers, Inc*, 529 US 205, 208 (2000).

37 *Traffix Devices, Inc v Marketing Displays, Inc*, 532 US 23, 29 (2001); *In re MortonNorwich Products, Inc*, 671 F.2d 1332, 1340-1341 (CCPA 1982).

38 *Traffix Devices, Inc v Marketing Displays, Inc*, 532 US at 29-30.

39 J Thomas McCarthy, 1 *McCarthy on Trademarks and Unfair Competition*, Section 7:93, 7323 (4th edn, 2008).

40 *Wal-Mart*, 529 US at 215.

41 *Ibid*, at 211.

amounts and advertising expenditures, as well as consumer surveys and direct witness testimony.

3.3 Registration procedure

US trademark law provides protection for both unregistered[42] and registered[43] trade dress. However, procuring a federal US trademark registration on the principal register for trade dress provides the owner of an industrial design with many advantages. A US trademark registration is *prima facie* evidence of the validity of the registered trade dress and the registration itself, the registrant's ownership of the trade dress, and the registrant's exclusive right to use the trade dress in connection with the goods identified in the registration.[44] Further, if a trademark registration is recorded with the customs authorities, infringing items can be prevented from entering the United States.[45]

Trademark registrations for trade dress are obtained by filing applications with the Patent and Trademark Office. Electronic applications are preferred and benefit from lower filing fees than paper applications. The application includes the applicant's name and address, a depiction of the mark ('the drawing'), a description of goods/services for which the mark/trade dress is being used and a filing fee. The applicant must be the owner of the mark, namely the person or entity who controls the nature and quality of the goods/services identified by the mark. Applications for three-dimensional product designs must include a 'special form' drawing uploaded in .jpg format. The drawing "must depict a single rendition of the mark, and the applicant must indicate that the mark is three dimensional".[46]

The applicant has the burden of proving that the trade dress has acquired distinctiveness. Proof of substantially exclusive and continuous use of a design as a mark by the applicant in commerce for the five years before the date on which the claim of distinctiveness is made may be accepted as *prima facie* evidence that the mark has acquired distinctiveness.[47]

Many applications for trademark registration for product designs are denied based on the existence of advertisements or promotional materials emphasising the utilitarian advantages of a feature of the design.[48]

3.4 Term of protection

If registered, a trade dress registration is valid for 10 years after the date of registration, provided that the first maintenance document is filed before the end of the sixth year after the registration date and other maintenance documents are filed thereafter. Provided the trade dress continues to be used as a distinctive source of origin in commerce in the US, its registration can be renewed in perpetuity, long after any design patent or copyright in the product design has expired.

---

42 15 USC Section 1125.
43 *Ibid*, Section 1114.
44 *Ibid*, Section 1057.
45 *Ibid*, Section 1124.
46 37 CFR Section 2.52.
47 15 USC Section 1052(f), 37 CFR Section 2Al(b); TMEP Section 1212.05.
48 See, eg, *In re Caterpillar Inc*, 43 USPQ.2d 1335 (TTAB 1997); *In re Gibson Guitar Corp*, 62 USPQ.2d 1948 (TTAB 2001).

3.5 Infringement of trade dress rights in industrial designs

Trade dress rights may be enforced in the courts through claims under federal law.[49] State law statutory and common-law unfair competition causes of action are also available. Such state law claims usually correspond to and are pled in conjunction with federal law claims. To succeed in a trade dress infringement action, a plaintiff must prove a valid, protectable trade dress right and the likelihood of confusion caused by the defendant's activities. Dilution claims are also possible for trade dress rights that meet the high threshold of establishing fame. In dilution cases, the owner of a famous trade dress can seek relief against infringers whose product design dilutes the trade dress either by blurring or by tarnishment, regardless of whether a likelihood of confusion can be established.[50]

If a trade dress is registered as a trademark, the rights holder can rely on evidentiary presumptions of validity, ownership and exclusivity when pursuing infringement actions. For unregistered trade dress, the owner must prove all of these elements. If a trade dress registration is challenged on the basis of functionality, the initial burden is on the challenger to rebut the presumption of validity (including non-functionality), whereas in the case of unregistered trade dress, the owner has the initial burden of proving that the trade dress is not functional. However, registration alone will in practice not be enough to succeed on a claim for trade dress infringement or dilution. The rights holder must be ready to submit substantial proof of non-functionality and secondary meaning, and must also be able to prove a likelihood of confusion.

3.6 Damages and other relief

If a court finds that infringement of trade dress has occurred, the plaintiff may seek an injunction against further infringement,[51] monetary damages, including the infringer's profits, any damages sustained by the owner, and court costs,[52] and destruction of the infringing articles.[53] The court may increase damages by up to three times the amount found as actual damages. In exceptional cases, attorneys' fees may also be awarded.[54]

Owners of trade dress in industrial designs can also seek preliminary injunctions against infringers. Factors that courts will consider in weighing their equitable discretion include:

- the rights holder's likelihood of success on the merits;
- irreparable injury to the rights holder pending a full trial;
- whether a preliminary injunction will preserve the status quo;
- whether hardships balance in favour of the rights holder; and
- whether a preliminary injunction serves the public interest.[55]

---

49 15 USC Section 1114 for registered rights and 15 USC Section 1125(a) for unregistered rights.
50 *Ibid*, Section 1125.
51 *Ibid*, Section 1116; *Reno Air Racing Ass'n, Inc v McCord*, 452 F.3d 1126 (9th Cir 2006).
52 *Ibid*, Section 1117.
53 *Ibid*, Section 1118; *Fendi Adele SRL v Filene's Basement, Inc*, 696 F.Supp.2d 368 (SDNY 2010).
54 *Ibid*, Section 1117; *Attrezzi, LLC v Maytag Corp*, 436 F.3d 32 (1st Cir 1006).
55 J Thomas McCarthy, 5 *McCarthy on Trademarks and Unfair Competition*, Section 30:32, 30-85 (4th edn, 2010); *Fiji Water Company, LLC v Fiji Mineral Water USA, LLC*, 741 F.Supp.2d 1165 (CD Cal 2010) (preliminary injunction granted against competitor accused of infringing trade dress in water bottle).

3.7 Licensing of trade dress rights in industrial designs

Trade dress is owned by the entity that uses it in the marketplace. However, it may be assigned or licensed to other parties. Assignments of registered trade dress must be in writing.[56] An assignment of trade dress must be accompanied by the goodwill of the business connected with the use of or symbolised by the trade dress.[57] It is also possible to grant an exclusive or non-exclusive licence to exploit certain interests in trade dress.[58] Licences in registered trade dress can be oral or written.[59] A trade dress licence must include provisions for quality control by the rights holder.[60] Only exclusive licensees may sue for infringement.

3.8 Compulsory licences

A compulsory licence requirement for trade dress rights would be incompatible with the concept that trade dress owners, like trademark owners, must control the quality of goods sold under their marks. However, where the courts deny injunctive relief (if, for example, the plaintiff fails to establish irreparable harm), the denial of relief could be interpreted as effectively operating as a compulsory licence.

4. Copyright protection for industrial designs

4.1 Nature of rights

The Copyright Act sets out a number of different categories of copyrightable works of authorship. Those applicable to industrial designs are pictorial, graphic and sculptural works, defined as including "two dimensional and three-dimensional works of fine, graphic and applied art, photographs, prints and art reproductions, maps, globes, charts, diagrams, and models".[61,62] Copyrights give the rights holder the exclusive right to:

- reproduce the copyrighted work;
- make derivative works based on the copyrighted work;
- distribute copies of the copyrighted work by sale, lease or rental;
- perform certain types of copyrighted works in public; and
- display the copyrighted work in public.

However, as discussed below, copyright protection for designs of useful articles (other than vessel hulls and decks) is limited by the requirement that the artistic elements of the design are separable from the functional features of the article.

The Copyright Act provides a unique, special area of protection for designs of vessel hulls and decks.[63] A 'vessel' is defined as "a craft that is designed and capable of independently steering a course on or through water through its own means of

56 15 USC Section 1060.
57 *Ibid.*
58 *Intellectual Property Development, Inc v TCI Cablevision of California, Inc*, 248 F.3d 1333 (Fed Cir 2001).
59 *Watec Co Ltd v Liu*, 403 F.3d 675 (9th Cir 2005).
60 *Freecyclesunnyvale v The Freecycle Network*, 626 F.3d 509 (9th Cir 2010).
61 17 USC Section 102(a)(5).
62 *Ibid*, Section 101.
63 *Ibid*, Section 1301.

propulsion; and that is designed and capable of carrying and transporting one or more passengers". A 'hull' is "the exterior frame or body of a vessel, exclusive of the deck, superstructure, masts, sails, yards, rigging, hardware, fixtures, and other attachments". A 'deck' is "the horizontal surface of a vessel that covers the hull, including exterior cabin and cockpit surfaces, and exclusive of masts, sails, yards, riggings, hardware, fixtures, and other attachments". The copyright protection for such vessel hulls and decks is 10 years, provided application for registration is made within two years of the date on which the design is first made public.

4.2 Requirements for copyright protection

All product designs not covered by the vessel hulls and decks provisions may be protected under copyright if they are an original work in a solid medium and the design does not have a purely practical function.[64]

(a) *Originality*

In the copyright context, 'originality' refers to a work created by its author rather than copied from another source.[65] It is not the same as the novelty requirement of patent law. Thus, two identical works of art, each independently created, are both eligible for copyright protection, provided that no copying is involved.

(b) *Works of authorship – useful articles – conceptual separability*

'Useful articles' are defined as "having an intrinsic utilitarian function that is not merely to portray the appearance of the article or to convey information". They are not entitled to copyright protection. However, the design of a useful article is eligible for copyright protection to the extent that the design "incorporates pictorial, graphic, or sculptural features that can be identified separately from, and are capable of existing independently of, the utilitarian aspects of the article".[66] This is referred to as 'conceptual separability'. Conceptual separability is generally found "when the artistic aspects of an article can be conceptualized as existing independently of their utilitarian function".[67] Thus, if the artistic elements reflect the author's artistic judgment exercised independently of functional elements, then conceptual separability exists.

Examples of articles accorded copyright protection under the doctrine of conceptual separability include china statuettes of dancing figures used as table lamp bases,[68] belt buckles with sculptured designs cast in precious metals,[69] the design of a bareheaded female human head with an expressive face and no makeup or hair,[70] and mannequins that support mounted animal skins.[71] Conversely, sculptures modified

---

64 *Ibid*, Section 102(a).
65 Melville B Nimmer and David Nimmer, *Nimmer on Copyright*, Section 2.01[A] (2011).
66 17 USC Section 101.
67 *Universal Furniture Int'l, Inc v Collezione Europa USA, Inc*, 618 F.3d 417, 432 (4th Cir 2010).
68 *Mazer v Stein*, 347 US 201, 216-217 (1954).
69 *Kieselsten-Cord v Accessories by Pearl, Inc*, 632 F.2d 989 (2nd Cir 1980).
70 *Pivot Point Int'l Inc v Charlene Prods Inc*, 372 F.3d 913, 931 (7th Cir 2004).
71 *Superior Form Builders v Dan Case Taxidermy Supply Co*, 74 F.3d 488, 493-495 (4th Cir 1996).

into bicycle racks[72] and life-sized mannequins of human torsos[73] have been found not to be entitled to copyright protection.[74] In the *Brandir* case involving the bicycle racks, the court noted:

> *While the RIBBON Rack may be worthy of admiration for its aesthetic qualities alone, it remains nonetheless the product of industrial design. Form and function are inextricably intertwined in the rack, its ultimate design being as much the result of utilitarian pressures as aesthetic choices ... Thus, there remains no artistic element of the RIBBON Rack that can be identified as separate and 'capable of existing independently, of, the utilitarian aspects of the article'.*[75]

(c) Fixation in tangible form

The final requirement for copyright eligibility is that a work of authorship must be "fixed in any tangible medium of expression now known or later developed from which they can be perceived, reproduced, or otherwise communicated, either directly or with the aid or a machine or device".[76] Thus, concepts and ideas are not eligible for copyright protection.

4.3 Copyright registration procedure

It is not necessary to register works created on or after January 1 1978 for them to be entitled to copyright protection.[77] The rights come into existence at the time a work is fixed in tangible form. However, registration is a prerequisite for an action for copyright infringement[78] (unless the work was created outside the United States in a Berne Convention country),[79] and a prerequisite for claiming statutory damages and reimbursement of attorneys' fees to the successful party.[80]

To obtain a registration of a copyright, the owner must submit an application for registration of the copyright claim to the Copyright Office. The application must include information about the author of the work, the copyright claimant and the work itself.[81] The application must be accompanied by the appropriate fee and by a deposit of copies of the work.[82]

The effective date of copyright registration of a work is the day on which the

---

72 *Brandir International, Inc v Cascade Pacific Lumber Co*, 834 F.2d 1142, 1147-1148 (2nd Cir 1987).

73 *Carol Barnhart Inc v Economy Cover Corp*, 594 F.Supp 364, 370 (EDNY 1984), aff'd *Carol Barnhart Inc v Economy Cover Corp*, 773 F.2d 411 (2nd Cir 1985).

74 Clothing designs are generally held to be non-copyrightable because of the inability to separate their intrinsic function from their decorative elements. See, eg, *Whimsicality, Inc v Rubie's Costume Co*, 891 F.2d 452, 455 (2nd Cir 1989). However, it is currently generally accepted that fabric designs, including those applied to clothing, are entitled to copyright protection. See, eg, *Knitwaves, Inc v Lollytogs Ltd (Inc)* 71 F.3d 996, 1002 (2d Cir. 1995); *Peter Pan Fabrics, Inc v Brenda Fabrics, Inc*, 169 F.Supp 142, 143 (SDNY 1958); *Peter Pan Fabrics, Inc v Acadia Co*, 173 F.Supp 292, 299 (SDNY 1959), aff'd *Peter Pan Fabrics, Inc v Acadia Co*, 274 F.2d 487 (2nd Cir 1960). Recently proposed legislation, the Innovative Design Protection and Privacy Prevention Act, would extend copyright protection to fashion design. HR 2196, S3728 Section 2(a)(2) and (e)(3).

75 *Brandir International, Inc*, 834 F.2d 1142, 1147-1148.

76 17 USC Section 102(a).

77 *Ibid*, Section 408(a).

78 *Ibid*, Section 411(a).

79 *Ibid*, Section 411(a) (1998); *Master Sound Int'l, Inc v Polygram Latino US*, 52 USPQ.2d 1060 (SDNY 1999).

80 *Ibid*, Section 412.

81 *Ibid*, Section 409.

82 *Ibid*, Section 408(a).

application, deposit and fee are received by the Copyright Office, assuming that the office or a court of competent jurisdiction determines that the submitted materials are acceptable for registration.[83]

4.4 Term of protection

The copyright in a work generally subsists from its creation and endures for a term consisting of the life of the author plus 70 years after the author's death.[84] For 'works made for hire' (ie, created by employees of a company in the normal course of their duties), the copyright endures for a term of 95 years from the year of first publication or 120 years from the year of creation, whichever expires first.[85]

4.5 Infringement of copyright

The federal district courts have exclusive jurisdiction over copyright infringement claims. To establish copyright infringement, a plaintiff must demonstrate both ownership of the copyright and copying by the defendant.[86] Copyright registration constitutes evidence of most of the elements listed in the copyright registration, provided the registration is obtained within five years of first publication. To prove copying, a plaintiff must demonstrate that the defendant had access to the copyrighted work and that the allegedly infringing material is substantially similar to the it.[87]

4.6 Damages and other relief

Preliminary injunctive relief is available in copyright actions relating to industrial designs.[88] The rights holder may also seek a permanent injunction preventing further infringement,[89] an order requiring destruction of the infringing products[90] and actual or statutory damages.[91] Courts may also, at their discretion, award costs and attorneys' fees to a successful copyright plaintiff.[92] However, copyright registration prior to the infringement or within three months of first publication is required to obtain statutory damages and attorneys fees.[93] If the copyright registration is recorded with the Department of Homeland Security, Customs and Border Protection, infringing items may be barred from importation.[94]

4.7 Licensing of copyrights

Copyrights may be assigned or licensed.[95] Exclusive licensees of any right under the

---

83 *Ibid*, Section 410(d).
84 *Ibid*, Section 302(a).
85 *Ibid*, Section 302(c).
86 *Feist Publ'ns, Inc v Rural Tel. Servo Co*, 499 US 340, 361 (1991); *General Universal Systems, Inc v Lee*, 379 F.3d 131, 141 (5th Cir 2004); Nimmer and Nimmer, note 65 above, Section 13.01[A].
87 *Arica Inst, Inc v Palmer*, 970 F.2d 1067, 1072 (2nd Cir 1992); *General Universal Systems*, 379 F.3d at 141.
88 See, eg, *Stanislawski v Jordan*, 337 F.Supp 23 1103, 1118 (ED Wis 2004); *Gucci Timepieces Am v Yidah Watch Co*, 47 USPQ 2.D (BNA) 1038 (CD Cal 1998); *Severin Montres, Ltd v Yidah Watch Co*, 997 F.Supp 1262, 1265 (CD Cal 1997).
89 17 USC Section 502.
90 *Ibid*, Section 503.
91 *Ibid*, Section 504.
92 *Ibid*, Section 505.
93 *Ibid*, Section 412.
94 *Ibid*, Sections 602, 603.
95 *Ibid*, Section 101.

Copyright Act may sue for infringement of a right they have been licensed to have.[96] However, non-exclusive licensees have no standing to sue.[97]

Both exclusive licences as well as assignments must be recorded in writing. Non-exclusive licences may be oral or implied. Any document concerning copyrights, including transfers of copyrights, may be recorded in the Copyright Office provided that the document is signed by the person who executed it or it is accompanied by a certification that it is a true copy of the original, signed document.[98] Upon submission of the recording document and a fee,[99] the office will return the document with a certification of recordation.[100] The recording document must comply with certain specificity requirements which provide constructive notice of the transfer, and the underlying work to be transferred must be registered.[101] Once recorded, the document will be publicly searchable. Transfers of copyright need not be recorded, but recording them may confer certain advantages. For example, a prior transferee will prevail over a subsequent conflicting transferee if the prior transfer was properly recorded in the Copyright Office.[102]

4.8 Compulsory licences

Except for compulsory licences for making and distributing recordings of musical works, the Copyright Act generally forbids involuntary transfers, unless they are required by bankruptcy law.[103]

5. International obligations

5.1 Design patents: foreign filings based on US application

While a US design patent application can claim priority to an earlier filed international patent application filed under the Patent Cooperation Treaty (PCT), a PCT application cannot be based on a US design patent application.[104]

5.2 Trade dress registrations: foreign filings based on US application

A US trade dress application may claim priority to an earlier filed international application for six months from the filing date of the foreign application.[105] The United States is also a contracting party to the Madrid Protocol.[106]

Most countries do not have copyright registration requirements as exist in the United States. However, several countries do consider a US copyright registration as evidence of ownership. Thus, obtaining a US copyright registration can be helpful evidence when pursuing copyright protection and enforcement in other countries.

---

96 *Ibid*, Section 501(b).
97 *Sybersound Records, Inc v UAV Corp*, 517 F.3d 1137, 1144 (9th Cir 2008).
98 17 USC, Section 205(a).
99 *Ibid*, Section 708(a)(4) (1990).
100 *Ibid*, Section 205(b).
101 *Ibid*, Section 205(c)(1).
102 *Ibid*, Section 205(d).
103 *Ibid*, Section 201(e).
104 Patent and Trademark Office, note 3 above, Section 1504.20.
105 15 USC Section 1126(d)(1).
106 *Ibid*, 1141.

6. Infringement

In cases of design patent infringement, there is no requirement to prove copying by the infringer in order to succeed in an infringement action. This means that independent creation is not a defence in design patent law as it is in copyright law. The design patent rights holder benefits from the presumption of validity of the patent and has to prove only that the patented design and the accused design are substantially the same in overall appearance. No technical expertise is necessary for a judge to decide whether the infringing product is substantially the same in overall appearance as the patented design. Minor differences in detail are generally insufficient to avoid infringement. Invalidity defences are subject to the clear and convincing evidence standard. Thus, when the case for infringement is strong, design patentees have a good chance of obtaining a preliminary injunction in court.

In cases of copyright infringement, the copyright owner must prove copying, usually by proof that the defendant had access to the copyrighted work and that the defendant's work is substantially similar. Although the copyright owner benefits from the *prima facie* evidence afforded by a US copyright registration (provided it was obtained within five years of first publication), the burden of proving invalidity is not as high as that for design patents. Nevertheless, decisions holding copyright registrations invalid are quite rare.

7. Infringement litigation relating to industrial designs

7.1 Procedure

Infringement litigation for claims relating to industrial designs is initiated by filing a complaint in a court that has subject matter jurisdiction over the claims and personal jurisdiction over the defendant.

7.2 Courts

There are no specialised intellectual property courts (with the exception of the Federal Circuit Court of Appeals for claims relating to patents).

Claims for design patent infringement and copyright infringement must be filed in the federal court. State law claims, such as unfair competition, may be filed with the federal claims.

Trade dress infringement claims may be filed in the federal court or in the state court. However, in practice most trade dress infringement claims are filed in the federal court, or removed by defendants to the federal court if they are filed in a state court. State unfair competition claims can also be filed with federal claims for trade dress infringement.

7.3 Interim remedies

Preliminary injunctive relief is available for design patent, copyright and trade dress infringement claims. Generally, in determining whether to grant preliminary injunctive relief, the courts will consider:

- the likelihood of success on the merits;
- the irreparable injury to the plaintiff pending a full trial;

- whether a preliminary injunction will preserve the status quo;
- the balance of hardships; and
- whether a preliminary injunction serves the public interest.

7.4 Final remedies: damages/delivery-up/final injunction

As discussed above, statutory damages are available for infringement of design patents and copyrights (subject to the requirements discussed above). Alternatively, awards for actual damages are available, if proven. For trade dress infringement claims, only actual damages are available, unless counterfeiting can be proven. Damages awards may be enhanced in certain circumstances, particularly in cases of wilful infringement. Delivery-up remedies and permanent injunctive relief are also available in cases of design patent, copyright and trade dress infringement.

7.5 Costs

Litigating claims relating to industrial designs in the United States can be expensive, particularly because of the discovery process in US litigation. However, the costs of litigating design patent claims are generally far less than the costs of litigating utility patent claims. With design patents, construction of the claims consists of interpreting the drawings. There is no need for expert opinions or Markman hearings for a judicial determination of claim construction. In general, there is no provision for the loser paying the winner's costs, unless the loser committed some egregious conduct that would cause the court to order such costs as a sanction.

In copyright infringement cases, costs, including attorneys' and experts' fees, may be awarded to the successful party (at the court's discretion), provided that the copyright registration was obtained within three months of first publication of the work, or before the infringement. This requirement also applies to works created in foreign countries that are party to the Berne Convention. Thus, although works created in foreign Berne Convention countries are not required to be registered, such registration is required in order for them to benefit from the provisions regarding reimbursement of costs and attorneys' fees and the provisions relating to awards of statutory damages.

In trade dress infringement and unfair competition cases, there are no provisions for reimbursement of costs or attorneys' fees, unless the court imposes them as a sanction, which is not common. Therefore, the plaintiff must expect to finance the litigation and must pursue monetary remedies through damages claims.

General liability and other types of insurance policies often provide insurance coverage (usually under 'personal and advertising injury') for legal fees and damages awards incurred in defending copyright infringement and trademark/trade-dress infringement claims. This type of coverage is more difficult to obtain for defence of allegations of design patent infringement.

7.6 Validity issues

Invalidity defences are often asserted in response to patent, copyright and trade dress infringement claims.

In the case of design patents, the patent is presumed valid by law and the accused infringer has the burden of proving by clear and convincing evidence that the design patent is not novel, is not ornamental, or would have been obvious to a designer of ordinary skill in the art. This is a heavy burden, with the result that few design patents have been held to be invalid.

Copyrights that have been registered with the Copyright Office within five years of first publication benefit from a presumption that the design is valid as a copyrightable work and owned by the party named on the certificate. This presumption may be rebutted by a preponderance of the evidence (rather than the higher 'clear and convincing' standard for design patents).

For trade dress rights, invalidity defences usually relate to allegations on the functionality of the design, allegations of lack of distinctiveness and/or abandonment of the trade dress rights through non-use or lack of control over third-party use. If the trade dress is registered as a US trademark, the registrant benefits from certain evidentiary presumptions that may be rebutted.

8. Licensing and exploitation

Ownership of US design patents initially vests in the individual inventor(s).[107] Patents and patent applications are treated as personal property, and may be assigned or licensed to other individuals or companies.[108] A licence may be 'exclusive', meaning that the licensee is the only party permitted to sell the specified products or in the specified location, or 'non-exclusive', meaning that other people or companies may be granted the same right to sell the specified products or sell in the specified location. Licences and assignments may be recorded in the Patent Office.[109] Recording a licence provides notice to third parties of an equitable interest in a patent.[110]

A trade dress owner may grant an exclusive or non-exclusive licence to exploit certain interests in the trade dress.[111] Licences in registered trade dress can be oral or written.[112] A trade dress licence must include provisions for quality control by the rights owner.[113] Licences in registered trade dress may be recorded with the assignment division of the Patent and Trademark Office, although it is not a requirement.[114] The recording of a licence provides notice to third parties of an equitable interest in trade dress.[115]

107 *Arachnid, Inc v Merit Indust, Inc*, 939 F.2d 1574 (Fed Cir 1991).
108 *Ibid*; see also 35 USC Section 261.
109 35 USC Section 261; Patent and Trademark Office, note 3 above, Section 313.
110 Patent and Trademark Office, note 3 above, Section 313.
111 *Intellectual Property Development, Inc v TCI Cablevision of California, Inc*, 248 F.3d 1333 (Fed Cir 2001).
112 *Watec Co, Ltd v Liu*, 403 F.3d 675 (9th Cir 2005).
113 *Freecyclesunnyvale v The Freecycle Network*, 626 F.3d 509 (9th Cir 2010).
114 Patent and Trademark Office, *Trademark Manual of Examining Procedure*, Section 503.02 (7th edn, 2010).
115 *Ibid*, Section 503.01.

About the authors

David Aylen

Managing partner, Gowlings Russia/CIS
david.aylen@gowlings.com

David Aylen is certified as a specialist in intellectual property (trademarks, patents and copyright). In addition to his JD degree in law, he holds an engineering degree from Carleton University, Canada. David is a regular committee member within the International Trademark Association (INTA). In 1999, David was appointed by INTA to the board of governors of the Brand Names Education Foundation. In 2009, he was elected by INTA as a vice-chair of the alternative dispute resolution committee. Currently, David is the only INTA-certified alternative dispute resolution expert for Russia.

David's notable achievements in intellectual property include acting as co-counsel in the well-known 'patent diaper wars' between Kimberly-Clark and Procter & Gamble and the telecommunications wars between AT&T, MCI and others on the pioneer patents for 800 and calling-card services. In 2009 he was appointed managing partner of Gowlings in Russia.

Anne Bateman

Partner and head of intellectual property & technology, Philip Lee Solicitors
abateman@philiplee.ie

Anne Bateman is a partner in the Dublin office of Philip Lee Solicitors. She specialises in intellectual property, technology and pharmaceutical law. In the intellectual property field, she advises on commercial agreements, portfolio management and infringement issues, and she acts in a general advisory capacity on all intellectual property issues. Anne has extensive experience in acting for a range of intellectual property owners and users, representing the Irish interests of large multinational owners and prominent Irish businesses, as well as a number of Irish public bodies.

Anne is a graduate of University College Dublin, King's College London and King's Inns Dublin. She has been a qualified Irish and Community trademark attorney since 1999. Anne has written for numerous publications in the field of intellectual property, including the European Intellectual Property Review. She has lectured in intellectual property at University College Dublin and Trinity College Dublin and currently lectures at the Irish Law Society.

David Brophy

Partner, FRKelly
d.brophy@frkelly.com

David Brophy is a partner in FRKelly, a European patent attorney and a Community trademark and design attorney. David divides his practice between patents and designs and leads the firm's design practice. He holds a master's degree in UK, EU and US copyright law from Kings College, London, for which he wrote his thesis on the interface and boundary between copyright and design rights.

Mr Brophy is a contributor to the renowned IPKat Blog, one of the most widely read and respected sources of news and comment on IP law. He served for several years on the European Patent Office's examination committee for the qualifying exam in European patent law, which is taken by all prospective European patent attorneys, and has written and spoken widely on patent and design law.

Claus Barrett Christiansen
Partner, Bech-Bruun
clb@bechbruun.com

Claus Barrett Christiansen is a partner in Bech-Bruun's intellectual property and technology department. He has extensive experience in design law, copyright, trademarks, patents, marketing practice, intellectual property contracts and litigation. He is an external professor at the University of Aarhus and has run courses in international copyright, international trademark law and marketing practice law for several years. He has taken a leading role in advising Danish and international clients in the retail, fashion and pharmaceutical sectors and is a widely used and experienced litigator before the Danish courts in intellectual property litigation.

Jared C Bunker
Partner, Knobbe Martens Olson & Bear LLP
Jared.Bunker@kmob.com

Jared C Bunker is a litigation partner in Knobbe Martens' Orange County, California, office. Jared represents and counsels clients in disputes involving patents, trademarks, copyrights and trade secrets. He received his JD in 2006 from the University of California, Los Angeles, and his BSc in chemistry from Brigham Young University in 2003.

Lodewyk Cilliers
Partner, Spoor & Fisher
L.Cilliers@spoor.com

Lodewyk Cilliers is a patent attorney and a partner at Spoor & Fisher. He specialises in the preparation, filing and prosecution of patent and registered design applications. Before joining the legal profession, Lodewyk was a mechanical engineer in the nuclear energy industry for a number of years. He has been practising intellectual property law for the past nine years.

Lodewyk is a council member of the South African Institute of Intellectual Property Law and is the lecturer and examiner in design law for both that institute and the Patent Board. Lodewyk serves on the institute's design law subcommittee.

Shlomo Cohen
Senior partner, Dr Shlomo Cohen & Co
shlomo.cohen@shlomocohen.co.il

Dr Shlomo Cohen is the founder and managing partner of Dr Shlomo Cohen & Co, a firm specialising in intellectual property law in Israel. Shlomo has written extensively on intellectual and industrial property matters and has appeared in court cases which have set several major precedents. Shlomo taught intellectual property courses at the Hebrew University and Tel Aviv University law schools and was an adjunct professor at New York University Law School from 1976 to 1995.

Shlomo chaired a committee appointed by the Ministry of Justice to revise the Israeli Registered Design (Design Patent) Act and was a member of the committees appointed to revise the Patent Act and the Copyright Act. Shlomo represented the Israeli government at a diplomatic conference leading to the Treaty on Intellectual Property in Respect of Integrated Circuits. He has been a member of the board of the Israeli chapter of AIPPI, the president of the Israel Bar Association (1999 to 2007) and founded the Licensing Executive Society in Israel, serving as its president from 1998 to 2006.

Owen Dean
Consultant, Spoor & Fisher; professor of intellectual property law, Stellenbosch University
O.Dean@spoor.com

Owen Dean is a former partner and chairman of Spoor & Fisher, specialist intellectual property solicitors, and holds the Chair of Intellectual Property Law at Stellenbosch University. He practised as a specialist intellectual property lawyer for 38 years, specialising in trademark and copyright and design law, primarily as a litigator. He was involved in many of the leading South African cases in these fields. He served for many years on a statutory advisory committee on intellectual property law to the South African government and had a role in drafting many of South Africa's current intellectual property statutes.

Throughout his professional career and beyond, Owen has been a regular speaker at conferences, both in South Africa and abroad, and has lectured on intellectual property law at several South African universities. He is the author of the *Handbook of South African Copyright Law* and chapters in several compilations dealing with intellectual property law. He has published numerous articles in South African and international legal journals on intellectual property topics.

Roland Deissenberger
Partner, Deissenberger Rechtsanwälte
rd@deissenberger.com

Dr Roland Deissenberger is an Austrian lawyer in private practice in Vienna. He has advised local and foreign clients on intellectual property, information technology, corporate law and commercial law for 30 years. He is the senior lawyer of Deissenberger Rechtsanwälte and is based in Vienna. Besides his law firm in Vienna, in 1998 Dr Deissenberger set up Deissenberger & Partners Ltd in Bangkok, a law firm focusing on legal counselling in Thailand and South East Asia in the same areas of practice as the Vienna office.

Marc de Kemp
Senior associate, Houthoff Buruma
m.de.kemp@houthoff.com

Marc de Kemp is a senior associate of Houthoff Buruma in Amsterdam, working in the firm's intellectual property, media and information technology department. For more than 10 years Marc has assisted various national and international clients in a wide-ranging variety of intellectual property and media- and entertainment-related issues. He has assisted a number of bicycle companies in the infringement of copyright and design rights. Marc is an experienced litigator in media and entertainment law, copyright-related matters and design rights law. He has been involved in some leading court cases in the Netherlands in these fields. He is a member of several intellectual property law and media law associations.

Graeme Deuchars
Articled student, Stikeman Elliott LLP
gdeuchars@stikeman.com

Graeme Deuchars is a third-year student at the University of Toronto, Faculty of Law. He holds a BBA from the Schulich School of Business at York University, with a specialisation in marketing. Outside the classroom, he has played a leadership role in Pro Bono Students Canada's not-for-profit corporate law project.

Graeme will be completing his articles with Stikeman Elliott LLP in 2012/13. He has an interest in corporate, intellectual property and competition law.

Kaia Bugge Fougner
Senior associate, Grette
kafo@grette.no

Kaia Bugge Fougner is a senior associate at Grette. She specialises in design, copyrights, trademark and unfair competition law, and is part of the firm's life science, food and health group. Her practice includes litigation, drafting contracts and intellectual property strategic advice.

Kaia gained a Masters degree in international business law, specialising in trademark law, competition law and the EU internal market, from Kings College, London, in 2007. She started as an associate in Grette in 2008 and was awarded her practising certificate in 2010. During 2011 she worked as an associate judge in a district court just outside Oslo for six months.

Ida Gjessing
Partner, Grette
idgj@grette.no

Ida Gjessing is a partner at Grette, housing one of Norway's largest practice groups within intellectual property law. She specialises in design, copyrights, patent, trademark and unfair competition law. Her practice includes litigation and non-contentious work such as licensing agreements, R&D agreements and intellectual property strategic advice. Clients include larger international enterprises, small and medium-sized enterprises, universities, government bodies, research foundations and innovative companies. She regularly advises the largest Norwegian brand company on trade dress matters and package design, and government departments and design organisations. She has litigated one of the few design infringement and validity cases heard by the Courts of Appeals in Norway, and recently succeeded in clearing a leading lighting company of an alleged infringement of an Arne Jacobsen design.

Ms Gjessing is the head of the Norwegian industry and commercial enterprises dispute resolution panel, which is a vehicle for out-of-court resolution of disputes under Norway's Marketing Control Act. She is a member of the standing expert committee on intellectual property law of the Norwegian Bar Association.

Moritz Hüsch
Partner, Heymann & Partner Rechtsanwälte
M.Huesch@heylaw.de

Moritz Hüsch is a partner in the intellectual property and information technology department of Heymann & Partner. Moritz studied law at the Universities of Freiburg, Hamburg, Hanover and Bologna. He holds a doctor of law degree from the University of Hamburg and a master of law degree from the University of Hanover, both specialising in intellectual property law.

Moritz has extensive experience in cross-border intellectual property and information technology transactions, outsourcings, complex intellectual property and information technology licensing, anti-trust law, and intellectual property and information technology litigation. In recent years, Moritz has advised, amongst others, E.ON AG in a complex cross-border outsourcing of its entire information technology infrastructure, one of the leading German car manufactures in a number of information technology outsourcing transactions, and in various marketing and acquisition transactions in the solar and renewable energy sector.

Stephen Jiew
Senior associate, Al Tamimi & Co
s.jiew@tamimi.com

Stephen Jiew heads Al Tamimi & Co's patent and design practice and has been practising in intellectual property since 1996 in multiple jurisdictions, including Japan, Singapore and Malaysia, with leading names in the intellectual property arena in both private practice and in-house. He was formerly the regional intellectual property counsel of Cadbury Schweppes Asia Pacific. Stephen's multijurisdictional experience brings an added dimension to the intellectual property aspects of mergers and acquisitions, complex licensing structures and intellectual asset management across all intellectual property subject matters, including copyright, patent, trademark and designs. Stephen's particular expertise is in devising strategic patent, industrial designs and trademark protection programmes for large-volume intellectual property owners in managing their portfolios, locally and across multiple jurisdictions. He is well versed in orchestrating appropriate measures in alignment with clients' corporate intellectual property agendas, where the local piece is part of a global filing and prosecution strategy.

Stephen has experience in managing landmark patent litigation cases for foreign multinational litigants where the boundaries of the law are tested. He is managing the first ever patent infringement and nullification court proceedings, including at an appellate level, in the United Arab Emirates.

Alban Kang
Managing partner, ATMD Bird & Bird LLP
alban.kang@twobirds.com

Alban Kang has been in legal practice for more than 28 years and is the managing partner of ATMD Bird & Bird LLP. He is a founding partner of the firm and practises in the intellectual-property and technology group. He is currently involved in complex patent litigation and other contentious intellectual-property-related cases.

Alban has been recognised as a leading practitioner in intellectual property law. He has been named as a leading Singapore intellectual property lawyer in the Asia Pacific Legal 500 in the 2012 edition, and in the previous ten editions. He has also been ranked as a leading intellectual property lawyer in Chambers Asia 2012. Alban has written and presented many articles and papers on various aspects of intellectual property law. He is the author of *Enforcing Injunctions*, a contributor to *Essays on Computer Law* and the general editor of *A Guide to Singapore Patent Law*. He is the author of the patent section of *Halsbury's Laws of Singapore* and the Singapore chapter in *Patent Claim Interpretation.*

Vorarit Karadist
Legal counsel, Deissenberger & Partners Ltd
vok@deissenberger.co.th; vk@veisz.com

Vorarit Karadist is the legal counsel of Deissenberger & Partners Ltd, Bangkok and head of the division of intellectual property and international trade in the firm's Bangkok office. Vorarit has extensive expertise in commercial proceedings, corporate matters, intellectual property and international trades, including litigation in disputes of several multi-million dollars-worth of government procurement projects in various specific fields. He has a leading role in providing legal consultancy and advising on civil and commercial laws. He is a managing director and president of Veisz Alliance Ltd, a firm specialising in the niche market of Thai government public procurement and tender projects providing business consultancy and legal services.

Anna Mae Koo
Associate, Vivien Chan & Co
Annamae.koo@vcclawservices.com

Anna Mae Koo practises transactional and intellectual property law at Vivien Chan & Co. She regularly advises on all areas of intellectual property, including licensing, franchising, intellectual property due diligence and strategic acquisitions, prosecution, technical assistance and technology transfer agreements, trade practices, and unfair competition law. She is involved in devising anti-counterfeiting strategies and intellectual property rights portfolio management for a number of multinational corporations in China. Anna Mae is actively involved in international associations and is a member of both the litigation committee of the International Bar Association and the Internet committee of the International Trademark Association. Anna Mae was a Prince Philip Scholar at the University of Cambridge, where she graduated with an MA in law. She has a Masters degree in real estate from the University of Hong Kong. She is fluent in English, Mandarin and Cantonese.

Simone Lahorgue Nunes
Senior partner, Levy & Salomão Advogados
slahorgue@levysalomao.com.br

Simone Lahorgue Nunes is senior partner at Levy & Salomão Advogados, a full-service law firm based in São Paulo, Rio de Janeiro and Brasilia, Brazil. She has a wide-ranging entertainment law practice and advises clients in connection with a broad variety of broadcasting, cable television, Internet and regulatory matters. Ms Lahorgue previously served as general counsel in the Brazilian financial market and Organizações Globo, the largest media group in Latin America, where her entertainment law practice extended to communications, intellectual property and sports law, as well as to contractual and corporate matters.

Ms Lahorgue is a professor with the judge-training programme of the State of Rio de Janeiro and is a member of the International Bar Association, where she is vice president of the technology subcommittee. She is an arbitrator with the World Intellectual Property Organization, with the Court of Arbitration for Sports and with the Brazilian National Association of Financial Market Institutions, and she speaks at national and international legal events. She received an official Commendation of the Order of Merit granted by the Brazilian Superior Labour Court in 2007, and a cultural merit award issued by the Brazilian Institute of Magistrates in 2000. She is the author of *Origins and Limits of Regulatory Power in Financial Markets* (Renovar, 2000) and *Copyright, Antitrust and other Constitutional Principles* (Campus/Elsevier, 2011, 2nd edn), as well as several articles. Ms Lahorgue holds Doctor and Masters degrees in economic law, both from the University of São Paulo.

AL Mary
Principal associate, Anand and Anand
loordma@anandandanand.com

AL Mary is a principal of the designs department at Anand and Anand, specialising in intellectual property law relating to industrial designs. She graduated in law at the Mysore University and went on to complete a postgraduate diploma in personnel management and industrial relations. She has been closely involved in all stages of design filing and prosecution both in India and internationally and has 11 years' extensive experience of handling design matters, including filing, prosecution, cancellation and infringement. Her practice also includes consultation, advice and research work specifically related to industrial designs.

Ms Mary joined Anand and Anand in January 2011, having previously worked in the Honourable Delhi High Court, the Supreme Court and intellectual property firms since 2001.

Stuart C McCormack
Managing partner, Stikeman Elliott LLP
SMcCormack@stikeman.com

Stuart C McCormack is currently the managing partner of Stikeman Elliott's Ottawa office and head of the firm's intellectual property practice group, and he sits on the partnership board of the firm. Stuart obtained the first Anton Piller order in Canada. He was previously the head of Sony Corporation's anti-counterfeiting group and worked in its licensing division in Tokyo for several years.

Stuart is a member of the International, American, New York State and Canadian Bar Associations, the Intellectual Property Institute of Canada, the International Trademark Association (past member North American sub-committee – anti-counterfeiting and enforcement, and the international trademark committees), the Law Society of Upper Canada, the Computer Law Association, the European Community Trademark Association (past member, anti-counterfeiting committee) and the IEEE.

Stefan Naumann
Partner, Hughes Hubbard & Reed LLP
naumanns@hugheshubbard.com

Stefan Naumann is a partner with Hughes Hubbard & Reed LLP and heads the firm's intellectual property practice in Paris. He is admitted to practice in France and in California, and is an independent neutral for the World Intellectual Property Organization, particularly for domain names. Stefan acts for well-known entertainment, medical device, advertising, new media, publishing, personal care and manufacturing companies. His patent litigation practice covers additional industries.

Stefan and his team handle litigation, arbitration and advisory and transactional work on patents, trademarks, copyrights, designs, neighbouring rights, image rights, trade dress, and data protection. His media work includes French media regulations, film production, distribution and merchandising, contract negotiation and collective bargaining, anti-piracy, and enforcement for a number of studios. Stefan has been repeatedly ranked among the leading French trademark practitioners by Chambers and the European Legal 500 Guide. His patent litigation and media practice has also been ranked repeatedly.

John Ng
Patent attorney, Vivien Chan & Co
johnng@vcclawservices.com

John Ng has been practising intellectual property law for more than 12 years and has experience in patents in a wide range of technical fields. He has prepared and prosecuted patent applications in major jurisdictions (including Greater China, the United States and Europe) in mechanical and electromechanical inventions, electronics, telecommunications, semiconductor technologies, wireless communications, computer hardware and software, medical devices, automation and industrial systems, Internet-related inventions and business methods. John is experienced in chemical and pharmaceutical patent applications in Greater China. John's practice areas include patent specification drafting and submission, patent searching and patentability advice, patent infringement and validity opinions, and patent litigation and revocation proceedings. He advises on patent enforcement, assignments and licensing matters in Greater China, and patent and design portfolio management.

John holds a bachelor's degree in mechanical engineering from the Hong Kong University of Science and Technology and a bachelor's degree in law from the University of London. He is fluent in English, Cantonese and Putonghua.

Karel Nijs
Associate, NautaDutilh, Brussels
karel.nijs@nautadutilh.com

Karel Nijs specialises in commercial and intellectual property law, with a particular focus on distribution, trademarks, designs and copyright. He regularly works with major clients from various industries against unfair trade practices and competition, both in contentious and non-contentious matters. Karel has published several articles on trademark law and trade practices and is the co-author of a theme code on Belgian corporate criminal law.

Karel obtained his law degree from the University of Leuven in 2005. During his studies, he spent one year at the University of Fribourg, Switzerland, as part of the Erasmus exchange programme. He graduated *cum laude* from the LLM programme for foreign students at the University of Münster, Germany. Karel joined NautaDutilh in November 2006. He is fluent in Dutch, French, English and German.

Massimiliano Pappalardo
Partner, La Scala
m.pappalardo@lascalaw.com

Massimiliano Pappalardo joined La Scala in 2006

and has been a partner in the firm's intellectual property and information technology practice since 2009. He advises national and international companies on intellectual property, information technology and data protection law, and on related commercial law matters. Massimiliano has 15 years' experience in litigation, focussing on trademarks, designs and patents, unfair competition, and consumer law. He has extensive experience in drafting and negotiating international commercial contracts, including licence, distribution and franchising agreements.

Massimiliano has tutored courses on information technology law and computer sciences law at the Università dell'Insubria and frequently lectures on intellectual property and information technology matters. Massimiliano has written extensively on the subject. His publications include: *Elementi di diritto dell'informatica* (Giappichelli Editore, 2003); 'Profili giuridici del linking', in *Diritto e società dell'informazione* (Nyberg Edizioni, 2005); 'Il difficile equilibrio tra valore sostanziale e carattere distintivo della forma', in *Il Diritto Industriale*, no. 4, 2008; 'Il caso "Smart" e il valore sostanziale della forma', in *Il Diritto Industriale*, no. 6, 2008; and 'Italy: user generated contents, liability and ISPs', in *Data Protection Law and Policy*, vol. 06, Issue 07, 2009.

Philippe Péters
Partner, NautaDutilh, Brussels
philippe.peters@nautadutilh.com

Philippe Péters specialises in intellectual property and information technology. He has significant experience in trademark, design, patent, information technology and commercial litigation. Philippe has represented Unilever, The Scotch Whisky Association, GlaxoSmithKline, Warner Bros, Nestlé, Henkel, Coca-Cola, L'Oréal, Balterio and NOS, among others.

Philippe is a member of various international intellectual property associations and a former president of both the Belgian Computer Law Association and the standing committee on intellectual property and new technologies of the Association Internationale des Jeunes Avocats. Philippe taught IT law at the Haute Ecole Commerciale Saint-Louis for eight years and has been a deputy judge in Brussels since 1988. He has published various articles and has given lectures on intellectual property law within and outside Belgium. Together with Jean-Jo Evrard, he co-authored a (Belgian) treatise on Benelux trademark law, published in 1996 and reissued in 2000. He is listed in Chambers and Pritchard's European Legal 500.

Michael Plogell
Partner, Wistrand
Michael.Plogell@wistrand.se

Michael Plogell is a partner of Wistrand Advokatbyrå and head of the firm's intellectual property and marketing and media law department. He has been a member of the Swedish Bar Association since 1993. Michael primarily advises on intellectual property and marketing law and is considered one of Sweden's leading experts in these fields.

Michael is an appointed mediator for both the World Intellectual Property Organization's Arbitration and Mediation Centre and the International Trademark Association panel of neutrals. He appears in both Legal 500's and Chambers & Partners' rankings for Sweden and is the author of several articles and books on intellectual property and marketing law. Michael is often engaged as a lecturer in intellectual property law and marketing law. He has been a part-time researcher at the legal faculty of the Gothenburg School of Economics since the autumn of 2008.

Justyna Rasiewicz
Partner, LDS Łazewski Depo & Partners
justyna.rasiewicz@lds-ip.pl

Justyna Rasiewicz is a partner at LDS Łazewski

Depo & Partners, a Polish niche intellectual property office. Justyna has extensive experience in intellectual property matters, including litigation. She has represented clients in the Polish Supreme Court in several cases that have helped to set precedents. She has expertise in multi-jurisdictional intellectual property disputes, including pharmaceutical and biotechnology patent protection. Justyna also advises in contentious matters concerned with the validity of exclusive rights and preparing contracts on intellectual property rights.

Justyna is a co-author of the *Commentary to the Law on Combating Unfair Competition* (2011 edition), where she has analysed provisions concerning claims and issues relating to litigation.

Katharina Scheja
Partner, Heymann & Partner Rechtsanwälte
K.Scheja@heylaw.de

Katharina Scheja is head of the intellectual property and information technology department of Heymann & Partner. Katharina studied law at the University of Frankfurt and holds a doctor of law degree from the University of Munich, specialising in intellectual property law. Before joining Heymann & Partner in 2007, Katharina was a partner with Clifford Chance, Willkie Farr Gallagher and FPS Fritze Paul Seelig.

Katharina has extensive experience in complex intellectual property and information technology litigation and arbitration, cross-border intellectual property and information technology transactions, outsourcings, complex intellectual property and information technology licensing and anti-trust law. In recent years, Katharina has advised, amongst others, E.ON AG in a complex cross-border outsourcing of its entire information technology infrastructure and in a number of complex patent litigation cases.

Archana Shanker
Senior partner and head of patent practice,
Anand and Anand
archana@anandandanand.com

Archana Shanker is a senior partner at Anand and Anand and heads the firm's patent practice. A graduate of the Law School at Delhi University, North Campus, she went on to complete her postgraduate diploma in bioinformatics and pharmaceutical regulatory affairs. She is an active contributing member of various international bodies, such as the Asian Patent Attorneys Association, the Association Internationale pour la Protection de la Propriété Intellectuelle and the Fédération Internationale des Conseils en Propriété Industrielle.

Archana's extensive experience enables her not only to represent clients in contentious matters in the pharmaceutical industry, but also to advise on protection and prosecution across a number of business sectors, including bioinformatics, pharmaceuticals, biotechnology and chemicals, not only in India but also in the United States, Europe, Japan and other key geographies. She leads Anand and Anand's efforts in nascent legislation of geographical indications and plant variety. Archana handles complex patent litigation issues before various judicial and quasi-judicial forums in India, such as the High Court and IPAB, and has been involved in advising her clients on patent strategies and regulatory affairs.

Archana is a regular speaker and panellist at various national and international forums, the author of articles in publications such as *Managing Intellectual Property*, *Asia Law Practice*, *IAM Magazine* and *Getting the Deal Through – Patents*, to name a few. Her contributions in the field of patents have earned her international recognition and she was named the leading patent lawyer by Asia Law. Archana has received credible peer-to-peer recognition. An array of prominent international accolades and awards have recounted her expertise as leading 'Patents Practitioner'. Her legal acumen and businesses know-how of patent monetisation are highly valued by the clients.

Takamitsu Shigetomi
Partner, Oh-Ebashi LPC & Partners
shigetomi@ohebashi.com

Takamitsu Shigetomi is a partner at Oh-Ebashi LPC & Partners and runs the intellectual property practice department. Mr Shigetomi specialises in intellectual property licensing and litigation and has prepared, tried and argued intellectual property cases in various fields, including mechanical engineering, electrical engineering, computer software, pharmaceuticals, biotechnology and chemistry.

Mr Shigetomi is an experienced author and lecturer in intellectual property practice. He is an adjunct assistant professor of the Graduate School of Intellectual Property at the Osaka Institute of Technology.

Paul Sumpter
Consultant, Chapman Tripp
p.sumpter@auckland.ac.nz

Paul Sumpter is a consultant in the litigation department of Chapman Tripp, one of New Zealand's largest law firms. He is also an academic in the Faculty of Law at the University of Auckland and a member of the New Zealand Copyright Tribunal.

Paul is the author of *Trade Marks in Practice* (Lexis Nexis, 2004; 2nd edition, 2011). He is also the author of *Intellectual Property: Principles in Practice* (CCH, 2006). He teaches undergraduate and postgraduate courses in intellectual property law. He has practised in this field since 1977.

Clive Thorne
Partner, Reynolds Porter Chamberlain LLP
Clive.Thorne@rpc.co.uk

Clive Thorne is a partner in Reynolds Porter Chamberlain's IP, technology and outsourcing group. He practises all areas of IP law, including patents, designs, copyright, trademarks and trade secrets. He has a particular interest in the arbitration of IP disputes. He has been appointed an International Chamber of Commerce arbitrator on an IT dispute and is on the World Intellectual Property Organization (WIPO) panel of arbitrators. He is also on the WIPO panel of experts for domain name disputes and has been on the Nominet panel of experts. He has been involved in many of the leading IP disputes in the United Kingdom and overseas. He is particularly experienced in multi-jurisdictional litigation.

Mr Thorne is admitted in Hong Kong and Australia. He practised in Hong Kong between 1984 and 1987 and continues to retain practice links in Asia. He has extensive experience in all areas of intellectual property and has authored a number of books, including *Users Guide to Design Law*, *Users Guide to Copyright* and *Intellectual Property – The New Law*.

Kukka Tommila
Partner, Juridia Ltd
kukka.tommila@juridia.com

Kukka Tommila is a renowned intellectual property expert. She advises on contentious and non-contentious intellectual property law and has extensive experience in and knowledge of trademark and design law. Kukka's areas of expertise include dispute resolution, negotiation and agreements, and protection and defence strategies both in Finland and internationally. She has advised and represented clients in numerous trademark and design-issue cases. Kukka is recognised in international rankings as a leading intellectual property lawyer in Finland.

Erik Ullberg
Senior associate, Wistrand
Erik.Ullberg@wistrand.se

Erik Ullberg is a senior associate with Wistrand Advokatbyrå's intellectual property and marketing and media law department. He has been a member of the Swedish Bar Association since 2009. Erik works primarily in intellectual property, marketing and media law, as well as EU and competition law. His professional experience includes intellectual property litigation and prosecution before national and EU courts and offices, intellectual property due diligence, and the negotiation and drafting of licence agreements.

Erik has also contributed to various publications on intellectual property and marketing law and lectures on these topics to students and professionals.

Dilek Ustun
Partner, Istanbul Patent & Trademark Consultancy Ltd
dilekustun@istanbulpatent.com

Dilek Ustun, a founder partner of Istanbul Patent & Trademark Consultancy Ltd, leads the foreign trademark and internet domain name disputes-resolution department. She is a registered trademark attorney and a legal attorney licensed by the Bar of Istanbul. She holds an LLB from Istanbul University. Dilek specialises in intellectual property conflicts, including those arising from patent and trademark rights. She has been working as a trademark attorney since 1997. Her articles have been published in various newspapers, periodicals and books in Turkey. Dilek serves as an expert in her area of specialisation, especially in domain name disputes. Dilek is the World Intellectual Property Organization's first panellist from Turkey under the organisation's Uniform Domain Name Dispute Resolution Policy. Dilek is a member of the International Trademark Association internet committee and panel of neutrals committee.

Dilek is an active member of the Women Entrepreneurs Association of Turkey, the International Trademark Association, the Association of European Trademark Owners and AIPPI. She is fluent in Turkish and English.

Markus Wang
Partner, Bär & Karrer
markus.wang@baerkarrer.ch

Markus Wang is a managing partner of Bär & Karrer and heads the firm's IP department. His practice covers a wide range of contentious and non-contentious patent, trademark, design, copyright and other IP-related issues, in particular in the consumer goods, pharmaceutical, biotechnology and IT sectors. He also specialises in regulatory matters in the life sciences and healthcare fields. He is recognised as a leading Swiss practitioner in intellectual property in professional publications and is listed in *Chambers Europe*, *WTR 1000: The World's Leading Trademark Professionals*, *IAM Patent 1000: The World's Leading Patent Practitioners* and *PLC Which Lawyer*. Mr Wang lectures in IP law at the University of Fribourg. He has written two books on design protection, contributed chapters to the latest Swiss commentary on trademark law and to a number of other books on intellectual property, and published several articles for periodicals in these fields.

Timothy Webb
Senior associate, Clayton Utz
twebb@claytonutz.com

Timothy Webb is a litigation and dispute resolution lawyer and has acted for a diverse range of public- and private-sector clients. He specialises in disputes concerning intellectual property, contract law, torts and trade practice issues, particularly in the technology, media and telecommunications sectors.

Mr Webb has acted for clients in many jurisdictions, including the High Court of Australia, the Federal Court of Australia, the Federal Magistrates Court, the Supreme Courts of New South Wales, Victoria, the Australian Capital Territory and Northern Territory (and their inferior courts), the Copyright Tribunal, the Trademarks Office and the Commonwealth Administrative Appeals Tribunal. He has acted for the Department of Defence in litigation concerning the construction of the Collins class submarines; for the commercial free-to-air television broadcasters in a dispute regarding the licence scheme applicable to the broadcast of commercial sound recordings; and for the Internet Industry Association in the landmark proceedings brought by the major film studios against an internet service provider alleging authorisation of copyright infringement.

Mr Webb has significant experience in alternative dispute resolution and has been involved in numerous arbitrations and mediations. He is a fellow of the Chartered Institute of Arbitrators and a member of the Dispute Resolution Committee of the Law Society of New South Wales.

Wolter Wefers Bettink
Partner, Houthoff Buruma
w.bettink@houthoff.com

Wolter Wefers Bettink specialises in intellectual property law, information technology law, e-business and privacy law. As an intellectual-property litigator, he has represented clients in trademark, copyright, model and design, database, breeders' rights and patent cases. He successfully defended the UK-based Landmark Group in a historic case on database protection of government data.

Mr Wefers Bettink assists clients with complex information technology projects, including outsourcing and business processes. He is experienced in dispute resolution relating to unsuccessful information technology projects for both providers and their customers. He has worked on a variety of internet-related matters, including intellectual property and contract formation, and is a specialist in data protection under both the EU Data Protection Directive and the national privacy legislation. Mr Wefers Bettink is a World Intellectual Property Organization arbitrator and mediator and an arbitrator for the Netherlands Arbitration Institute. He is a member of various specialist associations, including AIPPI and INTA. He has written numerous publications on topics relating to copyright, trademarks, domain names, electronic contracting, electronic dispute resolution and jurisdiction over websites.

Lynda Zadra-Symes
Partner, Knobbe Martens Olson & Bear LLP
ljs@kmob.com

Lynda Zadra-Symes is a litigation partner in Knobbe Martens' Orange County, California, office, where she has practised for more than 20 years. She represents clients through all stages of US litigation, from pre-action through trial and appeal, in federal courts throughout the country and before the Trademark Trial and Appeal Board of the US Patent and Trademark Office. Lynda's practice involves all types of intellectual property, including patents, trade secrets, trademarks and trade dress, copyrights, false advertising, unfair competition, and rights of publicity. She also advises on customs and anti-counterfeiting issues, international trademark and copyright matters, advertising, and competition issues. Her clients come from a wide variety of industries, from beverages, toys and fashion to medical devices, computer chips, software, e-commerce and video games, among others.

Lynda was called to the Bar of England and Wales in November 1989 and was admitted to the California Bar in 1991.